GUSTAV MAHLER
The Wunderhorn Years

Chronicles and Commentaries
by
DONALD MITCHELL

UNIVERSITY OF CALIFORNIA PRESS
BERKELEY AND LOS ANGELES

Copyright 1975 in London, England
by Donald Mitchell
University of California Press
Berkeley and Los Angeles, California
First California Paperback Edition 1980

Library of Congress Cataloging in Publication Data
Mitchell, Donald, 1925 -
   Gustav Mahler: the Wunderhorn years.
   Bibliography: p.
   Includex index
   1. Mahler, Gustav, 1860-1911.
Ml410.M23M63   780'.92'4   75-23204
ISBN 0-520-04220-4

Printed in the United States of America

1 2 3 4 5 6 7 8 9

To BENJAMIN BRITTEN

Contents (detailed Contents pages precede each Part)

Illustrations

Line

Plates

between pages 136 *and* 137

Preface and Acknowledgements

Although this volume picks up, musically speaking, from where my first book on Mahler, *The Early Years* (1958), came to an end, I want to make clear that *The Wunderhorn Years* has been designed as a self-contained, independent study, complete in itself. Now that I have, at long last, finished this work on Mahler's 'Wunderhorn' period, I hope it will not be too long before I can bring out *The Early Years* in a revised edition and make a start on writing the final volume (or volumes), for which I have already done much of the basic research. In any event, I feel I must offer an apology to the many students and lovers of Mahler who have written to me in the past, to inquire about a possible re-issue of *The Early Years* and about the fate of the long-promised continuation. That I am, at this moment, writing this prefatory note lifts a little of my feeling of guilt at having postponed my promises so many times for so many years.

There have been many reasons for the delay. One major factor since 1958 has been the vast increase of available materials and documents associated with Mahler, which has meant a corresponding expenditure of time on scrutinizing and assimilating those sources which have seemed to me to be the most important. Another post-1958 factor, of major significance for me at least, was the problem of how to plan the rest of the enterprise. It was not altogether the case that I gave up the ghost when writing *The Early Years* and arbitrarily applied the closure with a commentary on the first volume of the *Lieder und Gesänge*. I felt, rightly or wrongly, that my first book had, by that stage, methodically covered all the music associated with the early years (excluding, of course, the 'Blumine' movement from the First Symphony, which in those days I did not know had still survived) and that the 'Wunderhorn' years, the onset of which was marked by the *Gesellen* cycle, should be dealt with as an integral whole in the next volume.

I do not think I was mistaken in the view I took. *The Early Years* did have a natural shape as an intensive study of a composer's origins, and I hope that *The Wunderhorn Years* will, for those who have the patience to read it, reveal a comparable unity of purpose and subject matter, even though the materials, and the organization of them, are so much more elaborate. I am in no doubt that it makes good sense to write about Mahler's 'Wunderhorn' period *as a* period, that in so doing, one is unfolding a pattern that is there in the composer's art, not imposing one from without; and it will be my lack of skill, not any want of substance in my case, if this does not come across clearly in the present book.

In *The Early Years*, as I have implied, the task was less complex because the field was much the more restricted. My main business in the 1950s was not original research, for which in any case I had no funds, and of which I had no experience whatsoever, but an attempt to bring some sort of order into the established literature on Mahler and clarify, through study of his early works, the origins of his musical character. It soon became evident through my scrutiny of the early drafts of *Das klagende Lied* that there was an immense amount to be learned from Mahler's MSS, about the actual evolution of the works themselves and about his working methods—it should be remembered that in 1954, when I was first in Vienna, serious assessment of Mahler's MSS was an entirely novel undertaking, not only to me but to everyone else—and this line of approach, first adumbrated in *The Early Years*, has had a powerful influence, as readers will soon find for themselves (I hope not to their dismay), on *The Wunderhorn Years*. Hence indeed much of the present volume's elaborate detail.

The organization of *The Wunderhorn Years* differs from that of *The Early Years* in two ways. First, I have dropped the idea of a continuous, musically 'explanatory', biography. I was interested in Mahler's early life, partly because it was shrouded in obscurity and partly because I believed very strongly in the 1950s in the influence of the early years on a composer's subsequent life *and* art (a document typical of this area of interest of mine was my 1955 broadcast on Mahler and Freud, which I include here as an Appendix to Part II). I would not suggest that this old interest has melted away, but I have come increasingly to think that it was for a composer's early years, rather than for his later life, that the kind of biographical method I pursued in my first book was peculiarly appropriate. Moreover, there is M. de La Grange's huge work in this field, which there would be no sense in duplicating, even marginally. Second, since completing *The Early Years*, where I offered, or tried to offer, a more or less comprehensive account of each work I surveyed, I have become far less convinced that that sort of analysis is really necessary or even illuminating. Too often one has no option but to lapse into the purely descriptive, to try to match in words what only the music can, in fact, 'speak'. I do not claim to have avoided altogether this form of redundant commentary in the present volume, but I certainly have tried, for the most part, to offer an alternative method, to seize on what I take to be some of the principal and unique features of a given work and look at these in close detail, both in the narrow context of the isolated work and in the broader perspectives of Mahler's art as a whole.

It is an approach which avails itself of the resources of the microscope and the telescope, and which is responsible for the juxtaposition of magnified close-up and long-distance view which is emphatically one of the structural principles around which the book is built. It is this same principle which expresses itself in the alternation of Chronicles and Commentaries—the magnifying Commentaries focusing on points touched on in the broadly conceived, generalizing and chronologically-minded Chronicles—and is, I think, no less evident (if somewhat differently expressed) in the deliberate mix of the chronological and the anti-chronological, which is also a feature of *The Wunderhorn Years*. This is not untidiness on my part. Indeed, though much less systematically, my earlier book also ranged pretty far forward in its references to music of Mahler's which, strictly speaking, was outside the book's scope. If I do not believe in descriptive analysis, no more do I believe that one should accept unquestioningly the tyranny, the convention, of chronology. Thus when I have thought it relevant and important, I have not hesitated to look at and discuss in detail the consequences and significance for the future of, say, certain techniques or creative stimuli first revealed in the 'Wunderhorn' period but which Mahler was to develop later, perhaps even at the very end of his life, in works which chronologically belong to the next volume. I hope that readers will find this procedure more enlightening than confusing. Though I may seem to be anticipating the future too liberally in this volume, I shall be no less generous, if needs be, in making comparable retrospective gestures in the next.

I also ought to make clear perhaps that almost everything in this book is new. I have included a few items that have been published or broadcast before, though they appear here mostly in a radically revised and expanded form. It was in these particular writings that I began to concern myself with the special preoccupations of this book, and, I believe, to develop the kind of approach to the music that I have outlined above. As a result, these contributions provide an easy and logical transition from *The Early Years* to the main body of *The Wunderhorn Years*—Parts III and IV—where almost every word is published for the first time.

Finally, while I certainly hope to have advanced Mahler studies a little in this book, I am quite sure that we are as yet nowhere near the stage where we can be entirely confident about our interpretation of many of the facts (about the music, about the life). This, I think, is particularly true of the MS situation, where by no means all the facts are yet uncovered (or accessible) and where much still remains to be investigated. It will come as no surprise to me if fresh information reaches me that will require the modification, or contradiction even, of some of the speculation in this volume, as carefully argued as I hope it is. There can be no 'last word' on Mahler (a futile ambition), only various contributions to our understanding of him, made from our own personal points of view, though supported of course by the best data available to us. Sufficient reward if some aspect of one's own comprehension of his art proves to be an illumination for someone else or a point of departure for another student. It is in that spirit that this book has been written.

*   *   *   *   *   *

I must now thank everyone who has helped me in putting *The Wunderhorn Years* together.

First, I must thank the members of what was virtually a secretariat, without whose devoted labours the book would never have got done. I know it is the custom to thank one's wife last, but I must thank my wife, Kathleen, first; for nothing could have been accomplished without her encouragement, which has meant so much to me, and her patient typing of the many successive drafts of the book. I must next thank Colin Matthews, who drew the music examples for me, and Judith Osborne, Charles Ford and David Matthews, who at various stages were involved in the editing of the MS or the reading of the proofs. I also wish to thank Belinda Bartram, who typed the fair copy of the complete MS. Both Colin and David Matthews are Mahler specialists in their own right and I have greatly benefited from the ideas and comments they have put forward throughout their association with the book. Where a note appears with the initials 'C.M.', this is a contribution (or communication) from Colin Matthews. Finally, before closing this section, I want to thank Bill Hopkins, who drafted many of the translations for me, and Peter Moldon, of Faber and Faber, for his painstaking work on the design of the book.

Next I would like to give special thanks to two friends who are also colleagues in the Mahler field, Dr. Edward R. Reilly (Vassar) and Knud Martner (Copenhagen). Both have been unstintingly generous in sharing their own knowledge and research with me, and have never failed to help with the queries or calls for aid with which I have often bombarded them. This book owes them a substantial debt of gratitude.

To the following individuals, who have helped me at various times in often diverse ways, I should like to express my warm thanks: the late F. Charles Adler and Mrs. Hannah Adler (in particular for the use of the sketchbook for the Ninth Symphony and the sketch for the Chorale of the Second Symphony); Deryck Cooke; Jack Diether (New York); Berthold Goldschmidt; Dr. Laton E. Holmgren (New York); Dr. Albrecht Joseph; Hans Keller; Mrs. Christa Landon (Vienna); Dr. and Mrs. H. C. Robbins Landon (Vienna); Anna Mahler; Terence Miller; Margot Milner; Henry Pleasants; Frederik Prausnitz; Dr. Zoltan Roman (Calgary); Prof. Alfred

Rosé (London, Ont.); Harold Rosenthal; Prof. Ronald Taylor (Sussex); Dr. J. Ujfalussy (Budapest); and Philip Winters (New York).

I also wish to acknowledge, most gratefully, the help rendered me by the following institutions (and individuals): Central Music Library, Westminster; Staatsbibliothek Preußischer Kulturbesitz, Mendelssohn Archiv, Berlin (Dr. Rudolf Elvers); Music Room, British Museum (Alec Hyatt-King and O. W. Neighbour); Music Library, University of London; Mengelberg-Stiftung, Amsterdam (Miss W. H. Bijsterus Heemskerk); Mary Flagler Cary Music Collection and Lehmann Deposit, Pierpont Morgan Library, New York (Herbert Cahoon and Rigby Turner); G. Schirmer Inc., New York (Hans W. Heinsheimer and George Sturm); Library, University of Southampton; Library, University of Sussex; Österreichische Nationalbibliothek, Musiksammlung, Vienna; Universal Edition, Vienna and London (W. M. Colleran); Music Division, Library of Congress, Washington (Edward N. Waters and Mrs. Frances C. Gewehr); Josef Weinberger Ltd., Vienna and London (Dr. Otto Blau and Richard Toeman); Osborn Collection, Yale University Library (Dr. S. R. Parks) and the Beinecke Rare Book and Manuscript Library, Yale (Dr. Louis Martz).

I should like to acknowledge the first volume of M. de La Grange's biography of Mahler. This was published after the MS of this book had reached a very late stage. I have endeavoured where possible to take account of the wealth of information that he has placed at the disposal of all students of Mahler, and which places us in his debt, though as I point out in DM[3] (see Bibliography), caution has to be exercised in the use of his book. Nonetheless it is right to recognize the imposing scale of his achievement.

I must finally thank Faber and Faber and the University of Sussex, both of which institutions allowed me the periods of leave without which *The Wunderhorn Years* would never have materialized; and apologize to two old friends and colleagues in publishing, John Murray and Frank Upjohn (King, Ont.), for whom originally this book was to be written as a kind of everyman's guide to Mahler (it was to be simple and short). In the writing of it, I fear the book turned into something different from what was planned for them; but I hope to be able to rely on their forbearance until I have an opportunity to discharge the debt. It will not be forgotten.

All the merits in this book may be attributed to those who have helped me so generously. All the errors are mine.

D.M.

Barcombe Mills,
Sussex
January, 1975

Part I

Contents: Part I

CHRONICLE

MAHLER'S WORKS divide into three categories—songs, song-cycles and symphonies.[I] For many composers these categories have proved to be sealed-off compartments: for example, we do not find a significant connection between a song of Beethoven's and one of his symphonies. With Mahler, however, the interrelationship between the few media in which he worked was close and complex.

To recognize this fact is not to fall into the trap of regarding him as a 'song-symphonist', a horrid cliché that belongs to the dubious history of Mahler's critics and not to the history of his music. When Mahler uses material from a song or songs as building material for a symphony, then the song proves to offer the kind of symphonic, i.e. developmental, possibilities that a large-scale structure demands (e.g. the Scherzos of the Second and Third Symphonies).

It is also important to remember that the fertilizing process works in reverse: some of the songs are symphonically organized, for instance the first song of the *Kindertotenlieder* cycle, which presents elements of exposition, development and reprise. It is this type of practice that makes Mahler's song-cycles symphonic, rather than the breadth and continuity of their overall shape.[II]

[I] Roman numerals refer to the Commentaries that follow each Chronicle.

COMMENTARIES

I. Short List of Works and Dates of Composition

Das klagende Lied [Revised 1893 and 1898/1899.]	1880
Lieder und Gesänge Vol. I	1880–1883
Der Trompeter von Säkkingen [It was in this Suite of incidental music for the theatre that the discarded 'Blumine' movement in the First Symphony had its origins.]	1884
Lieder eines fahrenden Gesellen [Orchestral version materialized between 1891 and 1895.]	(December) 1883–(January) 1885
Symphony No. 1	1884 (?)–1888
Lieder und Gesänge Vols. II and III [Texts from *Des Knaben Wunderhorn.*]	1887–1890
Symphony No. 2	1888–1894
Des Knaben Wunderhorn Nos. 1*–10 (see table, pp. 140–3) [*Some writers propose 1888, Leipzig, as the probable date of the conception of this song, but as I explain later (see n. 33 p. 259–60) there is very little evidence to support this early year.]	1892–1898
'Revelge'	1899

'Der Tamboursg'sell'	1901
'Das himmlische Leben' (Symphony No. 4)	1892
'Urlicht' (Symphony No. 2)	1893
'Es sungen drei Engel' (Symphony No. 3)	1895
Symphony No. 3 [*Some early sketches apparently belong to this year.]	1893*/1895–1896
Symphony No. 4 [*The song-finale, 'Das himmlische Leben', was composed in 1892 (see above).]	1892*/1899–1900

II. Mahler: Song-Cycle and Symphony

In March 1960 I wrote a script for the BBC Third Programme entitled 'Mahler: Song-Cycle and Symphony' in which I set out in some detail certain musical relationships between two of Mahler's three orchestral song-cycles—the *Lieder eines fahrenden Gesellen* and *Kindertotenlieder*—and his symphonies. I have edited the script for its first publication here, annotated it, and in some places considerably amplified it (such extensions or diversions are indicated by square brackets), but I have not attempted to alter radically the character of the main text, which was designed to be spoken:

I shall always remember a remark made to me by that exceptional man and musician, the late Erwin Stein (1885–1958). He knew a great deal about Mahler, and I was always bothering him with problems and queries. Once I took to him one of the many mysteries of Mahlerian chronology, an important one, as it happened: how did Mahler originally conceive his first song-cycle, the *Lieder eines fahrenden Gesellen*? For voice and piano, or, as is still widely assumed, for voice and orchestra?

Stein was not able to help with any dates or information; instead, he tapped the score of the work with his finger and said, 'The answer is *there*. You must make up your mind on the evidence of the music.'[1]* A simple enough answer, I dare say; but I must confess that it had not occurred to me—which goes to show how unthinkingly dependent one can become on dates and documents, so much so, that when these props are suddenly removed one forgets that the most important document of all, the music itself, is there to guide one, providing one can read the signs aright.

On the musical evidence, indeed, it seems most probable that the *Lieder eines fahrenden Gesellen* were composed in 1883–5 (see pp. 119–23) in a version for voice and piano (though it may have been that Mahler *thought* of the cycle in orchestral terms from the start); and that it was not until much later that he orchestrated the cycle, for a concert of his own music in Berlin in 1896 (see also pp. 265–7).

By then, he had behind him his First and Second Symphonies, and was working on his Third, and it seems to me to make sense that the brilliant, mature and above all refined orchestral style of the *Gesellen* cycle

---

* See p. 44. All notes designated by arabic numerals are to be found at the end of each Part.

should emerge from the experience Mahler had gained in his early symphonies; otherwise we must imagine that this perfect instrumental technique flowered with startling suddenness, without any very convincing precedents. His early cantata, *Das klagende Lied*, composed four years before the cycle, has many authentic Mahlerian features in its orchestration; but there are not enough, I think, to make the orchestral version of the *Gesellen* cycle seem a logical, immediate next step in Mahler's development in the orchestral sphere.

So, strangely enough, when we hear Mahler quoting his *Gesellen* cycle in his First Symphony, it is more than likely that this was, in fact, the cycle's *first* appearance in orchestral dress. My Ex. 1 comes from the First Symphony's third movement, from the middle section of the famous funeral march. Mahler makes a perfectly straight quotation of part of the last song of the cycle, itself a funeral march:

Ex. 1

The first movement, too, makes use of material from the cycle, but not, by any means, in the shape of simple quotation. On the contrary, though the movement's themes and motives have their origin in the second song of the cycle, the way in which they are treated and developed is quite peculiar to Mahler's symphonic technique.

This important aspect of Mahler's symphonic technique has been admirably described by Stein (ES, pp. 6–7)*: 'His development sections expand, not by sequences, but by variations. Sometimes he shuffles the motifs like a pack of cards, as it were, and makes them yield new melodies. The motifs of the theme reappear, but in a different arrangement.'

In so far as it is possible to reduce a highly complex and sophisticated procedure to a general principle, this technique might be described as a breaking-down or fragmentation of a theme into its constituent motives, which are then re-presented in ever-changing chronological sequence and fresh contrapuntal combinations. Mahler brought this technique to a consummate pitch in the Fourth Symphony's first movement (from which Stein chooses his illustration), and it seems that he himself was aware of the implications of the technique. Of the symphony's second movement (where the same technique prevails, if in somewhat less concentrated form), he said (NBL, p. 144): '. . . often the thousand little fragments of

---

* See Bibliography, pp. 432–4 where the bibliographical keys are explained.

the picture change so kaleidoscopically that it's impossible to recognize it again'.

Stein was certainly right to emphasize Mahler's variation technique, which was a topic that Mahler often touched on, if not directly then at least by allusion. In 1899, for example, he said—inaccurately as it happens—of his songs (NBL, p. 119): 'In my writing from the very beginning you won't find any more repetition from strophe to strophe; for music is governed by the law of eternal evolution, eternal development—just as the world, even in one and the same spot, is always changing, eternally fresh and new.' In 1900, he was again asserting that 'a work of art must evolve perpetually, like life', a remark made in the course of a grotesque mis-assessment of Schubert, whose 'repetitions'—'each repetition is already a lie'—prompted Mahler's indignation (NBL, p. 138).

[When one genius misunderstands another, the misunderstanding is likely to be total. On the other hand, how revealing these blank spots are, though *not* of the genius who is criticized. Composers who talk critically about composers (and in particular about composers by whom they have been substantially influenced, as Mahler was by Schubert) are for the most part talking about themselves. The same holds true for critics, but they, alas, have no creative gifts to make their misunderstandings interesting.]

In 1901 (NBL, p. 176), Mahler was wondering if the public would realize that the second movement of his Fourth Symphony was in fact as much 'variations' as the work's third movement. When one takes into account his own musical practice and his recorded speculations, it is clear that Mahler's concept of 'eternal evolution, eternal development', backed up by his evident dread of repetition, was not far removed from the idea of perpetual variation, which was to be a significant preoccupation of Schoenberg and his associates. Here, surely, there is one of the many links between Mahler and the younger generation of Viennese composers by whom he was surrounded.

While it is true that it is in the Fourth Symphony that we encounter Mahler's variation technique at its most subtle and elaborate, it is exercised there in relation to thematic materials which are not exclusively built on prime song-sources (though the overall source for the symphony is the *Wunderhorn* song, 'Das himmlische Leben'). Nonetheless—and this, I think, is a point of crucial importance—Mahler adopts just the same fragmentation procedure even where prime song-sources are involved. Indeed, it is precisely in this technique that the relationship between his songs and his symphonies subsists.

For example, in the first movement of the First Symphony, which is based on the second song of the *Gesellen* cycle, we meet in the development section exactly that rearrangement and re-shuffling of motives described by Stein, motives derived from the long span of the song's melody. (Note that in the exposition too, i.e. from Fig. 4, Mahler reshuffles the order of the strophes in the song, opening in the symphony with the *third* strophe of the song and only later exploiting the first and second strophes. For a detailed analysis see MT, pp. 26–8.) Naturally enough, the technique is handled more simply than in the Fourth Symphony, but in essence, the variation principle is already there, fully established in the first of Mahler's series of symphonies; and it is a song, not a 'symphonic' theme, that offers Mahler the possibilities of symphonic extension and elaboration. It is of no little significance that, though the character of Mahler's building materials changed from the Fourth Symphony onwards (i.e. the incidence of prime song-sources diminished), his symphonic *technique*, on the whole, remained constant. This tells us something about the symphonic potentialities latent in the songs.

Those who want to do their own homework on the First Symphony, where Mahler's variation principle first emerged in symphonic guise, should compare the development section of the first movement (Fig. 12 to Fig. 26) with the exposition (four bars after Fig. 4 to Fig. 12), when it becomes clear how Mahler in his development re-orders the sequence of motives and phrases extracted from the song-source as it is initially exposed. It is altogether characteristic, for instance, that in the development (Fig. 16) he picks up the song's melody at its mid point (when indeed it functions as the continuation of a new melody which takes shape five bars before Fig. 16) and does not re-introduce the song's opening motive until later (Fig. 17), in contrapuntal combination with a cluster of motives derived from the prime song-source (see the four bars from Fig. 17 onwards) and the movement's exposition, which in itself already represents the song-source viewed from a fresh angle. There are in fact three blocks of invention involved in any detailed consideration of Mahler's symphonic treatment of 'Ging heut' morgens übers Feld': (1) the song itself; (2) the exposition of the first movement of the symphony, a re-statement of the song which is appropriately varied and extended to accord with its new formal status and context; and (3) the development of the movement, in which the motivic fragmentation of the exposition's materials (themselves one stage removed from the song-source) takes place.

One might add, for good measure, (4) the recapitulation, if only for the reason that we encounter there further evidence of Mahler's exuberant distaste for established chronological sequence or repetition. It will not escape the keen listener that the recapitulation opens not with the return to the principal song-theme (two bars before Fig. 29) but with the triumphant D major assertion of a theme from the development (scored for horn quartet, two bars after Fig. 15). When the song-theme does re-appear, Mahler unfolds it in the main in its original shape and sequence, but there is one fascinating insertion: this final statement of the tune now includes in its seamless flow the new melody to which, in the development, the second half of the song-theme appended itself as a continuation![2] (Cf. the recapitulation, seven bars after Fig. 29 to Fig. 30, et seq., with the development, five bars before Fig. 16, et seq.) Mahler, as can be seen by any patient student of the score, continues to play his motivic cards in unpredictable combinations and sequences until the very end of the movement. More than that, he takes care to demonstrate the unity that underpins the ceaseless variation.

Ex. 2 shows in skeletal form the outline and sequence of the principal song-theme in the exposition: (x) is the first limb of the theme, (y) the continuation:

Ex. 2

In Ex. 3, from the development, (x) is missing, but the new melody (z) leads to (y), the continuation of (x) in Ex. 2 above:

Ex. 3

In Ex. 4, from the recapitulation, (x), (z) and a version of (y) (in that order) all appear as one continuous melody:

Ex. 4

When Mahler has done with his development-by-dislocation, all the pieces fall back into place, into an eminently satisfying logical pattern.

We meet Mahler's variation procedure in all those instrumental movements of Mahler's that are bound up with specific songs, movements that

are confined to his first period as a symphonist, from the First Symphony
to the Fourth. [The movements are:

SYMPHONY I:

First movement: the song-source is 'Ging heut' morgens übers Feld',
    the second song from the *Gesellen* cycle.
Second movement: the song-source is 'Hans und Grete', from Vol. I
    of the *Lieder und Gesänge*.
Third movement: the song-source is 'Die zwei blauen Augen', the
    fourth song from the *Gesellen* cycle.

SYMPHONY II:

Third movement: the song-source is 'Des Antonius von Padua
    Fischpredigt', from *Des Knaben Wunderhorn*.
Fourth movement: itself a song, 'Urlicht', originally (see pp. 136f.) an
    independent setting of a *Wunderhorn* text.

SYMPHONY III:

The basic song-source for the whole symphony is 'Das himmlische
    Leben', originally an independent *Wunderhorn* setting, later used as
    the Finale of Symphony IV. (See pp. 127f. and 311f.)
Third movement: the song-source is 'Ablösung im Sommer', from
    Vol. III of the *Lieder und Gesänge*.
Fourth movement: itself a song, 'O Mensch! Gib Acht!', a setting of
    words by Nietzsche. (See also n. 21, p. 252.)
Fifth movement: a choral setting, 'Es sungen drei Engel', of a *Wunder-
    horn* text, from which Mahler later derived a solo song version. See
    pp. 129f.

SYMPHONY IV:

The basic song-source for the whole symphony is 'Das himmlische
    Leben', the *Wunderhorn* setting which is the Finale of this work'.
    (See pp. 311f.)]

Song, after the completion of the Fourth Symphony, ceases to fertilize
Mahler's symphonies in so explicit a manner; and of the song-cycles, it
is only the first, the *Lieder eines fahrenden Gesellen*, that plays a direct
thematic role in one of the symphonies. The *Kindertotenlieder* cycle,
which belongs to his middle period, bears another sort of relation to the
symphonies altogether, one I hope to demonstrate a little later. For the
moment, I might leave it at this: an intimate identity of style between
cycle and symphony. The third and final song-cycle, *Das Lied von der
Erde* (see also pp. 361f.), a late work, is song *and* symphony, *not* song-sym-
phony, something that Mahler never composed or attempted to compose,
despite the persistence with which this pernicious and misleading label
was at one time affixed to his works.

Mahler was a strongly developing composer, and so it was inevitable
that in a sense his widely spaced-out song-cycles should have more to do

with the works by which they are surrounded than with each other. But one thing they do all share in common (and one certainly cannot say this of his symphonies, though the generalization is often made)—each cycle ends in death. *Das Lied* offers a final dissolution into oblivion; the end of the *Kindertotenlieder* needs no explication; and the hero of the *Gesellen* cycle undoubtedly comes to rest in a grave beneath his lime tree. As I have mentioned before, the last song of the cycle is a funeral march that ends decisively in F minor. It would be possible, perhaps, to interpret the hero's farewell to life as typically romantic posturing, not a declaration of fact. But if, once again, we apply Stein's test of applying music to music to find out what music is about, we find ourselves able to reach a precise conclusion. It is not just Mahler's chilling F minor summing-up that I find significant, or the fact that the cycle's funeral march is quoted again in the funeral march of the symphony. (Death of a hero, indeed.) What clinches the matter for me is a *Wunderhorn* song, for voice and piano, that Mahler wrote some years later than the *Gesellen* cycle. It is entitled 'Nicht Wiedersehen!' (from Vol. II of the *Lieder und Gesänge*, see pp. 125f.), and in the very place where the lover, in the poem, is bidding farewell to his sweetheart in her grave, the song clearly recollects the funeral march from the *Gesellen* cycle. Ex. 5 is the relevant passage from the song-cycle and Ex. 6 the comparable passage from the song. The image of the loved one in a grave summons up not a mere reminiscence of Ex. 5 but the very same musical thought and conception:

Ex. 5

Ex. 6

That parallel, for me, settles the matter. The funeral march of the *Gesellen* cycle is a real one, not just romantic apostrophe. (In a paper read before the American Musicological Society in Toronto, November 1970, Dr. Zoltan Roman of the University of Calgary, to whom I am indebted for allowing me to read both a copy of his paper (ZR[1]) and his doctoral thesis on Mahler (ZR[2]), suggests that 'Nicht Wiedersehen!' might be one of the 'missing' songs from the original set of six that Mahler mentions in a letter of 1 January 1885 (GMB[1], pp. 33–4). On pp. 123–5 below, I go into some of the reasons why I think it wholly improbable that this could be the case, though Dr. Roman is certainly right in responding to 'Nicht Wiedersehen!' as a song that is very close indeed to the world of the *Gesellen* cycle.)

[On pp. 62–3 I show (what I could not know in 1960) that the musical imagery surrounding the last sleep of Mahler's hero in the *Gesellen* cycle was directly anticipated in the original first part of his early cantata, *Das klagende Lied*, at the point in the narrative where the younger knight seeks rest beneath a willow tree. This is the sleep that precedes his murder by his jealous brother. (Readers should turn to p. 63 and consult there Exx. 30/31.) Could there be clearer musical signs that in fact we must take the last song of the cycle to be a 'real' funeral march? The consistency of the imagery is overwhelming. Furthermore, we surely uncover here the dramatic justification for the cycle's progressive tonality (D minor→F minor). The Traveller travels and arrives at a destination that is wholly different from the point from which he has set out on his journey, and Mahler's overall key-scheme faithfully records the course of his hero's destiny. One might claim that Mahler's tonality, travelling along with his Traveller, is not only dramatic but also strictly realistic, even factual, perhaps. It seems to me that the same association of tonality and dramatic truth underlies the overall key-schemes of many of Mahler's symphonies. There is certainly another important relationship here between the song-cycles and the symphonies: the roots of Mahler's use of progressive, dramatic tonality in the instrumental works are obviously to be found in the song-cycle which preceded the first of his symphonies. Even when the drama of the symphonies becomes increasingly interior, it continues to be served by, and indeed made comprehensible through, the use of tonality as narrative. In short, the majority of Mahler's key-schemes tell a story.]

We again meet problems of chronology when we approach the *Kindertotenlieder* cycle. They are somewhat complicated, but I think they may be summarized with reasonable brevity. There are no dates on the manuscript of the work (which was in the possession of Bruno Walter, whom I consulted), and two of the main sources of information are contradictory. The first, Guido Adler (GA, p. 103), tells us that the cycle was written between 1900 and 1902, the first three songs between 1900 and 1901, the fourth and fifth songs between 1901 and 1902. This chronology was accepted for many years, though to my ears it had always gone against the evidence of the music.

A more convincing overall chronology was provided by the composer's widow in her first book of reminiscences. There (AM⁵, p. 70), she allots the composition of three *Kindertotenlieder* to the summer of 1904, an addition to the two songs already extant, according to her diary. So this gives a much later date of completion than any suggested by Adler, and also makes a different estimate of the number of songs actually written in each of the two stages of the cycle's composition. (To add confusion to a confused record, in her later autobiography (AM⁸, p. 34), Frau Mahler attributes the completion of the work to 1905 (but this date is excluded by the known date of the cycle's first performance), writes of six songs (when there are only five), and suggests that Mahler wrote three to begin with, whereas in her first book she had said only two.)

[In fact, this not particularly momentous matter of whether the successive stages in the composition of the work equalled 2+3 songs (Adler) or 3+2 songs (Frau Mahler) seems to have been settled decisively by HG¹, p. 941, n. 62, in which it is stated 'Natalie [i.e. NBL, pp. 165–6] does not indicate how many of the *Kindertotenlieder* were composed during this summer [1901]. However, before [Mahler] returned to Vienna, he gave her, in token of friendship, a manuscript of seven Lieder which included *three Kindertotenlieder*' (my italics). This would seem to clear up the point and also to elucidate a little the somewhat obscure statistics embedded in the section of her recollections that Bauer-Lechner entitled 'Sieben Lieder'. (The four remaining songs in this MS collection would have been, presumably, 'Der Tamboursg'sell', 'Ich atmet' einen linden Duft', 'Ich bin der Welt abhanden gekommen' and (one supposes) 'Um Mitternacht'. HG¹, pp. 631–2, like NBL, pp. 165–6, is not absolutely clear as to which Rückert songs—the three *Kindertotenlieder* apart—formed part of the MS gift. If one wants to include both 'Um Mitternacht' *and* 'Blicke mir nicht in die Lieder' in the MS collection (both of which songs belong to the summer of 1901), then it would mean excluding the one *Wunderhorn* setting, 'Der Tamboursg'sell'. Perhaps that is the answer to this query: three *Kindertotenlieder* plus four independent Rückert settings made up the gift to Natalie.) It may be of interest in this general context to mention the four MSS of the *Kindertotenlieder* cycle (all for voice and piano and without instrumental indications) that are to be found in the Pierpont Morgan Library (Lehmann Deposit), New York. There are what would appear to be fair MS copies of 'Wenn dein Mütterlein' (No. 3) and 'Oft denk' ich' (No. 4), both of which are written on identical MS paper and with the inscription 'aus Kindertotenlieder von Rückert'. 'Nun seh' ich wohl' (No. 2) is written on a quite different kind of MS paper, bears no collective or source title (like No. 5, also), and includes some intriguing pencil marks by the composer, above all an alternative version of one crucial vocal phrase 'zu drängen eure ganze Macht zusammen' (4 bars before Fig. 1a)—that runs like this:

Ex. 7

This particular phrase evidently gave Mahler some cause for special thought, because on p. 4 of this sketch there is further evidence of his working away to get this particular phrase precisely right, an especially interesting example of his working methods in evolutionary progress. The remaining MS is of the last song, 'In diesem Wetter' (No. 5), which is written on the same brand of MS paper as No. 2. It is tempting to match up paper types and periods of composition—and paper undoubtedly is very often a reliable indicator of chronology—in which case one finds that the identity of the paper for songs Nos. 2 and 5 cuts right across the chronology of the songs and their established order. As NBL does not name the songs, and as we do not know exactly which three *Kindertotenlieder* Mahler handed to her in MS form at the end of the summer of 1901, a characteristic ambiguity prevails. We must also remember that it could be the case that the songs were not composed in the order in which they finally emerged as a cycle. Should that prove to be so, then the chronology would have to be differently interpreted.]

We come up with some significant results if we once more apply the test of internal musical evidence. The first two songs of the *Kindertotenlieder* are both clearly connected with the Fifth Symphony, which we know Mahler was working on in 1901, and it was in that year, according to Frau Mahler (AM[8], p. 34), that her husband encountered Rückert's melancholy poems. To establish the links between the Fifth Symphony and the cycle, I show first a phrase from the first song (Ex. 8), the final cadence of which is of particular significance:

Ex. 8

In the funeral march (the first movement) of the Fifth Symphony—

just before the second trio begins—the long theme of the slow march
makes a clear reference to the first song of the cycle. Ex. 9, which is the
cadence with which the symphony's march tune closes, is identical with
Ex. 8, the cadence from the song:

Ex. 9

Ex. 9 is a clear quotation; but at the same time it is strictly thematic. In
other words, the shared cadential phrase crystallizes into an immediately
recognizable shape the concealed or less explicit melodic relations that
exist between the song and the first movement of the symphony.

I wrote earlier that with the *Kindertotenlieder* we meet 'an intimate
identity of the style between cycle and symphony'; and this is made
particularly clear in a general but convincing way if we compare the
cycle's second song with the famous Adagietto, the slow movement, of the
symphony. First, the song (Ex. 10):

Ex. 10

The melodic style of the song, above all its thrusting appoggiaturas, is
very close indeed to that of the Adagietto (see Ex. 11), and so is the sound
of the song's instrumentation. The combination of strings and harp, a
predominant impression one has of the song, is precisely the orchestral
colour of the Adagietto:

Ex. 11

[One of Mahler's five independent orchestral settings of Rückert, 'Ich
bin der Welt abhanden gekommen' (composed, not surprisingly in view
of its style, in August 1901), is also related to both the Adagietto from the

Fifth Symphony and the second song of the *Kindertotenlieder*. 'Ich bin der Welt' dissolves in a sublime cadence that is close indeed to the cadential dissolution of the Adagietto and it shares an appoggiatura-laden melodic style with both the symphony's slow movement and the cycle's second song. Even if we did not know the date of composition of 'Ich bin der Welt' (we owe it to NBL, pp. 106–7),[3] we could guess it pretty accurately from the internal musical evidence. In this connection, perhaps I ought to mention a fascinating pre-quotation of the cycle's second song in the slow movement of the Fourth Symphony, three bars before Fig. 3 (Ex. 12):

Ex. 12

This is, of course, none other than the principal motive of 'Nun seh' ich wohl' (Ex. 13):

Ex. 13

Mahler, as we know from various sources, completed the composition of the Fourth Symphony in August 1900—we learn from HG[1], p. 587, that the MS of the Adagio is inscribed 6th August, Maiernigg—and if Frau Mahler was correct in suggesting that Mahler did not come across the *Kindertotenlieder* poems until 1901, then we are right to speak of a pre-quotation. In this instance, then, the ensuing song from the cycle was anticipated in the symphony's lament. What is of greater interest is the fact that Exx. 11 and 12 have a common origin in the final duet of the lovers in Verdi's *Aida* (1871), an opera that Mahler frequently conducted. Ex. 14 (from Verdi) shows the relationship:

Ex. 14

When one bears in mind the dramatic situation of the lovers in the opera—their entombment—it is not surprising that Verdi's melodic shape emerges in the context of the *Kindertotenlieder* and the plaintive E minor section of the Fourth Symphony's slow movement.

I think it unlikely that Ex. 12 is anything other than an intimation of things (a song!) to come, but of course if Frau Mahler were wrong about her husband making the acquaintance of the *Kindertotenlieder* texts in 1901—suppose it were 1900, for example—then it could be that Mahler started the cycle (or started thinking about it) in the year that he was engaged on the Fourth Symphony; in which case Adler's first date (1900) for the first stage in the conception of the cycle would be valid. But all this really only emphasizes what was always a prominent aspect of Mahler's composing method, an aspect that became more pronounced as he grew older: the *overlapping* between individual works, whether song and symphony, or symphony and symphony. In part, the conspicuous interrelationships between one work and another must be attributed to the hectic conditions of Mahler's life. His obligations as a conductor meant that he sketched a work at one stage, composed it (during his summer vacations, almost always) and established a final score later in the year (and thereafter pretty continuously subjected it to revisions of the instrumentation). I do not doubt that this stretched time-table (sometimes covering a number of years) meant that a fresh project was already in his head (or being sketched) while he was still completing or applying the final touches to the work in hand. Hence the intriguing cross-references that are the subject of the last part of these notes.]

The links between the Fifth Symphony and the *Kindertotenlieder* that are illustrated in Exx. 8 to 11 suggest that we can with reasonable confidence regard 1901 as the year in which the cycle was begun. But although we may have confirmed the date when Mahler started composing the cycle, we have yet to confirm another, the probable date of completion. Here the Sixth Symphony can help us out.

The Sixth was completed in the summer of 1904, and a fair copy of the full score (in the archives of the Gesellschaft der Musikfreunde, Vienna) bears the date May 1905; and we learn from Frau Mahler that her husband finished off the *Kindertotenlieder* at the same time as he completed the Sixth (AM[5], p. 70). So I think we might reasonably expect to find a relation between the cycle and the symphony that would support the probable chronology in terms of musical invention. The clearest link obtains between the last song of the cycle and the finale of the symphony. Ex. 12 is from the song, 'In diesem Wetter', where we should pay particular attention to the contours of the melody and above all to its dominant rhythmic pattern. I quote the first two strophes of the song, the vocal line only; but we should remember that Mahler's scoring of the song gives noticeable prominence to the horns:

Ex. 15

In the slow introduction to the Finale of the symphony occurs Ex. 16, an important theme for the horn that very swiftly discloses a decisive rhythmic and melodic relation to the theme of the song:

Ex. 16

The relationship is later consolidated, again in the Finale's introduction and again by the horn (Ex. 17):

Ex. 17

It seems to me that these examples show that Mahler's sketchbooks for 1903 and 1904 contained ideas that fertilized both the current symphony and the current song-cycle, invention that plays a quite independent role in either work and yet preserves a recognizable common source. We can then, again with reasonable confidence, allot the completion of the song-cycle to 1904, and remark upon the singular fact that, for whatever reason, the composition of the *Kindertotenlieder* was spread over at least four years, an unusual stretch of time for the mature Mahler, even when taking into account the interruptions of his creative life. The first performance of the cycle was given in Vienna on 29 January 1905 (it must have been this date Frau Mahler was thinking of in her second book of memoirs), with Mahler conducting, and Friedrich Weidemann (1871–1919), a principal baritone of the Vienna Opera, as soloist. This date not only fits into place the last piece of the chronological jigsaw puzzle but also establishes as a momentous presence on the historical stage that most influential medium of the twentieth century, the chamber orchestra.

Two final points. First, those fragments (Exx. 16 and 17) from the introduction to the Finale of the Sixth Symphony are eventually welded together to form the chief theme of the huge movement's second group. The distraught atmosphere of the *Kindertotenlieder* has been dispelled, and the symphonic theme, when it emerges fully fledged, is of a quite clear-cut optimistic character. It appears thus (Ex. 18) in the recapitulation of the movement:

Ex. 18

It is interesting to note that a basic musical idea can serve with equal success what are pretty well opposite moods, agitation in the song-cycle, confidence in the symphony.

My second and last point is bound up with the continuation of Ex. 18, which I quote as Ex. 19:

Ex. 19

What constitutes the special interest of Ex. 19 is the fact that it contains, in concentrated form, a clear anticipation of the fourth movement of the Seventh Symphony, the second of the two serenade movements, both of which Mahler entitled 'Nachtmusik'. Above all, the prominent violin solo in Ex. 19—a serenade-like gesture in itself—emphatically prefigures a motive (Ex. 20) that it is of the first importance in the nocturne in the later symphony:

Ex. 20

However, it is not only an anticipation of Ex. 20 that Ex. 19 unfolds. The continuation and spontaneous expansion of the solo violin's motive by the strings opens, as it were, a door, through which we glimpse—or overhear —melodic shapes characteristic of the second nocturne, still to be composed, as Ex. 21 shows:

Ex. 21

In this curious but palpable way, one senses in Ex. 19 that Mahler, albeit unconsciously, touches on a world of invention and sensation that he was to explore and elaborate in a symphony yet to be written.

To recapitulate: Exx. 12 to 21 represent a whole complex of references. First there are the echoes of the last song of the *Kindertotenlieder* in the

introduction to the symphony's Finale, echoes that then achieve independent status as an extended symphonic theme; and growing spontaneously out of the symphonic theme, an intimation of part of the next
symphony on the stocks, already active in Mahler's mind. Here, indeed,
we seem to find not a cross between song-cycle and symphony, but symphony fertilizing symphony. Nothing could be more suggestive of the
unusual unity—not uniformity—of inspiration that is a marked feature of
Mahler's middle-period works.

[I mention in the Chronicle the 'symphonic' organization explicit in
the first song of the *Kindertotenlieder* cycle. What I have in mind is this:
the first two strophes of the song are virtually identical (but for the subtly
varied instrumentation). The third strophe, however, departs from the
pattern established by the first two. It presents, in fact, a closely worked
development, shared between the voice and the orchestra, of the song's
basic motives, which now appear in all manner of new continuations and
combinations. The fourth strophe returns us to the pattern of the first. A
special point of interest here is the way in which Mahler introduces his
'recapitulation' (oboe) while the leadback from the 'development' (flute)
is still in motion (see Ex. 22), a telescoping process that the composer
often used at similar junctures in his symphonies:

Ex. 22

The outstandingly brilliant example of Mahlerian 'telescoping' occurs
in the first movement of the Fourth Symphony, which undoubtedly left
its mark on this first song of the *Kindertotenlieder* cycle. A more detailed
account of the procedure appears on pp. 320f.]

Notes

1 Stein's advice holds good, but as will be seen on pp. 91f., further important musical evidence has come to light since this script was written.

2 The new melody (five bars before Fig. 16), having first found the 'wrong' continuation (Fig. 16), eventually finds the 'right' one (see six bars before Fig. 22), i.e. the one that proves to disclose the main theme of the Finale. In connection with my remarks about the sequence of principal thematic motives in the recapitulation (see pp. 30–1 and Exx. 2–4) it is instructive to compare the recapitulation with the onset of the development (from Fig. 15 onwards), when it will be seen that the ordering of events in the recapitulation has much more to do with the development than with the exposition. Note too that the version of (y) in Ex. 4 comes from the development. (See Fig. 18, where (y), characteristically, is contrapuntally combined with (z). The linear sequence is restored in the recapitulation.)

3 The date is confirmed by the manuscript sketches (for voice and piano) of the song that form part of the Mary Flagler Cary Music Collection in the Pierpont Morgan Library, New York, one of which is dated 16 August 1901. See the catalogue of the Collection published in 1970, p. 32 (Item 139).

Part II

Contents: Part II

CHRONICLE

THE INTERACTION—or perhaps tension would be the better word—between song and symphony is the essential and enlightening backcloth against which Mahler's music as a whole may be viewed. If we disregard his student efforts, many of which were abandoned and lost,[1] his first creative achievement, which he himself recognized as bearing the stamp of personal authenticity, was the cantata, *Das klagende Lied*, for soloists, mixed chorus and large orchestra. This early work, the original three-part version of which was completed in 1880 (but much revised and condensed—Part I (*Waldmärchen*) was eliminated—before its first performance under the composer's direction in 1901), reveals many Mahlerian finger-prints, among them a dramatic use of key symbolism, fresh vocal melody in a Slav-inflected, quasi-folk style, and the prophetic incorporation of an off-stage band which, at the dramatic climax of the work, presents a bold contrast in mood and music, a deliberate intrusion of the commonplace upon high drama which was to remain a unique feature of Mahler's art.[II]

---

[1] Roman numerals refer to the Commentaries that follow each Chronicle.

COMMENTARIES

I. The Early Works (supplementary notes)

IN MY FIRST book (DM[1]) on Mahler (1958), I spent a good deal of time scrutinizing all the available information on Mahler's student works, almost all of which were lost and perhaps some of which never existed in any very material sense. It is not necessary to go over that tedious and largely barren ground again. Readers who are interested in the results of my researches can turn to DM[1], pp. 116–20, where I listed all the information known to me at that time.

They should also consult the substantial Appendix 3 in HG[1] (1973), in which M. de La Grange lists a number of lost or unpublished works that his own research has uncovered. So far as my own work is concerned, I have come across some new facts and sources that affect the list I compiled in DM[1], and in order to round off the picture that I presented in 1958 I shall tabulate here, as concisely as possible, any fresh information of significance that has a bearing on the juvenilia of Mahler that I discussed in *The Early Years*. Undoubtedly, the most intriguing document of all is an article by Paul Stefan (1879–1943), the Austrian critic and writer on music who was a passionate advocate of Mahler and one of his earliest biographers. This first appeared in *Musical America* (issue of 10 April 1938, p. 20), and I am grateful to Mr. Jack Diether (New York), who first brought it to my attention. (I show any editorial additions of my own in square brackets.)

FOUR UNKNOWN EARLY MAHLER SYMPHONIES FOUND IN DRESDEN

Mengelberg Tells of Coming Upon the Manuscript-Scores in Possession of the Widow of Weber's Grandson

by Dr. Paul Stefan

Zurich, March 25

Willem Mengelberg [1871–1951, the eminent Dutch conductor and outstanding Mahler interpreter and enthusiast], in the course of a recent conversation with the writer, said that there are in Dresden the manuscripts of four complete symphonies of Gustav Mahler's youth. Mengelberg, long a personal friend of Mahler, whose music he made popular in Holland with his many performances, came upon the track of these otherwise wholly unknown works at a music festival in Dresden some time ago. Recently he examined them there again and was delighted with them.

It does not sound at all improbable that archives, which Mengelberg specifically designates, should include manuscripts of Mahler. These archives belong to the Baroness Weber, who must be about seventy years old, the widow of an officer with literary tastes, who was Carl Maria von Weber's grandson. Mahler, as a young Leipzig conductor, was a frequent visitor at the Weber house. He was a great admirer of Weber, and thus the late Hauptmann von Weber [the composer's son] and Mahler conceived the idea of supplementing and revising the posthumous fragments of Weber's opera *Die drei Pintos* ('The Three Pintos'). The work was frequently performed in their version.

[Mahler's version of *Die drei Pintos* was first performed at Leipzig on 20 January 1888, under his own direction. For an admirably full account of the work, and of the circumstances that gave birth to it, see John Warrack, *Carl Maria von Weber*, London, 1968, pp. 245–61. See also the *Correspondence of Hans von Bülow and Richard Strauss* (ed. Schuh and Trenner, trans. Anthony Gishford, London, 1953), for an amusing exchange of views about the piece, and in particular about the merits of Mahler's instrumentation (see pp. 61, 68–9, and 70–1). Strauss, as may be seen, finally agrees, in a somewhat craven manner, with Bülow's strictures; but curiously enough Mahler himself, in later years, seems to have come round to Strauss's point of view. Bauer-Lechner writes in 1901 (NBL, p. 170): 'Mahler says that his scoring of the *Pintos* is rather clumsy, as he lacked experience and skill at the time.' See also HG[1], Chapter 12, for further valuable documentation of the *Pintos* enterprise; and Ludwig Hartmann's guide to the opera, published by Hermann Seemann, Leipzig, n.d., but after 1897.]

But Leipzig was a rather late stage in Gustav Mahler's life [he conducted there from 1886–1888]. His real career began, after a short period of preparation (in Bad Hall, Laibach and Olmütz), at the Court Theatre in Cassel, where the romantic and romantically inclined artist found an outlet in his music. After Cassel came Prague, and only after the Prague years, Leipzig. The Webers lived in Leipzig at that time.

The beginnings of the preserved and frequently played First Symphony of Mahler go back to the Cassel period. He was twenty-three-years old at the time. This First Symphony was completed at the age of twenty-eight. Before that he had composed the cantata *Das klagende Lied* ('The Plaintive Song'), perhaps conceived of originally as an opera [not so: see DM[1], pp. 144–45], and allegedly also an opera, *Rübezahl* [see D below, p. 56]. When one considers the rapidity and impetuosity of Mahler's creating, it may very well be that as many as four symphonies came into being in the ten years between the completion of 'The Plaintive Song' (1878) and the First Symphony (1888). [Stefan overestimates the period. *Das klagende Lied* was completed in 1880, not 1878, and though the First Symphony was completed in its first version in 1888, Mahler had probably been working on the symphony for a number of years.]

Mengelberg maintains that the First Symphony shows such perfection that it most certainly could not have been actually the first symphonic work of a young composer. He finds this in itself reason enough to believe in the four preceding early symphonies. Not only because he has examined the pieces does one have all the less cause to doubt his statements. He might after all, have been dealing with rough outlines. But he and Max von Schillings [1868–1933, the German composer and conductor] once got hold of the manuscript-scores. It was an evening's visit in the archives of Baroness Weber—and when the two musicians discovered the scores, they immediately played them through on the piano, taking all night. Not until six in the morning did they stop, profoundly moved by the musical content of the unknown works.

Now, if all this is so, the friends of Mahler will have to make every possible effort to enable a circle of connoisseurs at least to examine the manuscripts, and, if feasible, to perform the works. Baroness Weber promised young Mahler, to be sure, to use every possible means to prevent a performance of these scores, which Mahler wanted to burn, just as he destroyed many another work of his youth. [In fact, there seem to have been more losses than destructions. When it came to the point, Mahler tended to preserve his early manuscripts, for all his threats of incineration.] But such a promise must not be allowed to bear more weight than the interest of the musical world in such works, which may, after all, be significant not merely for Mahler, but for a whole epoch.

The suggested cache of 'four complete symphonies' is indeed astonishing. I was certainly not able to commit myself to anything as bold as this when assembling the evidence of symphonic projects, conjectured or actually composed, during Mahler's youth (see DM[1], p. 117 (i) and (j), and p. 120 (p)), though I did (on p. 133) suggest that if all the enigmatic recorded hints were added together, the total of Mahler's symphonic attempts would be brought to five. We have no reason to doubt Stefan's seriousness, and it is hard to imagine that Mengelberg would have recklessly perpetuated yet another Mahler legend. One must be cautious, of course, because Stefan is only reporting a conversation he had with Mengelberg, and second-hand evidence is notoriously unreliable. Nonetheless, though one may perhaps be a shade sceptical about the probable existence of four symphonies, each of them completely carried through, the strong possibility remains that some important manuscripts, either early symphonies or parts of early symphonies, were to be found in Dresden just before the beginning of the Second World War. It is ironical indeed that the history of Europe seems to have played the chief role in cutting off possible sources of information about the manuscripts. Stefan died in 1943, before the war was over, Mengelberg in 1951, his last years clouded by political controversy. In 1938, when Stefan published his article, not only was war imminent, but Mahler's music was itself banned in Germany, and elsewhere there was not the degree of interest in it that obtains today. It was scarcely an auspicious moment for launching a Mahler investigation. Worse still, there was the war itself, and the massive British air-attack on Dresden in 1945. Efforts have been made in post-war years to trace these early Mahler works, but if they existed, and I think one must presume that something substantial—and symphonic—did, if not in quite the clear-cut shape described by Stefan, then it seems most likely that the manuscripts were destroyed on the night of 13 February 1945. In any event Stefan's article must now be taken into account when assessing the creative output of the years of trial and error which preceded the composition of Mahler's First Symphony.

The remaining unpublished or lost works for which supplementary information can be provided are as follows (I shall henceforth follow the order adopted in DM[1]):

A. First movement of Quartet for piano and strings in A minor
(DM[1], p. 116 (c)).
A performing edition, prepared from the manuscript by Dika Newlin, was heard for the first time at an ISCM concert, Philharmonic Hall, New York, on 12 February 1964. (See also HG[1], p. 720, who conjectures that this piano Quartet first movement was *not*, in fact, the prize-winning work of 1876 that I suggested it was in DM[1], pp. 34-5. The first movement of the prize-winning *Quintet*, if that indeed *was* what it was, has not survived.) An edition of the movement, edited by Peter Ruzicka, was published by Hans Sikorski, Hamburg, in 1973 (Edition Sikorski 800). The edition also includes a transcription of Mahler's sketch for a projected Scherzo.

B. Two songs [fragments] (DM[1], p. 116 (c)).
Some useful further notes on these fragments are included in JD, pp. 65-76. Mr. Diether identifies the text of the D minor fragment as a folk-song, 'Weder Glück noch Stern', collected in the 1830s by Heine, and also shows that Mahler, though he did not finish the song, was busy, as was his custom, adapting and supplementing the text to suit his own purpose. (See also p. 168 and pp. 416-18.)

C. Herzog Ernst von Schwaben, opera. Libretto: Josef Steiner.
(DM[1], p. 116 (f)):
For the following notes on Mahler's youthful librettist, I am indebted to Josef Steiner's daughter, Miss Annie Steiner. As I wrote in a paper for the Royal Musical Association in 1961 (DM[2], pp. 85-6), it was surprising to receive confirmation of the work's bodily existence, 'some eighty-two years after the opera was abandoned, left incomplete and probably destroyed. I had

not, after all, been pursuing a total fantasy.' Miss Steiner's reminiscences (see also pp. 118–19) provide a fascinating footnote to the history of Mahler's early works. My editorial additions are in square brackets.

My father Josef Steiner was born on 29 August 1857, in a village near Iglau, where his father had a shop. [The Mahler family moved to Iglau (first to Pirnitzergasse, No. 4, and twelve years later, next door, to No. 6) in December 1860. Iglau is now Jihlava (Yugoslavia).] As he studied at the Gymnasium (grammar school) in Iglau, away from his home, he had to live in lodgings. My father was three years older than Mahler, so he must have been two or three years in advance with his grammar school studies, but the two young men certainly shared their enthusiasm for music and poetry. [Mahler entered the Iglau Gymnasium in 1869. For a brief period he attended the Prague Gymnasium (1871–2), returning to Iglau until he departed for Vienna in 1875. He matriculated at Iglau in 1877 (see also HG[1], pp. 50–1 and DM[1], pp. 24–6).] My father was also a very good pianist and studied piano playing besides his grammar school studies in Iglau, and I feel it is more likely that my father and Mahler were studying music together in their earlier years (with 'Melion' probably, who is mentioned in Mahler's first letter to my father). [See GMB[1], p. 8, n. 3.] Mother told us that my father formed an 'orchestra' in his grammar school class, performing easy orchestral works vocally, each performer singing a certain instrumental part, and my father conducting. I do not know whether Mahler ever took part in these activities. He was a 'Privatist' of the grammar school from 1875 to 1877 and Privatists in Austria did not attend classes regularly, but were mainly taught by a coach and only went in for exams at the end of terms. [This was the period when Mahler attended the Vienna Conservatoire, which he had entered in 1875.]

My father's main interest was German literature and poetry, and at Vienna University he studied German literature and was afterwards a school teacher for some time. The time of his studies in Vienna (1875–9) coincided with his close friendship with Mahler in Vienna, and for some time they shared lodgings there.

In the years 1875 and 1876 Mahler and my father spent some of their holidays at a farm at Ronow in Bohemia, at the home of one of my father's aunts. During the holidays in 1875 my father wrote, or finished, the libretto of an opera, *Herzog Ernst von Schwaben*, and worked with Mahler on the musical score. At the end of this holiday—as he often told my mother—they packed all the papers they were working on in a box and stored them in an attic room. When they returned to Ronow for a holiday in 1876 and wanted to continue their work, the papers had gone. My father's aunt just shrugged, and said there was such a mess of papers about that she had simply burned them when she tidied up the attic. The two young men were rather upset, but apparently did not write down the libretto or opera again—although my mother told us that my father, about thirty years later, played fragments of *Herzog Ernst* to her from memory.

My father stayed on in Vienna, afterwards studying the law and settling down as a solicitor. He must have lost touch with Mahler soon after 1879, as Mahler was not resident in Vienna. My father died in April 1913, and unfortunately never told us about Mahler, as we were all young children at the time.

D. Rübezahl, fairy-tale opera. Libretto: Mahler. (DM[1], p. 117 (k).)

The text (but no music) of this early operatic project has survived, as I reported in AM[5] (see pp. xxv–xxvi and plate facing p. 83). Mahler's autograph text is in private hands in the U.S.A. An article about the libretto by Dika Newlin appeared in *Opera News*, New York, 18 March 1972. In it, she suggests where Mahler might have used his early song, 'Hans und Grete', as part of the opera's music.

E. Das klagende Lied, cantata. Text: Mahler. (DM[1], p. 117 (m).)

I wrote in no little musical detail about the published two-part version of *Das klagende Lied* in DM[1], pp. 141–96. If nothing else, I at least hoped in 1958 to establish the fact that the cantata was conceived as such and not as a fairy-tale opera, a widespread belief echoed by Stefan in his article above. But alas, the myth is hard to kill. H. F. Redlich carelessly repeats it in the 1963 edition of his *Bruckner and Mahler*, London, pp. 173–4—in a passage that is a positive nest of misinformation—and as late as 1967 the hoary old legend turns up yet again in the Mahler chapter of Vol. II of *The Symphony* (Penguin Books, 1967), along with other wrong facts. I am sorry to find M. de La Grange lending even half-hearted support to this notion (see HG[1], pp. 732–3), for which there is not a shred of hard musical or textual evidence, only hearsay on the part of a few witnesses scarcely noted for consistent reliability. Possibly Mahler did say (something like): 'I thought once of making *Das klagende Lied* a fairy-tale opera . . .', but to convert that disembodied speculation into a 'fact' that the cantata was 'originally conceived for the stage' (with all that the phrase implies) is to endow a void with solidity.

'Waldmarchen' : The unpublished first part of 'Das klagende Lied'.

In 1958, I knew of the whereabouts of the manuscript of the unpublished first part, *Waldmärchen*, but was unable to consult it as the owner (Mr. Alfred Rosé) was reluctant to open the manuscript to inspection. In 1969, however, the situation changed, and I was able to offer some first thoughts on the 'missing' first part of the cantata in the supplementary introduction which I wrote in the same year for the American edition of AM[3]. This new material, slightly amended, was published in the *Musical Times*, April 1970. I reproduce the article below, amended where necessary (in the main, to bring its views into line with the impressions I gained on hearing the music), and with added music examples; and as it now stands, I think the article on *Wald-märchen* completes the account of the cantata I began in 1958.

I ought to add perhaps that although, when I wrote this introduction, I had not heard the music, the London performance of *Waldmärchen* in April 1970 did not cause me to modify my view that Mahler demonstrated good sense in making his radical excision. On the contrary, such revelations as there were only went to confirm it and indeed strengthen it further. It struck me forcibly at the performance, for instance, that Mahler's inimitable 'voice' (which he himself thought he had established for the first time in *Das klagende Lied*) was less consistently heard in the original first part than in the succeeding parts (despite a marvellous Mahlerian inspiration like the ravishing lyricism of the passage beginning 'Du wonnigliche Nachtigall' (bar 421, et seq.)). In fact, it seems to me that it was only after the composition of the first part—and possibly because of it—that Mahler found a style relatively free of the eclecticism (natural enough, in all conscience) that is typical of *Waldmärchen* but less obtrusive in Parts II and III; and bound up with this response was my feeling that the original first part was less skilfully, less adroitly composed than the succeeding parts. Here again it struck me that Mahler had learned a remarkable amount through the experience of composing *Waldmärchen*, experience that he put to good use in the second and third parts. If these observations have any validity, then they provide further reasons why Mahler himself decided to omit *Waldmärchen*. It would not have been just a question of superfluous repetition: quality and maturity of invention, too, would have been a consideration.

Now the introduction, a revised version of the *Musical Times* article:

In my first Introduction to the new edition of Alma Mahler's *Gustav Mahler: Memories and Letters* (AM[5]), I wrote:

> ... there is little now that we may expect in the way of new Mahler discoveries. The only major manuscript source that still remains to be made accessible is the first part of the early cantata, *Das klagende Lied*, the *Waldmärchen* section, which was omitted when Mahler came to publish his revised version of the work in 1899–1900.

By a stroke of unexpected fortune, I was able, in 1969, to consult a manuscript source of *Waldmärchen*, a vocal score (in Mr. Alfred Rosé's hand) of Part I of what was originally a tripartite cantata, and thus am able to report on this last and hitherto missing link with Mahler's youth. This fascinating document was among Alma Mahler's papers (Frau Mahler died in 1964, in New York), and I am most grateful to Anna Mahler, the composer's daughter, for allowing me access to it.

The history of the unpublished first part of *Das klagende Lied* is a complicated one. The owner of a manuscript full score of the tripartite version of the cantata (in what appears to be a copyist's hand) was, for many years, Mr. Alfred Rosé, the son of Arnold Rosé and Mahler's sister, Justine; and it was Mr Rosé who mounted performances of *Waldmärchen*, under his own direction, in 1934 and 1935.[1] Recently, however, this manuscript (which probably belongs to 1881) has passed into the hands of Yale University (the Beinecke Library), an acquisition facilitated by the generosity of the family of Mr. James M. Osborn, of New Haven, Connecticut.[2] The change in ownership has meant that at long last *Waldmärchen* is not only available for comment but also for performance.[3] (A vocal score of *Waldmärchen*, with a Foreword by Jack Diether, was published in 1973 by Belwin-Mills Publishing Corp., Melville, N.Y.)

It seems to me that there were two good reasons why Mahler applied the surgeon's knife. First, there is the question of overall shape. *Waldmärchen*, we find, begins with an impressively and elaborately worked out orchestral prelude of over 120 bars (complete, it runs to over 600 bars), very close in length, style and manner to the prelude that opens the next section, *Der Spielmann*. (The prelude to *Hochzeitsstück*, on the other hand, is very much briefer, indeed only about one-third of the length of the other preludes, and in no way as elaborate in the meticulous, mosaic-like exposure and combination of leading themes and motives.) I have little doubt that it was, so to speak, an embarrassment of preludial riches that in part prompted Mahler to make his revision also an abbreviation: in a very real sense, the cantata in its original version gives the impression of beginning twice over.

Why then, one may well ask, did Mahler not confine his revisory strategy to adjusting the proportions of the preludes to his original Parts I and II? The case, I think, is altogether less simple than that. On my reading of *Waldmärchen*, concede though one may its conspicuous inspirations, one also has to admit that the section is very close indeed in its mingling of lyrical and dramatic incident to the style and matter of the immediately ensuing *Der Spielmann*; and also, of course, in its alternation of solo, choral and orchestral passages, though this is characteristic of the cantata as a whole. (One notes too that *Waldmärchen* introduces a bass soloist, who is not employed elsewhere in the work, an extravagance that might well have influenced Mahler to economize in his revision.) In short, though the best inspirations of *Waldmärchen* may be quite the equal of those in *Der Spielmann* or *Hochzeitsstück*, they may also be regarded as largely duplicate inspirations and thus expendable when scrutinized by a composer in his maturity.

More important, and here perhaps we approach the heart of the matter, it seems that Mahler's later dramatic sense must intuitively have told him that the excision of *Waldmärchen* greatly served to heighten and intensify the drama. Because, with all three sections *in situ*, we have a needless duplication of the narrative, i.e. although the first section unfolds the actual murder of the young knight by his envious elder brother, the essentials of the tale are told in retrospect during the succeeding second and third sections, through the medium of the bone-flute (the instrument that the wandering minstrel fashions unknowingly out of one of the murdered youth's bones). It is surely undeniable that the drama of the fairy-tale is immeasurably tightened by the omission of the expository first part, which, if anything, blunts the edge of the macabre narrative by making too much explicit at an early stage. The retrospective narrative device is altogether more telling.

Though there may be good reasons why Mahler deleted the first part—and I think on the whole his judgement was completely sound[4]—this is not to suggest that an occasional performance of the cantata in its entirety would be anything but welcome. The music of *Waldmärchen* is often as fresh and enchanting as any music in the published version, and knowledge of the unfamiliar score enables us to see how the young Mahler envisaged the cantata as a whole. It is fascinating, for instance, to trace in this original first part the source of themes and motives that we have come to know so well in the bipartite final version of *Das klagende Lied*. The descending minor scale that winds—or unwinds, rather—*Hochzeitsstück* to its A minor close (Ex. 23), and that also appears in *Der Spielmann*, is continuously used in *Waldmärchen*, as indeed is the octave motive ('Ach Leide!') that the scale fills out (see Ex. 24). Another link is the urgent, thrusting phrase to which the minstrel places the flute to his lips in *Der Spielmann* (Ex. 25); again, in *Waldmärchen*, this particular idea is prominently used, at one stage, appropriately enough, in close association with the incident of the murder itself (Ex. 26).

These are only two examples among many, of course; and they represent only what we should expect: evidence of Mahler's use of thematic and motivic connections between the parts to secure an overall unity and a cogently worked-out scheme of themes, motives and keys with specific dramatic associations (Ex. 26, for instance, clearly symbolizes the elder brother's aggressive jealousy). It is a mode of operation that means, inevitably, that we have *always* known something of *Waldmärchen*, simply because its materials

Ex. 23

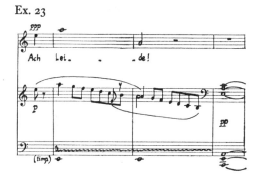

Ex. 24

Ex. 25

Ex. 26

were necessarily deployed later in *Der Spielmann* and *Hochzeitsstück*; and in the published version of the cantata there are indeed extensive stretches of music, as distinct from themes or motives, that are, in substance, based on comparable passages from *Waldmärchen*. (A prominent instance is Mahler's evocative 'forest murmurs' music, with its cascades of bird-song figuration, that is established early on in the prelude to *Waldmärchen* (bar 50, et seq.) and preserved in *Der Spielmann* (e.g. one bar after Fig. 7, et seq.).) This duplication of musical incident was doubtless another reason why Mahler felt able to declare his first section redundant: the best of *Waldmärchen* lived on in *Der Spielmann* and *Hochzeitsstück*.

On the other hand, *Waldmärchen* certainly has its own distinctive invention—the ingenious quasi-chorale treatment of some of the choral commentary is an example (see Ex. 27), not to speak of the flowering of an acutely poignant lyricism—and also clearly reveals an expository relationship to the succeeding sections. We find on occasion that what we know today as a prominent theme or motive in the revised version was much more extensively treated in the omitted first section. This is true, for instance, of the two

Ex. 27

quotations I introduce above, the descending scale (Ex. 23) and the phrase which carries the crucial text, 'Der Spielmann setzt die Flöte an' (Ex. 25), both of which are more insistently stated in *Waldmärchen* than in the ensuing sections. Thus part of the unique character of *Waldmärchen*—and one has to recognize the loss of it—was its function as a formal musical exposition (I cannot now understand Dr. Hans Holländer's description of it as 'a preliminary sketch'). This impression is further strengthened by the discovery of the detailed extent to which, as it were, Mahler foreshadowed the development and end of the work in its beginning: the haunting 'Ach Weh' motive of *Der Spielmann* (see Ex. 28a) is already clearly articulated in bar 28 of the prelude to *Waldmärchen*, though it is not developed in *Waldmärchen* itself (see Ex. 28b); and likewise in bar 70 we encounter the germinal motive of the festive 'castle' music (see Ex. 29a) that only attains its apotheosis in the celebrations of *Hochzeitsstück* (see Ex. 29b).

Ex. 28a

Ex. 28b

Ex. 29a

Ex. 29b

One may respect Mahler's judgement in making his revision, but there is no doubt that the original version of *Das klagende Lied* shows how the ambitious young composer—and we have to remind ourselves that Mahler was little more than twenty when he completed the work—was very much in control of the thematic and motivic detail of his cantata, even though the sheer abundance of ideas and fertile expression of them may later have been a cause of concern to him.

One point of overall formal organization is certainly—and interestingly—established by the manuscript of *Waldmärchen*: whereas the published version of *Das klagende Lied* opens in C minor (the prelude to *Der Spielmann*) and ends in A minor (the close of *Hochzeitsstück*), inspection of the original Part I (*Waldmärchen*) shows us that the first version of the cantata was less arbitrary in its tonal scheme; i.e. the prelude to *Waldmärchen* is launched with a tremolo on A that clearly looks forward to the clinching A minor of the cantata's final bars. (Also, F sharp minor, the key that eventually rounds off the unpublished first part, emerges early in *Waldmärchen*, in bar 5 of the prelude, and as I suggest in n. 5, p. 61, a special significance may be attached to this key.) To have the whole work before us may indeed confirm the impression, that was perhaps Mahler's, that here was too much of a good thing. But one is also left inescapably admiring the thorough organization that underpins the total concept.

Possibly, though, the most illuminating aspect of *Waldmärchen* is the extent to which it confirms the importance for the youthful Mahler of the world of *Des Knaben Wunderhorn*, the world which embraces not only his *Gesellen* cycle and *Wunderhorn* songs but the first four symphonies. In *Waldmärchen*, the use of fanfares (poetic and dramatic), the quasi-folk vocal melodies, the juxtaposition of major and minor, the march rhythms, the outbreaks of impassioned lyricism, the colourful key contrasts, the tramping basses founded on drum fourths—all these typical gestures fill out, most valuably, our knowledge and experience of Mahler's first period. Most striking of all, the murder of the fated younger knight beneath the willow tree[5] gives rise to musical imagery that is virtually identical with the famous passage in the *Lieder eines fahrenden Gesellen* (that Mahler later quoted in his First Symphony) where the travelling hero sinks to sleep and oblivion claims him. Only the tree is different: a lime, not a willow. My music examples (Ex. 30 from *Waldmärchen*, Ex. 31 from the *Gesellen* cycle), reveal this remarkable anticipation of a masterpiece still to come, for which reason alone *Waldmärchen* must be reckoned a historic document of the first significance.

I cannot resist pointing out two further relationships between *Waldmärchen* and other early works by Mahler. First, when one hears the bass soloist ascending his E flat minor scale in the fourth strophe (only to descend again in conformity with Exx. 23 and 24 above), one is inescapably reminded of another scale-ascending theme yet to come, the principal theme of the

Ex. 30

Ex. 31

[contd.

finale of the First Symphony. My Exx. 32 and 33 show the relationship (I quote the symphonic theme (Ex. 33) as it appears first in the development section of the First Symphony).

Ex. 32

Ex. 33

But what is far more entertaining and instructive is the relationship between the first song of the *Lieder und Gesänge*, Vol. I, 'Frühlingsmorgen', and a crucial juncture in *Waldmärchen*, when the younger knight plucks the flower he has been seeking, sticks it in his hat and lies down to rest (bar 338, et seq., Ex. 34).

Ex. 34

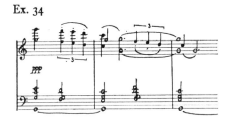

This is, of course, the sleep that precedes his murder, and we find that the composer in fact launches the unfortunate youth's final rest on a rocking lullaby motive (see Ex. 34) that, in the song, functions as an energetic (!) call to a laggard in bed to wake up (Ex. 35). Alas, the younger knight in *Wald-*

Meister RICHARD WAGNER in tiefster
Ehrfurcht gewidmet.

Symphonie

in (D moll)

für grosses Orchester

componirt

von

Anton Bruckner.

Partitur Pr. Fl. 18. / Mk. 30.   Stimmen Pr. Fl. 22.50. / Mk. 40.

Clavier-Auszug Vierhändig Pr. Fl. 7.20. / Mk. 12.

(Arr. v. Gustav Mahler.)

Eigenthum der Verleger für alle Länder. Eingetragen in's Vereins-Archiv.
Den Verträgen gemäfs deponirt
— Verlag von —
A. BÖSENDORFER'S Musikalienhandlung.
(Bussjäger & Rättig.)
WIEN, I. Herrengasse 6.

Jos. Eberle & C?

The title-page of Mahler's piano-duet arrangement of Bruckner's Third Symphony
(See pp. 68–9)

Symphonie in D moll.

Secondo.

I. SATZ.

Anton Bruckner.

Die mit ∧ bezeichneten Töne sind überall deutlich markirt zu spielen und durch das Pedal festzuhalten.

Moderato, con moto.

B. & R. 165.

The opening of the first movement

Symphonie in D moll.

Primo.

I. SATZ.

Anton Bruckner.

Die mit ⌃ bezeichneten Töne sind überall deutlich markirt zu spielen und durch das Pedal festzuhalten.

B. & K. 165.

märchen cannot be presumed to have known Mahler's early songs, in which case he might have been spared the cruel fate that overtakes him.

Ex. 35

Steh' auf Lang - schlä - fer!

Mahler's first book of published songs certainly belongs to the time when he was working on *Das klagende Lied*. It may well be that the quotation from 'Frühlingsmorgen' in the cantata tells us that the composition of the song preceded the cantata, in which case Mahler's reference to it was deliberate, a witty private reminiscence. If not—and the chronology is not itself of the first significance—then we have another clear instance of the consistency of Mahler's imagery, consciously or unconsciously deployed even at this very early stage.

(For a contrasted point of view about *Waldmärchen*, see JD, pp. 3–65, an ample survey of the original first part in which is quoted in its entirety a long synopsis of the piece by Mr. Alfred Rosé, written in connection with the performances he conducted in the 1930s.)

F. Der Trompeter von Säkkingen, incidental music. Poem: Joseph Viktor von Scheffel. (DM[1], p. 120 (q).)

As in the case of the four early symphonies mentioned by Stefan (see above), efforts have been made to trace the manuscript score (or at least the orchestral material) of this work. So far, without success; it appears likely that the score and parts were destroyed during the Second World War, when so many German theatres lost their archives. On pp. 217–24, however, I suggest that one movement of Mahler's *Trompeter* music has survived in the shape of 'Blumine', the original second movement of the First Symphony. (For further documentation, see HG[1], pp. 114–15 and p. 705.)

G. Bruckner, Symphony in D minor (No. 3). Piano-duet arrangement by Mahler and R. Krzyzanowski.

I mentioned this piano-duet version in DM[1], pp. 67–8, and described it there as Mahler's 'first publication'. On this occasion I reproduce the title-page of the printed edition, a rare item, and the opening page of the first movement. (See pp. 65–7.) The title-page enables us to identify the publisher correctly (I had the imprint not quite right in my earlier book), and although it is only Mahler's name which appears thereon, an entry in GMSZ, p. 76, tells us that Mahler was responsible for the arrangement of the first three movements and Rudolf Krzyzanowski for the Finale. If that information is correct, then the query I put in DM[1], p. 246, about the disposition of the partnership can be answered. I doubt, however, if 1878 is the correct date of publication. It is more likely to be 1879 or 1880, whichever year it was, in fact, in which Rättig brought out the score of Bruckner's Third Symphony. (According to HG[1], n. 17, p. 845, the transcription was published on 1 January 1880. In n. 18, same page, M. de La Grange quotes Alma Mahler's statement that the Finale was not transcribed by Mahler but by Ferdinand Löwe (and thus not by Krzyzanowski). There seems to be a confusion here that requires final clarification.)

II. Mahler and Freud

THIS PARTICULAR OBSERVATION in the Chronicle (p. 49) has become something of a cliché and it is now almost obligatorily accompanied by a reference to Mahler's famous interview with Freud in 1910. Though this incident is common knowledge today, it may be of some interest to record here how the disclosure came to be made. I had always been intrigued by the reference to the meeting with Freud in Frau Mahler's first book (AM⁵, p. 175) and wrote to the late Dr. Ernest Jones, who at the time had already brought out the first volume of his biography of Freud, seeking further information. He had not been aware of Frau Mahler's reference to Freud and at first doubted if any fresh facts would come to light. But they did, in the shape of a communication Freud made to Marie Bonaparte in 1925, material that Dr. Jones used in the second volume of his biography (*Sigmund Freud, Life and Work*, London, 1955, Vol. II, pp. 88–9). He was kind enough to send me this information when he found it, and further, was generous enough to let me use the Bonaparte document as the basis of a BBC Third Programme talk given in March 1955, before his own second volume had appeared. I was naturally anxious to spread this new knowledge, which greatly excited me. The charge of 'banality' was often made against Mahler's music and here, for the first time it seemed to me, there was made available information of a unique character that might assist general understanding of what, in turn, was a unique feature of Mahler's art. In so far as my talk (which I gave on 28 March 1955) was the first occasion on which the newly discovered facts about the Mahler-Freud interview were released and placed in a musical context, I think it retains a certain documentary value. I reproduce it here with only slight modifications and amplifications, and with indications, in the shape of music examples, of the excerpts from the symphonies I used in the broadcast.

If I were asked for a single term which described the characteristic flavour of Mahler's music, and which had both emotional and technical relevance, I think I should suggest 'tension' as the most appropriate word. It seems to me that when Mahler is expressing this basic tension—translating it into musical technique—he is at both his most characteristic and most inspired. Tension presupposes some kind of conflict between two opposed poles of thought or feeling, and often in Mahler's music we have just this situation exposed. Sometimes, of course, we have music from Mahler, anguished and turbulent, which does not state the conflict but expresses his reaction to it. Here the premises from which the conflict derives are not revealed but repressed; from the repression emerges the characteristic tension. Often, however, Mahler does express—or achieve— his tension through vivid contrast, through the juxtaposition of dissimilar moods, themes, harmonic textures—even whole movements. On these occasions, the conflict is exposed; we feel strongly the pull between two propositions which superficially seem to have little in common. The tension which results is typical of his mature art, where continually we are confronted with the unexpected. What seems to be reposeful and straightforward suddenly develops into something agitated and complex. There is a characteristic and relevant passage in the nocturnal fourth movement of the Seventh Symphony where the guileless serenade atmosphere is surprisingly disrupted, and the level of tension intensified through the abrupt dislocation of the prevailing mood [see Ex. 36]:

Ex. 36

This overwhelming tension in Mahler's music has, of course, been noted before, but its function has been little appreciated. Indeed, for the most part, it has been criticized or produced as evidence of his emotional instability, his stylistic inconsistency. The violent contrasts about which so much of Mahler's music pivots have been interpreted as an inability to maintain his inspiration—hence that view of his art which suggests that utter banality mingles with and deflates noble intentions, that dire lapses in taste inexcusably ruin otherwise impeccable conceptions. On a broader view, this misunderstanding of the nature of his tension has led to derogatory contrasts made between the size of his ideas and the size of his symphonies, not to speak of the strong body of opinion that sees the symphonies as inflated songs. Altogether, Mahler's tension, at all levels of expression, has been regretted rather than applauded, whereas to my mind it is just this tension which, as a composer, makes him tick.

If there has been little real understanding of his characteristic tension, there has been much analysis of it, much of it ill-founded, most of it in-adequate. Mahler's conflict—sensed alike by friend and foe—has been explained as the result of his activities tragically split between the tyranny of conducting and the urge to compose. It has been suggested that he was born at the wrong moment, on the tide of a musical fashion that was rapidly running out; his creative efforts to stay the retreating current imposed a strain on his music that it could not withstand. Or there is the socio-logical viewpoint, that he lived in a disintegrating culture, at the centre of a soon-to-collapse Austro-Hungarian empire, and his music therefore faith-fully reflects the social tensions of his epoch. Taken to excess, as it has been, this latter analysis almost assumes that history wrote Mahler's symphonies for him; his works become little more than musical com-mentaries on political events.

Mahler was a man of many talents and many tensions, and it would be rash indeed to suppose that the world in which he lived and his mode of life did not influence his art. Yet it is hard to imagine—it almost goes against plain common sense—that his music was shaped down to its finest detail by his historical environment. On the contrary, acquaintance with his music and the inner facts of his life suggests that his charac-teristic tension stems from sources much nearer home, from himself and his early relationship to his family, to his mother especially. His later environment, in the widest sense, may have done nothing to lessen his tension—it may, in fact, have exacerbated it—but it seems likely that the basic tension was a creation of his childhood years, was private and a part of his personality, not public and a part of history, either musical or political.

I may as well say at once that even when one has stumbled on what appears to be unconscious forces motivating a composer's work and directly influencing the character of his invention, the task of evaluating his music is made no easier. Music remains good or bad in itself, however far and factually we may penetrate a composer's mind. The discussion of a composer's neurosis is only musically relevant in so far as it enables us to see clearly what he did with it in terms of his music. If what may have appeared to be purely arbitrary in the music is shown to spring from deep personal sources, to present a consistent artistic attitude, extended and matured across the years, it may well be that the impression of musical arbitrariness is removed. Certain biographical data may actively assist musical understanding, and since understanding is a necessary stage on the way to evaluation, one can claim that such information is, at the very least, a proper study for musical research.

We are particularly fortunate in the case of Mahler that the kind of information I have in mind comes from a meeting he had in 1910 with none other than Sigmund Freud. The fact that the meeting took place has been known for some time; Frau Mahler mentions it in her remini-scences of her husband and gives there a brief account of the interview, based upon what she was told by Mahler. What has come to light recently is Freud's own account of his conversation with Mahler, made by Freud in a personal communication to Marie Bonaparte in 1925. Perhaps I may add at this point that it is entirely due to the courtesy and most generous co-operation of Dr. Ernest Jones, Freud's biographer, that I am in possession of this new material.

First, a word about the meeting itself. In 1910, Mahler became seriously alarmed about his relationship to his wife. He was advised to consult Freud, wrote, was given an appointment—cancelled it. He cancelled his appointment—significantly—no less than three times. Finally the meeting took place in Leyden, Holland, towards the end of August. [Probably 26 or 27 August, according to TR, p. 343.] The two men met at a hotel, and then, in Dr. Jones's words, 'spent four hours strolling through the town and conducting a sort of analysis'. The interview over, Freud caught a tram back to the coast, where he was on holiday, and Mahler returned by night train to the Tyrol.

Apart from what was said, it is impossible not to be intrigued by the very thought of this confrontation between two men of exceptional genius. Mahler, of course, was an artist, Freud a scientist. Yet Mahler's passionate seeking after musical truth was scarcely less ruthless than Freud's investigations; and no one, perhaps, either layman or expert, can fail to appreciate the consummate artistry with which Freud expounded his humane science. It is no accident that Lionel Trilling, the literary critic, can write in an essay on Freud of 'the poetic qualities of Freud's own principles, which are so clearly in the line of the classic tragic realism' [*The Liberal Imagination*, London, 1951, p. 57]. Perhaps it was this common ground between psychoanalyst and patient that explains why Mahler, who had never before encountered psychoanalysis, surprised Freud by understanding it with remarkable speed. [Freud, in his letter to Reik (see below), expressed again his admiration for 'the capability for psychological understanding of this man of genius'.] Perhaps Mahler, in his turn, was surprised by Freud's analysis of himself, as partial as it had to be in the peculiar circumstances of the interview. In a letter of 1935 to Theodor Reik [see TR, pp. 343-4], Freud wrote: 'In highly interesting expeditions through [Mahler's] life history, we discovered his personal conditions for love, especially his Holy Mary complex (mother fixation).' Mahler, his wife tells us, 'refused to acknowledge' this fixation— the denial confirms rather than contradicts Freud's diagnosis—but it seems that the meeting had a positive effect and Mahler's marriage was stabilized for the brief remainder of his life.

It was doubtless during those 'highly interesting expeditions through his life history' that Mahler—I quote Dr. Jones—'suddenly said that now he understood why his music had always been prevented from achieving the highest rank through the noblest passages, those inspired by the most profound emotions, being spoilt by the intrusion of some commonplace melody. His father, apparently a brutal person, treated his wife very badly, and when Mahler was a young boy there was a specially painful scene between them. It became quite unbearable to the boy, who rushed away from the house. At that moment, however, a hurdy-gurdy in the street was grinding out the popular Viennese air "Ach, du lieber Augustin". In Mahler's opinion the conjunction of high tragedy and light amusement was from then on inextricably fixed in his mind, and the one mood inevitably brought the other with it.'

Mahler's confessions strike me as being of genuine musical significance and relevance. It is not possible to deal here with all the questions they raise. We must overlook, for example, Mahler's estimate of his own achievements, remembering that composers are often the worst judges of their own value: what they value in themselves may be not at all what they are valued for by posterity. Moreover, we do not know by what standards Mahler judged his own music. He may even, quite sincerely, have wanted to be another kind of composer altogether. In this context, his own comment on 'noblest passages . . . spoilt by the intrusion of some commonplace melody' is of particular interest. Mahler himself seems to have regretted the conflict, to have viewed it as a disability; to agree, almost, with the views of his own sternest critics. I, on the contrary, as I have already suggested, regard the inevitably ensuing tension as a mainspring motivating his most characteristic and striking contributions to the art of music. But this, I feel, is not the moment to discuss whether Mahler was wrong or right about his own art, whether, in fact, the sublime in his music was fatally undermined by the mundane. I believe he was wrong, that he felt insecure about his music, that in a sense he did not even fully understand it himself. It would certainly not be unnatural for an artist in the grip of a violent tension from which he was unable to escape, to curse it rather than praise it, to imagine that to be rid of it would necessarily be an improvement. I am inclined to share Ernst Křenek's opinion that 'it is quite frequently not possible for an innovator to grasp fully the implication of his venture into the unknown. He may sometimes even be unaware of having opened a new avenue . . .', that 'the disconcerting straightforwardness of Mahler'—'his regression to primitive musical substances'—'is a striking foretoken of the great intellectual crisis which with extraordinary sensitivity he felt looming in the oncoming twentieth century' [see EK, p. 163, p. 207].

But it is not my purpose on this occasion to attempt a critical evaluation of specific features of Mahler's music. I only hope to show how frequently in his music, if by very various means, he re-enacted his traumatic childhood experience, how the vivid contrast between high tragedy and low farce, sublimated, disguised and transfigured though it often was, emerged as a leading artistic principle of his music, a principle almost always ironic in intent and execution.

Mahler himself confused the issue by crudely over-simplifying it.

It would be easy to point to the parallel between his music and his child-hood experience, if comedy always relieved tragedy, or a commonplace thought mechanically succeeded every noble one. But his music, merci-fully, is more interesting than that; the trauma, as it were, assumes com-plex shapes. However, in his First Symphony, in the slow movement, we have a clear instance of the basic conflict at work. The movement is a sombre funeral march. Mahler's use of the 'Frère Jacques' round as the basis of the march is symptomatic both of his ironic intention and of his ability to make old—even mundane—musical material serve new ends by reversing its established meaning [see Ex. 37]:

Ex. 37

Already in the movement's first section, the funereal mood has been interrupted by outbreaks of deliberate parody. In the gloomy recapitula-tion, the very march itself is juxtaposed with these mundane invasions—not quite hurdy-gurdy music perhaps, but close to it. The result is almost a literal realization of the tragic mood inextricably mingled with the commonplace [see Ex. 38]:

Ex. 38

Many like examples of this kind of simultaneous expression of seeming opposites could be found in Mahler's early music. As he matured the gap between his contrasts narrowed. There is a greater degree of thematic and formal integration. One might say that in disciplining his tension, Mahler succeeded in subduing the most strident features of his contrasting materials. The Seventh Symphony's first movement offers an interesting instance. The movement begins with an exalted, mysterious slow intro-duction [see Ex. 39]:

Ex. 39

This compelling mood is abruptly terminated in a passage in Mahler's favourite march rhythm that bumps us down to earth, a common function of Mahler's march-inspired motives [see Ex. 40]:

Ex. 40

The sudden drop in the level of harmonic tension and the sudden change in the character of the musical invention are, I think, striking. That the march motive grows thematically out of the opening paragraph integrates the contrast but does not lessen its effect. It is rather as if Mahler were expressing the conflict in terms of pure music, demonstrating that even the most far-reaching and profound musical idea can have a commonplace consequent, and one, moreover, which is thematically strictly related to its exalted antecedent. It is, so to speak, still his childhood experience; still the hurdy-gurdy punctures and deflates and makes its ironic comment. But now the experience is lived out at the subtlest artistic level. Even the mundane march motive [Ex. 40] is occasionally transformed into something sublime.[6] But for the most part it ranges the movement as a free agent, as a saboteur, stressing a rough world's impingement upon the eternal. My final example from this symphony shows how the rudely triumphant march cuts across the ecstatic convolutions of the first movement's lyrical second subject [see Ex. 41]:

Ex. 41

Perhaps the most significant musical consequence of Mahler's childhood trauma was this, that his unhappy experience endowed the hurdy-gurdy—the symbol of the commonplace—with a quite new weight. Its music became as highly charged with emotional tension as the tragic incident to which it is related. The conjunction of high tragedy and the commonplace meant that the commonplace itself, in the right context, could bear a new meaning. Its ironic comment could intensify a region of tragedy, or it could be used as a new means of expression; and here Mahler remarkably foreshadowed a main trend in twentieth-century art—not only in music, but also in the literary and visual arts—in which banality was to be systematically exploited. Undoubtedly this discovery of the potentialities of the commonplace vitally influenced Mahler's style. The first movement of his Third Symphony, a movement of massive proportions, forty-five minutes long, symphonically elaborated and organized to a high degree of complexity, largely draws its material from the world of the military band, from marching songs and military signals. These mundane (hurdy-gurdy) elements derive their tension from the new context in which they are placed. The movement's development is typical. The commonplace is made to sing a new and unprecedented song [see Ex. 42]:

Ex. 42

In the Third Symphony, Mahler, as he had done in the funeral march of the First, obliged the commonplace to serve his own singular purpose; the contrast between means and achieved ends could hardly be stronger. Elsewhere, we have seen how he used the mundane as comment upon nobler conceptions. Mahler, however, was nothing if not thorough in his contradictions, and his attitude to the commonplace itself was often sceptical. In the Fifth Symphony we see this reverse process in action. The work's Scherzo first offers an unblemished, winning, slow waltz [see Ex. 43]:

Ex. 43

But just as the tragic mood aroused its opposite, so too does even this kind of attractive commonplaceness undergo savage transformation. We do not have tragedy, it is true, but ironic comment on the deficiencies of the commonplace, on its musical unreality, on its inability to meet the realities of a tragic world. If the mundane often succeeds the tragic, Mahler seems to say, there is no guarantee that the easeful security of the commonplace is anything more than a deceitful fantasy [see Ex. 44]:

Ex. 44

I hope I have shown some of the ways in which Mahler in his music actively and, I believe, fruitfully reacted to that central event of his child-hood which I have discussed. There is little doubt to my mind that it played a main role in the formation of his musical character, in the creation of the tension that is so conspicuous a feature of his art. It was, I think, the basis of his musical conflict and certainly responsible for the remarkable irony of his utterance. If there were another tension of almost equal weight that played a part in determining the nature of his art, I would suggest that it was the conflict he witnessed, felt and registered between the old concept of musical beauty and the emerging new. But while not excluding the influence wielded by historical circumstance, I cannot but believe that an analysis of Mahler's personality is the surer guide for those bent on discovering why his genius took the shape it did.

The relationship of psychology to the art of composing has as yet been little investigated. Perhaps, as Hindemith wrote in *A Composer's World* (Harvard, 1952, pp. 24–5), 'We are on the verge of entering with our research that innermost field in which the very actions of music take place: the human mind. Thus psychology, supplementing—in due time perhaps replacing—former mathematical, physical and physiological *scientiae*, will become the science that eventually illuminates the background before which the musical figures move in a state of meaningful clarity.'

Notes

1 For further details, see DM¹, pp. 118, 153–57. There I had to rely in my account of *Waldmärchen* on reports generously contributed by Mr. Rosé and Dr. Hans Holländer. Clearly, these must now be revised in the light of information I bring forward on this occasion.

2 The MS of the original version of *Das klagende Lied* at Yale, which I have now seen, is a document of great interest. It is a beautifully written out fair copy of the full score, the neatness of which perhaps indicates that this was the copy of the work that Mahler had prepared for him and then submitted unsuccessfully for the Beethoven Prize (according to the researches of M. de La Grange, this was in 1881: cf. HG¹, pp. 79–81, with DM¹, pp. 145–50). The MS, which may well have been copied in 1881, bears many marks, most of them in Mahler's hand (in pencil, sometimes in colour), but some (in red ink) in another—perhaps the copyist's?—hand. The marks for the most part are associated with the revision or addition of dynamics and tempo indications, and with the re-touching of the instrumentation (superfluous doubling struck out, for example). These are all marks that are characteristic of the refining process to which Mahler subjected his scores throughout his life. There is one minatory marginal comment from the copyist (or was it from one of the youthful composer's examiners?) that draws attention to the faulty disposition of the parts among two B flat clarinets, the lower part of which is impractical as written. This bit of evidence Mahler took to heart, and he made a note in the MS that the part in question was to be transferred to the bass clarinet; and thus it appears in the revised version (in the published edition, see clarinets nine bars after Fig. 10). What did not give rise to marginal comment—though of course it was to be modified by Mahler himself when he prepared the two-part version of the cantata for publication (the first revision was completed in Hamburg, in December 1893, again a date we owe to M. de la Grange (HG¹, pp. 730–1))—was the evidently exuberant expectation of the youthful composer that there were no constraints to be observed in the field of orchestral resources. Thus we find no less than six harps specified in the original score of *Das klagende Lied*! This perhaps indicates the extent to which Wagnerian practice influenced the aspiring composer in the 1880s. (Mahler found himself able to manage with two harps when he came to revise the piece in the 1890s.) However, to be just—and this is one of the fascinating aspects revealed by a scrutiny of the original version—the six harps (sometimes

reduced to four) are intelligently rather than mindlessly deployed, i.e. to secure a really memorable splash (or wash) of colour at a crucial juncture. A good example can be found at Fig. 25 in the published edition, an eruption of glittering E flat minor arpeggios, for which Mahler employs four harps in his original version; or, to take another example, all six harps are brought into play for the similar eruption of F sharp minor arpeggios that close Part I (*Waldmärchen*) of the original version. Clearly, Mahler wanted to make an emphatic feature of those steely harp arpeggios, which are of course dramatically motivated and dramatic in impact. So even here, and in these early days, one finds Mahler piling on colour, not for the sake of colour alone, but rather for the sake of articulating certain dramatic features. There is no doubting the excessive means; but the intent was also functional. Besides the array of harps, there are other instrumental points of interest: that Mahler (again following Wagner?) sometimes specifies the use of *Waldhörner*, especially in overtly lyrical passages, and, in Part III, establishes as 'Orchestra B' (in opposition to 'Orchestra A', which is the main orchestra), the famous offstage band which, for the first time in Mahler's music, introduces the element of the mundane, the commonplace, into a tragic context. (See also pp. 70–8.) 'Orchestra B' also introduces for the first time the E flat clarinet into Mahler's orchestra (cf. pp. 327–8 and n. 18, pp. 369f.), on this occasion as member of a properly constituted wind band. (This was an instrument that was to play a major role in Mahler's orchestra of the future.) The specification of the band in its original form was as follows: piccolo, 2 flutes, 4 clarinets (2 in E flat), 3 bassoons, 4 *Flügelhörner*, 2 cornets (cornets-à-pistons), and percussion (triangle, cymbals, and timpani). A not insubstantial swelling of the orchestral resources already involved in the cantata! But, as Mahler found when working on the final version of this score, there was no room for economy here if the dramatic spatial juxtaposition of conflicting kinds of music was to be retained. The wind band had to be kept, virtually unchanged, but for a minor instrumental modification and the substitution of horns and trumpets for *Flügelhörner* and cornets.

Parts II and III of the MS are the most heavily worked over, which suggests that these corrections were made in connection with the revised, two-part version of the work. A detailed comparison of the tripartite version with the revisions of 1893 and 1898 would doubtless reveal many variants of significance. This I did not attempt. But I did notice, even on a cursory inspection of the MS under review, that one excised passage in Part II, which was re-composed in the revised version (from Fig. 14 onwards in the published score), includes a motive in the trumpets—a fanfare figure ('in the distance')—that was peculiar to the passage in question and thus disappeared altogether when the music was deleted (I show below the fanfare's rhythmic outline). (What was also lost was an elaborate bit of percussion that Mahler designated 'Like the distant tolling of bells'.) The general character of this passage is in fact preserved in a passage (from Fig. 7 in the published score) that has already appeared as part of the orchestral prelude. It would seem that this was the only major bit of re-composition that Mahler found it necessary to undertake. (The whole deleted passage, in its own right, is clearly worth detailed investigation.) For the rest, the revised Part I of 1893 is very close in substance to the original Part II of the cantata.

3 The first performance in England was given at the Royal Festival Hall, London, on 21 April 1970 by a quartet of soloists and the London Symphony Orchestra and Chorus, conducted by Pierre Boulez. Only *Waldmärchen* was heard in London, whereas at New Haven (where the U.S. première took place on 13 January) the original first part was followed by *Der Spielmann* and *Hochzeitsstück* (in the revised version).

4 As in my view was his eventual exclusion of the 'Blumine' movement from the First Symphony. See AM[5], pp. xvii–xix and pp. 217–24 of this book.

5 *When* is the fatal blow struck? Mahler's text is not really explicit, and Mr. Rosé and Mr. Diether seem to me to assume too easily that the murder is enacted during the penultimate choral strophe. It is my feeling, however, that while this strophe sets the scene for the murder, it does *not* include the act itself. Does not the blow fall during the lengthy interlude for orchestra alone (of which Ex. 30 forms part), which follows the eighth strophe? The interlude surely depicts the sleeping, dreaming youth—I believe Mr. Diether reads too much into the last line of the preceding strophe, 'Der Junge lächelt wie im Traum', when translating it as '*In death the lad a smile doth wear*' (my italics)—whose smiling dream is brutally interrupted by an outburst of F sharp minor (bar 575, et seq.). It is this interruption which, in my view, represents the blow of the sword itself. If so, it would certainly lend the dramatic significance to F sharp minor which its musical status would seem to propose. (There could be no doubting of the dramatic logic of rounding off *Waldmärchen* with the 'murder' key, which has been so judiciously—and thematically—touched on in the first few bars of the opening prelude.) Furthermore, compare the similar dramatic outbursts of minor keys (similar figuration) in *Der Spielmann* (Fig. 25, E flat minor) and *Hochzeitsstück* (two bars after Fig. 72, A minor), outbursts clearly related to the precedent in *Waldmärchen* and each of them directly associated with the enunciation of the murder by the bone-flute. There is little doubt in my mind that in the F sharp minor eruption in this scene of *Waldmärchen* we have the key of—and the key to—the dramatic and musical timing of the fatal sword-stroke. It is the orchestra alone which tells this part of the tale.

6 Looking at this script afresh in 1974, and at this passage in particular, I wonder why I did not in fact demonstrate the transformation, in the movement's development, of the 'commonplace' Ex. 40 into the sublime chorale motive (see over), which is one of the most telling instances of Mahler showing us that sometimes the commonplace and the sublime are not opposites at all but simply two aspects of the *same* idea:

It seems worth while taking the opportunity to make this point now.

Part III

Contents: Part III

Das klagende Lied, for all its youthful exuberance and pronounced echoes of Weber and early Wagner, already shows a finely calculated and original orchestral style, and its intensity of narrative power clearly anticipates Mahler's extraordinary capacity to re-live and musically re-experience the fairy tales or romantic poems he chose as his texts. Thus this early cantata significantly prefigures not only Mahler's first song-cycle, the *Lieder eines fahrenden Gesellen*,[I] but also his various settings of poems from *Des Knaben Wunderhorn*, the influential anthology of folk poetry collected in the early nineteenth century by Arnim and Brentano. Mahler must have known of this collection in his youth (far earlier than has been commonly supposed by most Mahler students), but it was probably between 1887 and 1890, in what we know now as the second and third volumes of the *Lieder und Gesänge aus der Jugendzeit*,[II] for voice and piano (published in 1892),[1] that he set *Wunderhorn* texts substantially for the first time. (The texts of the *Gesellen* cycle, modelled after the *Wunderhorn* manner by Mahler himself—and in the first song a *Wunderhorn* text is used—were written some four years earlier.) The spirit and invention of these wholly characteristic songs, whose collective title ('aus der Jugendzeit' was the publishers' invention) underestimates their originality and importance (the first volume, too—also published in 1892[2]—though it owes something to the tradition of Schumann and of the *Lied* proper, was by no means without its exceptional inspirations), are a marked influence on the first group of Mahler's symphonies. But much more substantial and far-reaching in effect are the later *Wunderhorn* settings, for voice and orchestra,[III] the pervasive influence of which enables one confidently to designate the first four of Mahler's symphonies as '*Wunderhorn*' symphonies.

These unique songs, imagined orchestrally with piercing clarity, do not represent a nostalgic yearning for an antique past. On the contrary, they are remarkable for their pungent immediacy, an intensification of the vivid actuality already established in the best moments of *Das klagende Lied*. No less remarkable, and equally typical, is the frequent extremity of the emotions explored. It is not accidental that the characteristic 'contents' of the songs, whether light-hearted or broken-hearted, sunlit or spectral, caustic or gay, and the musical imagery (e.g. military fanfares) and forms (e.g. funeral marches, *Ländler*-like dances) associated with them, should emerge so powerfully in those symphonies which in a very meaningful sense were born out of Mahler's immersion in the *Wunderhorn* world. Nor does one forget the sometimes ironic and parodistic tone of these unconventional, indeed often uncomfortable texts, for which Mahler found a comparably biting musical voice, thus creating a musical sarcasm (a genuine extension of the vocabulary of music) which, as he proved as early as in the slow movement of the first of his symphonies, did not necessarily depend on the stimulus or presence of words.

Though his first song-cycle, the *Lieder eines fahrenden Gesellen*, was not strictly speaking a setting of *Wunderhorn* poems, the cycle patently belongs to Mahler's *Wunderhorn* period. One might regard it as a kind of overture to the subsequent symphonies. The intimate thematic relationship between the cycle and the First Symphony (1884?–8) is so well known that it scarcely requires more than a brief acknowledgement here. But there are two other important issues, one of which has a direct bearing on the cycle, the other on both the symphony and one of Mahler's lost early works. First, it is possible that the composition and completion of the symphony preceded the orchestration of the cycle, which would mean, paradoxically, that the first appearance of the cycle's materials in an orchestral guise was made in the context of the symphony. Second, it is probable that the discarded second movement of the original five-movement version of the symphony, first performed at Budapest in 1889, the so-called 'Blumine' movement, was part of the suite of incidental music that Mahler wrote to accompany a stage production ('living pictures') of Scheffel's narrative poem, *Der Trompeter von Säkkingen* (Cassel,[3] 1884). The singular chronology and mode of assembly of the four *Wunderhorn* symphonies throw a revealing light on Mahler's compositional processes at this time.[IV]

COMMENTARIES

I. *Lieder eines fahrenden Gesellen*

O N 27 S EPTEMBER 1897, Mahler signed a contract with the Viennese publishing firm of Josef Weinberger for the publication of his first song-cycle, the *Lieder eines fahrenden Gesellen*. (I reproduce the document below.)

Verlags-Schein.

Hiermit verkaufe ich das ausschliessliche und unbeschränkte Verlags-g Vertriebs- und Aufführungs-Recht meiner nachgenannten Composition

Lieder eines fahrenden Gesellen
No 1. Wenn mein Schatz Hochzeit macht
  2. Ging heut Morgen über's Feld
  3. Ich hab' ein glühend Messer
  4. Die zwei blauen Augen

für alle Länder, für alle Zeiten und demgemäss für alle Auflagen, ohne alle Beschränkung in Betreff der Zahl und der Grösse derselben, sowie auch für alle Veröffentlichungsarten, überhaupt das Recht der ausschliesslichen und unbeschränkten Verfügung über diese Werke. an die Musikalien-Verlagshandlung J o s e f W e i n b e r g e r in Leipzig und Wien, für ihn selbst und seine Rechtsnachfolger.

Zugleich erkläre ich, dass ich das hierfür vereinbarte Honorar laut besonderer Quittung empfangen habe.

Wien am 27 Sept. 1897.

Gustav Mahler

The agreement with Weinberger for the *Gesellen* cycle
(By kind permission of Dr. Otto Blau and Josef Weinberger Ltd.)

We know from Mahler's own correspondence and from an inscription on the published vocal score of the work (albeit a somewhat ambiguous inscription—see pp. 119f. below) that the *Gesellen* songs belong to the Cassel period and were probably composed between 1883 and 1885. The cycle was published, according to Hofmeister, in 1897, in two versions, i.e. for voice and piano and for voice and orchestra. (HG[1], p. 707, gives 1912 as the date of the publication of the orchestral version by Weinberger, but without comment or amplification. This cannot be correct.)

As I have suggested elsewhere (see AM[5], pp. xx–xxiii), the chronology of the *Gesellen* cycle presents peculiarly complex problems. In trying to sort out the steps that led towards the final materialization of the work as we know it today, however, revealing light is thrown on the processes of Mahler's creativity and his technique of composing. So it is a far from worthless investigation, even though some facts uncovered by it may still continue to baffle us. Before any conclusions are reached or attempted, it seems to me obligatory to scrutinize in some detail the four sources—two manuscript sources, and two printed sources—which between them offer (to the best of my knowledge, at least) the most complete account of the cycle's genesis.

The earliest MS source known to me (which I designate OV, i.e. Original Version) is in the possession of Mr. Alfred Rosé, to whom I am indebted for supplying me with much of the following information. I ought to add that I have not seen the manuscript itself, and thus rely entirely on Mr. Rosé's own description of it. I referred to the OV in the context of the chronological problems surrounding the *Gesellen* cycle in DM[1], pp. 254–55, n. 10; but Mr. Rosé has sent further details since I made my first inquiry of him.

(According to HG[1], pp. 741–2, who has the information from Mr. Rosé, there was yet an earlier MS than the OV described here; i.e. the OV—so Mr. Rosé recalls—was a copy Mahler made from his original MS for the use of his sister, Justine. The earlier MS, from which the OV apparently derives, seems to have disappeared, though I doubt if its discovery would in fact throw much fresh light on the query which hangs over the chronology of the cycle's orchestration. In any event, if the OV, as Mr. Rosé thinks, was a *copy* made from the original MS, then the OV tells us most of what we need to know musically about Mahler's initial conception of his *Gesellen* songs.)

The OV, which is a voice and piano version of the cycle, is bound up in a single volume which also contains the manuscripts of Mahler's nine *Wunderhorn* settings from the *Lieder und Gesänge* (i.e. Vols. II and III) and the five songs which comprise the published Vol. I of that collection. The order of the songs in the manuscript corresponds to the published editions, with the exception of Vol. I where, in the manuscript, the order of the last two songs is reversed, i.e. 'Phantasie' precedes 'Serenade'. However, as may be seen from the list below, there are certain differences between the manuscript and printed sources of the *Lieder und Gesänge*, not only minor variations in individual song titles and sequence, but also in overall grouping and collective titles, i.e. what we know now as the three-volume *Lieder und Gesänge* collection stands here in two independent groups, on the one hand the sequence of nine *Wunderhorn* songs ('Lieder'), and on the other the collection of five songs ('Gedichte'), a division which reflects the different periods in which each group was composed. One must not read any chronological significance into the bound-up order of the manuscripts as they appear in this volume nor impose any kind of chronological uniformity on the volume as a whole. This is simply a collection of early Mahler manuscripts, the sequence of which is arbitrarily disposed:

> Geschichte von einem 'fahrenden Gesellen' in 4 Gesängen
> für eine tiefe Stimme mit Begleitung des Orchesters
> von Gustav Mahler
>
> Clavierauszug zu 2 Händen
>
> Lieder des fahrenden Gesellen—ein Cyclus

Aus 'des Knaben Wunderhorn'
9 Lieder von Gustav Mahler

Um schlimme Kinder artig zu machen!
Ich ging mit Lust
Aus! Aus!
Starke Einbildungskraft
Zu Strassburg auf der Schanz
Ablösung im Sommer
Scheiden thut weh!
Nicht Wiedersehen!
Selbstgefühl

5 Gedichte componiert von Gustav Mahler

Frühlingsmorgen
Erinnerung
Hans und Grethe
Phantasie aus 'Don Juan' von Tirso de Molina
Serenade aus 'Don Juan' von Tirso de Molina

Before launching out on an examination of the problem raised by the OV's suggested first title, i.e. that part of it which implies an orchestral accompaniment ('mit Begleitung des Orchesters'), let us first compare the OV (the earliest known vocal score) with the vocal score of the work which was published in 1897 (and is hereafter designated VS). Some of the differences are indeed startling. For example, in the OV the second song, 'Ging heut' morgens übers Feld', is in *D flat*, not in D, and the third song, 'Ich hab' ein glühend Messer', in *B minor*, not in D minor.[4] Thus when we are discussing the carefully planned and progressive key-sequence of the cycle, we should remember that this now familiar and much commented-on disposition of keys was a later development, though already rudimentarily present in Mahler's OV. The tabulation below sets out the similarities and the contrasts:

	Song 1	2	3	4
OV	D minor→G minor	D flat→F	B minor→C minor	E minor→F minor
VS	D minor→G minor→	D→F sharp→	D minor→E flat minor→	E minor→F minor

It is fascinating, when comparing these two sources, to see how, in the VS, the refinement and sophistication of the final overall tonal scheme (which most ingeniously combines concentric and progressive features in a finely balanced partnership) emerges from the bold but relatively crude and arbitrary key-sequence of the OV.

While it is the variations in the overall key-scheme which appear to constitute the biggest and perhaps most important differences between the OV and VS, there are some other variants which, although of an altogether more minor order, are of no little interest. The very first song, for example, brings us a fascinating example. Who would have guessed that in the earliest version of the *Gesellen* cycle, when the opening instrumental ritornello of the first song returns as a tail-piece, the voice joined in with a repeat of the poem's first line? Ex. 45 shows the vocal line in the OV (cf. Fig. 7 in the VS, where, of course, the vocal part is omitted):

Ex. 45

As it happens, this was an altogether crucial passage for Mahler, one which evidently cost him no small amount of labour. To the rhythmic problems it posed him, we shall return later. Meanwhile, we do not have to spend much time debating the prudence of Mahler's change of mind so far as the vocal part was concerned. The instrumental character of the ritornello cannot arbitrarily be adopted by the voice. To test the good sense of Mahler's later rethinking, try singing Ex. 45 up to speed. It simply does not work.

For the second song of the OV (in D flat, remember) Mr. Rosé's list of variants includes what appears to be more than one possibility for 'Zink! Zink!' (Ex. 46: to see what Mahler finally settled for, cf. the VS, five bars before Fig. 10):

Ex. 46

Zink, zink!   zink, zink!

and this version (Ex. 47) of 'Ist's nicht eine schöne Welt?' (cf. the VS, five bars after Fig. 16):

Ex. 47

Ist's nicht ei-ne schöne Welt?

The third song (in the OV, in B minor) presents a different version of the great vocal cry of despair (Ex. 48) which forms the final climax of the song (cf. the VS, Fig. 25):

Ex. 48

Ich wollt', ich wollt'ich läg'auf der Tod - ten - bahr, könnt'

For the rest, the variants comprise a minor textual discrepancy three bars after Fig. 23 ('seh' ich das blonde, blonde Haar' instead of 'seh' ich von fern das blonde Haar'); a significant omission; and a no less significant inclusion. The omission in the OV consists of the repeat of the 'O weh!' motive (see one bar before Fig. 22 and bars 3–5 after Fig. 21) which is, as it were, floated across the instrumental lead-back to the resumption of the song at 'Wenn ich in den Himmel seh' (six bars after Fig. 22). This re-introduction and augmentation of the motive—an inspired afterthought—does not appear in the OV.

The inclusion which in itself introduces a complicating factor into our discussion of the cycle's sources, concerns the four bars preceding Fig. 20. I quote here the bars from the VS (Ex. 49 the vocal part only):

Ex. 49

So tief!__   So   tief!__ Es schneid't so weh und tief!

Mr. Rosé confirms that in this passage the OV and VS are identical. Why then is there a problem? Because if we consult the published orchestral score we find, oddly enough, another reading for these bars (see Ex. 50 below), where the phrase 'Es schneid't so weh und tief!' is dropped from the voice part and transferred to the orchestra (violins and horns):

Ex. 50

There are, therefore, not only expected differences between the OV and the VS (and the list of variants I have supplied above constitutes, according to Mr. Rosé, a complete account of the differences: it seems that the fourth song in the OV manuscript is identical with the published VS) but unexpected discrepancies between the VS and the published orchestral score (hereafter PS), two items which one would reasonably assume should match up. The fact that they do not is certainly confusing; on the other hand the confusion itself is undoubtedly revealing of the various stages of composition through which the cycle passed. (I raised the matter of these textual discrepancies as long ago as 1958, in DM[1], p. 183.)

What is immediately clear, as soon as one starts trying to reconcile the OV with the VS, and the VS with the OV and PS, is the ambiguous nature of the VS, scrutiny of which tends to suggest that it occupies an intermediate documentary position, on the one hand obviously serving as an adjunct to the PS, on the other, still manifesting many links with the OV.

We have seen one of those links exemplified in Exx. 49 and 50, where the OV and VS match up, but not the VS and PS. A much more important and intriguing example involves Ex. 45, the instrumental ritornello which opens and closes the first song of the cycle. Note especially (my example is taken from the OV) Mahler's notation of the changing metre— $\frac{4}{8}$ | $\frac{3}{8}$ | $\frac{4}{8}$ | $\frac{3}{8}$, etc.

If we next turn to the VS and compare the identical passage (from Fig. 7), we find there the *same* notation of the metre as in the OV (all that is different in the VS is the omission of the voice part). Thus here (see Ex. 51), the VS follows the OV; and we may assume from the evidence of Ex. 45 that the VS (to which Ex. 52 corresponds) and OV are likewise identical in their notation of the song's very opening, when the ritornello first presents its characteristic metrical scheme, the fluctuating tempo of which Mahler was anxious— explicitly so—that performers should precisely observe (see also n. 6, p. 244):

Ex. 51

Ex. 52

It is this particular example which obliges us to introduce both the PS and its hitherto little-known predecessor, an earlier version of the full score of the cycle which is in the possession of the Willem Mengelberg-Stiftung, Amsterdam (hereafter EV). I write 'little-known', for such is indeed the case. In fact, here again is one of these curious blank spots that one repeatedly runs across in Mahler research. There seems no reason why the Mengelberg archive should not have been scrutinized, above all after the big Mahler Centenary Exhibition in Vienna in 1960, in the invaluable catalogue of which the EV was listed. Yet even this prominent display of an important manuscript item did not stimulate anyone at the time to follow up the clues it offers to the cycle's genesis (the MS is, of course, listed in HG[1], p. 741, et seq.). The EV comprises fifty-eight pages of manuscript full score (twenty-nine sheets of score paper) and is inscribed thus: 'Older autograph score of the Lieder eines fahrenden Gesellen by Gustav Mahler, received as a present from the author at the end of 1895.' There follows the signature of Hermann Behn[5] (1859–1927), a lawyer and musician who was a close friend of Mahler's during the Hamburg years. Mahler's gift to Behn must then have passed at some stage into the hands of Mengelberg, most probably after the death of Behn in 1927.

What does the EV tell us? It gives us, of course, a fascinating demonstration of the gradual refining process by which Mahler finally arrived at the renowned economy and precision of the PS. To provide a blow-by-blow

(*above*) A page copied from the early MS full score of the *Gesellen* cycle (EV)
(*opposite*) The corresponding page from the published full score (PS)

(*above*) A page copied from the early MS full score of the *Gesellen* cycle (EV)
(*opposite*) The corresponding page from the published full score (PS)

account of all the instrumental variants which are uncovered by a detailed comparison of both scores would be a lengthy business. Those who want to check every instrumental detail will need to scrutinize the EV and PS, side by side and page by page. In the context of this book, it seems most useful to present two typical sections from each score for the purpose of comparison. On pp. 98–9 I reproduce a page from the second song, 'Ging heut' morgens . . .', in both orchestrations, the EV on the left, and facing it, the page as it appears in the PS; and on pp. 100–1 appears a page from the third song, 'Ich hab' ein glühend Messer', in which the EV and PS are similarly juxtaposed. There is no point in my duplicating in words what Mahler himself demonstrates so clearly and economically. The first pair of excerpts shows us very practically and immediately the evolution of that refinement and lucidity of instrumental texture, after which Mahler sought so patiently and persistently and which—in his own estimation—he rarely found; while the second, which reveals an extensive redistribution of parts among the strings and woodwind, shows that it was not always refinement that was Mahler's practice but sometimes a radical substitution of one category of sonority for another. To study these scores in detail is to enjoy the benefit of lessons in orchestration with a master of the art.

I mentioned above in connection with Ex. 45 and Exx. 51 and 52 the crucial importance of the notation of the rhythm of the song's opening ritornello, a passage that clearly gave him some trouble before he alighted on a satisfactory formulation. As we have seen, it seems pretty certain that the VS follows the formula established in the OV (cf. Exx. 51 and 52 with Ex. 45). If we now turn to the PS, the published full score, we could reasonably assume to find there a notation of the ritornello that matches up with the VS —after all, these are (supposedly) the complementing published items. But not at all. The PS presents what was Mahler's final solution (which was also the simplest) of how to notate the combined duple and triple metres. He solved the problem thus, at one stroke (Ex. 53):

Ex. 53

Ex. 53, as one readily sees, is not identical with Ex. 52,[6] which in the main still clings to the notation of the OV (see Ex. 45). In the comparable passage in the intervening EV, however, we find that Mahler had already alighted on what was virtually the straightforward notational solution embodied in the

PS (Ex. 53), though he still felt it necessary at this stage to spell out above the flute stave in his manuscript score, the basic rhythmic pattern of his alternating 2s and 3s as in Ex. 54 below. The final step that remained to be taken was

Ex. 54

to get rid of the alternation of $\frac{2}{4}$ and $\frac{3}{4}$ bars and incorporate the $\frac{3}{4}$ bars as triplets within the overall $\frac{2}{4}$ scheme. Mahler, at the very beginning of the EV, was within a hair's breadth of achieving this tidy solution of his problem, and indeed, as the first song progresses in the EV, the final rhythmic scheme emerges ever more clearly amid (or rather, because of) the cancellations and scratchings out. By the time the coda is reached, in fact, the EV and PS (see Ex. 58) are virtually identical in notation (what differences there are, subsist in the instrumentation, not in the notation or the actual notes).

I mention above the scratchings out in the EV, which consist almost exclusively of the deletions of redundant time-signatures. I think the confusions still persisted, principally because Mahler was scoring from the OV (in which score the 'wrong' time-signatures were installed), but also because he still had not quite seen that the conversion of the $\frac{3}{4}$ bars into triplets in a $\frac{2}{4}$ scheme was the simple answer to his problem.

From what can still be deciphered on p. 11 of the EV, for example, it seems clear that Mahler wrote in at one stage a scheme of time-signatures that ran thus from one bar before Fig. 7 (Ex. 55):

Ex. 55

$$\frac{3}{4} \left| \frac{2}{4} \right| \frac{3}{8} \left| \frac{2}{4} \right| \frac{3}{8} \left| \frac{2}{4} \right. \text{(to end of song)}$$

The comparative scheme from the same point in the OV and VS runs as follows (Ex. 56):

Ex. 56

$$\frac{3}{4} \left| \frac{4}{8} \right| \frac{3}{8} \left| \frac{4}{8} \right| \frac{3}{8} \left| \left(\frac{3}{8}\right) \right. \text{(to end of song)}$$

Ex. 55 is evidence of the uncertainty in Mahler's mind that persisted to a very late moment in the writing out of the score, though in fact Ex. 55, when compared with Ex. 56, registers the influence of Ex. 54 (i.e. the EV consistently substitutes $\frac{2}{4}$ for the OV's (and VS's) $\frac{4}{8}$. Eventually Mahler scratched out all the time-signatures after the $\frac{2}{4}$ established at Fig. 7, thereby arriving in the coda at a notation which, as I have said above, is identical with the PS (Ex. 58) in all essentials.

It is by following in such detail as this the curious notational history of the metre of Ex. 45 (and the related passages) that we are enabled to follow Mahler's own steps as he progressed from the OV to the PS, with the EV, as now seems certain, functioning as an interim, mid-way shot at converting the OV, for voice and piano, into a cycle for voice and orchestra.

The EV and PS, without doubt, are more closely related than the OV and PS; or to put it another way, whereas the VS is clearly related to what we know of the OV, and the EV is clearly a stage *en route* towards the PS, the VS and PS—which are the two published items—do not match up, because each has its origin in a chronologically different source. H. F. Redlich, in his Preface to the Eulenburg edition (No. 1053, 1959) of the miniature orchestral score of the *Gesellen* cycle, demonstrated quite clearly (pp. v–vi) that the published vocal score (VS) did not adequately represent the published full score (PS). He chose to illustrate this by juxtaposing the opening bars of the first song from the VS with the identical passage from the PS, and the point is well made. But perhaps an illustration drawn from the closing bars of the song is even more telling. Ex. 57 gives us the coda as it appears in the VS, and Ex. 58 the same passage as it appears in the PS; and the attentive reader will not fail to notice how paradoxically discrepant are the published materials:

Ex. 57

Ex. 58

It is, perhaps, this example of the kind of variants one encounters in the printed vocal and orchestral scores of the *Gesellen* songs that is one of the most intriguing. To attempt to list all the passages where the vocal score and orchestral score differ, even if one were to confine oneself only to substantial differences, would be tedious and indeed superfluous. What is required is an entirely new vocal score, which should be made direct from the final orchestral score, and thus at long last bring the two published versions of the cycle into a precise relation. The vocal score issued by Weinberger in 1897 could then be discarded; or, rather, retained as an interesting historic document. What, certainly, it does not document, are Mahler's final intentions.

This is not the place in which to assemble, bar by bar, the new vocal score that is urgently needed. But it is probably worth listing a few further examples of the variants that we find in the four sources known to us (the OV, VS, EV and PS), even some of the most minor of which tell us something about the character and chronology of Mahler's composing methods. In the following examples, I shall try to keep all the sources within view and divide the examples of variants into specific categories. (It should be remembered that I exclude from consideration here the whole field of instrumentation.)

A. Variant readings

(i) On p. 95 above, I pointed to a significant omission in the OV, i.e. the repeat of the 'O weh!' motive (one bar before Fig. 22) was evidently a later addition. This is how Mahler finally shaped it, in the PS (Ex. 59):

Ex. 59

In the VS, however, it appears thus (Ex. 60):

Ex. 60

In the EV, on the other hand, the repeat of the motive appears as it was finally established in the PS. For some reason or other, and despite the improvement already carried through in the EV, Mahler did not bring the VS into line with his final decision.

(ii) Likewise, I mentioned on pp. 95–6 above the four bars preceding Fig. 20, where the VS and PS present alternative readings (see Exx. 49 and 50). In this instance the EV follows the precedent of the VS (and OV), and the phrase in question (Ex. 49) is retained in its vocal form. The omission of it from the PS must have been a final thought, and one which, yet again, was not registered in the VS.

(iii) A characteristic variant is to be found by comparing the piano accompaniment of the VS, three bars before Fig. 27, with the comparable passage in the PS. One notes at once that the VS does not in fact completely represent the violins' accompaniment (in thirds) of the vocal line that we find in the PS. (The VS omits the thirds in semiquavers.) Here, the PS follows the EV, in which the violins' accompaniment is identical with Mahler's final version. Thus the chronology of this passage is clearly (OV)/VS→EV→PS.

(iv) At one time I thought there was sufficient evidence to suggest that, whatever the radical revisions in instrumentation and refinements of notation, Mahler rarely amended the substance of a composition. It was, I think, my research into the evolution of *Das klagende Lied* (see DM[1], pp. 141–96) that led me to this conclusion, the substance of which I would now wish radically to revise. Perhaps the assumption still holds largely true for the early pieces, even for big stretches of the First Symphony, though it is clear now (see pp. 196–217 below) that some major modifications of substance were made as that work progressed towards its final formulation. We can be sure that it would not be safe to assume anything of the sort in relation to later works: if nothing else, the fascinating facsimile publication of Mahler's draft score of the first three movements of the Ninth Symphony (ed. Erwin Ratz, Vienna, 1971) shows how radically he could subject his invention to revision even after a movement had achieved virtually a complete outline in full score.[7] However, though it is no longer possible (or prudent) to draw wide conclusions from particular cases, it would seem as if the *Gesellen* cycle may fit into the pattern of early Mahler MSS, i.e. the musical substance of the work was not transformed in any major way during its long progress from the OV (of 1884) to the PS (of 1897). In this respect, the early song-cycle seems to stand on an equal footing with the early cantata.[8]

The only (insubstantial) variant of substance occurs in the EV, in the last song, where the C minor end of the first half of the song is extended by two bars, thus (Ex. 61):

Ex. 61

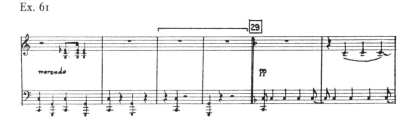

Mahler quite rightly thought that this part of the proceedings could usefully be speeded up, and by cutting bars 3 and 4 from the above example, arrived at the onset of F major that much earlier (compare two bars before Fig. 29 in the PS). I believe it more than probable that the EV here was following the OV—Mr. Rosé did not send me any information on this particular point, which in any event would only catch a manically scrutinizing eye—but oddly enough, in this instance, the VS gets it (largely) right, i.e. the two extra EV bars are excised. On the other hand, the VS introduces, typically, its own brand of discrepancy by adopting the change of time-signature in a bar (Fig. 29 in the VS) which coincides with neither the PS nor the EV, both of which register the move to F major in the bar where the harp's syncopated figure first begins. This small muddle in the VS confirms my view that in fact the two redundant bars in the EV *did* form part of the OV and VS but were retrospectively cut out of the VS when Mahler was getting the orchestral score into final shape; and it may well be the case that in the OV (which the VS would have followed), the double bar is established where it is presently placed in the published vocal score (one notes, too, that Fig. 29 in the VS is comparably misplaced[9]).

B. Refinements

Two examples:

(i) In the first song, two bars after Fig. 4, the VS gives us this reading of the bird-song figuration (Ex. 62):

Ex. 62

The PS gives us Ex. 63 below, a minor revision but one which rhythmically enlivens the regular semiquavers of Ex. 63. We find this revision already embodied in the EV.

Ex. 63

(ii) There are countless instances of Mahler's punctilious notation of rests, one of the means by which he clearly hoped to achieve—more than that, to impose—an articulation of the phrasing of motives and melodic shapes which would precisely correspond to his conception of the music and to the way in which he wanted it to sound. What I mean can easily be seen by comparing an earlier stage in the presentation of a theme with a later. Ex. 64 comes from the PS, the cello counter-theme which accompanies the singer's 'Guten Morgen! Ei, gelt? Du!' at Fig. 9 in the second song. Mahler could hardly go further notationally in expressing exactly how he wants the cellos to articulate the theme:

Ex. 64

This is a characteristic example of Mahler's passion for notational detail, and characteristic of the PS as a whole. The EV on the other hand, though already showing an advance in delicate, nervous detail of this kind (cf. (i) above), presents the theme thus (Ex. 65), a still relatively straightforward version of Ex. 64, with little of the anxious aids to correct articulation which

Ex. 65

are a feature of the later version. (It is just through studying minutiae of this kind that one gains a picture, from Mahler's notation, of what a typical Mahler performance might have been like: it must have been fantastically rich in organized detail.)

That the PS should continually demonstrate the results of Mahler's search for ever more refined means of articulating his phrasing in specific notational terms is not surprising; and it is only logical that the EV (as Ex. 65 above shows), the earlier orchestral version, should represent a less sophisticated stage. We would expect the VS, in this respect, to have more to do with the EV than the PS, and thus it is surprising to find that the printed vocal score for once reflects, to a degree at least, the characteristic refinements of the PS. For example, if one compares Exx. 64 and 65 above with the comparable passage in the VS, the VS is closer to Ex. 64 (from the PS) than to Ex. 65 (from the EV). Or compare, in the same song, the passage three bars after Fig. 13, where in the PS the part for the violins is meticulously articulated (Ex. 66).

Ex. 66

Once again Mahler's rests, his carefully graded dynamics and the distri-
bution of the tiny phrase (each with its stint and quota of differently weighted
accents) between violins I and II, are designed to achieve an exactness of line
and tone that one might associate with the finest etching. There is not
quite the wealth of refinement in the VS, but nonetheless, if one compares the
relevant passage from the VS (see Ex. 66), and then goes on to place it alongside the comparable bars from the EV (see Ex. 67), it is clear that the VS is
closer to Mahler's final thoughts than to the interim EV.

Ex. 67

This is an interesting example to select for discussion because the addition
of the rests—the insistence on a particular kind of articulation through the
manipulation of rests—is, in my experience at least, wholly characteristic of
the kind of difference we normally find between an early Mahler version and
a later or final version. For instance, it was just such a refinement that I
singled out as a feature that distinguished the revised and published version
of *Das klagende Lied* from the early manuscript (see DM[1], p. 163). (For
another example of a passage where, in a way rather similar to Exx. 66 and
67, the VS seems to reflect the PS, while the EV shows less refinement of
articulation, compare Fig. 12 et seq. for three bars in the VS with the comparable passage in the PS and EV.)

Perhaps at this stage it is pertinent to remember that there is another
Gesellen source apart from the four sources (two manuscript and two printed)
which have formed the basis of our exploration so far. I refer to the First
Symphony, in which Mahler made use of materials from the *Gesellen* songs
(see also pp. 29f.). I shall touch on the complex chronological relation between
the symphony and the orchestral version of the cycle when I come to deal
with the chronology of the symphony, itself a dauntingly complex subject.
Our purpose here—to throw light on the small but significant puzzle presented by Exx. 64–7—can be carried a step further by looking at (1), the
published first edition of the symphony, brought out by Weinberger in 1899,
and (2), the surviving manuscript score of the symphony, which includes the
revisions Mahler made in 1893.

Not surprisingly, when Ex. 66 turns up in the symphony's first movement
(two bars before Fig. 9, et seq.) the notation in the main is identical with that

of the PS of the *Gesellen* songs, the publication of which (in 1897) had preceded the score of the symphony. This correspondence makes sense, revealing as it does a consistency of notation between two late revisions of two
intimately related scores.

What does the 1893 revision of the manuscript tell us? (I use '1893
revision' or '1893 manuscript' simply as a convenient form of reference to the
earliest known manuscript source for the symphony. As I hope to make clear
later (see pp. 196–203), I believe substantial portions of this MS to be of an
earlier date than the 1893 revisions.) If we consult the manuscript of the first
movement, and locate there the relevant passage, i.e., Ex. 66 in its symphonic
parallel, we find that the manuscript includes the rests and most of the accents.
In short, the 1893 manuscript and the printed version of the symphony are,
as it were, of one mind, at least where the articulation of this particular
passage is concerned.

An important factor to bear in mind is this: that the actual passage we are
scrutinizing was the subject of, or part of, a revision by Mahler, a fact we can
be sure of because the manuscript paper used in the autograph of the symphony for the whole of the first movement is of a brand that Mahler bought
and used during his Hamburg years, from 1891 to 1897. (For a detailed survey of the various manuscript papers on which the 1893 revision of the First
Symphony is written, see pp. 197–9 below.) This means that the relevant
passage, in its articulated form, i.e. in the manner of Ex. 66, must have been
established not later than 1893. If we now return for a moment to the EV, the
early manuscript full score of the *Gesellen* songs, we can use this same passage both to help us date the EV more precisely and draw a conclusion about
the original puzzle which has led to these labyrinthine investigations. All we
have in the way of a written date for the EV is 1895, at the end of which Behn
was given the score by Mahler as a gift. (See p. 97 above. Incidentally, this
in itself *must* mean that Mahler had already completed an alternative full
score by that time. How otherwise could he have parted with the EV?) We
know, however, from the type of manuscript paper involved, that the EV
belongs to the Hamburg years. The available facts so far narrow us down to
1891–5 for the genesis of the EV. What narrows the period down even
further, is the useful intervention of the 1893 manuscript version of the First
Symphony, and in particular the revision of the first movement. As we have
seen, the articulated form of the passage we are considering was already
established by 1893 in the symphony. It is inconceivable in my view that the
EV, which presents the passage in a notational form which lacks all the
touches of refinement characteristic of a Mahler revision, could have come
after the sophisticated notational version which appears in the symphony,
which would stand on its head everything we know about Mahler's revising
methods; and this means, on the assumption that the symphony's first move-

ment was written out again by 1893 at the latest, that the EV must have been completed *before* that date. Since we know moreover that the EV is written on Hamburg manuscript paper, then the EV must have been written out between 1891 and 1893, and presented to Behn in 1895, by which time, I repeat, another manuscript full score of the *Gesellen* cycle must have existed, almost without doubt the version which Mahler revised and refined in preparation for the Berlin performance in 1896.

Thus extending the scope of our inquiries to include the manuscript score of the First Symphony has brought in return a small harvest of improved chronological facts, while leaving the initial puzzle unsolved. There is no doubt in my mind that the EV's version of Ex. 66 (see Ex. 67) was based on the OV (though I have not been able to scrutinize this passage in the OV myself), and that Mahler introduced the refinement of articulation into the VS as a result, in all probability, of his work on the PS (and after all, he had already got the passage 'right', as we have seen, in the manuscript of the First Symphony). The puzzle, then, is not so much a matter of *how* this discrepancy arose, as *why*, when Mahler bothered to bring the VS into line with the PS *in this one* respect—albeit a detail which clearly was of much importance for him—he neglected to adjust all the other discrepancies, some of them major in character and therefore downright misleading or confusing, which I have outlined above (see pp. 95–107). Thus the puzzle is still unsolved, and is likely to remain so, especially as the prime documentary sources—the copy of the vocal score from which the engraver worked and the manuscript full score of the revised orchestral version—seem to have disappeared.

The last point that needs an airing is this: why did Mahler make no effort (for such seems to be the case) to perform the *Gesellen* cycle before 1896? (HG¹, p. 707, gives 20 April 1886 as the date of the first performance of the second song, at Prague, in its voice and piano version, but the account of this occasion on p. 143 is altogether less specific. But even if this performance actually took place, it scarcely affects my argument.) Here was a young (and ambitious) composer, anxious—indeed determined—to make his name, with a seminal work completed, but making no attempt to bring it to performance. Why?

I think I have outlined at least a substantial part of the reason for the long postponement in n. 13, p. 246, namely, that the *Gesellen* cycle was not finally completed until the 1890s because it was not until then that the realization of it as an orchestral cycle was achieved. One remembers in this context that it was in any event at this time that Mahler was busy in the sphere of the orchestral *Wunderhorn* song (which would have made it particularly natural for him to pick up the *Gesellen* project again). One remembers further—and this is surely a point that suggests that there was a time-lag between the conception of the songs and their materialization in orchestral dress—that Mahler not infrequently included his orchestral songs in his concerts in the early 1890s—well before 1896, that is. It is hard to imagine why, if Mahler had an already completed orchestral song-cycle (from 1884!) in his bottom drawer, even if this were a score that required radical revision, he would not have made use of it—in short, have performed it.

I do not think there was an orchestral version to perform, but even had there been, I wonder very much if the cycle would have been released any earlier; which is to say that I believe the real motive behind the 'suppression' of the *Gesellen* cycle rested in the delicate issue of the songs' relationship to the First Symphony, which Mahler was, as it were, reluctant to reveal—did he fear the charge of 'song-symphonist', that was indeed later to be levelled at him?—until the symphony had at least been launched. I think some such defensive reasoning as this was responsible for the protracted period that intervened before Mahler was ready to divulge the bond between the cycle and the symphony. (See also n. 13, where I suggest in what a close chronological relationship the composition of the songs and the inception of the symphony may in fact stand.) It was not only a practical matter—of scoring the songs—but a revelation of method, of his inner life, also, which he must have realized would lead to grotesque confusions and misinterpretation. In retrospect, it was optimistic of Mahler to think that by 1896 the chances of such miscomprehension had appreciably diminished.

II. *Lieder und Gesänge* ['aus der Jugendzeit']; the *Gesellen* Songs continued

As I MENTION in the Chronicle (p. 89), 'aus der Jugendzeit' was the later invention of the publishers. When the songs were first published by Schott's, Mainz, in 1892 (see notes 1 and 2, p. 242); there was of course no sub-title, which certainly could have made no sense in relation to the last two volumes of the songs, which were published not all that long after their composition. I reproduce the title page of the original edition of Vol. I on p. 114. The same point arises with the later publication of the so-called *Sieben Lieder aus letzter Zeit*, where 'aus letzter Zeit' is again the publishers' additional description. When the songs were first published in 1905 (except for 'Liebst du um Schönheit', which was published two years later), they were issued as separate Lieder in editions for voice and piano and voice and orchestra, not as a collection. Both sub-titles were probably added after Mahler's death, to make the distinction clear between the early and late song collections.

Vol. I of the songs I dealt with in some detail in DM¹, pp. 197–225, and I have nothing significant to add to what I wrote there.¹⁰ It may be useful, however, to repeat here the projected dates of composition I allotted to the songs in Vol. I, 1880–3, and to mention again (see p. 93) what I apparently overlooked when I compiled the information about Mahler's early works in my book: that Mr. Alfred Rosé possesses not only an autograph manuscript of the songs that comprise Vol. I of the *Lieder und Gesänge* but also a manuscript (evidently undated) of the nine settings of *Wunderhorn* texts that make up Vols. II and III. The order of the nine songs in the manuscript (see p. 93) corresponds with the order of the published volumes, though there is no indication in the autograph of the division into two volumes.

We have, at least for the moment—and as is not the case with the orchestral *Wunderhorn* songs—no precise dates for the composition of the individual *Wunderhorn* songs which make up Vols. II and III of the *Lieder und Gesänge*. Thus it is a question of determining the overall period during which the songs were written. It seems likely (see NBL, p. 12, and HG¹, pp. 171–2) that Mahler was prompted into writing these songs by turning up a copy of the Arnim and Brentano anthology in the Weber household, and realizing (to the

Lieder und Gesänge

für

eine Singstimme und Klavier

Ausgabe für hohe Stimme. **Heft I. Pr. Mk. 2 50** Ausgabe für tiefe Stimme.

Ausgabe für hohe Stimme. **Heft II. Pr. Mk. 2.50** Ausgabe für tiefe Stimme

Ausgabe für hohe Stimme. **Heft III. Pr. Mk. 3.—** Ausgabe für tiefe Stimme.

von

GUSTAV MAHLER

Heft   für hohe Stimme.   Heft   für tiefe Stimme.

Eigenthum der Verleger

LONDON
SCHOTT & Cº
159 Regent Street

MAINZ
B. SCHOTT'S SÖHNE
Weihergarten

BRÜSSEL
SCHOTT FRÈRES
82 Montagne de la Cour

PARIS
P. SCHOTT & Cⁱᵉ
70 rue du Faubourg St Honoré

The title-page of the first volume of *Lieder und Gesänge*
(By kind permission of the Library, University of Southampton)

full, for the first time) the musical potentialities of the *Wunderhorn* texts. (According to Mahler, it was for Frau Weber's children that these early *Wunderhorn* songs were initially conceived.) M. de La Grange (p. 171) suggests that it was towards the end of 1887 that Mahler began to draft these songs, which certainly would seem to be a better proposal than 1888, the year specified by most other authorities (e.g. Adler, Stefan, etc.), if only on the grounds that it is difficult to see how, in 1888, Mahler could have found time to compose them: this, after all, was the year in which he completed the First Symphony (in March),[11] conducted for the first time (on 20 January) his reconstruction of Weber's opera, *Die drei Pintos*, and was also engaged on the composition of 'Todtenfeier' (to become the first movement of the C minor symphony), which he completed in September. Some reminiscences by Max Steinitzer of the Leipzig years (they appeared in *Musikblätter des Anbruch*, II, 7–8, Vienna, April 1920) tell us that Mahler sang to his friend—'with deliciously vivid expression'—some of the *Wunderhorn* songs that were ready, and no doubt these were the first fruits of Mahler's discovery of the potentialities of the famous anthology. Moreover, in so far as Steinitzer's recollections seem to refer to the 1887–8 Leipzig season, they would at least tend to support the possibility of the first songs being conceived and drafted in 1887, somewhat earlier, that is, than most commentators have previously assumed. (Steinitzer, alas, is not specific in his article about titles, which makes all the more puzzling the reference to an already extant 'Das himmlische Leben' (in 1887–8!) which M. de La Grange includes in his account of Steinitzer's recollections. This fact is not only inherently improbable but also is not to be found in the article in question.) There is another documentary point which may further strengthen the likelihood of 1887 as the year in which the songs first materialized: we have a letter of Mahler's in which he himself clearly refers to the *Lieder und Gesänge* in a chronological context. In April 1896, he wrote from Hamburg to Max Marschalk (GMB[1], p. 195), 'By the way, I shall send you by book-post some volumes of songs of mine. They belong to the time before my D major symphony. Perhaps in this way you will best learn much of that which has intimate significance in my life.' The volumes to which Mahler refers can only have been the *Lieder und Gesänge* (no other songs by Mahler were available in published form at the time he writes), and on the assumption that Mahler's 'before' means pre-1888, the year when he laboured at top pitch to complete the first draft of the First Symphony, this letter at least lends substance to the belief that the first of the early *Wunderhorn* settings probably belong to 1887.

If 1887 probably represents the point of germination, where may one place the point of termination?

1888, as I have suggested, was an excessively congested year, towards the end of which Mahler left Leipzig to take up his appointment as Director of

the Opera at Budapest (he had joined Nikisch at Leipzig as his assistant in
the summer of 1886). This certainly makes it likely that the next batch of
early *Wunderhorn* songs belong to the period after Mahler had taken up his
Budapest position. Here the researches of M. de La Grange prove extremely
valuable. According to his biographical text, there is evidence to suggest that
(1) a new (unspecified) *Wunderhorn* song was composed at Hinterbrühl in
June 1890 (HG¹, p. 214); and (2) this same summer, i.e. the summer of 1890,
'probably consisted of finishing the first lieder of the *Wunderhorn*' (p.
215).

This would appear to be a reasonable and convincing chronology, and it is
one to which M. de La Grange gives further support in the entry on the songs
in his own Appendix (pp. 760–1), where he writes 'The last songs [of the
Lieder und Gesänge] were probably composed during the summer of 1890, for
Mahler had no time to compose the following summer [i.e. 1891] due to his
Scandinavian journey.'

However, something of a contradiction seems to develop when in fact we
move on to the summer of 1891. For M. de La Grange suggests (p. 236) that
it was in June, in Vienna, that Mahler probably completed 'the first *Wunderhorn* songs with piano accompaniment, which were published by Schott the
following year.' M. de La Grange adds in the next sentence, 'He may also
have sketched out, during that month, some of the great orchestral songs
that he was to compose during the winter.'

M. de La Grange seems to re-introduce the composition and completion
of the *Wunderhorn* songs in the summer of 1891 because of a reference by
Mahler in an unpublished letter (see HG¹, n. 29, p. 877) to the composition
of 'six lieder'. An enigmatic reference, indeed; but surely it is more likely
to be a (forward-looking?) reference to the later (orchestral) *Wunderhorn*
songs than to the voice and piano series? (This is something that M. de La
Grange appears to allow for himself by his juxtaposition of his two sentences,
each of which offers a different possibility.) Consider what has to be accepted
if the reference to 'six lieder' is taken to be a reference to the *Lieder und
Gesänge*. There are only nine *Wunderhorn* songs in all. Are we to suppose that
two-thirds of them were composed as late as 1891, that only a minimal start
was made in 1887, when the creative impetus was at its most fresh and the
motivation strongest? Moreover, if it is correct that a song was *added* in the
summer of 1890, then this would reduce the number of songs that had been
completed between 1887 and 1890 to two!

This seems unlikely; and at the other end of the time-span, the reality of
the reference to the 'six lieder' looks scarcely more convincing. Are we to
assume, that is, that Mahler wrote or completed two-thirds of the songs in
June 1891, that these were fair copied, and then with the rest of the contents
of the three volumes, engraved, proofed, corrected, printed and published by

February 1892? Even by modern standards this would be a very speedy publishing operation indeed. We cannot even assume that Vol. II might have been engraved by Schott's while waiting for Vol. III to arrive, because among the songs in the *last* volume is 'Scheiden und Meiden', which we know to have been performed in Budapest in November 1889 (see also p. 155), which means that this song in fact must have been among the *first* of the songs to have been composed. Thus Mahler must have delayed making his final disposition of the published order of the songs until the series was complete.

There the matter must rest, awaiting further analysis of the letter on which M. de La Grange bases his suggestion about the summer of 1891; and should the letter in fact prove to refer to the *Lieder und Gesänge*, then we should have to revise radically our placing of the songs, which would not really belong to Mahler's Leipzig period in any substantial sense, and in fact would virtually be divorced from his alighting on the *Wunderhorn* anthology in 1887. Until the chronology is finally clarified, the best dates seem to me to be 1887–90. (M. de La Grange should surely correct the date in his list of works, p. 707, to read 1887, not 1888, if only to match up with his own chronology on p. 171.)

* * * *

Adler's seemingly definitive statement that it was in 1888 that Mahler came to know *Des Knaben Wunderhorn*, the famous anthology of Arnim and Brentano, has led to a good deal of misunderstanding. It looks now as if 1888 was *not* in fact the year of discovery; and I doubt furthermore if 'discovery'—for this is what Adler seems to imply—accurately represents the true state of affairs.

I have already in AM[5], pp. xxiii–v, set out certain facts about Mahler's relationship to *Wunderhorn* poems which suggest by any reckoning that his acquaintance with the *Wunderhorn* literary style must have long preceded his Leipzig period. There seems little point in going over that ground again except perhaps to repeat that the first song of the *Gesellen* cycle (composed in Cassel) is modelled on an actual *Wunderhorn* text, a fact that first seems to have been brought to light by Siegfried Günther as long ago as 1920 (see PB, p. 357, and PS[1], pp. 100–1). Some well-informed commentators, e.g. Dr. Mosco Carner in a programme note written for the BBC in May 1955, have made the correct textual attribution, but in general this small but significant fact has had a quite unnatural difficulty in establishing itself, which is my justification for repeating it here.

If nothing else, then, the use of the *Wunderhorn* text in the *Gesellen* cycle tells us that Mahler must have known individual *Wunderhorn* poems well before 1888, and certain private communications I have received over the past few years make it hard to believe that Mahler could have remained unaware of the *Wunderhorn* anthology until he was introduced to it by the Weber family in the late 1880s. For example, Miss Annie Steiner, whom I have previously quoted in connection with her father's libretto for *Herzog Ernst von Schwaben* (see pp. 54–6), writes as follows:

> Most of the words of Mahler's songs (also the text of *Das klagende Lied*) show the substantial influence of early German folk-songs, as collected in *Des Knaben Wunderhorn* by Arnim and Brentano at the beginning of the nineteenth century. Some of my father's own poems are likewise influenced by the *Wunderhorn*. I do not doubt that, as German poetry was the subject of my father's early University studies just between 1875 and 1880, and since he was an enthusiastic teacher as well as a pianist and singer, he must have discussed the *Wunderhorn* Lieder [i.e. the poems] with Mahler very extensively, read them to him, and roused his enthusiasm, when they lived together for some time.

It is surely likely that Miss Steiner's speculation is correct and indeed that it was probable that the *Wunderhorn* 'tone' of both *Das klagende Lied* and the *Gesellen* cycle springs directly from the stimulus of a literary climate prevailing in Mahler's youth. (Mahler himself, however, insisted otherwise in a letter to Bauer-Lechner (HG[1], pp. 284–5) about the text of *Das klagende Lied*: 'You will also see that at a time when I did not even suspect the existence of the *Wunderhorn*, I already lived completely in its spirit.')

Further confirmation of that literary climate reached me from Vienna, from Anna and Karl Fränkel, who took up a question I asked in DM[1], p. 260, n. 98, about a friend of Mahler's in his early Vienna years: 'Who was Kralik?'

> [Richard Kralik von Meyrswalden], wrote my correspondents, 'was an historian [he taught at Vienna University], romantic poet, composer of his own ballads, plays, etc. He was born in 1852 [d. 1934: his son is the well-known Viennese music critic, Heinrich Kralik] at Eleonorenhain in the 'Böhmer Wald'. His father was a glass manufacturer. He had a house in the 'Cottage' [Währing Cottage-Verein, Vienna] where Mahler was a guest. Kralik's sister, Mathilde—pianist, composer and music-teacher [1857–1944]—was a pupil at the Musik Akademie, together with Mahler [she seems to have had the same teachers]. This he [Kralik] told us in 1926, when we used to visit his house and listen to his lectures and readings of his literary work and music. He told us that Mahler first came to know folk-song through him.'

I think if we add these fascinating personal reminiscences to what we know of the historic cultural influence exercised by the *Wunderhorn* anthology

—and folk-song for Kralik must have largely, if not exclusively, meant *Des Knaben Wunderhorn*—we cannot but conclude that Mahler absorbed the *Wunderhorn* spirit and style along with the very air he breathed as a student in Vienna, if indeed he had to wait until then for his first acquaintance with the collection. It is certainly hard to imagine that what was patently a topic of consuming interest to some of his closest youthful friends, especially those with literary ambitions, should somehow and mysteriously have passed him by. In any case, even if we were to discard all other documentary evidence and rely only on the music, and in particular on the *Gesellen* cycle, it would be impossible to maintain that it was not until the late 1880s that Mahler got to know of the existence of the *Wunderhorn* anthology. Such documentary evidence as there is simply goes to confirm what might be deduced from the music alone: a natural, in fact predictable, familiarity with the *Wunderhorn* world.

It has been suggested, of course, that Mahler might have known only individual *Wunderhorn* texts up to the time he ransacked the anthology for his first series of settings in the *Lieder und Gesänge*. This seems highly improbable when one takes into account the nature of the literary community of which he was an ardent member and the expertness of his own pastiche *Wunderhorn* texts. What surely *is* probable is this: that when Mahler was prompted to write a series of songs at Leipzig by rubbing shoulders, as it were, with the Weber family's copy of *Des Knaben Wunderhorn*—and there is reason to believe that the Arnim and Brentano anthology may have been a specially cherished and thus specially prominent volume in the Weber household[12]—he was not so much launching out on a new voyage of discovery as fulfilling a development that had already made itself musically manifest and was already very much part of his way of thinking in so far as a choice of texts for music was concerned. This is not to underrate the happy and fruitful accident that set him off on a solid and extensive exploration of the *Wunderhorn* anthology. But it was not, in my view, the introduction of a 'new' strand into Mahler's thought but, rather, the crystallization of a pre-occupation that had long been established. One doubts, for example, if the creative spark would have been blown into a flame by a volume of texts *other* than the *Wunderhorn* poems, however enthusiastic the Weber family might have been.

If the chronology outlined above for the early *Wunderhorn* settings is correct (i.e. 1887–90), then there was probably less of a gap than we have hitherto imagined between Mahler rounding off the composition of the *Gesellen* cycle and starting work on the first batch of songs. We have some kind of documented dates for the *Gesellen* cycle, first an inscription on the printed vocal and full scores, 'December 1883', placed somewhat ambiguously beneath the composer's name on p. 1 of the music, and secondly, Mahler's own reference to the completion of the cycle in a letter to his close friend, Dr. Friedrich Löhr, dated Cassel, 1 January 1885 (GMB[1], p. 33), where he writes: '. . . I have written a cycle of songs, six for the time being, which are all dedicated to her [i.e. to Johanna Richter, a singer at the Cassel theatre with whom Mahler was passionately in love]. She does not know them. What else could they tell her but what she knows already. I shall send you the closing song, though the paltry words cannot even convey a small part of it. The songs are planned as a whole in such a way that it is as if a fated travelling journeyman now sets out into the world and wanders solitary.'

The obvious explanation of 'December 1883' is this: that Mahler wrote this date into the published edition of the voice and piano version of the cycle in order to make clear the work's youthful origins. He was to do the same later in the case of *Das klagende Lied*, where, in the published revised version of the cantata, 'Vienna, 1880' is added after Mahler's name on p. 1 of the music in the vocal and full scores of the work. The publication of the cantata did not take place until the turn of the century (1902, according to Hofmeister), a long time after its composition; and so there was good sense in making clear that this was the first publication of an early work. It was surely a further important consideration in the case of the *Gesellen* cycle that its publication coincided with the period when the publication of Mahler's symphonies was beginning. All the more reason, then, to identify the chronological situation as precisely as possible.

But how precise—how accurate—was Mahler's date? M. de La Grange (HG[1], p. 741) thinks Mahler got it wrong (along with Adler, Stefan, et al.), and boldly states: 'The poem [*sic*] and the music for these songs were written (with piano) between Christmas 1884, and 1 January 1885', i.e. the date which Mahler should have entered on his published vocal score of 1897 was 'December 1884' (not 1883): he was just one year out in his calculations. This is certainly a tidy solution, which ties in neatly with M. de La Grange's belief that the MS drafts of the poems of the third and fourth songs, dated respectively 19 and 15 December 1884, represent as it were the initial stage in the composition of the work. But as I try to show in laborious detail in n. 14, p. 247, we cannot in my view be quite so confident that these autograph texts were those which Mahler then proceeded for the first time to set to music: the reverse might be the case, i.e. these particular texts might have been copied out *after* the settings had been completed and probably were. Moreover, on 1 January 1885, we find, as we have seen above, Mahler writing to Löhr that 'The songs are planned as a whole in such a way that it is as if a fated travelling journeyman now sets out into the world and wanders solitary.' Are we to suppose that the planning of the cycle as an integral unit, 'as a whole'— which must mean the conception of the songs as a continuous dramatic structure (its unique aspect)—was all achieved (including the actual composition of all the music) between 15 December and 1 January? (For 'zusammengedacht', the crucial word that Mahler uses in his letter, M. de La Grange finds no adequate equivalent in his translation (HG¹, p. 120):'The cycle deals [*sic*] with a young *Gesell*...' etc. 'Deals' scarcely conveys the meaning of 'zusammengedacht'.) I must confess that I find this proposed time-table extremely difficult to accept. As I point out in n. 14, p. 247, the draft texts of the poems are in fact numbered respectively II and I, from which one would have to infer (if one adopted M. de La Grange's reckoning) that Mahler had no idea of sequence at all in the middle of December, even as late as the 19th. Again, if one works from the reasoning set out in HG¹, p. 741, there were still two poems to be written *after* the 19th (not to speak of the music); and yet, magically, by 1 January 1885, the overall, integrating idea had emerged, the closing song was now in its right place, and all the music (presumably) composed. We are to assume that all this was accomplished within, at most, twelve or thirteen days, perhaps in even less time than that. The chronology of Mahler's music, as one knows to one's cost, is full of surprises, and it may be that the chronology of the *Gesellen* cycle will reveal itself as yet another surprise—a virtuosic display of ultra-high-speed planning and execution. However, until such time as we know that to be established as fact, I prefer to accept the inscription 'December 1883' and Mahler's letter of 1 January 1885, as offering two dates which, between them, indicate 1884¹³ as the year in which Mahler worked substantially on his *Gesellen* songs, though it was clearly towards the end of the year that a final, intense bout of creative activity developed.

There is perhaps one other speculation that ought to be made and kept in mind. Although 1 January 1885 without doubt represents a terminal date of a kind for the composition of the *Gesellen* cycle, for reasons that I set out later (see pp. 123–5)—e.g. Mahler's own enigmatic reference to *six* songs and the blurring of the distinction between songs and song-texts (both of them 'Lieder')—this closing date was clearly itself somewhat tentative and open-ended, i.e. we cannot exclude the possibility of the composition of the *Gesellen* cycle continuing *after* 1 January. If we assumed indeed that the drafts of the poems for the third and fourth songs in December did represent the *first* compositional stage, then it would be more than probable that the point that Mahler had reached by 1 January was the overall disposition of the order of the songs, with the 'Schlusslied' placed and composed, but still (I would guess) with compositional decisions to be made and settings to be composed. But this hypothesis does nothing to illuminate 'December 1883' and I do not give much weight to it.

A final point: it might be that we shall never know for sure what private meaning 'December 1883' had for Mahler (on the assumption, that is, that he meant that month and that year). 1884, however, was undoubtedly the

year in which his passion for the singer Johanna Richter was a dominant preoccupation. Indeed, it was during this year that he wrote at least two lyrical
poems (which he did not in fact set to music) in which the image of the
'fahrende Geselle' appears (see also n. 14, p. 247). In the spring of 1884,
moreover, as M. de La Grange himself observes (HG[1], p. 114), Mahler wrote
to Löhr: 'Heinrich told me, my dear Fritz, of the sorrows that befell you on
Christmas Day. So I may as well tell you that I was afflicted in the same way
on the same day, and that with that day there began a period of unceasing
and intolerable struggle to which there is as yet no end in sight, a struggle I
have to endure day in, day out, indeed hour by hour.' (GMB[1], pp. 26–7.)
M. de La Grange surmises—and surely correctly so—that Mahler is referring in this letter to some incident in his unhappy love affair with Johanna
Richter: clearly he was prompted into making this disclosure by what was
apparently a like experience of Löhr's on the same day. The day in question
was Christmas Day 1883, and while we do not know precisely what the
sorrowful event was, we are left in no doubt that it made its mark on Mahler.
Is it not possible, in fact, that here we have a clue to the inscription 'December
1883', an indication of a time or incident that set Mahler off on the creation
of his *Gesellen* cycle? (One wonders, for example, if the first song, the opening
lament, may not have been conceived or drafted at this moment of high
emotional drama, in which case it might be that the two poems from mid-
December represent the closing stage in the composition of the cycle.) There
is certainly no doubt that the songs were autobiographical, that the dramatic
narrative of the cycle reflected his own anguished relationship to Johanna
Richter. It was a charged personal experience in which, oddly, a harrowing
Christmas of 1883 and a scarcely less harrowing New Year's Eve of 1884
seem to have played a vital structural role. It may be, then, that Mahler's
inscription was not simply a slip of the pen or the memory but on the contrary an accurate indication of the inception, the onset, of the cycle that was
so intimately bound up with the structure of his personal life throughout the
ensuing year—'a period of unceasing and intolerable struggle'.

* * * *

In view of the variety of proposed solutions, perhaps it might be helpful
if I summarise them very briefly:

(a) The work—texts and music—was drafted, organized and completed
between 15 December 1884, and 1 January 1885. (This, I think, represents
the view of M. de La Grange.)

(b) The work was initiated (in whatever sense) in December 1883 (the date on the published vocal score) and essentially completed by 1 January 1885. (This is more or less my position.)

(c) The texts and music were initiated in December 1884, and the shape of the cycle determined by 1 January 1885, but substantial compositional work continued *after* 1 January.

* * * *

Mahler, in his letter of 1 January 1885, speaks of *six* songs. What then happened to the surplus two? The earliest known autograph of the *Gesellen* songs (see above, pp. 92f.) contains only four songs and one knows of no hint that the 'missing' songs physically survived in Mahler's possession or the possession of anyone else. It certainly cannot be ruled out that the songs were composed and later destroyed, lost or given away to some still undiscovered source. But did they exist? At first sight, Mahler's reference seems clear enough, but if we examine the relevant paragraph from his letter more closely there are distinct ambiguities. For instance, Mahler writes of 'six [songs] for the time being' as if the cycle were still open to enlargement, though a sentence or two later he writes of the 'closing song ['Schlusslied']' which was clearly already in existence. It is conceivable, of course, that he might have thought of adding further songs to the five that supposedly at this stage preceded the sixth and last, though once again we are reminded by Mahler's own words, 'The songs are planned as a whole . . .', etc., that the overall, integrally 'dramatic' conception of the *Gesellen* cycle, which is so conspicuous a feature of the work, was already established by 1 January 1885, even if the final decision about the number of songs still had to be taken. But what is also surely significant and revealing is Mahler's reference to the 'Schlusslied' that he is sending his friend Löhr: we soon come to realize that it is not the song, i.e. words and music, that he is dispatching, *but only the words*;[14] and I suggest that it could be an ambiguous and interchangeable use of the word 'Lied' that has since led to confusion.[15] One remembers, for instance, that the texts of the *Knaben Wunderhorn* poems are themselves sub-titled 'Alte deutsche *Lieder*' (my italics), and I believe it quite probable that when Mahler referred to a 'cycle of songs ['Lieder'], six for the time being', he was making no distinction between the four songs it is likely that he had already composed and the two 'songs' which only existed as projected texts—'Lieder' as yet without music. If this hypothesis is correct, it may throw some light on the poem by Mahler, dated Cassel, December 1884, and first published in *Der Merker*, the Mahler issue of 1 March 1912, p. 183, and reproduced here from the pages of the journal itself:

EIN JUGENDGEDICHT GUSTAV MAHLERS.

Die Nacht blickt mild aus stummen ewigen
Fernen
Mit ihren tausend goldenen Augen nieder.
Und müde Menschen schließen ihre Lider
Im Schlaf, auf's neu vergessnes Glück zu
lernen.
Siehst du den stummen, fahrenden Gesellen?
Gar einsam und verloren ist sein Pfad,
Wohl Weg und Weiser der verloren hat
Und ach, kein Stern will seinen Pfad erhellen.
Der Weg ist lang und Gottes Engel weit

Und falsche Stimmen tönen lockend, leise —
,,Ach, wann soll enden meine Reise,
Wann ruht der Wanderer von des Weges Leid?
Es starrt die Sphynx und droht mit Rätselqualen
Und ihre grauen Augen schweigen — schweigen.
Kein rettend Wort, kein Lichtstrahl will sich
zeigen —
Und lös' ich's nicht — — muß es mein Leben
zahlen"

Kassel, Dezember 1884.

Mahler's 'Jugendgedicht' of 1884

The night looks down tenderly from silent eternal distances
With its thousand eyes of gold.
And tired men close their eyelids
In sleep, to learn anew the happiness they have forgotten.
Dost thou see the silent journeyman?
His path is very lonely and forlorn,
Perhaps he has lost his way and his bearings
And alas, no star will shine on his path.
The way is long and God's angels far
And false voices are heard enticing, gentle—
"Ah, when shall my journey end,
When will the wanderer rest from the sorrows of the road?
The Sphinx stares and threatens with its tormenting riddle
And its grey eyes are dumb—dumb.
No saving word, no ray of light will appear—
And I cannot solve it—I must atone with my life".

It has been generally assumed (e.g. GE, p. 43, or JD, p. 68), though without outright documentary proof, that this poem, a typical example, surely enough, of Mahler's early versifying, originally formed part of the *Gesellen* sequence of texts; and indeed this seems likely in view of the reference to the wanderer in the fifth line—'Siehst du den stummen, fahrenden Gesellen?' The anguished tone of it, moreover, suggests that this was almost certainly a poem 'dedicated', like the rest of the *Gesellen* songs, to Johanna Richter in 1884, the object of Mahler's unhappy love. If all this is a true interpretation, then we have here the survival of one of the two additional 'Lieder' mentioned by Mahler in his letter of January 1885, in just the form that fits my hypothesis, i.e. as a 'song' without music; and that this 'song' never came to be composed seems to me to be perfectly comprehensible when one tries to accommodate the text into the known *Gesellen* narration. It does not function in the overall dramatic scheme, for which reason, I have no doubt, Mahler discarded it.[16]

If one were asked to select one song from the *Gesellen* cycle on the grounds of its unique Mahlerian features, one might choose, I think, the last, 'Die zwei blauen Augen', both for its stamp of authentic personality and for its significance as a type of song which was to have a far-reaching influence on Mahler's development. I am not thinking here of the purely instrumental works, with their many funeral-march movements, nor have I in mind related general considerations, e.g. the self-evident importance of the symbolic role that the funeral march was to play in Mahler's music, whether in a symphony, song-cycle, or independent song. I am aware, too, that all slow songs conceived as slow marches are of necessity bound to have something in common. 'Zu Strassburg auf der Schanz', for example, another march song from Vol. III of the *Lieder und Gesänge*, follows virtually the same basic pattern as 'Nicht wiedersehen!'. What I wish to emphasize here is the fact that 'Die zwei blauen Augen' initiated a mode of expression and more particularly a type of structure, which accumulates a history of its own as we chart its course down the years, from the mid 1880s to the last years of Mahler's life.

I have already (see pp. 33–4, and Exx. 5 and 6) touched on the relationship between 'Die zwei blauen Augen' and 'Nicht wiedersehen!' (one of the early *Wunderhorn* settings, from Vol. III of the *Lieder und Gesänge*), a relationship which, in my view, casts a revealing light on how we are to understand, to interpret, the final unfolding of the dramatic narrative in the song-cycle. The consistency of the imagery makes its own point, but what must be further stressed, and can be confirmed by the briefest examination of the two songs in juxtaposition is the fact that 'Nicht wiedersehen!' follows almost exactly the formal scheme established in 'Die zwei blauen Augen', the first of Mahler's slow funeral marches for voice and orchestra, and the first of what might be described as his 'farewell' finales. It is indeed, in the precise context of Mahler's orchestral song-cycles that 'Die zwei blauen Augen' proves to throw a very long shadow. We find, for example, that the last song of the middle-period *Kindertotenlieder* cycle, for all its outward differences (lullaby instead of funeral march) corresponds in formal organization and poetic scheme to the type of song which 'Die zwei blauen Augen' exemplifies; and even in the concluding 'Abschied' of the late-period *Das Lied von der Erde*, what we meet there is a huge elaboration of the principles clearly articulated in the last song of the early *Gesellen* cycle. The dissolution in which each cycle ends has its origins in a conception first formulated in the very first cycle of all.

Here again, then, we have an example of that prominent consistency of quasi-dramatic idea and type of musical invention, on this occasion extending beyond thematic interrelationships to considerations of form. It is this factor which was undoubtedly responsible for 'Nicht wiedersehen!' re-evoking the specific melodic shapes and overall form of 'Die zwei blauen Augen'. The *Wunderhorn* setting was a song of farewell to a dead lover in which Mahler paid, as it were, his last respects to his similarly misfortunate Traveller; and in so doing, whether consciously or unconsciously is beside the point, executed his farewell in invention and song-type very closely approximating to the Traveller's own farewell to the world. (See Exx. 5 and 6, p. 33, and also compare in the same songs Mahler's treatment of his 'Ade!' refrain, i.e. from one bar after Fig. 28 et seq. in 'Die zwei blauen Augen' with, say, the last eight bars of 'Nicht wiedersehen!'. One notes above all the pervasive interval of a fourth, the basic unifying interval of the *Gesellen* cycle and the First Symphony, and similarly prominent in 'Nicht wiedersehen!'.) It is thus that 'Nicht wiedersehen!' functions as an informative footnote, an amplifying appendix, to the *Gesellen* cycle, completing the story in more ways than one, and reinforcing the special status which 'Die zwei blauen Augen' must enjoy in Mahler's output.

III. The Chronology of the *Wunderhorn* Songs

THE CHRONOLOGY of Mahler's music is complex, and not least so among his orchestral songs known as *Des Knaben Wunderhorn*. Some dates, however, are precise, and these I include where they are known. We know for a fact that five of the songs were completed in full score at Hamburg (where Mahler was chief conductor at the Opera) on 26 April 1892. (The manuscript full score of the songs is in the archives of the Gesellschaft der Musikfreunde, Vienna.) These are: 'Der Schildwache Nachtlied', 'Verlor'ne Müh', 'Trost im Unglück', 'Wer hat dies Liedlein erdacht?' (at one time one of the best-known of Mahler's songs, which Elisabeth Schumann did much to popularize), and 'Das himmlische Leben'. This last setting Mahler wrote first in a voice and piano version (the MS is in the Berlin Staatsbibliothek* dated 10 February 1892), and then as an independent orchestral song (the manuscript is separately inscribed 12 March 1892) which he later projected as a possible finale for the Third Symphony and finally used as the now familiar last movement of the Fourth. When the songs came to be published, some years after they had been written (in 1899, by Josef Weinberger)[17], 'Das himmlische Leben' was excluded from the collection. By then, the song was destined to find another home, in the Fourth Symphony.[18]

As was the case with 'Das himmlische Leben', and as, indeed, was Mahler's general custom (see n. 21, p. 252), the other four songs in this 'quintet' of *Wunderhorn* Lieder were first drafted in voice and piano versions: 'Der Schildwache Nachtlied' on 28 January 1892; 'Verlor'ne Müh' on 1 February; 'Trost im Unglück' on 22 February; and 'Wer hat dies Liedlein erdacht?' on 6 February. (The dated MSS of the voice and piano versions of these four songs are in the Berlin Staatsbibliothek. HG¹, confusingly, on p. 249, misdates the orchestral scores of 'Das himmlische Leben' and 'Trost im Unglück'.) Thus for 'Das himmlische Leben' and the first four of the *Wunderhorn* orchestral songs we can trace the chronology exactly and compactly, from their inception in voice and piano versions to their final formulation in full score.

---

* The institute I designate here, and similarly throughout the book, is properly the Staatsbibliothek Preußischer Kulturbesitz, (West) Berlin. It is not to be confused with the Deutsche Staatsbibliothek, (East) Berlin.

For 'Das irdische Leben', a song which Mahler clearly thought of as a contrasting complement to 'Das himmlische Leben' (see p. 139), I have no exact date, but it must have been composed in, or before, the summer of 1893, when Mahler referred to it in conversation with Bauer-Lechner (see NBL, pp. 10–11). It is probable that it was written at about the same time as 'Des Antonius von Padua Fischpredigt', the voice ('low voice') and piano version of which (with meticulous instrumental indications) is dated 'Steinbach, 8 July 1893',[19] and the MS full score, 'Steinbach, 1 August 1893', which was followed nine days later by the enchanting 'Rheinlegendchen', also composed at Steinbach, and then entitled (on the full score, dated 10 August, which forms part of the Lehmann Deposit at the Pierpont Morgan Library, New York) 'Tanzlegendchen'. The voice and piano version of the song was composed a day earlier at Steinbach, on 9 August (the MS is in the Berlin Staatsbibliothek: HG[1], p. 775, transposes the dates of the two versions). In July, also at Steinbach, the orchestral version of 'Urlicht' had been completed (on the 19th). This was a summer particularly rich in *Wunderhorn* activity and in cross-relations between song and symphony.

The information so far assembled means that we can already establish a chronology for the first volume[20] of the *Wunderhorn* songs (as we know it today), and as we shall see, a chronology can likewise be put together for the second volume. One has to bear in mind, however, that some dates may be open to various interpretations (especially when the MS sources are not available for verification), e.g. the completion date of the full orchestral score of a song in one case, and in another, the completion of a first draft of a song, probably in a version for voice and piano.[21] All the dates, as so often with Mahler, may fix certain points or stages in the process of the composition of a given work but do not necessarily tell us when the work was actually composed, i.e. set down for the first time, in whatever manuscript form. (One often feels that the only safe method of dating much of Mahler's music is to use the formula 'not composed later than — ', and fill in the blank with the appropriate year.)

*   *   *   *

For the second volume of songs, we have dates for the 'Fischpredigt' and 'Rheinlegendchen' (see above); for 'Lied des Verfolgten im Turm' and 'Wo die schönen Trompeten blasen' (the voice and piano drafts of both of which are dated July 1898, and thus do not belong to 1895 as conjectured (wrongly) in HG[1], pp. 776–7, though he gets the date right in n. 27, p. 917!); and Bauer Lechner (in NBL, p. 40) enables us to attribute the last song of the set, 'Lob des hohen Verstandes', to the summer (June) of 1896 (probably between the 21st and 28th of the month).[22] A voice and piano sketch of this song, once in the possession of Webern, is now in Northwestern University Library, Evanston, Illinois. It is entitled 'Lob der Kritik'.

The two remaining independent orchestral settings of *Wunderhorn* texts, 'Revelge' and 'Der Tamboursg'sell', were written somewhat later (and published in 1905 by C. F. Kahnt); the former was completed in July 1899 (NBL, p. 120), and the latter (the MS full score of which is in the Lehmann Deposit at the Pierpont Morgan Library, New York, together with an early MS draft of the song (see also the table on p. 142–3)) in August 1901 (NBL, pp. 165–6).

(The dates that we glean from Bauer-Lechner are supported in more detail by M. de La Grange, who adds fresh and valuable detail about the composition of these two great songs. In HG[1], n. 27, p. 917, it is suggested that the first sketch of 'Revelge' might belong to the summer of 1898 (to be completed in the summer of 1899). It is certainly fascinating to learn (p. 523) that Mahler considered 'Revelge' to be 'the most beautiful and the most successful of his *Humoresken*, perhaps even "the most important of all his lieder"' (here M. de La Grange quotes from an unpublished part of Bauer-Lechner's reminiscences). No less fascinating (and again emanating from the same source) is Mahler's remark that 'The first movement of the Third Symphony now seemed to have been only "a simple rhythmic study" for this lied, which he could never have composed without it'. This comment brings a sudden and brilliant illumination, in the composer's own words, of the unique relationship between his songs and his symphonies.)

These chronological observations deal in the main with the *Wunderhorn* settings with which we are familiar today as a collection of ten orchestral songs in two volumes. But there were, of course, other *Wunderhorn* settings made during these years which we know not as independent orchestral songs but as symphonic movements, though it now seems certain that, besides 'Das himmlische Leben', one other song—'Urlicht'—was in fact first conceived as an independent song. The movements are (see also the list on p. 32): 'Urlicht', the fourth movement of the Second Symphony; 'Es sungen drei Engel', the fifth movement of the Third Symphony; and 'Das himmlische Leben', the Finale of the Fourth. (For a note on 'O Mensch! Gib Acht!', the Nietzsche setting which is the fourth movement of the Third Symphony, see n. 21, p. 252.) We have precise dates for 'Das himmlische Leben', and it is clear from the composition sketch (dated 24 June) that Mahler produced his choral setting of 'Es sungen drei Engel' ('Was mir die Morgenglocken erzählen') in the summer of 1895 (see also NBL, p. 19,[23] and n. 21, p. 252).

What is of particular interest about the composition sketch of 'Es sungen drei Engel' is the fact that the date shows that, as late as the summer of 1895, Mahler was still working—still planning—on the assumption that 'Das himmlische Leben' would emerge as the symphony's Finale, the climactic point of the programmatic scheme: hence, of course, the close thematic relationships between the two conceptions, 'Es sungen drei Engel' and 'Das himmlische Leben'. They were, of course, intended to hang together, thematically speaking; and the shared imagery of their texts—two childlike visions of heaven—made it all the easier for the thematic links to unfold quite spontaneously. Indeed, it is no exaggeration to suggest that the musical 'model' for—or behind—'Es sungen drei Engel' was again that most creatively influential of all Mahler's solo songs, 'Das himmlische Leben', with the poetic and musical world of which so many major aspects of Mahler's *Wunderhorn* period are associated. In a very real sense, we witness the solo song from 1892 giving birth to an extension of itself (at one remove, so to say) in the choral symphonic movement of 1895. (From this point of view, indeed, one might say that the fifth movement of the Third Symphony again follows the traditional pattern established by Mahler, i.e. the generating of a symphonic movement by a solo song.)

The MS documentation in the case of 'Es sungen drei Engel' is, for once, ample rather than scarce. Those with a taste for following step by step Mahler's compositional processes are generously catered for, where this particular movement is concerned. One can start with the 'model', the *fons et origo*, 'Das himmlische Leben', move on to the composition sketch of 'Es sungen drei Engel', of June 1895, and then on to the draft full score from August of the same year. The next document is the fair copy, in full score, of the movement that Mahler made in Hamburg in May 1896; and that in turn can be compared with the published full score of 1899. The last stage in this fascinating hatching-out process would be an examination of the authentic solo voice version of the choral movement that Mahler published in 1899 as part of the voice and piano *Wunderhorn* set. With that, as it were, the wheel turned full circle, the solo version of 'Es sungen drei Engel' complementing the solo song, 'Das himmlische Leben', out of which—and for which—the choral symphonic movement was born. It is also a happy accident that the majority of these MS sources are all housed under the roof of one library. The three MS versions of the choral movement of the Third Symphony may all be inspected at the admirable Pierpont Morgan Library, New York, where they form part of the Cary Collection and Lehmann Deposit.

As I point out in n. 17, p. 249, Mahler himself, despite the fact that he had prepared a solo voice and piano version of 'Es sungen drei Engel', never took the one step further that remained, i.e. he did not go on to produce a version for solo voice and *orchestra*, which would have been the logical development. Perhaps it was just a question of time (or lack of it, rather). True, 'Urlicht' emerged as part of the series of independent *Wunderhorn* orchestral songs, but then 'Urlicht' was a different proposition. Unlike 'Es sungen drei Engel', 'Urlicht' was first conceived and composed as an independent song, and no instrumental modifications were entailed by the publication of the original 1893 orchestration of 'Urlicht' as No. 12 of the Weinberger *Wunderhorn* full score series (see also p. 136). For 'Es sungen dre Engel', however, it was a question of devising an orchestration for a solo voice version, though no doubt Mahler would have used the orchestration of the symphonic movement as a model. Perhaps Mahler intended to do this; but he never got round to it, and it was Josef Wöss who finally completed the gap (post-1923) in the series by making an arrangement which at long last supplied the hitherto missing orchestration of No. 11 (see n. 17, p. 249).

Although Mahler published his voice and piano version of 'Es sungen drei Engel' in 1899 as an 'arrangement', i.e. the song is identified as a movement from the Third Symphony: 'Frauenchor aus der 3. Symphonie/Bearbeitung für eine Singstimme' ['Women's chorus from the Third Symphony/Arrangement for solo voice'], the version really stands up in its own right as an independent solo song rather than an arrangement proper.[24] However, Mahler had no option but to describe the song as such. The full score of the Third Symphony was itself published in the same year as the *Wunderhorn* volumes (1899). (The full score of the Second Symphony, with 'Urlicht' *in situ*, had already been published in 1897.)

If Mahler's own voice and piano version of 'Es sungen drei Engel' is more a genuine solo song than an authentic arrangement, a later voice and piano version of the movement published by Universal Edition (Edition No. 3649a/b, *c.* 1914 (?)) was an arrangement proper, i.e. it reproduces as precisely as possible the symphonic movement. There is no doubt that this voice and piano reduction is the 'arrangement' that Mahler's voice and piano version was not.

To confuse matters (when are matters not confused where Mahler is concerned?), this U.E. edition—in an advertisement (dated 1920) on the back cover of the publication—is attributed to Mahler: 'Bearb. für Ges. u. Klav. v. Komp.' But this cannot be correct. As we have seen, Mahler had already published in 1899 what he described as his solo voice arrangement of the choral movement. The later U.E. arrangement was undoubtedly more faithful to the symphonic movement than was Mahler's, and that presumably was its *raison d'être* as a posthumous publication. (In retrospect, however, it seems to have been a curiously redundant publishing operation.)

The U.E. arrangement is quite ingeniously done. It is plain, moreover, that in making it, the U.E. editor (Josef Wöss, as I believe him to have been[25]) took into account Mahler's voice and piano version (the Weinberger text), departing from it where necessary (in order to reproduce as precisely as possible the symphonic movement, not always to good musical effect, however) and occasionally clarifying the layout of Mahler's idiosyncratic piano writing. Wöss must have known Mahler's voice and piano version, because, for some reason, Mahler amended a line of the *Wunderhorn* poem ('Bete zu Gott nur alle Zeit') to read in the published version of the symphonic movement, 'Liebe nur Gott in alle Zeit!' (see Fig. 8), although—strangely enough—in his 1895 composition sketch it was the original *Wunderhorn* line that he had set. When he came to write his solo voice version, he *restored* the original line again, 'Bete zu Gott . . .' (compare the parallel bar in the song with Fig. 8 in the symphonic movement), a restoration, paradoxically, followed by Wöss, because in doing so he departs from the text of the symphonic movement that he was supposedly arranging. In this instance, Wöss is closer to Mahler's voice and piano version (and to the *Wunderhorn* poem itself) than to the original choral movement.

*   *   *   *

Perhaps it may be of some interest at this point to illustrate some of the details that distinguish Mahler's voice and piano version of 'Es sungen drei Engel' from Wöss's arrangement of the symphonic movement, which means that we shall see for ourselves how Mahler concentrated on producing a genuine solo song rather than a pedantic transcription. It may also be revealing from time to time to bring in the early composition sketch of 1895.

Here, to start with, is a minor but telling example of Wöss's arrangement practice against Mahler's. Ex. 68 (Wöss) is absolutely faithful to the texture of the symphony (three bars before Fig. 2), whereas in Ex. 69 Mahler rethinks the second bar in terms of a continuing (and musical!) voice and piano relationship:

Ex. 68   Ex. 69

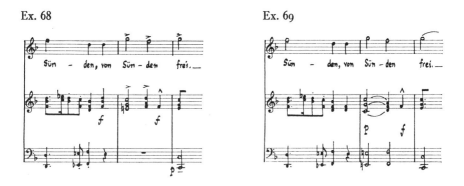

To take another example of the same kind, compare Ex. 70 (Wöss) with Ex. 71 (Mahler). Once again Mahler's doubling of the voice in the piano part shows, even at this very simple level, that the art of the composer has the edge on that of the arranger's:

Ex. 70

Ex. 71

But the differences between the solo song and the arrangement of the choral movement are not always as minor as these. Compare, for example, Ex. 72 (Wöss) with Ex. 73 (Mahler). Note the bass, in particular. Wöss is faithful to the symphony (see three bars after Fig. 7), whereas Mahler, in his solo song version (bar 76), comes up with a not insignificant modification of the bass in the second half of the bar, raising it a semitone in pitch:

Ex. 72

Ex. 73

This in fact was a passage where Mahler clearly was in some doubt about the most satisfactory articulation of the bass line. In the composition sketch of 1895, for instance, we find yet another version, as follows (Ex. 74):

Ex. 74

Another intriguing variant is embodied in the passage where, in the symphony, the women's chorus echoes the sighs and sobs of the contralto soloist (Fig. 5 et seq.). This was a passage for which Mahler himself devised an appropriate text for the chorus to sing. In the choral movement it appears thus (Ex. 75):

Ex. 75

Du sollst ja nicht wei-nen! Sollst ja nicht wei-nen!

In the Wöss arrangement of this passage, those bars appear as follows (Ex. 76), and exactly coincide with the symphonic movement, though of course the choral realization (for obvious reasons) has been incorporated into the piano reduction:

Ex. 76

In the Mahler version, however, the transcription (see Ex. 77) is again not exact, for the good reason that whereas Ex. 77 works in terms of piano texture and sonority, Ex. 76, for all its faithfulness as a transcription, does not. Indeed, Mahler teaches us here (an object lesson of its kind) that what is acceptable as a dissonance in a choral/orchestral texture will not necessarily transfer to the keyboard without modification:

Ex. 77

What perhaps is of even more interest is the fact that in the original composition sketch, this echoing of the 'weeping' idea did not appear at all in choral form, as we can tell from Ex. 78 below, which represents Mahler's sketch. The *motive* is there, of course (shaped as it appears in the symphony), but at this stage it had evidently not occurred to Mahler to convert it into a choral interpolation (for which, as I have said, he also had to contrive a text):

Ex. 78

Finally, let me draw attention to the ingenuity with which Mahler in his solo song version instates *the integral text* of the *Wunderhorn* poem. Wöss does an adequate arranger's job, but does not establish the final verse of the poem. Mahler, with only the tiniest (though not insignificant) modifications of his vocal line, concludes his song with the poem's conclusion. Those interested in such fine detail may compare Wöss's—an arranger's—approach with Mahler's—a composer's—to the textual problem by placing their solutions (see the composite Ex. 79 below) alongside the parallel choral passage in the symphonic movement (two bars before Fig. 9, et seq.):

Ex. 79

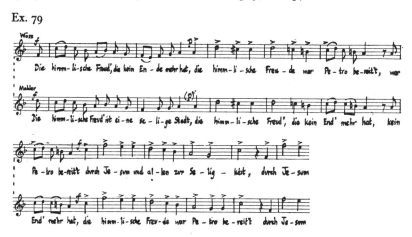

In the case of 'Urlicht', the *Wunderhorn* setting which forms the fourth movement of the Second Symphony, the movement existed first as an independent song before it was built into the symphony, as we know from the 1894 MS of the symphony (see n. 50, p. 270) and a letter of Mahler's written in 1895 (see p. 184). I have more to say about this matter when attempting to unravel the complex chronology of the composition of the symphony (see pp. 161–87). Here perhaps it is sufficient to note that the original voice and piano version of 'Urlicht' was published as part of the 1899 Weinberger collection (No. 12, 'Urlicht', 'Aus der Symphonie No. 2 in C moll') and that the orchestral version of the song, dated Steinbach, 19 July 1893, is identical with the orchestration of the voice and orchestra version issued by Weinberger as part of the series of *Wunderhorn* songs for voice and orchestra. So there must have been a later orchestral revision, when the song would have been brought into line with the orchestral resources deployed in the symphony. As I point out, however, in n. 50, p. 270, the 1894 MS of the complete symphony (Mengelberg-Stiftung, Amsterdam) contains a MS of 'Urlicht' still in its orchestral song format, which means that the final orchestral revision of the song post-dated the first complete MS of the symphony, i.e. was made later than December 1894.

This information necessarily suspends a query over Mahler's claim in his 1895 letter, mentioned above, that he did not set about the orchestration of 'Urlicht' until he had decided to incorporate the song into the symphony. It is difficult to reconcile this claim with the existence of, as it were, the 'wrong' orchestration. It seems certain, indeed, that 'Urlicht' existed as an independent song in both a voice and piano and orchestral version before Mahler decided to make symphonic use of it.[26] But however the enigmatic reference in the letter may be resolved, it is certainly possible—as I suggest in n. 26—that the decision to build 'Urlicht' somewhere into the symphony was taken during the summer of 1893, the same summer that saw the completion of the Andante moderato and the Scherzo (and the completion of the full score of the song—the 'Fischpredigt'—on which the Scherzo was based). A curious summer this, in which we observe Mahler's *ad hoc* assembly of the middle movements of the symphony, without a very clear idea of their sequence, their logical interrelationship or the destination to which they were to lead (though it is hard to imagine that he did not have at least a dim inkling of what he wanted, programmatically, in the way of a finale, when he chose to add 'Urlicht' to the pool of movements out of which the ultimate shape of the symphony was to emerge). It was in 1894 that the problem of the 'missing' Finale was to be solved. In 1893 he was still, as it were, marking time, a composer in a Pirandello-like search after a last movement.

Although it is clear that an instrumentation of 'Urlicht' was accomplished in July 1893, this does not mean of course that the song itself may not have

Jean Paul Friedrich Richter

J. B. Foerster in 1895

Mahler in 1897

Hans von Bülow in 1889

The first page of the voice and piano version, dated 10 February 1892

'Das himmlische Leben'

The opening of the final E major section

Mahler's handwritten 'programme note' for the Third Symphony been in existence for some time. Mahler's 1895 letter on the subject speaks indeed of the voice and piano version as the 'original version' of the song, and it might well be this first draft to which Foerster refers (in JBF, p. 406), where he writes that 'Urlicht' was composed in 1892. This could certainly be the year in which the song was first sketched out in voice and piano form as yet another *Wunderhorn* song, and before Mahler contemplated using it in the symphony, if his own account of the matter is accurate, at least in this respect. The chronology of 'Urlicht', then, is pretty firmly established: possibly 1892 for the voice and piano draft, and 19 July 1893, for the completion of the first orchestration of it.

These notes complete the best chronological account I can compile of all Mahler's orchestral settings of *Wunderhorn* texts, whether independent songs or songs built into the symphonies. To round off the *Wunderhorn* story, we must touch for a chronological moment on the two purely instrumental movements based on *Wunderhorn* songs. The Scherzo of the Third Symphony is the less complex matter to investigate. We know that Mahler was working on the symphony in 1895 and completed the work in the summer of 1896 (28 July, see NBL, p. 49). We have a date in fact for the final manuscript full score of the Scherzo: 'Hamburg, Saturday 25 April 1896'. Moreover, it was with the composition of the huge first movement that Mahler was primarily concerned in the summer of 1896, and it is reasonable to suppose that the Scherzo, like the other movements that comprise Part II of the symphony, had been pretty fully shaped in the preceding summer. (Mahler himself said to Bauer-Lechner in 1896, 'I should never have had the courage to finish this gigantic first movement if [the other movements] hadn't already been composed.' (NBL, p. 47.[27])) As for the *Wunderhorn* song itself on which the Scherzo was based, Mahler returned to a song, 'Ablösung im Sommer', that belonged to Vol. III of the *Lieder und Gesänge*, his earlier settings of *Wunderhorn* poems for voice and piano, published in 1892. As we have seen (pp. 113–15), it is probable that Mahler set about composing these songs (in all, nine of them) in 1887, when he was conducting at Leipzig. A likely completion date for the songs is 1890 (see pp. 115–17). At the least, then, there was a gap of five years between the conception of the song and the re-composition of it as a full-scale symphonic scherzo.

If the distance between the song-source and the Scherzo of the Third Symphony is a positively clarifying element—the sources are nicely separated and the sequence of events is not in doubt—the immediacy of the juxtaposition of the song-source (the 'Fischpredigt') and the Scherzo of the Second Symphony is well-nigh confusing. We have dates for the voice and piano and orchestral versions of the song (8 July and 1 August 1893, respectively) and we also know (from HG[1], p. 273) of a completion date inscribed on the first orchestral score of the Scherzo—16 July. (See also n. 19, p. 251).

Remarkably, as we see, the first orchestration of the Scherzo preceded that of
the song, the reverse, I think, of what one would have expected or predicted.
This striking chronological simultaneity, and unexpected sequence of
song/symphony/song, only brings fresh emphasis to the closeness, during this
whole period, of the relationship between the *Wunderhorn* songs and the
current symphonies: they did not so much run parallel as inter-cross and
inter-twine. It must have been the case, however, that the actual conception
of the 'Fischpredigt', the first sketch of it as distinct from the fair copy
which we know to be dated 8 July, preceded work on the Scherzo (the
symphonic movement undeniably derives from the song, which was the basis
of a discussion between Mahler and Bauer-Lechner (NBL, pp. 10–11)).
While we have no precise knowledge of when Mahler started to work on the
Scherzo, it appears that he was aiming to complete his work on sketches of
the movement that he brought with him (along with the Andante) on holiday (NBL, p. 7). If the chronology implied by these facts is correct, then
clearly the known dates (8 July and 1 August for the song, 16 July for the
first orchestral draft of the Scherzo) represent the period in which Mahler
brought both the song and Scherzo to their *final* compositional stages at
virtually the same time, and in an unorthodox sequential 'mix'. This fascinating accomplishment, if treated in isolation, would suggest a phenomenally
rapid conversion of the song into the elaborate symphonic movement that is
difficult to accept. It is almost certain, if Bauer-Lechner's recollections are
correct, that sketches for the Scherzo must date back at least to 1892; and
that likelihood in turn projects an earlier date for the concept of the song than
the date—8 July 1893—that is actually inscribed on the fair copy of the voice
and piano version. In other words, this dated fair copy does not diminish the
probability of the initial draft of the 'Fischpredigt' belonging to another year
altogether (probably 1892?). All of which goes to show with what caution it
is necessary to interpret the dates on Mahler's MSS.

*   *   *   *

Is all this no more than a dry-as-dust accumulation of dates and facts? I
think not. The dates, on the contrary, establish the uniquely close association
between *Wunderhorn* song and symphony at this time, a period when Mahler
crossed the frontiers between the two spheres so frequently and so rapidly
that, as we have seen, it is difficult on occasion to disentangle an ordered
sequence of compositional events. We hardly need to seek further confirmation of what is already sufficiently documented—the intimate relation between
in *Wunderhorn* songs and 'Wunderhorn' symphonies (I-IV)—but there is a
fascinating bit of further information in Paul Bekker's big study of Mahler's

symphonies (PB, p. 145), where he reproduces a draft (undated) for the programme of a (rather than 'the') Fourth Symphony. This is it:

SINFONIE Nr. 4 (HUMORESKE).

Nr. 1. Die Welt als ewige Jetztzeit, G-dur.
['The World as Eternal Present']

Nr. 2. Das irdische Leben, es-moll.
['Earthly Life']

Nr. 3. Caritas, H-dur (Adagio).

Nr. 4. Morgenglocken, F-dur.
['Morning Bells']

Nr. 5. Die Welt ohne Schwere, D-dur (Scherzo).
['The World without Care']

Nr. 5. Das himmlische Leben, G-dur.[28]
['The Heavenly Life']

The outline of projected movements scarcely represents the Fourth Symphony that we are familiar with today. However, 'Das himmlische Leben' is in its right place, and G major contains the whole scheme. What is of exceptional interest in the *Wunderhorn* context is the use of the 'Humoreske' title[29]—this was a title Mahler also used at one stage for his orchestral *Wunderhorn* settings ('Humoresken', as we know, is inscribed on the Vienna full score of five of the songs)—and above all his including as a second movement the *Wunderhorn* song 'Das irdische Leben'. More than that, the fourth movement—'Morgenglocken'—is none other than the *Wunderhorn* setting, 'Es sungen drei Engel', which is the fifth movement (same key) of the Third Symphony. Indeed, if Mahler had proceeded with this tentative scheme and stuck to six movements, then we should have had an equal number of purely instrumental movements[30] alternating with *Wunderhorn* settings. Once again, this little-known draft of a programme shows the dense intertwining of song and symphony characteristic of these *Wunderhorn* years.

The two last *Wunderhorn* settings, 'Revelge' and 'Der Tamboursg'sell', in a sense reverse the established relationship in Mahler's works between song and symphony, i.e. one is primarily conscious throughout these songs of Mahler the symphonist, and the middle-period symphonist at that. They are in fact, 'symphonic' in a way that the earlier songs are not. This has something to do with their unusual scale and weight, and in particular with the elaboration and independence of the orchestral part, which in both songs is strikingly characteristic of Mahler's mature symphonic style. It is the breath—or better, perhaps, the breadth—of the symphonist that is unmistakably felt in these

Songs		Dates of Composition[31]

VOL. I[32]
of *Des Knaben Wunderhorn*

Published Nos.	*MS Nos.*	
(1) 'Der Schildwache Nachtlied'[33]	(1)	The voice and piano versions of Nos. 1–4 are dated respectively: 28 January; 1 February; 22 February; and 6 February 1892. Completion date on MS full score of No. 3, 'Hamburg, 26 April 1892. The 5 Humoresques finished!' (No. 3, then, must have been the last song to which Mahler put the final orchestral touches.)
(2) 'Verlor'ne Müh'	(2)	
(3) 'Trost im Unglück'	(3)	
(4) 'Wer hat dies Liedlein erdacht?'	(4)	
[— 'Das himmlische Leben']	(5)	
(5) 'Das irdische Leben'	(6)	Composed after April 1892, and not later than the summer of 1893.

VOL. II

(6) 'Des Antonius von Padua Fischpredigt'	(8)	Voice and piano version dated Steinbach, 8 July 1893. MS full score dated Steinbach, 1 August 1893.
(7) 'Rheinlegendchen'	(9)	Voice and piano version (on which the title 'Tanzreime' was inscribed and then crossed out; see also NBL, p. 12) dated Steinbach, 9 August 1893. MS full score dated Steinbach, 10 August 1893.
(8) 'Lied des Verfolgten im Turm'	(8)	MS voice and piano draft dated Vahrn, July 1898 (title page inscribed 'Meiner lieber Nina [Hoffmann] . . .' and dated Vienna, May 1899).
(9) 'Wo die schönen Trompeten blasen'	(9)	MS voice and piano draft dated Vahrn, July 1898.
(10) 'Lob des hohen Verstandes'	(?)	Composed (21–28) June 1896.

Orchestral Settings of *Des Knaben Wunderhorn*

Publication   Notes

'Das himmlische Leben' was the fifth song in the MS, later to become the Finale of the Fourth Symphony (see below). It was excluded from the published collection of *Wunderhorn* songs. The RH numbers in brackets refer to the order of the five songs in the Hamburg MS, and continue with the numbers Mahler inscribed on his MSS. The LH numbers refer (throughout) to the overall sequence of the original publication of the songs. (See n. 17, p. 249.)

1899

Nos. 3, 4, 7 and 'Das himmlische Leben' were first performed at Hamburg on 27 October 1893 (see n. 18, p. 250), and Nos. 1 and 2 at Berlin on 12 December 1892 (see HG¹, pp. 707–8).

See below for reference to Scherzo of the Second Symphony.

1899

The first performances of Nos. 5 and 9 were given at Vienna on 14 January 1900; of Nos. 6 and 8 at Vienna on 29 January 1905. A first performance for No. 10 has not been located.

Independent settings	Dates of Composition
'Revelge'	July 1899.
'Der Tamboursg'sell'	August 1901.

Symphonic movements (songs)

'Das himmlische Leben' (5) (Symphony IV/4)	Version for voice and piano dated 10 February 1892. Completion date on MS full score, 12 March 1892.
(12) 'Urlicht' (7) (Symphony II/4)	MS full score of song dated Steinbach, 19 July 1893 (independent voice and orchestra version).
(11) 'Es sungen drei Engel' (Symphony III/5)	Composition sketch for choral setting dated 24 June 1895 (duration 4 min.); draft in MS full score inscribed 'Sunday August 1895 [*sic*]. Holiday work concluded' [i.e., 11 August: see HG¹, p. 807]; in the Hamburg MS full score of the complete symphony, the movement is dated 8 May 1896. Mahler's (solo) voice and piano version published 1899 as part of the Weinberger collection. The U.E. (hire) version for solo voice and orchestra is not Mahler's arrangement, nor is the U.E. publication of a (solo) voice and piano reduction. (See pp. 130–5.)

Symphonic movements (Orchestral)

Scherzo (Symphony II)	According to HG¹ (p. 273), the first orchestral score is dated 16 July 1893.
Scherzo (Symphony III)	Completion date on MS full score, Hamburg, 25 April 1896; composed in summer of preceding year.

Publication Notes

1905   There is no date on the MS full score or on an early and incomplete draft for voice and piano, both of which form part of the Lehmann Deposit at the Pierpont Morgan Library, New York. It is of some interest to note that the sketch is devoid of instrumental indications but for a notation, at the start, of a prominent and specifically *drum* rhythm above the piano part:

It is precisely this solo drum march rhythm which proves to open *Der Tamboursg'sell* in its final version!

These two late *Wunderhorn* songs were first performed at Vienna on 29 January 1905.

Symphony published 1901.   This song, in its orchestral form, bears an individual date in addition to the collective inscription. (See Vol. I above.) The number in brackets refers to the placing of the song in the Hamburg MS. A voice and piano edition of the song issued by Doblinger as an offshoot from the symphony was Mahler's original voice and piano version.

Symphony published 1897.   Conceived first as an independent song, then incorporated into the symphony. (The completion date on the full score of the symphony reads, 'Finished on Tuesday, 18 December 1894, at Hamburg.' See n. 50, pp. 270f., in which this MS is discussed.)

Symphony published 1899.

Symphony published 1897.   See above ('Des Antonius von Padua Fischpredigt') for reference to song on which this movement is based.

Symphony published 1899.   This movement was based on an earlier *Wunderhorn* setting for voice and piano, 'Ablösung im Sommer', from the *Lieder und Gesänge*, Vol. III, published in 1892 and probably composed between 1887 and 1890.

songs; and because both of them are conceived as extended marches, one is irresistibly reminded of the great march movements of, say, the Third, Fifth or Sixth Symphonies (Mahler, as I have said already (p. 129), remarked in 1899 that the first movement march of the Third seemed to have been only a 'rhythmic study' for 'Revelge', which 'he could never have composed without it'. (HG[1], p. 523)). (Despite the precedents set by Beethoven, Berlioz and Wagner, was Mahler the first composer to raise the march to enduring symphonic status?) 'Der Tamboursg'sell' was composed while Mahler was working on the Fifth Symphony and discloses, predictably, a family relationship with the symphony's slow funeral-march first movement. (There is an early and incomplete MS draft (on three staves) of 'Der Tamboursg'sell' in the Pierpont Morgan Library. When one sees this very tentative and early MS stage—possibly the first?—one realizes that the *scale* of the song must have emerged in the actual composition of it. The proportions of the song certainly could not be predicted from this early draft of it.) The more energetic and desperate 'Revelge', composed two years earlier, already seems to foreshadow the vast march canvases of the first movement and Finale of the Sixth Symphony. It is in those movements, indeed, that one can hear Mahler's dead drummer still marching on. Nonetheless, although it is by no means stretching a point to discern a link between the independent *Wunderhorn* songs and the middle-period symphonies, Mahler's last excursion into the world of *Des Knaben Wunderhorn* shows that the old relationship has essentially changed: the songs are no longer prime sources for the symphonies but, on the contrary, derive their unique characteristics from the nature and processes of Mahler's symphonic art.

The orchestra is so uppermost in one's mind as an integral part of Mahler's *Wunderhorn* songs that it is easy to forget that his first settings of *Wunderhorn* poems (Vols. II and III of the *Lieder und Gesänge*) were for voice and piano. However, a glance at the piano accompaniments makes it clear why he conceived the later settings as songs for voice and orchestra. Already, in some of these earlier songs, the orchestra is *there*, locked within the piano accompaniments and struggling to get out. Often, indeed, the accompaniments read more like the piano reduction of an orchestral score than an accompaniment proper. In 'Zu Strassburg auf der Schanz', for example, he calls for the sound of muffled drums from the pianist, an anxious insistence on an immediate and detailed sonorous *realism* which makes one realize that the later turn to the orchestra was not a luxury but an *obligation*. (A fascinating bit of information brought to light in HG[1], p. 764, is that 'a two-page orchestration of the first quarter of ['Zu Strassburg auf der Schanz'] exists, but it breaks off abruptly at the end of the first page (of the piano edition)'. This is certainly proof that Mahler himself recognized the orchestral implications latent in the song and makes it all the more logical that his next series of *Wunderhorn* songs were conceived orchestrally. Small wonder, incidentally, that it was with this song that Mahler chose to experiment.)

Here, we touch on one of the most remarkable aspects of Mahler's relation to his texts. As Dika Newlin puts it (in DN, p. 119), the *Wunderhorn* anthology of L. Achim von Arnim and Clemens Brentano (published in 1806/1808) was 'a typical product of the romantic *Zeitgeist*, with its stress on the simple, artless life of the "little people" and the glamour of bygone days'. There is no doubt that one of the reasons for the collection's popularity was just the appeal it made to the nineteenth century's yearning after the lost innocence of a vanished past. But Mahler's approach was stubbornly independent of any romantic indulgence. He eschewed all bogus medievalism and sophisticated, self-conscious 'folksiness', and accepted the texts at their face value. Hence the songs' reality, rather than their romanticism. Mahler did not adopt a fairy-tale, 'once upon a time' approach, but re-lived the texts as if they were of the present moment. It is the dramatic truth of his settings that exalts them far above the level of most manifestations of romantic historicism, whether literary or musical. 'Das irdische Leben', for example, or 'Revelge'— to choose at random—are conceived in a spirit of urgent immediacy that has little to do with the spirit of retrospective romanticism. It is the beauty of the moment of truth that we meet in these songs, not the beauty of romantic make-believe. (Mahler, we may notice, was always strictly true to the unhappy implications of his texts. There are no contrived 'happy endings', though there are, of course, some happy songs.) It is just the well-nigh *anti*-romantic character of Mahler's *Wunderhorn* settings—their actuality—that lends them their singular flavour.

The songs are too various to be arranged meaningfully in watertight compartments. A dominant group, however, consists of those songs which are marches or liberally infested with transfigured military imagery, i.e. 'Revelge', 'Der Tamboursg'sell', 'Der Schildwache Nachtlied' (with its magical and unexpected dissolution on the dominant!), 'Wo die schönen Trompeten blasen', and 'Lied des Verfolgten im Turm' (a miniature dramatic dialogue,[34] which form makes more than one appearance among the settings). The rest of the songs range widely in scope. At one extreme we have endearingly genial inventions like 'Rheinlegendchen' and 'Verlor'ne Müh', and at the other, 'Das irdische Leben', a piercingly plaintive cry of pain.[35] There are two charmingly droll songs, 'Wer hat dies Liedlein erdacht?' and 'Lob des hohen Verstandes',[36] and two songs in which Mahler's humour develops the sharp edge of irony, the renowned 'Fischpredigt' and 'Trost im Unglück', in both of which the irony is embodied in the choice and in the manipulation of the musical ideas. It is notable that the conventional, romantic 'love song' is conspicuous by its absence.

The contrasts in character presented by the songs are matched by the resourcefulness of Mahler's instrumentation: indeed, the individual character of each song is very much bound up with the individuality of its orchestration. Each song, in short, has its own sound. It would not be possible in the space available here to specify in detail the orchestral layout of all the songs, but responsive ears will not miss the primarily—and appropriately—wind and percussion-band instrumentation of 'Der Tamboursg'sell' (Mahler makes sparing use of only the *lower* strings, cellos and double-basses), or in 'Wo die schönen Trompeten blasen', the imaginative precision with which the composer reserves (in the main) the warm and expressive strings for the lyrical contrasting sections and deploys the woodwind and brass in the ritornello-like fanfares. Maximum clarity and vividness of orchestral sound: this is the common factor we find in all the songs, however distinct they may be in character. Mahler's ruthless insistence on clarity remained a constant preoccupation, whether it was serving the pungency of his wit or embodying the stark, factual enactment of a military narrative. The precision of his chamber-orchestral instrumentation, with its emphasis on the separation rather than the blending of colours, is yet another manifestation of the move away from romanticism.

I mention in n. 37, p. 261, Mahler's 'highly original treatment of his materials'. How inventive and original this was we can observe in the use he made of an identical principle—an undulating *moto perpetuo*—in three songs, the 'Fischpredigt', 'Wer hat dies Liedlein erdacht?', and 'Das irdische Leben'. The principle may be the same, but how different is each song! (It is interesting that the kind of rather sinister repetitiveness characteristic of the last song can also sometimes be found in Dvořák, e.g. at the opening of his symphonic poem, *The Water Goblin*, which belongs to 1896. Dvořák's piece was composed some two or three years after Mahler's song, but in any event, it is not the chronology that interests me but the occasional approximation of style of these two composers, which has its roots in a common musical culture, not in the cause-and-effect of chronology.) Finally, there is the question—a huge and complex one—of Mahler's audacious use of 'popular', everyday musical materials. Perhaps it will suffice in the present context if I content myself with this comment: that while many of the songs' forms and much of their imagery arouse familiar romantic expectations in the listener, Mahler treats his materials (the fanfares, marches, country-dances, quasi-ballads, etc.) in so realistic a manner that they acquire a quite fresh level of significance. We are led, all unsuspecting and unprepared, to expect a conventional romanticism, but our expectations are disappointed—contradicted, indeed,[37] —and we experience instead a sometimes traumatic *realism*. This curious procedure is wholly characteristic of Mahler's genius, and it is nothing less than his genius at its most characteristic that we encounter in his *Wunderhorn* songs. Keen ears, and a close reading of their texts, are all that is required for a response to their unique humour, terrors, drama and charm.

**A checklist of the whereabouts of the MSS of Mahler's
Wunderhorn Songs**

Vols. II & III of *Lieder und Gesänge*	MS (voice and piano) of these nine songs in the possession of Mr. Alfred Rosé

The Orchestral Songs

No. 1*	(a) Early draft (v. & p.) in Library of Congress (b) MS (v. & p.) in Berlin Staatsbibliothek (c) MS (Orch.) in archives of Gesellschaft der Musikfreunde, Vienna
No. 2	(a) MS (v. & p.), as for (b) in No. 1 (b) MS (Orch.), as for (c) in No. 1
No. 3	(a) Sketch (in private hands, see n. 21, p. 252) (b) MS (v. & p.), as for (b) in No. 1 (c) MS (Orch.), as for (c) in No.1
No. 4	(a) MS (v. & p.), as for (b) in No. 1 (b) MS (Orch.), as for (c) in No. 1
No. 5	MS (Orch.) in Pierpont Morgan Library, New York
No. 6	(a) MS (v. & p.), as for No. 5 (b) MS (Orch.) in Harvard University Library
No. 7	(a) MS (v. & p.), as for (b) in No. 1 (b) MS (Orch.), as for No. 5
No. 8	MS (v. & p.), as for No. 5
No. 9	MS (v. & p.), as for No. 5
No. 10	Sketch in Library of Northwestern University, Illinois.
No. 11	(a) Sketch, as for No. 5. (In the same location we find (1) a draft full score of the movement and (2) a complete MS of the symphony containing the movement.)
No. 12	Microfilm of MS (Orch.) in Library of Congress

* These numbers (*without* brackets) correspond to the LH numbers in the table on pp. 140–3. The order of the voice and piano versions in the Berlin Staatsbibliothek runs as follows, in what in fact is the chronological order indicated by the dates on the MSS: No. 1, 2, 4, (5), 3, 7. This, clearly, is merely the order in which the MSS have been bound up and is not to be confused with the numbers set out in the RH column in the table which are Mahler's own, though later modified.

| No. (5) | (a) MS (v. & p.), as for (b) in No. 1 |
| ['Das himmlische Leben'] | (b) MS (Orch.), as for (c) in No. 1 |

'Revelge'	?
'Der Tamboursg'sell'	(a) Sketch (v. & p.), as for No. 5
	(b) MS (Orch.), as for No. 5

Hangversenybérlet II. szám.

Budapest, szerdán 1889. november hó 20-án esti 7¹/₂ órakor

a magyar királyi operaház zenekarából alakult filharmoniai társulat

BRAGA HERMIN

asszony, csász. és kir. kamaraénekesnő és

MAHLER GUSZTÁV

úr, a' magyar kir. operaház művészeti igazgatója szives közreműködésével

ERKEL SÁNDOR

karnagy vezénylete alatt

FILHARMONIAI HANGVERSENYT

rendez

A FŐVÁROSI VIGADÓ NAGY TERMÉBEN.

M Ű S O R:

1. *Cherubini.* »Abencerage«, nyitány.
2. *Mahler.* »Symphoniai költemény« két részben.
   I. rész: 1. Bevezetés és Allegro commodo. 2. Andante. 3. Scherzo.
   II. rész: 4. A la pompes funebres; attacca. 5. Molto appassionato.
   Kézirat, *első előadás* a szerző vezénylete alatt.
3. *Mozart.* Magándal »Figaro lakodalmából«. (Cherubin dallama.)   *Braga Hermin* asszony.
4. *Bach-Abert.* »Präludium, choral és fuga«.

Jegyek kaphatók: Rózsavölgyi és társa cs. és kir. udv. zeneműkereskedésében, Kristóftér 3., valamint a hangverseny napján az esteli pénztárnál.

Előadás alatt az ajtók zárva maradnak.

III-ik filharmoniai hangverseny 1889. decz. 4-én

The programme of the 1889 Budapest performance of the First Symphony

IV. The Chronology of Symphonies I-III

The First Symphony

The first performance of Symphony I

MAHLER CONDUCTED THE première of his First Symphony at Budapest on Wednesday, 20 November 1889.

Three documents: first the letter, dated 19 November, which Mahler addressed to the Orchestra of the Budapest Philharmonic Society[38] after the *Generalprobe* (see p. 150). The translation runs as follows:

> Gentlemen!
>
> With today's full rehearsal still impressed on my mind I feel compelled to thank you and everyone concerned for the performance, both self-sacrificing and sustained by genuine artistic intelligence, through which you have assisted in bringing my modest work into reality.
>
> Today's rehearsal has already afforded me the certainty that I shall never again hear my work played to such perfection.
>
> I feel proud to be in charge of such a company of men who put themselves in the service of art with such devotion and disregard of every personal interest, and I ask you henceforward to remain as kind to me as I am grateful and indebted to you.
>
> Sincerely, your most devoted
Gustav Mahler

Second, the programme for the performance (opp.), which shows that it was only his own work that Mahler conducted. The remainder of the concert was conducted by Sandor Erkel (1846–1900), the son of Ferenc Erkel (1810–93), a notable figure in the history of Hungarian musical life (he was the founder of the Budapest Philharmonic Concerts and the creator for Hungary of a tradition of national opera). Sandor succeeded his father as conductor of the Philharmonic concerts. Hermin Braga, the singer in the excerpt from *Figaro*, was a member of the Vienna Opera (from 1878–88?), appearing at the time at Budapest as a guest artist.

Most important of all is the brief description of Mahler's work, which appears thus in the programme:

Mahler's handwritten letter to the orchestra of the Budapest Philharmonic, 1889

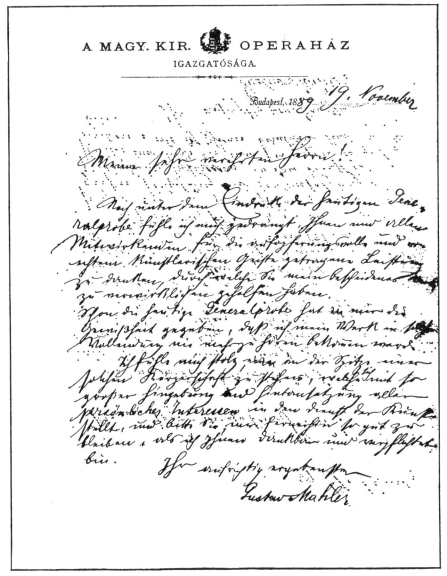

Mahler. 'Symphonic Poem' in two parts.

> Part I: 1. Introduction and Allegro comodo. 2. Andante. 3. Scherzo.
>
> Part II: 4. A la pompes funèbres [*sic*]; attacca. 5. Molto appassionato.

Manuscript, *first performance* under the composer's direction.

Third, a review by the critic, August Beer, of the première, which appeared in the *Pester Lloyd*, No. 321, Thursday, 21 November 1889 (see opposite).

Theater, Kunst und Literatur.

Philharmonisches Konzert.

Die Philharmoniker haben sich heute mit einer Novität eingestellt, die, abgesehen von ihrem inneren Werthe, durch die Persönlichkeit des Autors das lebhafte Interesse unseres Musikpublikums erwecken mußte; es ist die „Symphonische Dichtung" des Operndirektors Gustav Mahler, dem wir innerhalb Wochenfrist nun schon zum zweiten Male am Konzertpodium und — les extrèmes se touchent — merkwürdigerweise in entgegengesetzten Polen der musikalischen Komposition begegnen: das eine Mal im kleinen Genre des Liedes mit seinen einfachen Linien und bescheidenen Ausdrucksmitteln, heute in den großen, breit ausladenden Formen der Symphonie, der höchsten Gipfelung der Instrumentalmusik. Beide so grundverschiedenen Kompositionen tragen das gemeinsame Merkmal einer tief empfindenden, echt musikalisch veranlagten Künstlernatur, die mit einem reichen, lebhaft bewegten Einbildungskraft hoch entwickeltes Gestaltungsvermögen verbindet. Mahler nöthigt uns umso größere Achtung mit seiner Symphonischen Dichtung ab, als er das Werk bereits vor nahezu einem Lustrum fertig im Pulte liegen hatte und somit in einem Alter an die höchsten Probleme sich herangewagt, wo andere junge Talente kaum das musikalische Stammeln überwunden haben. Auch wenn der Autor uns die zeitliche Entstehung der Komposition unbekannt wären, könnte kein Zweifel darüber bestehen, daß wir es mit einem Jugendwerke, allerdings einem vielversprechenden Jugendwerke eines begabten Musikers zu thun haben, dessen Talent noch in voller Gährung begriffen ist. Alles deutet auf Sturm und Drang, auf ungestümes Ringen nach höchstem künstlerischen Ausdruck, auf das heiße Bestreben, die sich unablässig drängenden Bilder der Phantasie in charakteristischer Tonsprache umzusetzen. Gerade das ungewöhnliche technische Können, über welches Mahler verfügt, ist ihm hiebei eher hinderlich als fördernd. Er verblüfft uns geradezu durch seine Virtuosität in der Behandlung des modernen Orchesters, eine Beherrschung der instrumentalen Ausdrucksmittel, die ohne gründliche Vertiefung in die Partituren eines Berlioz und Wagner und ohne angeborenen koloristischen Sinn undenkbar ist. Er ist mit den Klangeffekten der einzelnen Instrumente und ihren Mischungen ebenso sehr vertraut, wie mit der Führung großer Tonmassen, nur verführt ihn gerade diese technische Superiorität leicht zu greller Farbengebung und zu Uebertreibungen des Ausdrucks, in welchem ja junge, überschäumende Talente sich ohnehin nicht genug thun können. Das gilt namentlich vom Finale, welches in seiner wilden Entfesselung von Orchesterstürmen selbst die Orgie Childe Harold's und die Höllenmusik in der Symphonie phantastique von Berlioz stellenweise noch überbietet. Dieses Ueberschreiten des künstlerischen Maßes erscheint immerhin als das geringere Bedenken gegen das größere, daß dem Werke der einheitliche Grundton abgeht und daß einzelne Theile, wie der erste Satz und das Finale zur Formlosigkeit neigen. Auch von einer symphonischen Dichtung, obwohl sie eine ungleich größere Freizügigkeit in Form und Anlage gestattet, verlangen wir musikalische Abgeschlossenheit und entsprechend ihrer Tendenz das Vorwalten einer bestimmten Gedankenrichtung, sei es nun die Illustration einer einzelnen poetischen Idee, oder einer Reihe von seelischen und äußeren Vorgängen, die in kausalem Zusammenhange zu einander stehen. So haben Berlioz, Liszt, Saint-Saëns die Hauptzüge eines Dramas, ein Gedicht, ein historisches oder selbsterfundenes Ereigniß in symphonischer Form wiedergegeben. Mahler's Komposition macht den Eindruck, daß ein Programm zu dieser Musik erst nachträglich entworfen wurde. Darauf läßt die große Lücke schließen, welche zwischen der ersten dreisätzigen Abtheilung und den beiden letzten Sätzen klafft. Dort das ausschließliche Vorwalten ländlicher, idyllischer Stimmung; eine poetische Waldszene, ein schwärmerisches Ständchen, ein lustiger Hochzeitsreigen, hier ein Trauermarsch und ein hochdramatisches Finale, eine in großen Dimensionen aufgebaute Apotheose, die auch durch ihre unverhältnißmäßig räumliche Ausdehnung die vorangehenden vielkurvierten Sätze erdrückt. Man muß von diesem jähen Uebergang der Stimmung und der Ungleichheit der architektonischen Anlage absehen, um die einzelnen Schönheiten des Werkes genießen zu können. Der erste Satz ist ein poetisch gedachtes Waldidyll, welches und durch die zarten, duftigen Farben interessirt, mit denen es ausgeführt ist. Jagdhörner erschallen, Vogelstimmen, charakteristisch durch Flöten und Oboen nachgeahmt, werden laut und eine warme, Lust und Frohsinn athmende Melodie der Geigen fällt jubelnd ein. Ueber den Satz ist echte Frühlingsstimmung gebreitet, nur ist die thematische Führung auf Kosten des Kolorits zu sehr in den Hintergrund gedrängt und es gibt einzelne leere Stellen: Farbe ohne Zeichnung. Interessant ist auch der lange Orgelpunkt auf A in der Einleitung, auf welchen Mahler sehr kunstvoll die Harmonien der Bläser aufbaut, freilich nicht ohne einen Stich ins Bizarre. Die folgende Serenade ist eine innige, schwärmerische Melodie der Trompete, welche mit einem schwermuthigen Gesang der Oboe alternirt, wir erkennen unschwer das Liebespaar, welches in verschwiegener Nacht seine zarten Gefühle austauscht. Die beiden obligaten Instrumente werden sehr feinsinnig von dem Streichquartett begleitet. Der dritte Satz führt uns in die Dorfschänke. Er führt den Titel Scherzo, ist aber ein echter, rechter Bauerntanz, ein Stück voll gesunder, dem Leben abgelauschter Realistik mit schnurrenden, surrenden Bässen, kreischenden Geigen und quiekenden Klarinetten, zu welchen die Bauern ihren „Gestrampften" tanzen; viel feiner ist das Trio gehalten, ein langsamer Walzer in Vollmann'scher Weise idealisirt. Der folgende Trauermarsch reißt den Hörer plötzlich aus der idyllischen Frühlingsstimmung, die der Autor bisher so glücklich festzuhalten wußte. Zudem berührt uns der parodistische Ton, der in den ersten zwei Absätzen angeschlagen wird, fremdartig genug. Der Todtenmarsch beginnt mit dem bekannten, auf die Note getreu wiedergegebenen Liede „Bruder Martin, schläfst Du schon", einem humoristischen Canon, der in Deutschland bei Liedertafeln und Burschenkneipen in erheiternd psalmodirendem Tone abgesungen wird, der zweite Absatz, in ungarischer Manier gehalten, ähnelt in Thema und Harmonie auffallend einer Nummer aus Schubert's „Momentes musicales", auch hier ist der parodistische Ton in den ironischen Accenten der Geigen unverkennbar. Erst das Trio in seiner schönen, mild tröstenden Kantilene entspricht dem wahren Charakter einer Leichenfeier. Das Finale mit seinem schwungvollen, leidenschaftlich gesteigerten ersten Thema; zu welchem ein feierlicher Hymnus als zweites tritt, ist ungemein breit ausgesponnen, es ermüdet durch die allzu häufige Wiederholung dieser Motive und betäubt durch das große Aufgebot von Instrumentalmassen, namentlich durch die intensive Verwendung der Pauken und Becken, die zu starken dynamischen Wirkungen herangezogen werden. Eine eingelegte Episode, in welcher Themen der ersten Abtheilung und des Trauermarsches, theilweise harmonisch verändert, sich wiederholen, stellt allerdings äußerlich — den Zusammenhang zwischen der ersten und der zweiten Abtheilung her. Die Aufnahme der Symphonie war so ungleichartig, wie die beiden Hälften des Werkes und in der That sind die erste Abtheilung wurde von unserem Konzertpublikum, welches sich heute minder vollzählig eingefunden, mit regstem Interesse angehört, und Direktor Mahler, welcher persönlich dirigirte, nach jedem Satze mit warmem Beifall bedacht. Nach dem Trauermarsche schlug die Stimmung um und nach dem Finale gab es eine kleine, aber immerhin hörbare Opposition. Die Philharmoniker spielten das schwierige Werk mit großer Präcision, nicht minder trefflich die vorangehende Abenceragen Ouvertüre von Cherubini und Abert's hier wiederholt aufgeführte Transkription von Bach's Präludium und Fuge mit eingelegtem Choral. Frau Braga, die Solistin des Abends, sang sehr geschmackvoll die Arie Cherubin's aus „Figaro's Hochzeit" und nach vielem Beifall als Zugabe die Romanze „Kennt Du das Land?" aus „Mignon". A. B.

August Beer's review of the Budapest première of the First Symphony in 1889

Beer, of Moravian-German origin, had been appointed music critic to that paper in 1888. These were days when ample space was available for reviews and critics deployed a style to match. Nonetheless, I print Mr. Beer's review complete, which was, after all, one of the first major reviews of Mahler as a composer. It is a fascinating document. What strikes one so forcibly, I think, is the combination of genuine insight on the critic's part (it is by no means an unsympathetic notice) with the manifestation of those familiar objections to Mahler's art—'overstepping of artistic moderation, 'formlessness', 'exaggerations of expression', 'extraordinary technical abilities [in orchestration] . . . which hinder rather than assist . . .'—that, Mr. Beer's review brings home to us, have been part of the history of Mahler's music from the very first moment it made its impact on its very first audiences. Moreover, how illuminating is Mr. Beer's account of the audience reaction at Budapest, which noticeably diminished in comprehension and enthusiasm from the Funeral March onwards! (In its way, and for its time, a genuine—even the 'right'—response, one must admit.) The translation runs as follows:

Theatre, *Art and Literature*

Philharmonic Concert. Today the Philharmonic came up with a novelty which, aside from its intrinsic worth, was bound to arouse lively interest among our music lovers on account of its composer's personality; this is the 'Symphonic Poem' by the Director of the Opera House, *Gustav Mahler*, whom we have now, within the space of a mere week, met with twice on the concert platform and—*les extrêmes se touchent*—strange to say, at opposite poles of the art of musical composition: once in the diminutive genre of the Lied [pp. 154–6], with its simple lines and modest resources, and today in the large, broadly expansive forms of the Symphony, the highest summit of instrumental music. Each of these compositions, so fundamentally different, bears the same mark of an artistic nature of profound sensitivity and genuine musical gifts, combining a wealth of lively imagination with highly developed powers of organization. With his Symphonic Poem Mahler demands all the more respect in that he put the work finished into his desk almost five years ago, so that at an age when other young talents have barely overcome their musical stammers he was pitting himself against the loftiest problems.[39] Even if we were ignorant of the author and of the work's genesis in time, there could be no doubt that we have here to do with an *early work*, even though an early work of much promise and by a talented musician whose gifts are perceptibly in full ferment. Everything points to Sturm und Drang [Beer's words], to a turbulent struggle for the highest artistic expression, to an ardent striving to transform into characteristic musical language the continuous swarm of the imagination's ideas. It is precisely the extraordinary technical abilities Mahler has at his disposal which hinder rather than assist him in this. He frankly staggers us by his virtuosity in handling the modern orchestra, a master over instrumental resources which would be unthinkable without a thorough absorption in the scores of Berlioz and Wagner and without an innate feeling for colour. He is just as familiar with the sonorities of individual instruments and their combinations as with managing large masses of sound, yet he is easily led astray by just this technical superiority into using harsh colours and exaggerations of expression, which indeed young, exuberant talents can never have enough of. This is especially true of the Finale, whose unleashing of orchestral fury in some places even outdoes the Orgy of Childe Harold [in *Harold in Italy*] and the music of Hell in the *Symphonie Fantastique* of Berlioz. This overstepping of artistic moderation nevertheless seems a smaller matter for concern than the more substantial fact that the work lacks a unifying underlying note and that certain parts of it, like the first movement and the Finale, tend towards formlessness. Even in a symphonic poem, although it permits of incomparably greater freedom in form and layout, we require the music to be self-contained and to show a corresponding tendency for a specific train of thought to predominate, whether this be the illustration of a poetic idea, or a sequence of mental and physical events standing in a causal relationship to each other. In this way, Berlioz, Liszt and Saint-Saëns have reproduced in symphonic form the main features of a drama, a poem, a historical event or an event imagined by the composer himself. Mahler's composition gives the impression that a programme for this music was only subsequently projected. This serves to close the large gap which yawns between the first three-movement section and the last two movements. In the former, the exclusive predominance of a pastoral, idyllic mood: a poetic forest scene, a fanciful serenade, a merry wedding roundelay; in the latter a funeral march and a Finale of high drama, an apotheosis constructed in large dimensions whose disproportionately spacious expansiveness swamps the much shorter preceding movements. One has to overlook this sudden transition of mood and the inequality of architectural design if one is to be able to enjoy the work's particular beauties. The first movement is a poetically conceived forest idyll, which catches our interest by the delicate, hazy colours in which it is painted. Hunting horns ring out, the voices of birds, characteristically imitated by flutes and oboes, become louder, and a warm violin melody, breathing delight and goodwill, enters exultantly. Spread over the movement there is a genuine feeling of springtime, only the thematic working is too often pushed into the background at the expense of colouristic effect and there are certain empty passages: colour without design. Also of interest is the long pedal point on A in the introduction upon which Mahler constructs the harmonies of the wind instruments, admittedly not without a tinge of the bizarre. The serenade which follows [Beer means the 'Blumine' movement] is a heartfelt, rapturous trumpet melody which alternates with melancholy song on the oboe; it is not hard to recognize the lovers exchanging their tender feelings in the stillness of night. The two obbligato instruments are accompanied very delicately by the strings. The third movement takes us into the village inn. It bears the title Scherzo, but is a real genuine peasant dance, a piece full of healthy, true-to-life realism with whirring, humming basses, screeching violins and squealing clarinets to which the peasants dance their 'hops'; the trio is maintained at a much more refined level, a slow waltz idealized in the manner of [Robert] Volkmann [1815–83]. The subsequent funeral march suddenly jerks the listener out of the idyllic vernal mood which the composer has hitherto been able to portray with such felicity. Moreover, the note of parody which is struck in the first two sections produces a strange-enough impression. The funeral march begins with the well-known song 'Bruder Martin, schläfst so schon', reproduced note for note, a humorous canon which in Germany gets reeled off in amusingly psalmodical tones in glee clubs and students' taverns, and the second section, performed in the Hungarian manner, is strikingly similar in its theme and harmony to a number from Schubert's 'Momentes musicales' [sic], and here too the parodistic tone is unmistakable in the ironic accents of the violins. Only the trio, with its beautiful, gently consolatory cantilena, corresponds to the true character of a funeral service. The Finale, with its spirited, passionately intensified first theme, to which is added a solemn hymn as second theme, is of uncommonly broad design, and it both tires through its all-too-frequent repetition of these motives and deafens by its great enrolment of instrumental forces, particularly by its intensive use of the timpani and cymbals which are called upon for strong dynamic effects.[40] An appended episode in which themes from the first section of the work and from the funeral march are recalled, in part subjected to harmonic alterations, establishes—though in a superficial way—the connection between the work's first and second parts. The symphony's reception was as contrasting as the two halves of the work in reality are. Our musical public, which today again turned out in full force, listened to the first part with the liveliest interest, and bestowed warm applause after each movement on Director Mahler, who was himself the conductor. After the funeral march, the mood suddenly shifted, and after the Finale there was a small but for all that audible element of opposition. The Philharmonic Orchestra played the difficult work with great precision, and no less splendidly the preceding Abencérages Overture by Cherubini and [J.J.] Abert's [1832–1915] transcription of Bach's Prelude and Fugue with added Chorale, a work much performed here. Frau *Braga*, the evening's soloist, brought much taste to her singing of Cherubino's aria from *The Marriage of Figaro* and, as an encore after much applause, the romance 'Kennst Du das Land?' from *Mignon* [Thomas].

A.[ugust] B.[eer]

The earlier recital mentioned by Beer in his notice of the symphony—Mahler's appearance 'in the diminutive genre of the Lied'—took place on Wednesday, 13 November 1889. I reproduce below translations of the advertisement for the concert and Beer's review. This again is of no little interest. We note that Mahler included two songs (Nos. 1 and 2) from what we know now as the first volume of the *Lieder und Gesänge* and one *Wunder-horn* setting, which was to form part (No. 3) of the third volume. (The volumes, as we have seen, were all published in 1892. See pp. 113–17, where I discuss in detail the chronology of the early *Wunderhorn* songs.) We note too that Mahler was *not* disposed to include in his Budapest programme the *Gesellen* cycle, even though the voice and piano version was ready. This was not the moment to reveal the link between the symphony, to be heard a few days later, and the cycle.

Pester Lloyd, 1889, No. 312. Tuesday, 12 November

Theatre, Art and Literature

On Wednesday 13th at 7.30 p.m. in the small assembly hall there will take place the second *evening of chamber music* (in the subscription series) given by *Krancsevics, Pinkus, Sabathiel, Bürger*, with the participation of Miss Bianca *Bianchi*, singer of the Royal and Imperial Court, and of Mr. Gustav *Mahler*, Director [of the Opera], with the following programme: 1. Cherubini. Quartet (D minor, No. 3) Allegro Comodo, Larghetto, Scherzo, Finale. 2. Mahler. a/, b/, c/ Lieder. 3. Mozart. Quartet (D major, No. 7) Allegretto, Andante, Menuetto, Allegretto. 4. Loewe. a/ Der Fischer. (Goethe). b/ Kleiner Haushalt. (Rückert).

Pester Lloyd, 1889, No. 314. Thursday, 14 November

Theatre, Art and Literature

Evening of Chamber Music. The *Krancsevics* Quartet had today come up with a programme that was substantial in its instrumental part and inter-esting in the additional vocal items, three songs by Director Gustav *Mahler*, performed by Miss *Bianchi*, accompanied by the composer at the piano. Thus the programme did not lack the attraction of novelty—and curiosity. In his songs, Mr. Mahler gives evidence of a sensitive, genuinely musical nature that goes its own way on paths untrod by known and popular musicians. His melodic writing is quite his own, the piano part rich in harmonic detail, and his utterance is distinguished. He is less happy in grasping and sustaining the mood that the poem exhales. Throughout Leander's poem 'Es klopft an das Fenster der Lindenbaum' there runs a fresh, lively strain; it roguishly makes mock of a late sleeper, each verse ending with a call to get up out of bed at last. One expects a waggish, popular melody in lively tempo instead of the delicate, misty, far too distinguished colours with which this simple text has been musically furnished. Evidently Mahler had the dreaming sleeper rather than the ironic knocker-up in mind, and yet it is the latter who speaks throughout the whole poem. On the other hand, the refrain 'Steh' Auf!' is absolutely in character. The second text, by Leander, too, 'Es wecket meine Liebe die Lieder immer wieder', eminently suited to musical composition by virtue of its unified, fanciful moods, is not entirely matched by the melancholy, though deeply felt melody. The right note is struck in the third song, 'Scheiden und Meiden'; this is kept in the manner of a genuine folk-song, and only at the end is one a little distracted by the artistically handled vocal part which, almost alla concertante, floats up two octaves. Miss Bianchi, very discreetly accompanied by Director Mahler at the piano, sang the three songs, and also two ballads by Löwe, 'Der Fischer' and 'Kleiner Haushalt'—the latter a specimen of refined humour and witty instrumental characterization—to lively applause, and with Mr. Mahler was repeatedly called back. Cherubini's D minor Quartet, interesting for its clear thematic work and painstaking craftsmanship rather than for any depth of thought or warmth of feeling, and Mozart's Quartet in D major (No. 7), as charming as its sonorities are beautiful, were performed with the accustomed accuracy by Messrs. Krancsevics, Pinkus, Sabathiel and Bürger, and here the subtly nuanced performances of the inner movements merit special praise.

A.[ugust] B.[eer]

The reproduction of the Budapest programme shows how Mahler launched his First Symphony, not as a symphony at all, but as a Symphonic Poem in two parts (which reminds us that the first movement of the Second Symphony was entitled at one stage 'Todtenfeier' ['Funeral Rite'][41], and that the Third Symphony was thought of as a possible sequence of symphonic poems). We also note the original scheme of five movements, with the 'Blumine' movement established as the second movement (the Andante) of Part I, and the interesting fact that in the case of the first movement Mahler actually specified the division of the movement into Introduction and Allegro comodo.[42] (At one stage in the composition of the Third Symphony, Mahler likewise spelled out the division of the first movement into Introduction and Allegro, each part with its own programmatic title.)

The First Symphony, then, was launched as a symphonic poem (though one of a most unusual overall shape), and without an indication of the 'programme' on which the work was based. The only way in which Mahler gave his first audience a helping hand was to hint at the funeral-march character of the opening movement of Part II. But of course the indication could hardly have prepared the audience for what they actually heard: an audacious *parody* of a funeral march. If anything indeed, the description 'A la pompes funèbres' might have led them to expect the very *opposite* of what they heard. In that case, the shock was all the greater. It is possible that the shock was an intentional part of Mahler's shock tactics, which undeniably played a role in the creation of the work, and which, as Beer's review shows, made an impression as such at the première.[43]

At what stage, and for what reason, did Mahler introduce a programme? The first part of the question can be answered with relative ease. It was for later performances of the work, at Hamburg and Weimar (in 1893 and 1894 respectively), that Mahler prepared the programme which is reproduced in HG[1], Plates 46 and 47.[44] The text (in translation) runs as follows:

1st Part. 'From the Days of Youth', Flower-, Fruit- and Thorn-pieces.
1. 'Spring without End' (Introduction and Allegro comodo). The Introduction depicts Nature's awakening from the long sleep of winter.
2. 'Blumine' (Andante).
3. 'In full sail' (Scherzo).

2nd Part. 'Commedia humana'.
4. 'Aground' (Funeral March 'in the manner of Callot'). The following may serve as an explanation: The external stimulus for this piece of music came to the composer from the parodistic picture, known to all children in Austria, 'The Hunter's Funeral Procession', from an old book of children's fairy tales: the beasts of the forest accompany the dead woodsman's coffin to the grave, with hares carrying a small banner, with a band of Bohemian musicians, in front, and the procession escorted by music-making cats, toads, crows, etc., with stags, roes, foxes and other four-legged and feathered creatures of the forest in comic postures. At this point the piece is conceived as the expression of a mood now ironically merry, now weirdly brooding, which is then promptly followed by:
5. 'Dall' Inferno' (Allegro furioso), the sudden eruption of a heart wounded to the quick.

The simplest method of showing the various stages in the development of a programmatic scaffold for the First Symphony is to set out all the available information in tabular form (see pp. 158–159).

If Stefan was right (see n. 44, p. 262), there were slight, but significant differences between the Hamburg and Weimar versions. At Hamburg, as we see above, the introduction to the first movement had its own programmatic explanation, 'Nature's awakening from the long sleep of winter', a conception which evokes memories of the similar poetic programmatic sequence that Mahler at one time formulated in connection with the first movement of the Third Symphony, i.e. summer marching in after the arousal and dispersal of winter.

At Weimar, again according to Stefan, it seems that the association of the fourth movement (the Funeral March) with its pictorial source (probably 'The

	Budapest: 1889	Hamburg: 1893	Weimar: 1894
Title	'Symphonic Poem' in two parts*	'Titan', eine Tondichtung in Symphonieform	As for Hamburg?
Part I	Part I indicated, but no title given	I. Theil. 'Aus den Tagen der Jugend', Blumen-, Frucht- und Dornstücke' [*sic*]	As for Hamburg
I	Introduction and Allegro comodo	'Frühling und kein Ende' (Einleitung und Allegro comodo). Die Einleitung stellt das Erwachen der Natur aus langem Winterschlafe dar	'Frühling und kein Ende'. Die Einleitung schildert das Erwachen der Natur am frühesten Morgen. (See PS¹, p. 113.)
2	Andante	'Blumine' (Andante)	'Bluminenkapitel' (See PS¹, p. 113.)
3	Scherzo	'Mit vollen Segeln' (Scherzo)	As for Hamburg
Part II	Part II indicated, but no title given	II. Theil. 'Commedia humana'	As for Hamburg
4	A la pompes funèbres; attacca	'Gestrandet!' (ein Todtenmarsch in 'Callot's Manier')	Gestrandet. Des Jägers Leichenbegängnis. (?) (See PS¹, p. 113.)
5	Molto appassionato	'Dall' Inferno' (Allegro furioso) folgt, als der plötzliche Ausbruch der Verzweiflung eines im Tiefsten verwundeten Herzens	'Dall' Inferno al Paradiso', then as for Hamburg

* All the details in this first column appeared originally in a mixture of Hungarian, French and Italian. I have translated the Hungarian but left everything else as it was published in Budapest in 1889. Readers who pursue a comparison of Stefan's transcription of the programme with the Hamburg original may notice that in two tiny details Stefan's

Berlin: 1896	Title page of EMS (1894?)	EMS (part-revised 1893)	Published full score: 1899
Symphonie in D-dur für grosses Orchester	Symphonie ('Titan') in 5 Sätzen (2 Abtheilungen)	Original title page missing	Symphonie No. 1 in D-dur
Sub-division into Parts I and II dropped	I. Theil: 'Aus den Tagen der Jugend'	Part I title probably omitted when Introduction revised in 1893	Sub-division into Parts I and II dropped
No inscription, except for Einleitung und Allegro comodo	'Frühling und kein Ende'	Nro. 1 'Frühling und kein Ende!'	No title. Langsam. Schleppend. *Wie ein Naturlaut.* Then: Im Anfang sehr gemächlich
This movement was omitted	'Blumine'	No title on MS, other than Nro. 2: Andante alegretto [*sic*]	Discarded
Now No. 2. No title, except for Scherzo	'Mit vollen Segeln'	Nro. 3 'Scherzo' Kräftig bewegt! (Langsames Walzertempo.)	Now No. 2. No title. Kräftig bewegt, doch nicht zu schnell
Omitted	II. Theil: 'Commedia humana'	2. Theil (sub-title scratched out)	Omitted
Now No. 3. No title, except for 'Alla Marcia funebre'	Todtenmarsch in 'Callots Manier'	Nro. 4 Todtenmarsch 'in Callots Manier'/Ein Intermezzo à la Pompe funèbre [*sic*]	Now No. 3. No title. Feierlich und gemessen, ohne zu schleppen
Now No. 4. No title, except for Allegro furioso	'Dall' Inferno al Paradiso'	'Dall' Inferno al Paradiso!'	Now No. 4. No title. Stürmisch bewegt

text diverges. His transcription of the title of Part I reads, ' "Aus den Tagen der Jugend", *Jugend-*, Frucht- und Dornen*stücke.*' (My italics.) The repetition of 'Jugend' makes no sense, and must have been a slip of the pen. See also p. 226 for the original Jean Paul title from which Hamburg (but not PS[1]) minimally departed.

Hunter's Funeral Procession', by Moritz von Schwind, the Austrian artist
(1804–71): see also pp. 235–7) was made even more emphatic. (To the
identification of this pictorial source I shall return later.)

As I point out in n. 44, p. 262, Stefan—maddeningly—gives no precise
indication of the overall title under which the work was performed at Weimar.
Was it identical with the cumbersome Hamburg formulation?[45] Or was it, I
wonder, closer to the designation—'Symphonie ("Titan")'—towards which
Mahler seems to have been moving, on the assumption, that is, that the title-
page of the EMS represents a late and perhaps final effort on Mahler's part to
organize a tidy title (with 'Symphony' upgraded) and minimal programme
before he decided to abandon the programme altogether (along with 'Blumine'). It is tempting to think that the EMS title-page was devised for
Weimar, the more so as this forms part of the MS score which Mahler may
have sent to Richard Strauss (see pp. 199–200). But this can hardly be so, as
the details of the EMS title-page and of the Weimar column (based on
Stefan's quotation of the programme) do not match up in the table that I set
out above. (For my view of the probable chronological placing of the EMS
title-page, see n. 45, p. 263).

Why a programme at all? Mahler wrote a letter to Max Marschalk, the
critic, in March 1896 (GMB[1], pp. 185–6), in which he makes clear that the
verbal explanation of the programme followed the actual composition of the
work: '. . . at the time my friends persuaded me to provide a kind of programme for the D major symphony in order to make it easier to understand.
Therefore, I had thought up this title and explanatory material after the
actual composition. I left them out for this performance,[46] not only because
I think they are quite inadequate and do not even characterize the music
accurately, but also because I have learned through past experiences [no
doubt, at Hamburg and Weimar] how the public has been misled by them.'[47]

That Mahler was correct when he told Marschalk that the symphony
preceded the programme is supported by the EMS.[48] The title-page (see
column 5 of the table, pp. 158–9) was clearly a later addition to the MS
(see also n. 45), and so far as the body of the MS is concerned, such titles
as are inscribed therein (see column 6) appear in a manner that would
certainly suggest their being written into the MS at a stage when the work
had been completed (and indeed already first performed at Budapest): the
method of inscription is, as it were, marginal.

My table sets out the history of the programmatic titles which were
first attached to the First Symphony and then discarded. The history is of
particular interest in relation to this particular symphony, but it also raises
general issues in connection with Mahler's whole approach to an explicit
literary scaffolding; and in touching on that topic, one has to broach the
subject of the curious and fascinating ambiguity which surrounds Mahler's

first symphonic essays. Clearly, a persistent question mark was suspended for him, and indeed by him, above those works which he composed for orchestra between 1884 and 1900. Each in turn settled down to be a symphony; but as one studies the chronology of their composition, it becomes evident that Mahler was not always absolutely clear in his own mind about the overall shapes of his works and their overall titles. (It was perhaps not until after the turn of the century, i.e. after the composition of the Fourth Symphony, that Mahler ceased to have doubts about nomenclature.) As one documents the first period of Mahler's symphonic output (Symphonies I–IV), one is increasingly aware not only of uncertainties about titles (which suggest certain ambiguities of basic concept) but also an unexpected variation of shape within a work and, even more surprising, a very strange co-evolutionary pattern between adjacent works, e.g. the Third and Fourth Symphonies.

We have seen from the table above, or can trace in it, the birth of Mahler's earliest large-scale orchestral work as a Symphonic Poem in two parts and its eventual metamorphosis into the first of his symphonies. The Second Symphony, too, shows its own curious evolutionary pattern in all the areas that are under discussion: title, overall shape, and programmatic content. For a start, the massive first movement was composed not as the first movement of a projected *second* symphony but as the first movement of an unnumbered Symphony in C minor, a first movement that was to remain without successors until these materialized—along with the unfolding of a complete programme for the work—over an exceptionally long span of years. Of all Mahler's symphonies, indeed, it is the Second which presents us with the most eccentric chronological history.

The Second Symphony

To savour to the full the idiosyncrasy implicit in the assembling of the symphony, it is first necessary to recall the completion date of the First Symphony, which was, as recorded in Mahler's own correspondence, March 1888, Leipzig (the precise date is unknown): 'Well! My work is finished!', Mahler wrote to his friend Friedrich Löhr (GMB[1], pp. 63–4). What is still a little-known fact about the movement that eventually became the first movement of the Second Symphony is this: that the earliest known full score of the movement is dated 'Prague, 10 September 1888 (Duration 20 min.)'. (According to HG[1], p. 708, there is evidence of a 'Sketch' for the movement which is dated 8 August. But no location is given, nor is the source of the information stated. This 'Sketch' is not mentioned on p. 783, where he writes further about the symphony's MSS, a commentary which itself requires substantial correction (see also DM[3]).) In other words, this huge symphonic movement, in many ways offering such a profound contrast in form and style with the First Symphony, was completed in its first orchestral draft by Mahler (one can only assume in a great fit of creativity) a mere six months at most after his labouring to the end of the First Symphony. (HG¹ (pp. 171 and 174), taking up a hint from Steinitzer (see *Musikblätter des Anbruch*, II, 7 and 8, Vienna, April 1920, p. 297) and a reminiscence of Bauer–Lechner's (NBL, p. 34), suggests that Mahler was working simultaneously on the C minor funeral march and 'Titan' (as early as the end of 1887). I think it well established that while Mahler was busy with his 'Titan' Symphonic Poem, ideas were coming to him for 'Todtenfeier' ['Funeral Rite'] and that he wrote these down (and perhaps even worked at them a little). But I doubt if it would be wise to place too much emphasis on the Steinitzer/ Bauer–Lechner documentation, which I interpret as evidence of Mahler's customary thinking ahead to the next piece, and noting down ideas for it—as we know, for example, he noted down ideas (sometimes quite extensively worked out) that later formed the basis of the A flat Andante—rather than methodical work on two huge projects at the same time. The Bauer–Lechner recollection is indeed vivid—an account of Mahler's vision of himself (early in 1888) dead on a bier, surrounded by flowers! (see also n. 112, p. 302)—and doubtless had a role to play in the forming of the psychological drama that 'Todtenfeier' enacts. Even so (and bearing in mind further that NBL was writing in 1896 of an event remembered by Mahler from January 1888!), it seems probable to me that (first ideas apart) the composition of 'Titan' and 'Todtenfeier' followed the conventional chronology, though it is clear from the sequence of dates known to us that Mahler must have been absolutely ready to launch into the new piece, just as soon as 'Titan' was rounded off. (See also n. 54, p. 277.))

Exceptional enough that after one great burst of creative energy in the spring of 1888, another should have followed so closely, and one of such a monumental kind. But this is by no means the end of the unique facts and incidents that attended the birth of the Second Symphony (but for Brahms's First, was there ever such a prolonged symphonic pregnancy in the history of music?). There is still intriguing and surprising information to be culled from the 'Todtenfeier' MS. For one thing, along with the programmatic title, the MS is inscribed 'Symphonie in C-moll/I. Satz'.[49] So the movement was, in 1888, projected from the very first as the opening movement of a symphony. Note, however, the absence of a number: we find neither No. 1, nor No. 2. No. 2, of course, could not have been possible in September 1888, because at that stage the First Symphony did not exist as such: it was still a Symphonic Poem in two parts. As for No. 1, which I suppose Mahler might have used—in September 1888, the 'Todtenfeier' movement did indeed represent his *first* shot at something he must himself have regarded as a Symphony proper (as distinct from the immediately preceding Symphonic

Poem)—if he ever thought of committing himself to the more-than-one that No. 1 inescapably implies, then his optimism would soon have been shattered by the difficulties and obstacles that he encountered as soon as he had finished his projected first movement. The chronological facts tell the story. It was not until the very end of 1894 (18 December)[50] that Mahler managed to bring the work to completion. Six years intervened between the composition of the first movement and the completion of the finale. Small wonder that Mahler crossed out the 'Symphony in C minor' designation of 'Todtenfeier'! He must have wondered if his original conception was ever to be achieved. The central difficulty, it seems to me, must have rested precisely in the matter of Mahler's 'original conception'; or rather in the *absence* of a conception that extended beyond the remarkably self-sufficient and dramatically self-contained 'Todtenfeier'. (One is not being simply facetious if one remarks that Mahler created real problems for himself by casting his first movement in the form of an epic funeral rite. It is in a sense putting last things first, always a risky business.)

The first movement of the C minor Symphony (to become the Second Symphony, but which remained Mahler's conjectured 'First' for as long as the First Symphony remained a Symphonic Poem) clearly shows us, as I have suggested in n. 41, p. 261, that Mahler was attempting to establish his credentials for entry into the great symphonic tradition, and thus also represents an important evolutionary step in his turning away from his exploration (in the First Symphony) of the predominant orchestral form of the late nineteenth century, which was the symphonic poem, the influence of which still has to be given due weight in the development and shaping of Mahler's unique symphonic art.

*   *   *   *

A few dates and facts may be helpful in this context. Liszt's long series of symphonic poems, by which Mahler was clearly influenced, spans the period 1848–82. (It is interesting to remember that Liszt's very last symphonic poem, *From the Cradle to the Grave*, was composed in 1881–2 and published in 1883, when Mahler was twenty-three!) The Liszt–Mahler relationship has never been adequately investigated and would surely repay serious research and documentation. Mahler certainly made consistent and brilliant use of Liszt's principle of thematic transformation (one remembers, of course, Berlioz's pioneering of this device in the *Symphonie Fantastique* (1830), a work of crucial importance for both Liszt and Mahler); and such works as Liszt's *Faust* Symphony (1854–7), with its choral Finale (not to speak of Schumann's Scenes from *Faust* (1844–53), likewise with a choral conclusion), must have profoundly fertilized Mahler's imagination. When one surveys the history of the symphonic poem, one soon comes to realize that Mahler, in launching his Symphonic Poem in two parts in 1889, was conforming to the fashionable programmatic spirit of the times. Between, say, the mid 1850s and the mid 1890s, there was scarcely a major composer in Europe who was not contributing to the gathering flood of symphonic (or tone) poems. Debussy, Dukas, Dvořák, Franck, Mussorgsky, Rimsky-Korsakov, Saint-Saëns, Sibelius, Smetana, Tchaikovsky: all these composers, and this list does not attempt to be a comprehensive one, succumbed to the lure of the symphonic poem, though each, of course, interpreted the concept in a highly individual way.[51] Mahler's leading German contemporary was Richard Strauss (1864–1949), whose brilliant symphonic poems established him as an outstanding musical personality in the 1880s. Undoubtedly Mahler became well acquainted in later years with the unique orchestral voice of Strauss, but when his Symphonic Poem in two parts was first performed at Budapest in 1889, Mahler could have heard none of Strauss's early works in this form. (What Mahler would have heard, presumably, was Strauss's F minor Symphony, conducted by Strauss in Leipzig in October 1887. It was this visit of Strauss's which led to Mahler and Strauss meeting for the first time (see HG1, pp. 168–9).) *Don Juan*, the second of Strauss's tone poems (the first was *Macbeth*, and I am discounting the earlier *Aus Italien*), was actually the first to be heard in public. It was completed in the summer of 1888 (a little later, that is, than the completion of Mahler's work) and first performed at Weimar on 11 November 1889, just two weeks before the first performance of the Mahler (on the 26th). Strauss's success at Weimar has become a legend. As his biographer, Norman Del Mar, writes: 'The appearance of *Don Juan* established Strauss once and for all as the most important composer to have emerged in Germany since Wagner, while the innovations in orchestral technique, then so startling, have become the recognized basic standards for orchestras of the present day. At twenty-four Strauss had written the first of the masterpieces on which his posthumous position in musical history firmly rests.' (NDM, pp. 76–7.) Mahler's first performance was perhaps more of a sensation than a success; but otherwise, with the switching round of titles, composers' names, ages, and the dates of the premières, etc., what Mr. Del Mar writes about Strauss could apply with equal precision to Mahler. It is an odd fact that both composers, so strongly contrasted in personality, who were in some sense to remain rivals, should have emerged into prominence within a few days of each other, both, moreover, exploiting a common medium, the orchestra, with exceptional and innovating mastery, and both declaring themselves as disciples of the now all-pervading fashion for the symphonic poem, or at least (in Mahler's case) reflecting its potent spell. Perhaps most fascinating of all, both young composers—Strauss explicitly so, Mahler more covertly—chose to depict the Artist as Hero as the principal subject matter of their symphonic poems. Very different artists, very different heroes, and of course, very different music; but the parallel is striking. Strauss and Mahler were to bend both the symphonic poem and the symphony substantially towards autobiography, a development of profound significance for the future of music in the twentieth century.

*   *   *   *

The problem of the continuation of the Second Symphony was not solved until Mahler had, as it were, alighted on a programme that enabled him to round the work off, to complete the programmatic concept embodied in 'Todtenfeier'. This did not happen at one stroke. On the contrary, the work extended itself in a curiously piecemeal, haphazard fashion, the chronology of which we can trace with some precision. It was not until the summer of 1893 that the second movement (the Andante) and the third movement (the Scherzo) were completed; some three years, that is, after the first movement was completed. Moreover, if the account is accurate, Mahler told Bauer-Lechner (NBL, pp. 116–17) that he was unhappy about the sharp contrast between the Andante and opening Allegro (the 'Todtenfeier') because the contrast was excessive. This was an unplanned excess, as 'I [Mahler] originally planned both movements independently of each other, without a thought of integrating them.'[52] No doubt this was why Mahler, when he finally succeeded in formulating a programme for the whole work, referred to the Andante and the Scherzo (and in fact to 'Urlicht' as well) as 'intermezzi', which quite neatly sidesteps the formal issue.

When Mahler completed the 'Todtenfeier' movement in full score in September 1888, he was just about to take up his post as Director of the Royal Hungarian Opera in Budapest. On 1 April 1891, he was appointed to Hamburg as first conductor at the Stadttheater. By the summer of 1893, the Second Symphony had grown to three movements, or perhaps it would be better to say, two further movements had been contributed to an area, the final, overall shape of which was still to be determined. It was during these Hamburg years that Mahler plunged into the world of the orchestral *Wunderhorn* song, from which—an expansion of the principle already adumbrated in the First Symphony—emerged the series of *Wunderhorn* orchestral movements, the first, brilliant example of which was the Scherzo of the Second Symphony, the so-called 'Fischpredigt' movement. One may think, indeed, that the materialization of this particular movement had more to do with Mahler's *Wunderhorn* preoccupations than anything else. No doubt he wanted to get on with his symphony, and no doubt he would have need, eventually, of a Scherzo. The Scherzo was written, but it was one strongly coloured by Mahler's current creativity rather than by any very clear idea about the ultimate shape of the symphony. The Andante, which was written at about the same time as the Scherzo (at Steinbach, in the summer of 1893),[53] was completed in a week in a 'grand sweep', that one may well think reflects the grand flow of the principal melody. This, however, was a theme, if the Mahler/Bauer–Lechner account is correct, that was noted down, along with others, at Leipzig, at the time of the *Pintos* première there, i.e., early in 1888.[54] Thus the origins of the Andante precede those of the Scherzo by some five years.

How to go on? This was Mahler's problem, which he put to a close friend, the distinguished Czech composer, J. B. Foerster (1859–1951). Foerster was resident in Hamburg[55], because his wife, the opera-singer Berta Lauterer, a noted dramatic soprano (1869–1936), was a member of the Hamburg company (from 1893 to 1901) and it was through this association that the Foersters and Mahler came together. Mahler had the habit, it is clear, of using his colleagues and friends as sounding-boards, and perhaps particularly so in the case of the unfinished Second Symphony. Possibly he thought that these trial runs through the incomplete work might stimulate a suggestion from someone or other that would help solve the puzzle. Mahler, of course, had tried out (probably in 1891) 'Todtenfeier' at the piano on Bülow,[56] with disastrous results: Bülow covered his ears with his hands (a precise image of his response to Mahler's music). (It is easy now to be impatient at Bülow's reaction. But we ought to remember how very unsettling and radical the music of the Second Symphony must have seemed to early audiences. Dr. Edward Reilly, in the MQ article (p. 447) on Adler which I have already mentioned (see n. 1, p. 242), quotes an illuminating comment of Adler's that makes this point very intelligently:

'In the Second Symphony . . . the bold power of combination builds up to harmonies previously not to be found in the literature. In this respect he oversteps the boundary previously accepted in our time for the purely beautiful. It is not impossible, and not improbable—indeed surmise based on the experience of history suggests—that the progressive artist leads his own age and especially posterity to another way of viewing and understanding sounds. Whether an enduring advance results . . . only the future can decide.'

(Adler apparently also referred to the 'unprecedented cacophonies' of the third movement of the Third.))

To Foerster, too, Mahler had played 'Todtenfeier' as an independent movement, and of course found there an altogether different, because sympathetic, response. In 1893, Mahler brought to Foerster, not only the first movement, but also the Andante and Scherzo, with the announcement that he had begun 'to write a new symphony'. One interpretation of these words could lead us to believe that it was not until 1893 or thereabouts that Mahler decided to add to the existing opening movement; or to put it another way, that it was *only* in 1893 that Mahler finally decided that 'Todten-feier' was to lose its acquired status as an independent, self-sufficient pro-grammatic piece and was to be built *on* and *from*. As I have already indicated, it is virtually certain that 'Todtenfeier' first emerged as a highly organized, greatly ambitious symphonic first movement (the symphonic poem idea was a later stage), and the difficulties Mahler encountered in trying to go on, make the first movement appear to be a more isolated act of creation than it was originally meant to be, I think. (There are, for example, sketches for the Andante from this time, which show that Mahler had other creative ideas to work on, though according to his own testimony (see n. 58, pp. 278f.), it was not his original intention to use the Andante in the projected C minor Symphony.) The title-page of the MS of the first movement precisely reflects what the overall form and character of the music irresistibly suggest between them—that it was a grand Symphony in C minor on which Mahler was embarking. In any event, there can be little doubt that 1892 began without Mahler seeing his symphonic way forwards. In a letter to Löhr in December 1891 (GMB[1], p. 97), he was still referring to 'my "Todtenfeier"', without any mention of an envisaged symphonic continuation.

When Mahler announced to Foerster that, of the new symphony, 'three movements are already done', I think we can assume that the internal order of the movements was still open to variation, though it may indeed have been the case (see JBF, pp. 403–4) that Mahler played them to Foerster at the piano in the sequence that they appear in the finished work. (I suggest in n. 57, p. 278, that at the Hamburg run-through in 1895 the order may have been different. I wonder, in fact, if the *detail* of Foerster's recollections was not retrospectively influenced by the published edition of the symphony, i.e. he forgot the intervening stages that were lived through before the final order was established?) Foerster's response to Mahler's performance at the piano was extremely interesting. He was immensely struck by the new movements and full of praise for the beauty of their individual inspirations. But he clearly found it difficult to discern any links between the movements. On the contrary, what troubled him was the feeling of disparate styles, of each movement existing in isolation. Mahler, on this particular occasion, did not agree, but was evidently of one mind with Foerster in thinking that after composing a first movement on such an epic scale, the problem of writing a finale to match it in weight was indeed a severe one. Foerster was undoubtedly an admirer of Mahler's, but he also showed himself to be a percipient critic. It is true, of course, that a performance of the first three movements alone could only sound strangely incomplete and inconsistent. With the Finale *in situ*, the intermezzi certainly make sense as such, as deliberate relaxations, that is, between the two great edifices of sound which constitute the first move-ment and Finale. Still, there was—and there remains—a real point of substance in what Foerster had to say to Mahler in 1893; and it is of significance that Mahler himself, as we have seen above, eventually came round to share, at least in part, the view of his friend.[58]

It was the death of Bülow in Cairo on 12 February 1894, that, ironically, solved Mahler's finale problem and provided him with a programmatic context for his intermezzi (with, as it were, a story line on which those otherwise unrelated movements could be hung). During Bülow's memorial service at Hamburg on 29 March 1894, which Mahler attended (and at which Foerster was also present), one of the items performed by the boys' choir of the Michaeliskirche (the church where Mahler was himself to be baptized in 1897) was a chorale setting of Klopstock's verses: 'Auferstehʼn, ja auferstehʼn wirst du mein Staub, nach kurzer Ruhʼ' ('Thou shalt rise again after a short sleep'[59]) and, as if mentally illumined by a flash of lightning, Mahler saw how to bring his work to an end. The answer was Resurrection, the only answer, one realizes with the benefit of hindsight, that could offer a continuation after the massive funeral rites of the first movement. This, as I suggested earlier, had created a real dramatic problem for Mahler: what can one do with a Hero whom one has just buried? Bülow's memorial service supplied Mahler not only with the dramatic idea that enabled him after years of fruitless questing to compose a finale for the incomplete symphony, but also to formulate a programme that retrospectively made sense of the whole enterprise. Further, the occasion supplied Mahler with his text—Klopstock's verses (see Appendix C, pp. 416–18)—which he then set about modifying and amplifying, as had always been his practice. (Those who are interested in Mahler's literary carpentry should consult HG[1], pp. 791–2, and Kurt Blaukopf's recent study of the composer,[60] where he aims to show the differences between Klopstock's original and Mahler's versions: sufficient to say here, perhaps, that Klopstock's text runs to twenty-five lines (many of which—three verses— Mahler did not use at all), while Mahler's own version runs to no less than thirty-three lines.[61]) One cannot help wondering, in addition, if even more came out of the Bülow memorial service than the solving of the new symphony's finale problem, though this was clearly the most important consequence to flow from it. Although Mahler in his letter to Seidl (see pp. 172–3) only refers to the impact made upon him by the choir's intoning of the Klopstock chorale (without describing the nature of the choir) Foerster has a good deal more to say, in particular about the effect made by the chorus of boys' voices, by whom in fact the chorale was sung:

> From Cairo came the news that Hans von Bülow had died there. . . . Mahler . . . was profoundly affected by the sad tidings. When we met in the afternoon he played through his 'Todtenfeier' in such a way that we both felt it as he expressed it in words: in memory of Bülow . . .
>
> The memorial ceremony had the following programme: a Prelude by

Johann Sebastian Bach, the chorale 'Wenn ich einmal muss scheiden' from Bach's [*St. Matthew*] Passion, a reading from the Holy Scriptures, then the chorale from the *Messias*: 'Auferstehen, ja auferstehen wirst du nach kurzem Schlaf' [*sic*]. The chorale was sung by the boys' chorus of St. Michael's Church. Behrmann, the chief clergyman, delivered the funeral oration; and the ceremony closed with Bach's chorale [from the *St. John Passion*] 'Ruhet wohl, ihr teuren Gebeine' [*sic*]. (See Addenda.)

Mahler and I were present at the moving farewell. But the church was overcrowded, even though admission had been restricted to invited guests, and my seat was nowhere near Gustav Mahler's, so that we did not see each other. The strongest impression to remain was that of the singing of the children's voices. The effect was created not just by Klopstock's profound poem but by the innocence of the pure sounds issuing from the children's throats. The Resurrection hymn died away, and the old, huge bells of the church opened their eloquent mouths—those bells which had already lamented so many famous dead—and their mighty threnody brought mourning to the entire port. The funeral train started. Frau Thode, Bülow's daughter, with her husband and Siegfried Wagner represented the family.

At the Hamburg Opera, where the master-conductor had so often delighted the fastidious townspeople, he was greeted by the funeral music from Wagner's *Götterdämmerung* [conducted by Mahler]. A great moment, full of reverence, remembrance and thankfulness . . .

Outside the Opera, too, I did not find Mahler. But that afternoon I could not restrain my restlessness, and hurried to him as if to obey a command. I opened the door and saw him sitting at his writing-desk, his head lowered and his hand holding a pen over some manuscript paper. I remained standing in the doorway. Mahler turned to me and said: 'Dear friend, I have it!'

I understood. As if illuminated by a mysterious power I answered: "Auferstehen, ja auferstehen wirst du nach kurzem Schlaf . . ."

Mahler looked at me with an expression of extreme surprise. I had guessed the secret he had as yet entrusted to no human soul: Klopstock's poem, which that morning we had heard from the mouths of children, was to be the basis for the closing movement of the Second Symphony.

This was patently a moment of intense feeling and drama, and it seems not far-fetched to suppose that it was an experience that established in Mahler's ear—creatively established as it were—the musical potentiality of boys' voices, an area of colour and symbolism that he was to exploit in his next symphony, the Third, and transcendentally so, in the Eighth.

* * * *

Mahler had an almost Ives-like capacity to incorporate sound-events into his music, taken, so to speak, 'from life', though Mahler's ear was a good deal more discriminating (more traditional and orthodox, some might say) than that of his great contemporary in the U.S.A. A kind of photographic, acoustical realism was not often among Mahler's objectives, though there are indeed many passages in the first movement of the Third Symphony that very closely approach the quality of unflinching documentation (rather than elegant composition) that is frequently a leading feature of Ives's music. (I am thinking of Mahler's audacious treatment of his march tunes, military signals and fanfares, and so forth, in the Third's first movement—audacious, because the treatment is not designed to disguise the materials but, on the contrary, to reveal them, to expose them, in a condition of maximum nakedness.) The connection in principle between Ives's approach and Mahler's has caught the attention of Mr. Elliott Carter, the distinguished American composer.[62] But one must not let the parallel, such as it is, carry one away. Ives's sometimes almost literal reproduction or simulation of the chaotic sound-world in which we live could never have attracted Mahler. It was surely only a tradition-less Ives who could be open to such a radical admission of everyday sound-events and random musical happenings into his music on anything like the scale that Ives permitted: we must remember that Ives's aesthetic, significantly, has been extremely influential in our own time in blurring or (in some extreme cases) negating the distinction between music and noise. Where Mahler chose to make creative use of an accidental sonorous event, then it was clearly a *musical* event that caught his imagination or a manifestation of nature (bird-song, for example) that could be musicalized, though very much in Mahler's idiosyncratic manner. There is no doubt, I think, that in a very interesting and novel way Mahler did enormously expand the scope of his music by a remarkable receptivity to sound-experiences and sound-stimuli, the context, location, and function of which were often remote from or even contrary to the sphere of 'pure' or traditional symphonic music. But however remote—and clearly it was often the conjunction of a sound-event and an unexpected location that was the point of ignition for Mahler—the experiences he set about digesting and incorporating in his music were, almost without exception, musical rather than non-musical in nature, and—no less importantly—in their potentialities. It might have been, one guesses, that Mahler would have been intrigued by the acoustic experience from life that gave rise to, say, Ives's 'Putnam's Camp' (the second of his *Three Places in New England*), but one does not need to guess at all that, had Mahler actually written a piece out of that experience, it would have been purely musical considerations that would have governed its composition: the original acoustic event would, so to speak, have been musicalized, would have played a far less prominent role than the one allotted it by Ives. For Mahler, the distance between music and aural experiences from life, even when they were of a directly musical character, represented a very significant and clearly defined gap. For Ives, and this is surely part of his prophetic importance, the gap was far narrower and indeed on occasions was altogether abolished. It is just that gap itself which divides the two composers.

*   *   *   *

This digression is not altogether off-centre, for the Finale of the Second Symphony, like the first movement of the Third, makes singular use of musical materials drawn from the world (marches, military signals, cadenzas of bird songs), and thus moves within that area in which Ives, in his inimitable manner, was also active.

But the question to which we must return now is the chronology of the composition of this last movement and the immediately preceding vocal movement, 'Urlicht', the setting of a *Wunderhorn* poem for contralto and orchestra, the nearest thing to a slow movement proper that the symphony possesses: no less than a slow movement for voice and orchestra. As Deryck Cooke correctly observes (in DC, p. 26), '. . . the voice is just one more instrument (a highly expressive one) in the motivic texture'. The precedent set by 'Urlicht' in this respect is of no little importance, especially when one thinks of *Das Lied* still to come.

Perhaps a brief table will help at this point, though readers must bear in mind that the order of the middle movements remained undetermined over a longish stretch of time, i.e., the movements were not composed with a pre-established sequence in view. As the dates show, indeed, the first full score of the Scherzo *preceded* that of the Andante, a sequence that in fact is in accord with Mahler's original intention to have the Scherzo follow the first movement; and while it is true that 'Urlicht' was first orchestrated in July 1893, this was the orchestral solo song version that was completed, and it should not be assumed that Mahler at this time had a precise location for 'Urlicht' in mind, even though he may have had a strong presentiment that the song was destined for the symphony; or if not that, an awareness, at least, of the song as an addition to the resources available to him. In other words, the middle part of the tabulation may look misleadingly tidy. The actual state of affairs was probably one of emphatic flux:

10 September 1888 Prague	First orchestral score of 'Todtenfeier' completed.
Summer months of 1893 Steinbach	Andante: First orchestral score dated 30 July. [Sketch for this movement completed *c.* 21 June.] Scherzo: First orchestral score dated 16 July. [NB: the orchestral version of the 'Fischpredigt' *Wunderhorn* song is dated 1 August.] 'Urlicht': Orchestral version of song [see also pp. 136–7 and notes 26, 50 and 68] dated 19 July.

12 February 1894 Cairo	Bülow dies.
29 March 1894 Hamburg	Bülow memorial service. Mahler hears Klopstock Chorale setting.
29 April 1894	Revision of first movement completed.*
25 July 1894 Steinbach	Finale completed [probably in draft score].
18 December 1894 Hamburg	Fair copy of Finale completed in full score.

* See n. 49, p. 269, and the Preface by Erwin Ratz to the Critical Edition of the Second Symphony (Universal Edition, Vienna, 1971).

The chronological ambiguity, if there is one, rests not in any doubt about the *completion* date—Mahler was quite explicit about this in a letter to Arnold Berliner (GMB¹, p. 134)—but about the actual period of composition. We know for a fact that it was *after* the Bülow memorial service in March 1894 that Mahler was able to bring his symphony to an end. Did he, then, compose the whole of the Second Symphony's gigantic Finale between the end of March and the end of July? Or had some work been done on the Finale before the sudden illumination was vouchsafed in March which enabled Mahler to top his edifice with a final chorale of his own devising?

I know of only two reasons which give us cause to question the theory that the Finale *in toto* was a direct result of the Bülow commemoration in March. There is, first, Mahler's famous letter to Arthur Seidl, written in 1897 (I use here the translation by Eithne Wilkins, see GMB¹, pp. 228–9, and the entry for GMB¹ in the Bibliography):

> Whenever I plan a large musical structure, I always come to a point where I have to resort to 'the word' as a vehicle for my musical idea. It must have been pretty much the same for Beethoven in his Ninth, except that the right materials were not yet available in his day. For Schiller's poem is, in the last resort, inadequate; it cannot express the wholly new, unique idea he had in mind. Incidentally, I recall R. Wagner's somewhere saying the same thing quite baldly. In the last movement of my Second I simply had to go through the whole of world literature, including the Bible, in search of the redeeming Word—and in the end I had no choice but to find my *own* words for my thoughts and feelings.
>
> The way in which I was inspired to do this is deeply significant and characteristic of the nature of artistic creation.
>
> I had long contemplated bringing in the choir in the last movement, and only the fear that it would be taken as a superficial imitation of Beethoven made me hesitate again and again. Then Bülow died, and I went to the memorial service. The mood in which I sat and pondered on the departed was utterly in the spirit of what I was working on at the time.

Then the choir, up in the organ-loft, intoned Klopstock's 'Resurrection' chorale. It flashed on me like lightning, and everything became plain and clear in my mind! It was the flash that all creative artists wait for—'conceiving by the Holy Ghost'!

On reading that letter, Seidl must have concluded that Mahler found himself in the midst of his Finale, only lacking the text that would enable him to bring it to a successful conclusion. Bülow's memorial service provided him with the verbal key to the solution—'Aufersteh'n'—in the guise of Klopstock's poem, which, as Mahler himself indicates ('I had no choice but to find my *own* words for my thoughts and feelings'), served as little more than the base upon which he erected his own text (see pp. 416–18 and n. 61). The letter is certainly perfectly clear in what it states, and the chronology which Mahler's account implies, i.e. a Finale already composed to the point where the 'redeeming Word' was the only missing component, which necessarily implies in the case of the Second Symphony a vast stretch of already completed music, seems to be supported by an article quoted by Theodor Reik in that part of his book[63] in which he attempts to analyse the psychological 'block' that seemingly prevented Mahler from finishing the movement. Reik quotes (p. 264) a newspaper article—'Aus GMs Sturm- und Drangperiode'—by Alfred Rosé (the son of Arnold Rosé and Mahler's sister, Justine), which appeared in a Hamburg newspaper in 1928,[64] and in which Mr. Rosé writes as follows:

> While composing the last movement of the Second he was so agitated and nervous that his sisters feared for his health and almost wished he would stop writing. In 1893 Mahler had to return to Hamburg without having accomplished his purpose: he had not managed to finish the last movement of the Second. Shortly afterwards Bülow died, and Mahler conducted [*sic*] a memorial service for him. A choral version of Klopstock's 'Auferstehen' was sung, and these words were what stimulated Mahler to write the ending of his Second. He retained the first verse of Klopstock's poem and composed the additional verses himself. The first movement of the Second had already been completed in Leipzig in about 1888 as a separate work, and had been called 'Todtenfeier'. Bülow knew the work, and it is curious that his own memorial service gave rise to the end of the symphony a few years later.

If one couples this information with Mahler's own letter to Seidl, it becomes necessary to put forward a chronology which assumes: (1) that Mahler's final (and programmatic) solution of the problem of how to continue his symphony, i.e. his grand conception of Judgement Day, of Resurrection, was not bound up with the moment of enlightenment and illumination experienced at Bülow's memorial service, but on the contrary had been formulated even before Bülow's death; from which follows (2), that in 1894

Mahler was not seeking a finale, but merely a text that would fit the overall, pre-determined dramatic scheme, and supply the edifice with its choral consummation.

One certainly cannot discount Mahler's letter to Seidl, though one notices that there is much that he does *not* say about the prolonged difficulties he found himself in when trying to complete the symphony; and while Alfred Rosé's article clearly stems from family sources of information, one has to remember that memories, however well founded, are notoriously unreliable when it comes to collating events with precise dates. (One notices, for example, that Mr. Rosé in his article confuses two quite separate events: Bülow's memorial service, which Mahler attended but did not conduct (only the funeral music from *Götterdämmerung*, after the service was over: see p. 169), and the memorial concert for Bülow, which Mahler *did* conduct.) Still, Mr. Rosé's mother was alive in 1928 (she did not die until 1938), a point to remember when assessing the evidence.

What tends in the other direction, so far as the complex history of this crucial movement is concerned? There is a variety of evidence, in fact, which can be produced, but the most important considerations seem to be the following:

(A) We know that in the summer of 1893 Mahler was working on the Scherzo of the symphony (which, as we have seen, he at one time thought of placing second in the sequence of movements), and also on the Andante, two MS sketch pages of which (according to HG[1], p. 781), he took with him to Steinbach, one containing the principal tune of the Andante (to Fig. 3), the other, the first episode (in the minor) complete, including the counter-melody (at Fig. 4). (See also n. 52, p. 274.) Natalie Bauer-Lechner, a faithful chronicler of this period, records the completion of the Scherzo and the Andante[65] but seems to have made only a relatively minor reference to Mahler working on the Finale of the symphony at this time. The reference, quoted by M. de La Grange from the unpublished part of Bauer-Lechner's recollections, appears thus in his text (HG[1], p. 276): '. . . [Mahler] began to note down', writes M. de La Grange, 'some sketches for the Finale, but they did not suit his purpose. "You can't imagine what tricks fate plays on one! [The source of the reported speech is attributed to Bauer-Lechner.] Instead of the ideas in quadruple time, which I need for my Finale, I now have only ideas in triple time, which are of no use at all!"' M. de La Grange himself concludes, and surely correctly so (p. 278), that when the end of August came and Mahler had to abandon his work, 'the Finale . . . was hardly sketched'. The reference in Bauer-Lechner certainly shows that Mahler was searching around for appropriate finale-ideas in the summer of 1893, but the slender scale and character of the reference scarcely suggest that Mahler was already in the grip of the fierce fit of creativity out of which the great Finale was eventually born in 1894. He was, in my view, marking time: obligatorily so, since the event that was finally to shape, clarify and release the inspiration that would enable him to complete his symphonic edifice, still lay in the future. If he had been in the throes of writing the movement, if he had in fact worked out a plan for the huge movement in which only the choice of 'redeeming Word' remained to be made, it is inconceivable that nothing of all this creative toil should have been registered and documented by the faithful Natalie. Mahler's sisters may have 'feared for his health' in the summer of 1893 but not, I think, on account of any excited or inspirational labour by their brother in connection with the Finale. (Interestingly enough, M. de La Grange (pp. 274–5) cites a passage from Bauer-Lechner that makes clear that Mahler was in a high state of nervous tension when working on the *middle* movements of the symphony. Here, perhaps, is another example of the blurring of memories that so often occurs with the passing of time.) We should also remember—and perhaps this is conclusive evidence that Mahler was not as involved as he might have wished to be in writing the Finale of the Second Symphony—that it was in August of this summer that he found time to make further progress with his revisions of the score of the First Symphony (his revising of the 'Blumine' movement is dated 16 August 1893).

Likewise, there is nothing in Foerster's important memories of Mahler to suggest that there was a stage when Mahler had the Finale part-finished and was hindered only by the search for a culminating text. Foerster's reminiscences of the Second Symphony divide into two clear parts: the occasion which must have been after the summer of 1893 when Mahler played him the first three movements and discussed the difficulty of writing a Finale of the appropriate scale, and the occasion of Bülow's memorial service. Had Mahler been in the midst of his Finale and still at a crucial point in it, at the time he played the first three movements to Foerster, it is scarcely credible that he would not have mentioned this fact to his friend. For this would have meant that he was not stuck for a Finale (or for a programme, indeed), but only lacked a text. Secondly, as Foerster himself makes explicit, it was the almost mystical experience vouchsafed Mahler at the Bülow commemoration by the intoning of the Klopstock chorale that provided him with the basis ('Unterlage') for the Finale of the symphony. As I shall indicate, there is strong musical evidence to support this view.

(B) Bauer-Lechner and Foerster are two valuable independent sources of information. What of Mahler himself, apart from his enigmatic letter to Seidl? Here again, there is nothing to support the summer of 1893 as a date at which Mahler was ferociously labouring at his Finale. In a long annotation to Letter 86 in GMB[1] (n. 77, pp. 487–8) Friedrich Löhr writes a quite extensive account of a visit he paid Mahler at Steinbach in July 1893, and reports the composition of further *Wunderhorn* songs for voice and orchestra and the completion of a symphonic movement 'in an astonishingly short time' (this was probably the Andante, to the composition of which Bauer-Lechner also refers (NBL, p. 7) in much the same way), Löhr gives no details of the new *Wunderhorn* songs made known to him, but presumably these would have been 'Urlicht' and the 'Fischpredigt', both of which would have been composed about the time of his visit. There is no mention by Löhr, however, of any work on the Finale of the symphony, nor any indication of a critical stage having been reached in its on-going composition.

It is surely significant that, Bauer-Lechner's diary entry excepted (see p. 174 above), there is nothing in Mahler's published correspondence from this period and nothing, it seems, in the recorded memories of his close friends, about the problems connected with a Finale that was launched but brought to a standstill for want of the 'redeeming Word'. The contrast is all the more dramatic when we move on to 1894 and to the months *after* Bülow's memorial service. On 29 June (GMB[1], pp. 100–1) Mahler makes an announcement to Löhr of the birth of the Second Symphony's Finale:

> Steinbach am Attersee
> Dear Fritz! This is to announce the happy arrival of a strong and healthy last movement of the 2nd. Father and child are faring appropriately in the circumstances; the latter is not yet out of danger.
>
> It received in holy baptism the name: 'Lux lucet in tenebris'. Quiet sympathy is requested, funeral wreaths declined with thanks. Other presents will however be accepted.
> Cordially,
> Gustav
> This is my birthday wish for you!

On 10 July, he writes to Arnold Berliner (GMB[1], pp. 133–4):

> Of course I am in the midst of work. The 5th movement is magnificent and closes with a choral hymn whose text is my own [*sic*].
>
> Let this remain strictly between ourselves (the *entire* communication).
>
> The sketches are complete down to the smallest detail and I am just on the point of writing out the score. It is a *bold* piece, of extremely powerful construction. The final climax is colossal.

On 25 July, again to Berliner (GMB[1], p. 135):

> The last movement (score) of the Second Symphony is finished! It is the most significant thing I have done up till now.

Here, in these communications, if anywhere, is the sense of creative excitement attendant upon the conception and execution of the huge Finale of the Second Symphony; and it seems that the inescapable conclusion must be that it was in 1894, and as a result of the Bülow commemoration, that the movement was composed.

(C) Lastly, but most important, the music itself directly supports this chronology rather than Mr. Rosé's, or for that matter Mahler's, as unfolded in his letter to Seidl. Briefly, if we were to accept the fact that the Finale had already reached a stage by March 1894, when it was only a *text* that was frustrating Mahler's ability to complete the movement, then we are obliged to believe that Klopstock's opening lines mysteriously proved to fit an already predetermined theme, and one already elaborately treated in the movement up to the point when the closing chorus is introduced. The theme of the (Resurrection) chorus is shown in Ex. 80, at the moment of the chorus's entry. But of course Ex. 80 is a transfigured version of a theme that represents the basic dramatic idea of the Finale—the evolution from the grave to resurrection—and which is stated in one of its many forms as early as Fig. 5 in the movement (see Ex. 81):

Ex. 80

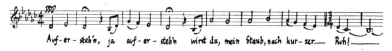

Ex. 81

The passionate, aspiring continuation of the Resurrection chorale (see Ex. 82), that eventually carries the final chorus to its grand culmination, is prefigured even earlier in the movement, six bars after Fig. 2 (see Ex. 83):

Ex. 82

Ex. 83

Words and music are indeed inseparable at the climax of the movement, and it is simply beyond the bounds of credibility that Mahler had reached this critical stage in his Finale, was illumined by the experience of the Bülow memorial service, and only *then* discovered that his pre-existing musical ideas magically fitted those crucial lines of Klopstock that he thereupon chose as a point of departure for his own extensions and amplifications of the text. If this were the case—and there are instances in Mahler where he remarked himself on texts that later proved to fit preconceived musical ideas—then surely he would have made something himself of an event that exceeds even the miraculous. What motive could he have had to hide or suppress it?

But this is speculation. All the musical signs point to a sudden conception of the nature of how the Finale must end, a consequence of the Bülow commemoration; and from that experience, which probably led to the first sketches of the Resurrection chorale (see p. 282, for what is certainly an early sketch for the 'Aufersteh'n' chorus[66]), the Finale derived. Or to put it another way, having alighted on the text and the music for the culminating chorus, Mahler then, in a fit of creativity all the more powerful for so long having been pent up, wrote his Finale with its pre-determined choral climax in view. Hence, no doubt, the thematic unity and integrity which underpin an otherwise conspicuously alfresco structure. There is no cause for surprise at this retrograde method of composing. We meet it at an even more sophisticated and complex level in the Fourth Symphony, the first three movements of which were written with an already established last movement—'Das himmlische Leben'—as their final destination. The Finale of the Second provides a clear technical and chronological precedent for the remarkable procedures of the Fourth.

To sum up: All the evidence, and most importantly, all the musical evidence, points to the composition of the Finale in 1894, as a direct result of the impact made on Mahler by Bülow's memorial service. That event not only provided him with the musical idea of a concluding chorus but also the text *for* it; and further still, it was the concept of Resurrection, naturally stressed at the service, that enabled him at long last to unfold a Finale of the right scale (both musically and dramatically) to balance the huge first movement which had, as it were, been dedicated to the idea of Death. Finally it must be emphasized again that it was through his experience at the Bülow service that Mahler alighted on the programmatic idea—Death→Resurrection: C minor→E flat major—that retrospectively made sense of what was hitherto a puzzling *ad hoc* assembly-line of movements and created for him the possibilities of the pre-Resurrection programmatic bonanza—the Last Trump, March of the Dead, Caller in the Desert, Judgement Day, etc.—that he seized on with such zest. It is an extraordinary story, the compiling of the Second Symphony, and certainly an extraordinary chronology, and raises any number of questions about the nature, consistency and integrity of a composer's inspiration.

Sinfonie in C-moll.

I. Satz.

[Mahler's handwritten draft — German cursive]

Wir stehen an dem Sarge eines geliebten Menschen. Sein Leben, Streben, Leiden und Wollen zieht noch ein mal, zum letzten Male an unserem geistigen Auge vorüber. — Und nun in diesem ernsten und im tiefsten erschütternden Augenblicke, wo wir alles Verwirrende und Herabziehende des Alltags wie einen dichten absterben greift eine fürchterliche ernste Stimme an unser Herz, die wir im betäubenden Treiben des Tages stets überhören: Was nun? Was ist dieses Leben — und dieser Tod? Gibt es für uns ein Fortdauern? Ist dieß Alles nur ein wüster Traum, oder hat dieses Leben und dieser Tod einen Sinn? — Und diese Frage müssen wir beantworten, wenn wir weiter leben sollen. —

Mahler's handwritten draft programme for the Second Symphony (Berlin, December 1901) [A complete translation follows on pp. 183–4]

die nächsten 3 Sätze sind als Intermezzi gedacht.

2. Satz – Andante: ein seliger Augen-
blick aus dem Leben dieses theueren
Todten, und eine wehmüthige Erinnerung an seine Jugend und verlorene
Unschuld.

3. Satz – Scherzo: der Geist des Unglau-
bens, der Verneinung hat sich seiner
bemächtigt, er blickt in das Gewühl der
Erscheinungen und verliert mit dem
reinen Kindersinn den festen Halt, den
allein die Liebe giebt; er zweifelt an
sich und Gott. die Welt und das Leben
wird ihm zum wirren Spuk; der
Ekel vor allem Sein und Werden packt
ihn mit eiserner Faust und jagt ihn
bis zum Aufschrei der Verzweiflung.

4. Satz Urlicht (Alt-solo). die rührende
die Stimme ~~des Glaubens~~ tönt an sein Ohr
„Ich bin von Gott, und will wieder zu Gott!

Der liebe Gott wird mir ein Lichtchen geben
wird leuchten mir bis in das ewig' selig' Leben!

—— · ——

5. Satz.

~~~~~~
~~~~~, und wir stehen wieder vor
allen fürchtbaren Fragen, und der
Stimmung am Ende des 1. Satzes. —
Es ertönt die Stimme des Rufers: das
Ende alles Lebendigen ist gekommen,
das jüngste Gericht kündigt sich an, und
~~~~~~ alles Schrecken des Tages aller Tage ist
hereingebrochen. — Die Erde bebt, die
Gräber springen auf, die Toten er-
heben sich und schreiten in endlosen
Zügen daher. Die Großen und die Kleinen
dieser Erde, die Könige und die Bettler,
die Gerechten und die Gottlosen — alle
wollen dahin, ~~~~~~~~~~~~~~~~~~~~~~
~~~~~~~~~~~~~; der Ruf nach Erbar-
men und Gnade tönt schrecklich an die
unser Ohr. — Immer fürchtbarer schreit es

dafür — alle Sinne vergehen uns, alles
Bewußtsein schwindet uns beim Her-
annahen des ewigen Gerichts.

Der grosse Apell" ertönt; die Trompeten
aus der Apokalypse rufen alles Fleisches
alle Farben; — mitten in der grausen,
stillen Stille glauben wir eine ferne,
ferne Nachtigall zu vernehmen, wie
einen letzten zitternden Nachhall des
Erdenlebens! Leise erklingt ein Chor
der Heiligen und Himmlischen:

Auferstehen, ja auferstehn wirst du!
Da erscheint die Herrlichkeit Gottes!
Ein wundervolles, mildes Licht durchdringt
uns bis in das Herz — alles ist stille und
selig! — Und siehe da: Es ist kein Gericht — Es ist kein Sünder, kein Gerech-
ter — kein Grosser und kein Kleiner
— Es ist nicht Strafe und nicht Lohn!
Ein allmächtiges Liebesgefühl durch-
leuchtet uns mit seligem Wissen und
Sein!

We may take away with us many different things from a detailed story of the prolonged composition of Mahler's Second, but one fact must surely dominate all others: the importance for him still at this stage of a coherent dramatic programme; for, as we have seen, without a viable programme, he was unable to complete the great work that he had begun. This shows without doubt how deeply involved he was in the idea of the dramatic association between music and a developing programme, and how essential it is not to overlook his first four symphonies when surveying the field of the symphonic poem at the end of the nineteenth century. They represent a very significant strand in the culmination of the new form fathered by Liszt.

Symphony in C minor

1st movement. We stand by the coffin of a well-loved person. His life, struggles, passions and aspirations once more, for the last time, pass before our mind's eye.—And now in this moment of gravity and of emotion which convulses our deepest being, when we lay aside like a covering everything that from day to day perplexes us and drags us down, our heart is gripped by a dreadfully serious voice which always passes us by in the deafening bustle of daily life: What now? What is this life—and this death? Do we have an existence beyond it? Is all this only a confused dream, or do life and this death have a meaning?—And we must answer this question if we are to live on.

The next 3 movements are conceived as intermezzi.
2nd movement—Andante: a happy moment from the life of his beloved departed one, and a sad recollection of his youth and lost innocence.

3rd movement—Scherzo: the spirit of unbelief, of presumption, has taken possession of him, he beholds the tumult of appearances and together with the child's pure understanding he loses the firm footing that love alone affords; he despairs of himself and of God. The world and life become for him a disorderly apparition; disgust for all being and becoming lays hold of him with an iron grip and drives him to cry out in desperation.

4th movement Urlicht (alto solo). The moving voice of naive faith sounds in his ear.
'I am of God, and desire to return to God!
God will give me a lamp, will light me unto the life of eternal bliss!'

5th movement.
[?... the cry of desperation starts up ... ?]
We again confront all the dreadful questions and the mood of the end of the 1st movement.—The voice of the caller is heard: the end of all living things is at hand, the last judgement is announced, and [all] the whole horror of that day of days has set in.—The earth trembles, graves burst open, the dead arise and step forth in [long] endless files. The great

and the small of this earth, kings and beggars, the just and the ungodly—all are making that pilgrimage, [shuddering and (?) in endless files]; the cry for mercy and grace falls terrifyingly on our ear.—The crying becomes ever more dreadful—our senses forsake us and all consciousness fades at the approach of eternal judgement. The *'great summons'* is heard; the trumpets from the Apocalypse call [every body and every soul];—in the midst of the awful silence we think we hear in the farthest distance a nightingale, like a last quivering echo of earthly life! Softly there rings out a chorus of the holy and the heavenly:

'Risen again, yea thou shalt be risen again!' There appears the glory of God! A wonderful gentle light permeates us to our very heart—all is quiet and blissful!—And behold: there is no judgement—There is no sinner, no righteous man—no great and no small—There is no punishment and no reward! An almighty feeling of love illumines us with blessed knowing and being!

In an unpublished and undated letter, which must however belong to 1895, Mahler writes to a friend: 'Regarding the *separate* edition [of 'Urlicht'], I beg you to consider that my "piano score" was really the *original version* of the composition, before I knew that I would instrument it and insert it into the Symphony.'[67] We have a date for the first orchestration of 'Urlicht' (see also notes 26, 50 and 68, pp. 256, 270 and 283, respectively)—the MS full score is dated Steinbach, 19 July 1893 (see also p. 171)—and as I have suggested earlier, it is possible that as Mahler brought this song into orchestral existence, he became aware of its possibilities as an addition to the stock of musical resources out of which he might build the middle movements of his symphony. On the other hand, I doubt very much if at this stage (the summer of 1893) the placing of 'Urlicht' could have been determined, i.e. I doubt if Mahler knew how, precisely, he intended to use the song. This was something that could only be settled when a clearer picture of his Finale emerged, and that was still to be conceived and written. Whether or not Mahler was accurate in claiming that the first orchestration of 'Urlicht' was tied up with the decision to incorporate the song in the symphony seems to me to matter not a great deal (if indeed that *was* what he meant to claim: see n. 26, p. 256), to be a secondary consideration. Of prime interest and significance is the fact that the song first existed as an independent creation and was not, as one had previously imagined from the evidence of overt thematic integration, written specially for the symphony. (This is not only apparent from Mahler's letter but also confirmed, as I point out in n. 50, pp. 273f., by the original 1894 MS of the complete symphony, with its *Wunderhorn* song-folder still *in situ*.)

The independence of 'Urlicht' was a fact that seems to have been known to Foerster, who suggests that the setting of the *Wunderhorn* poem was originally made in 1892 (see JBF, pp. 406–7). This may indeed have been the case, as I have suggested earlier (see pp. 136–7), if we are thinking in terms of the original voice and piano draft, i.e. the '*original* version' to which Mahler refers in his letter. 1892 was undoubtedly a year of pronounced *Wunderhorn* industry. Foerster, however, also suggests that the song was pressed into service when the Finale was complete in sketch form and Mahler found himself faced with the problem of how to bind together the Scherzo (now the third movement) and the Finale, and decided to insert the vocal movement, 'Urlicht', between the movements for that purpose. This information (see also n. 70, p. 285) seems to overlook the deliberately introduced, unifying thematic link between the song (Ex. 84) and the Finale (Ex. 85), which is surely a perfectly straightforward instance of the song having a hand in shaping the invention of the Finale. The MSS, moreover, do nothing to support the view that this was a link manufactured *after* the Finale was essentially complete.[68]

Ex. 84

Ex. 85

But Foerster, I believe, may have approached the truth of the chronological matter, none the less. *How* and *where* to incorporate—to integrate—the song: that decision may not have been taken until the Finale was well on the way towards completion. Indeed, as I suggest in n. 50, the evidence of the 1894 full score of the symphony supports the view that it was at a very late stage that the song was, as it were, thrust into its present position in the complete MS. (One cannot absolutely exclude the possibility that it was not until this late hour in the evolution of the work that the idea of incorporating 'Urlicht' *first* emerged.)

We know, after all, how uncertain Mahler was about the sequence of the middle movements. It is not only the alternation of the Scherzo and the Andante[69] that I have in mind. There was a stage, as we have seen (see n. 52, pp. 275f.), when Mahler thought of the Andante as his *fourth* movement, which in itself implies, at the time at least, a still undetermined structural role for 'Urlicht'. I think it quite likely that the final placing of the song was only fixed as the course of the last movement unfolded. The Finale's thematic links with the song do not declare themselves until the choral conclusion of the movement is reached, and it strikes me as a real possibility that it was at this crucial moment that Mahler decided on the role the song was to play, and its ultimate placing, where it functions dramatically as a promise of the resolution to come and musically as preparation for the culmininating and massive appearance of the 'redeeming Word', not to speak of providing an essential moment of repose after the energy of the Scherzo and before the tumult of the Finale. Thus it may have been that some vital decisions about 'Urlicht' were made very late in the day, though perhaps not quite as late as Foerster implies.

If, as I surmise, a fluidity of disposition of the inner movements persisted to a pretty late stage in the symphony's composition, I wonder whether at one time—until 'Urlicht' as it were decisively intervened—Mahler contemplated the Finale following *immediately* after the Scherzo, picking up from the point at which the Scherzo comes to rest? If so—and if what Foerster writes is correct,[70] Mahler must have envisaged this as a possibility —then doubtless one of the factors governing his final placing of 'Urlicht' must have been the need he came to feel at this point for contrast and relief *between* the movements.[71] By introducing the D flat 'Urlicht' after the biting sarcasm of the Scherzo, Mahler uses the song to give us a glimpse of the peak of affirmation that the Finale is at length to scale.

There can be no doubt that quite a complex history is attached to the placing of 'Urlicht', even though now we may never know the precise facts. But it is the end-result that matters, and what impresses one afresh, just because Mahler seems to have laboured at this particular symphony in such an *ad hoc* manner, is the extraordinary deftness with which everything (or at least everything that matters) is brought into the right kind of relation with everything else. 'Urlicht', as we have seen, was not originally destined for the symphony at all, but who could guess that to be the case from the song's close-knit integration with the symphony, not just motivically, but tonally too. The serene D flat of 'Urlicht' not only counterbalances the genial A flat of the

Andante which lies retrospectively the other side of the C minor Scherzo, but finds its fulfilment in the noble pages of D flat at Fig. 27 in the Finale, which in turn find their fulfilment in the G flat of the entry of the Resurrection chorus (Fig. 31); and eventually there is the triumphant E flat which brings with it the final conquest of C minor. In all the circumstances, one cannot but be surprised at the adroit dovetailing of 'Urlicht' into an elaborately dramatic and symbolic programme of tonalities. But in the long run, one's surprise is superfluous. There is always fascination in the sight of genius tying itself in knots, which is certainly part of the fascination of the history of Mahler's Second Symphony. On the other hand, it is one of the capacities of genius to untie those same knots with Houdini-like skill. There is no denying the tangle of anxieties, frustrations and uncertainties from which the work emerged. But when the last knot was cut—and perhaps with the final decision about the placing of 'Urlicht' this point was reached—the total shape that was released could well have been pre-ordained, not painfully pieced together over more than five years.

The Third Symphony

The Second Symphony is the clearest example in Mahler of the *programme* that had to be completed before the *symphony* itself could be rounded off. It is, I think, an extreme case—the difficulties that attended the work's birth were of an order that Mahler did not experience elsewhere—and in the two succeeding symphonies, the Third and Fourth, although the programmatic plan was again of no little importance (a governing formal factor in the Fourth, no less), things ran more smoothly, perhaps because Mahler had a clearer idea from the outset of the kind of terminal point at which he wished to arrive. This was certainly true in the Fourth, where, conveniently, the song 'Das himmlische Leben' was to comprise a pre-existing, predetermined finale, and also indeed of the Third, where for a time at least, the same song was to perform the same function. Though Mahler came to change his mind with regard to this particular movement, there was not, I think, any doubt in his mind as to the nature of the destination at which the Third was aiming.

It would be pedantic and superfluous to chart the progress of the Third Symphony in anything like the detail of my approach to the Second. I have already said something, here and there, of Mahler's changing conception of the work, and to the work's complex and fascinating inner relation with the Fourth Symphony (see also p. 139) I shall return at a later stage. Moreover, for those with the necessary patience, a remarkably rich documentation of the work's assembly can be achieved by bringing together all the sources of information. These are, principally, Mahler's own letters; the reminiscences of Anna Bahr-Mildenburg and Bauer-Lechner; Alma Mahler's memoirs;

and Paul Bekker's study of the symphonies (see Bibliography). What I shall content myself with here is a brief selection of some of the documents which, read through in sequence, show how Mahler's programmatic concept of the Third Symphony gradually evolved, with the number of movements, their titles, order and status, subjected to pretty continuous review and variation by the composer. (See also HG[1], pp. 798–9, where M. de La Grange attempts to tabulate methodically the various programmatic drafts.) First, two outline drafts of the symphony quoted by Bekker.[72]

Das glückliche Leben, ein Sommernachtstraum (nicht nach Shakespeare, Anmerkungen eines Kritikers [im Text durch gestrichen] Rezensenten): [The Happy Life, a Midsummer Night's Dream (not after Shakespeare, annotations by a Critic [struck out in the text] Reviewer):]

I.	*Was mir der Wald erzählt,*	[*What the forest tells me,*
II.	*Was mir die Dämmerung erzählt,*	*What the twilight tells me,*
III.	*Was mir die Liebe erzählt,*	*What love tells me,*
III.	*Was mir die Dämmerung erzählt,*	*What the twilight tells me,*
IV.	*Was mir die Blumen auf der Wiese erzählen,*	*What the flowers in the meadow tell me,*
V.	*Was mir der Kuckuck erzählt,*	*What the cuckoo tells me,*
VI.	*Was mir das Kind erzählt.*	*What the child tells me.*]

I. *Der Sommer marschiert ein* (Fanfare—lustiger Marsch. Einleitung nur Bläser und konzertierende Kontrabässe), [*Summer marches in* (Fanfare—lively March. Introduction only with Wind and solo Double-basses),]

II. *Was mir der Wald erzählt* (1. Satz), [*What the forest tells me* (1st movement),]

III. *Was mir die Liebe erzählt* (Adagio), [*What love tells me* (Adagio),]

IV. *Was mir die Dämmerung erzählt* (Scherzo, nur Streicher), [*What the twilight tells me* (Scherzo, strings only),]

V. *Was mir die Blumen auf der Wiese erzählen,* [*What the flowers in the meadow tell me,*]

VI. *Was mir der Kuckuck erzählt,* [*What the cuckoo tells me,*]

VII. *Was mir das Kind erzählt.* [*What the child tells me.*]

Next, a letter from Mahler to Friedrich Löhr, dated 29 August 1895 (GMB, pp. 106–7):

Hamburg, Bismarckstrasse 86,
29 August 1895

... My new symphony will last about 1½ hours—it is all in large symphonic form.

The emphasis on my personal emotional life (in the form of, 'what things tell me') is appropriate to the work's singular intellectual content. II–V inclusive are to express the successive orders of beings, which I shall correspondingly express thus:

II What the flowers tell me

III What the beasts tell me

IV What the night tells me (man)

V What the morning bells tell me (angels)

The last two numbers with sung text.

VI What love tells me, is a synopsis of my feelings towards all beings, in which deeply painful spiritual paths are not avoided, but gradually lead through to a blessed faith: 'the joyful science'. Finally d[as] h[immlische] L[eben] (VII), which I have finally however entitled 'What the child tells me.'

Nro. I, Summer marches in, should indicate the humorously subjective content. Summer is thought of as a victor—in the midst of everything that grows and blossoms, crawls and speeds, thinks and desires and finally all that we sense without seeing. (Angels—bells—in a transcendental sense.)

Over and above everything, eternal love acts within us—just as rays come together in a focal point. Do you understand, now?

It is my most individual and richest work.

Nro. I is not yet done and must be kept in reserve for a later date. . . .

Mahler enclosed on a quarto sheet, the following:

Symphony Nro. III
'THE JOYFUL SCIENCE'
A SUMMER MORNING'S DREAM

I Summer marches in.

II What the flowers in the meadow tell me.

III What the beasts of the forest tell me.

IV What the night tells me. (Alto solo.)

V What the morning bells tell me. (Women's chorus with alto solo.)

VI What love tells me.

Motto: 'Father behold these wounds of mine!
Let no creature be unredeemed!'
(from *Des Knaben Wunderhorn*)

VII Life in heaven. (Soprano solo, humorous.)

All but Nro. I is finished in score.

At this stage the work was still in seven movements, with 'Das himmlische Leben' (which had been composed in 1892) installed as the Finale. There is confirmation of this particular programme by Bauer-Lechner (p. 20), also writing in the summer of 1895, though in her version 'Das himmlische Leben' is given its alternative title of 'Was mir das Kind erzählt' (see the title which also appears in Bekker's drafts.)

The Bekker drafts are in themselves remarkably fascinating documents, not least for the intriguing marginal notes in the second draft on possible instrumental ideas. They must be early drafts, containing as they do titles which represent a very early stage in Mahler's conception, e.g. 'Was mir der Wald erzählt' (in association with the first movement), and a spate of duplications of one sort or another, e.g. the first draft includes two entries for a possible Scherzo under the title 'Was mir die Dämmerung erzählt' (presumably because Mahler at this stage was combining various possible sequences of movements within one draft) along with another title, 'Was mir der Kuckuck erzählt' (No. V), which was itself at one time a projected title for the Scherzo. This duplication persists in the second draft, and one begins to wonder in fact whether Mahler may not have had two 'character' movements in mind, the 'cuckoo' Scherzo which came to be written (based on the early *Wunderhorn* 'cuckoo' song, 'Ablösung im Sommer') and a 'twilight' Scherzo ('strings only'!) which did not. Ultimately, of course, all his ideas boiled down to one movement, the Scherzo with which we are familiar, and he settled for one title (before he dropped the idea of titles altogether), i.e. 'Was mir die Thiere im Walde erzählen'. The 'twilight' title remained as a possibility, however, even when the actual movement based on the 'cuckoo' song was drafted in full score. As I mention on p. 253, it is on this draft score that the 'twilight' title is amended to read 'Was mir die Thiere im Walde erzählen'. As interesting as what is included in these early drafts are the omissions: no hint in Bekker of the 'Morgenglocken' movement or of 'O Mensch! Gib Acht!' (itself variously titled 'Was mir die Nacht erzählt' ('What the night tells me') and 'Was mir der Mensch erzählt' ('What man tells me')). These movements we find installed in the drafts set out in the letter to Löhr, which represent a much later stage in the evolution of the work, when the music and the programme had almost attained their final shape and synchronization.

It would be a superfluous task to list *all* the variations of title and order that we encounter in studying the progress of this symphony's composition. What I quote here (and later) provides sufficient evidence of the multiplicity of stages through which Mahler's programme passed before it reached a defined sequence, a defined number of movements, and—while they were still a possibility—consistent titles. Though Mahler, as we have seen, often changed his mind about his titles, there remained throughout the variations and modifications an unmistakable consistency of evolutionary thought, i.e. we may find one *title* replacing another, but we do not find a title suddenly switched from one *movement* to another. The only (and mysterious) exception that immediately comes to mind is a sketch for the Minuet ('Was mir die

Blumen auf der Wiese erzählen') which was entitled 'Was [not 'Was mir']
das Kind erzählt' (the sketch is mentioned in an editorial footnote in NBL,
p. 20, and now resides in the Library of Stanford University, California). One
wonders when it was that 'Das himmlische Leben' was installed as the movement to represent the concept of the child's vision? And when the Minuet
was established as a 'flower' piece?[73]

*   *   *   *

From Bauer-Lechner's reminiscences, summer 1895:

My calling it a 'symphony' is really inaccurate [said Mahler], for it
doesn't keep to the traditional form in any way. But to me 'symphony'
means constructing a world with all the technical means at one's disposal.
The eternally new and changing content determines its own form. In this
sense, I must forever learn anew how to forge new means of expression
for myself—however completely I may have mastered technical problems,
as I think I may now claim to have done . . .

'Summer marches in' will be the prelude. Right away I need a regimental band to give the rough and crude effect of my martial comrade's
arrival. Such a mob is milling around, you never saw anything like it!

Naturally enough, it doesn't come off without a struggle with the
opponent, Winter; but he is easily worsted, and Summer, in his strength
and superior power, soon gains undisputed mastery. This movement,
treated as an introduction, is humorous, even grotesque, throughout . . .
And I'll call the whole thing 'Meine fröhliche Wissenschaft' [My joyful
Science]—for that's just what it is.[74]

A letter from Mahler to Max Marschalk, dated 6 August 1896 (GMB[1],
pp. 198–9):

My work is quite finished. It has the following titles, from which you
can probably put together something of a guide.

A Summer Noon's Dream.

Ist section.

Introduction: Pan awakes.

No. I: Summer marches in (Bacchanalian cortège).

IInd section.

No. II: What the flowers of the meadow tell me.

No. III: What the beasts of the forest tell me.

No. IV: What man tells me.

No. V: What the angels tell me.

No. VI: What love tells me.

I shall not bother with any commentary on this. You should get to
know the work before I take it to Berlin.

From Bauer-Lechner's reminiscences, summer 1896:

> He ... drafted the introduction to the first movement of the Third. Of this, hc said:
>
> 'It has almost ceased to be music; it is hardly anything but sounds of nature. I could equally well have called the movement "What the Mountain tells me"—it's eerie, the way life gradually breaks through, out of soul-less, rigid matter. And, as this life rises from stage to stage, it takes on ever more highly developed forms: flowers, beasts, man, up to the sphere of the spirits, the "angels". Over the introduction to this movement, there lies again that atmosphere of brooding summer midday heat; not a breath stirs, all life is suspended, and the sun-drenched air trembles and vibrates. At intervals there come the moans of the youth—that is, captive life—struggling for release from the clutches of lifeless, rigid Nature. At last he breaks through and triumphs—in the first movement, which follows the introduction *attacca*.
>
> 'The title "Summer marches in" no longer fits the shape of things in this introduction; "Pan's Procession" would be better—not the procession of Dionysus! It is no Dionysian mood; on the contrary, Satyrs and other such rough children of nature disport themselves in it.'
>
> On another occasion, Mahler remarked while talking about the symphony: 'Nothing came of the profound interrelationships among the various movements which I had originally dreamed of. Each movement stands alone, as a self-contained and independent whole: no repetitions or reminiscences. Only at the end of the ... "animal" ... movement [No. 3], there falls once more the heavy shadow of lifeless Nature, of still-uncrystallized, inorganic matter. But here, it represents a relapse into the lower forms of animal creation before the mighty leap towards the Spirit which takes place in the highest earthly creature, Man. There is another link, between the first and last movements—which will, however, hardly be noticed by the audience. What was heavy and rigid at the beginning has, at the end, advanced to the highest state of consciousness; inarticulate sounds have become the most perfectly articulated speech.'

Entry of 28 June:

> 'Having such a draft [of the first movement] finished [said Mahler] is like being a girl with her dowry in her pocket. Now, I've found the right title for the introduction: "Pan's awakening", followed by "Summer marches in". I wonder how on earth it will turn out! It is the maddest thing I ever wrote!':

A later entry:

> 'To my genuine horror, I discovered only today that this first movement lasts half an hour, perhaps longer. What will people say? They won't leave a hair of my head unscathed! But I can justify myself. Because of its manifold variety, this work, in spite of its duration of two hours, is short,

in fact, of the greatest concision. I shall consider the first movement as Part I, and shall have a long interval after it. But I have decided to call the whole thing "Pan: Symphonic Poems" [Symphonische Dichtungen].'[75]

Though Mahler may have decided to adopt 'Pan: Symphonic Poems' as a title in the summer of 1896, it was as his Third Symphony that the work was first performed on 12 June 1902, at Crefeld. However, in the programme, the symphony had a sub-title, 'A Summer Morning's Dream', and the titles of the six movements were set out for the guidance of the audience (the six titles are virtually identical with Nos. 1–6 as quoted in the letter above to Marschalk). When the score was published, all the titles were omitted, no distinction was made between the introduction and the march of the first movement, and it was only the division of the work into Parts I and II that was retained. Indeed, Mahler followed more or less the same principle with the Third that he had followed previously with the First and Second Symphonies; the programme in a very vital sense generated the work, and the work was then launched with at least enough of the programmatic scaffolding still visible to serve as an aid to the comprehension of the music by its first audiences. Later, even the vestigial verbal scaffolding was withdrawn; and in the published scores there are no programmes at all. However, despite Mahler's withdrawal of his programme and on occasion his downright hostility to any kind of analysis of his music, whether programmatic or otherwise,[76] the enormous importance of the dramatic programme for his early symphonies cannot be gainsaid: the symphonies *are* the programmes, embodied and transcended, it is true, but unthinkable without them, and also partly incomprehensible without them, at least if one is thinking of a complete penetration of the creative act which went to the making of each singular work. It was not for nothing that Mahler saw to the dissemination of sufficient evidence of his programmatic intent, even while vigorously insisting on the awful misunderstandings that resulted from false interpretation and on his preference for letting the music speak for itself. A programme can never save a bad piece, but it is conceivable that a good piece that is intimately bound up with a programme or inner drama will suffer if audiences are denied the keys that will enable them to break the code of the otherwise mysterious array of imagery. (Individual movements from the Third were performed *before* the complete first performance of the work in 1902, and for these fragmentary occasions Mahler made the titles of the movements and his programmatic ideas available to his audiences. The result, at least in Berlin in 1897, when Weingartner conducted the Minuet, Scherzo and final Adagio, was catastrophic. See HG¹, pp. 397–400, and in particular the review of the concert by Paul Moos, critic of the *Neueste Nachrichten*.)

Some programmatic keys, as we have seen, Mahler did make available, some we know of only by alighting on them in unpublished MS sources.

For example, we only learn how *detailed* a programme Mahler worked to in his Third Symphony, above all in the first movement, when we examine the complete MS full score of the work at the Pierpont Morgan Library (Lehmann Deposit). Here are some of the fascinating programme details,[77] all of them inscribed in Mahler's own hand at the specified locations in the score of the symphony:

1ST MOVEMENT	TITLES	
(opening)	*Der Weckruf!*	[*Reveille!*]
Fig. 11	*Pan schläft*	[*Pan sleeps*]
Fig. 12	*Der Herold!*	[*The Herald!*]
Fig. 44	*Das Gesindel!*	[*The Mob!*]
Fig. 49	*Die Schlacht beginnt!*	[*The Battle begins!*]
Fig. 51	*Der Südsturm!*	[*The South storm!*]
3RD MOVEMENT		
Fig. 14 and three bars before Fig. 27	*Der Postillion!*	[*The Postillion!*]
4TH MOVEMENT		
Fig. 6, two bars after Fig. 8, and one bar after Fig. 11	*Der Vogel der Nacht!*	[*The Bird of Night!*]

This table unfolds almost a complete scenario for the first movement—as it were, a cast-list introducing the characters in order of their appearance—and when confronted by this kind of evidence, it is impossible not to recognize the *dual* worlds that Mahler's works inhabited at this time: the symphonic poem and the symphony, inextricably mixed together. Mahler was never free of doubts, torments and contradictions about his programmes—like his conducting, they were something to be resisted and denounced and yet at the same time were indispensable to him—but his own actions guaranteed that his contemporaries knew enough about his programmatic intentions and that some sort of 'tradition' would be handed down to posterity, which is certainly the case, as this whole section of this book surely proves. One cannot discuss the early symphonies without immersing oneself in their programmes. The only alternative is one which Mahler himself created in the Fourth Symphony, where one needs to know nothing of a programme because it is built into the symphony in the shape of the final song, 'Das himmlische Leben', and the song gives us the key to all the dramatic imagery throughout the work. The Fourth was the last of Mahler's overtly programmatic symphonies and the first for which he was not obliged to suppress or withdraw the programme. It was fully written out in the music.

*   *   *   *

The First Symphony continued

It was the programme of the First Symphony that was responsible for this lengthy digression.[78] Now it is time to return to the work itself, the First Symphony, which in recent years has become an extraordinarily popular repertory piece. I do not intend to dwell on the music as a whole, which seems no longer to require exegesis. There is, however, some fresh information to be brought forward about the symphony, some of it minor, some of it major, but all of it (I hope) of musical significance.

To take a minor point first: the repeat of the exposition in the first movement, that somewhat unexpected classical gesture made in an ultra-romantic work. It was not installed in the first (manuscript) version of the symphony (see below), nor, interestingly enough, was the repeat incorporated in the first published edition of the score, issued by Weinberger in 1899. I have a copy of this before me, a score that was originally in the possession of Mahler himself.[79] Four bars after Fig. 4 Mahler has himself written in pencil the double bar and repeat sign and also made the necessary adjustment at Fig. 12, i.e., he has dropped into the cello stave the upbeat of two crotchets that marks the return of the main tune. So it was not until after 1899, and after the first publication of the score, that Mahler finally settled to commit himself in print to the repeat—a sensible addition, one may think, which doubtless grew out of Mahler's experience of performing the work. The repeat seems to me to lend a bulk to the first movement that it requires, especially in relation to the Finale, the movement that completes much that is deliberately left undone in the first movement. The first movement emerges as underweight without the repeat, and I think it must have been this consideration that influenced Mahler to make the modification.

To repeat or not to repeat? This was a relatively simple decision for Mahler to make in relation to the first movement: our main interest in taking note of it is to record the fact that it was a late rather than an early decision. There was a much earlier decision that Mahler had to take about another possible repeat, but this time not in the first movement but in the Finale. It was a decision taken when the work was still in MS and in five movements, and as a consideration of the point involves a scrutiny of the MS sources of the symphony, perhaps it would be best to clear the ground by describing the sources that exist. This is no matter of interest only to bibliographers or antiquarians: on the contrary, out of the patchwork of MS sources we see the symphony that is familiar to us today emerging and evolving. It is not manuscript paper that we have under the magnifying glass, but Mahler's creative process.

*   *   *   *

The earliest surviving MS of the symphony is in the possession of Yale University (Beinecke Library, Osborn Collection). (It is described at some length by Mr. Jack Diether in the 'Mahler Juvenilia' issue of *Chord and Discord*[80] (hereafter JD), which also includes some reproductions of pages from the MS. Perhaps the first fact to establish is this: that the MS does not wholly represent the score that was played at the Budapest first performance in 1889 but incorporates major revisions made in 1893 (Mahler presumably having started work on revising the symphony for the first time towards the end of 1892; see also HG[1], p. 267). The composer himself gives dates for these revisions at the end of some of the movements: at the end of the second movement, the Andante—and it must be remembered that this MS gives us the original *five* movements—there is the inscription, 'Renovatum 16 August 1893'; at the end of the Scherzo, '27 Jänner 93 renovatum'; and at the end of the Finale, 'Umgearbeitet 19 Jänner 1893'. That completes the tally of dates in Mahler's own hand. What can be deduced from them?[81]

It seems to me, for a start, that this bout of furious revising may have been triggered off by the prospect of the performance of the work that eventually came to be given at Hamburg under Mahler's direction on 27 October 1893. The experience of the Budapest première of the symphony clearly brought home to Mahler certain defects in his original conception that he was later to remedy, and it seems likely that he got down to the serious revising of his MS with the idea of a forthcoming second performance in mind.

Mahler took up his duties as first conductor at Hamburg (which meant not only conducting at the main Hamburg theatre but also at the smaller theatre at what is now Hamburg-Altona (Altona, on the right bank of the Elbe, and just below Hamburg, was incorporated into Hamburg in 1938)) from 29 March 1891. We certainly should not be surprised that it was not until January 1893 that we find him completing some of the major revisions of which the EMS provides evidence. He had to settle into his new job, and his duties were arduous indeed. Here is Mahler's conducting schedule for the last few days of March and for the whole of April 1891, i.e. for the period from the first engagement of his appointment to the end of his first complete month at the theatre[82]:

MARCH

| 29 | *Tannhäuser* |
| 31 | *Siegfried* |

APRIL

2	*Freischütz*
3 (Altona)	*Cavalleria Rusticana*
5	*Meistersinger*
7	*Cavalleria Rusticana*

8 (Altona)	*Freischütz*	
9	*Wasserträger*	(Cherubini: *Les deux Journées*)
10	*Zauberflöte*	
15	*Lohengrin*	
17	*Asrael*	(Alberto Franchetti (1860–1942))
22	*Fidelio*	
24	*Holländer*	
26	*Lohengrin*	
28	*Don Giovanni*	
30	*Götterdämmerung*	

Small wonder, in the face of *that* kind of immediate work-load, that it was some while before Mahler resumed revisory work on his symphony; and when one reflects on the fact that this exacting pattern of conducting was to be virtually a permanent feature throughout the whole of Mahler's life, to which was added in later years an increasing burden of administrative responsibilities, one's astonishment at his finding time for anything at all outside the theatre grows to very sizeable proportions. His mental energy alone must have been prodigious (but of course this in itself is a manifestation of the uncommonly gifted and creative personality).

* * * *

It seems probable to me that the score of the First Symphony at Yale comprises in the main two manuscript elements: (1) the 1893 revisions and interpolations, which can clearly be identified as such; and (2) the original score.

I append here my notes on the Yale MS of the First Symphony, which set out as briefly as is possible, some at least of the essential information that the MS divulges:

Title-page: inscribed on inside of cover, and clearly written in after the MS was bound up.

First movement: re-written on Böhme paper, of Hamburg origin ('Joh. Aug. Böhme, Hamburg' is the imprint) Nos. 11 (18 staves) and 12 (20 staves). The opening of the movement to two bars after Fig. 16 is written on Böhme No. 12, the rest of the movement on No. 11. This is a complete Hamburg revision made at the same time as the part-revision of the third movement, the latter being dated 27 January 1893.

One notes that the ink in which the title 'Frühling und kein Ende!' is inscribed is darker than the ink in which the music itself is written. This would suggest that the title was written in at a later stage.

['*Blumine*': the discarded second movement. The first two signatures (eight pages) of this movement are written on non-imprinted paper which is unlike any of the other papers used in the MS, i.e. it is of a small size not met with elsewhere and is obviously of an earlier origin than any other part of the MS. I wonder if these two signatures may not date back to the days of the score of the original incidental music for *Der Trompeter von Säkkingen* from which 'Blumine' was salvaged? The modest dimensions of the paper suggest that when Mahler was writing out this music he cannot have been involved in the actual composition of the symphony, the instrumental forces of which necessarily involved different, i.e. larger-size, papers. The remainder of the movement (in the Presser score (see p. 224) from one bar before Fig. 9 to the movement's end) is written on Böhme No. 11, and comprises the Hamburg revision. This is dated 16 August 1893. (It might be relevant to mention here the two chronological stages that may be distinguished with regard to the deletion and retention of 'Blumine' during this first bout of revisory activity: i.e. 'Blumine' was out in January, but back again in August. The much amended numeration, in Mahler's own hand, of the signatures that make up the MS clearly document the composer's initial decision and later change of mind. See also JD, p. 83, and HG[1], p. 752 and p. 267.)]

Second movement: The first two signatures of this movement are written on Böhme paper Nos. 11 and 12 (from the opening of the movement to one bar before Fig. 9). (Pp. 1–4 are on Böhme No. 12, pp. 5–8 on No. 11.) Thus this part of the movement was certainly revised at Hamburg. The remainder of the movement is written on non-imprinted (i.e. not Böhme) paper of a consistent weight, texture and appearance; but one notes that while this paper is clearly of an earlier origin than the Böhme paper, it is *not* identical with the non-imprinted paper used for the first two signatures of 'Blumine', which is clearly of an earlier origin still. The revision is dated 27 January 1893: see also my note on the first movement above.

Third movement: This movement is written on non-imprinted, non-Böhme paper *throughout*, of a character identical with the non-imprinted paper on which the preceding Scherzo is written (but for the first two signatures). (The 'Part II' title-page is also inscribed on the same type of paper.) One notes that the ink in which the actual title of the movement—'Todtenmarsch "in Callots Manier"', etc.—is written, is pale in comparison with the ink of the music itself, which might seem to contradict the chronology of the titles that can be deduced from the density of the ink, on which I rely in my note above about the title of the first movement. But when we come to the Finale, we find the case of a later Hamburg interpolation where the ink in which the music is written is noticeably paler than the ink in a passage which is indubitably of an earlier origin. That some of the ink Mahler used in Hamburg did not have the staying power of some of its predecessors seems to be the explanation for the faded title of the Funeral March.

Fourth movement: A 'mix' of Böhme and non-imprinted papers. The non-imprinted paper, which accounts for the bulk of the movement, is of the same type of non-imprinted paper that was used for the whole of the Funeral March and much of the Scherzo. (One notes, too, that those pages that show evidence of Mahler's deletions and modifications in this movement are again of the same type of non-imprinted paper.) The Hamburg revisions, on Böhme paper Nos. 11 and 12, can be detailed as follows: the first begins at Fig. 29 and continues until three bars after Fig. 35, this interpolation being written on No. 12; the second begins at fourteen bars after Fig. 44 (bar 509) and continues to Fig. 49, and is written on No. 11. The revision (re-composition?) is dated 19 January 1893.

Signature 14b is written on Böhme paper, and it is here that the ink of this later interpolation has faded (as against the ink used on the non-imprinted, earlier paper). My remarks on the significance of this appear above in the note to the third movement.

An oddity in the Finale, for which I have no immediate explanation, is the loose four-page signature which comprises pp. 15–18 of the last movement and is designated signature 5 by Mahler. This is inserted—not bound—into his signature 4, which means that the first two pages (pp. 13–14) of signature 4 are followed by pp. 15–18 of the inserted signature 5 and then run on with the ensuing two pages, which are the balance of signature 4 (pp. 19–20). Odder still, the inscription 5 on the loose folder appears on an *inside* page, i.e., on p. 17. Whatever the explanation for this feature of the MS at this point, the paper for signature 5 is of the same type of non-imprinted paper used elsewhere in the movement. But this loose insertion is otherwise a bit of a puzzle.

There is a long letter that Mahler wrote to Richard Strauss (see RSW, pp. 87–8) on 15 May 1894, which seems to support the view I take of the MS (see also n. 81, p. 288). Strauss, as the letter tells us, was organizing what was to be the third performance of the symphony, at Weimar (where Strauss was first conductor of the Weimar Orchestra), on 3 June 1894. (The second (Hamburg) performance had taken place in October 1893.) The letter suggests that the MS full score that Mahler first sent Strauss for his inspection—the MS that Mahler refers to as his 'original score'—was in fact the MS that we are discussing here, i.e. the score (now at Yale) that Mahler revised in 1893 and then used for the Hamburg performance. After that performance, as we know—and as Mahler writes himself in this letter—further revisions were made and a copyist's score prepared (see pp. 203f., where I give some information about this item), and it is this revised score that Mahler now offers to send to Strauss. I quote the letter almost in its entirety, not only because it would seem to confirm my assumptions about the provenance of the early MS full score but also because it contains some enlightening information about Mahler's performing practice: the size of the string band he had in

mind, etc. One notices that it is the *string* parts, and especially the string
parts in the introduction, that have apparently undergone extensive renovation (see also n. 97, p. 298, where I touch on the timing of the importation
of string harmonics into the introduction):

Dear Friend!
   ... Bronsart writes to me that you will be kind enough to prepare my
symphony. I am sending you the orchestral parts tomorrow.—In addition
I shall myself be bringing with me 2 copies of each of the different string
parts which are at present being written out here; for the preparation
in Weimar, five first violin parts, five second violin, four viola, four
cello and four bass should certainly be enough.—One thing more: the
manuscript that you have in your hands no longer corresponds in detail to
the parts sent over to you. The latter have been pretty well touched up in
accordance with the 2nd copy which is in my hands, and in which I
profited by my experiences of the performance here.—It has all become
altogether slimmer and more transparent.—Will the original score, without the touching-up, be adequate for you for purposes of preparation?
Or should I send you my copy straight away for these purposes? I would
anyhow have done this immediately if I had not been uneasy about knowing that the work would be then completely out of my hands and travelling
about in the post.—However, if you prefer it, then let me know by return
and I will then send it you immediately.—
   I would make one request even so: take the wind and string sections
separately—I was forced to do this here too.—I shall meet you in Weimar
on the 29th! When do I have my rehearsals? Would you be so kind as to
book me a room there somewhere and also a seat at the performances for
my brother [Otto, 1873–95], who would like to attend them (he is the
young man whose letter I sent on to you before).
   Is it really true, as Herr von Bronsart tells me, that the full complement of strings is given as a mere ten first violins and eight seconds? *This
would be a real blow*, for I do not in fact know what it would then sound
like! Can *nothing be done* there to obtain adequate reinforcements? I
would take some of the cost of this on myself with pleasure.
   I would like to remark too that the parts are *quite free from error*, and if
anything is doubtful priority must be given to *these rather than the original
score*. The instrumentation of the introduction has been completely
altered in the string parts and the scheme according to which this has
been done is included in the pile of notes I am sending. *When will Guntram
be printed?*
   I send you most cordial greetings until the happy time when we meet
again in Weimar.

In connection with this Weimar performance of the First Symphony
given under Richard Strauss's auspices, we have a further letter of Mahler's
(to Arnold Berliner, dated Weimar, 5 June 1894 (GMB[1], pp. 132–3), which

allows us a glimpse of the occasion itself as seen through the eyes of the composer, and of his brother, Otto, who it seems had suggested that a successful reception of the work would have been a sign of its worthlessness:

> My Symphony was received on one side with raging opposition, on the other with the most reckless appreciation.—Opinions burst upon each other in the street and in the salon in a delightful way!—Well—when the dogs bark we can see we're going somewhere! 'Of course I swept the field again!' (in my view, which however can't entirely have been shared by a good few people).
>
> His Royal Highness, Her Grace and Their Excellencies were extremely gracious, also in the bestowing of excellent sandwiches and champagne.
>
> Performance extremely skimped with severely inadequate rehearsal. Orchestra very happy on account of a keg of beer after the symphony, and sympathetically in tune with my manner of conducting. My brother present—extremely happy about half-failure—myself ditto about half-success!

(For a fuller account of the work's reception at Weimar, see HG[1], pp. 299–301.)

It is not possible—and I doubt if it will ever prove so—to be absolutely categorical about the pedigree of that part of the early MS—Mahler's 'Originalpartitur'—which is not explicitly of Hamburg provenance. One remembers, certainly, that in later years, there were successive drafts of some of the scores of Mahler's symphonies with some very substantial variations in the actual nature and ordering of the material effected between one draft and another (the Ninth Symphony is a case in point). But it is my view that this complex process of creative evolution, as it were, *across* a whole sequence of draft manuscripts, belonged to Mahler's later period rather than his earlier: possibly it was a development that reflected the increasing complexity and elaboration of the music itself, to which it became that much more difficult to bring a final definition. If one thinks of early works like the cantata, *Das klagende Lied* and the *Lieder eines fahrenden Gesellen*, all the evidence there is to be drawn from early drafts and sketches suggests that in Mahler's early period the articulation of the shapes and forms remained largely unaltered, however extensive and far-reaching later revisions might be in the sphere of orchestration. Thus the re-working of the recapitulation in the Finale of the First Symphony (see pp. 205f.) strikes me as exceptional.

I do not infer from that particular revision, or from the complete re-copying of the first movement in 1893 (which I attribute to a complete re-orchestration, not re-composition, of the movement, though I have to rely here on supportive confirmation offered by precedents embodied in Mahler's cantata and first song-cycle), the probability of similar re-structuring having taken place at some earlier stage.[83] On the other hand, while I do not doubt that the bulk of the Yale MS represents the 1889 version of the work (the mending of the recapitulation in the Finale apart, I would guess the 1893 revisions mainly to be in the field of orchestration), there must of course have been many sketches and drafts (and a short score?) that preceded the materialization of the MS that is under review, none of which MS sources appears to have survived.[84] We should remind ourselves, then, that when we talk about an 'original' or 'earliest' version, a whole evolutionary process has already preceded its creation, and, in the case of the First Symphony, since disappeared. However, what this MS does tell us is of sufficient interest on its own account: with the exception of the one structural alteration in the Finale, the MS (if I am right in my assumptions about it) represents the *work* (if not in its entirety, the *score*) performed at Budapest in 1889; and (questions of orchestration and the discarded Andante apart) it is the same work that we hear today, in the same sense that (the problem of the omitted *Waldmärchen* apart) we can be confident that what we hear performed today as *Das klagende Lied* is substantially the work that Mahler composed in his teens.

The interior title-page of the MS (which is reproduced in Mr. Diether's article) I have already set out in the table on p. 159 and discussed in some detail in n. 45, p. 263. There is some interest, however, in the way in which the titles actually appear on the MS. In the case of the first movement, the title 'Frühling und kein Ende!' would have been re-copied along with the rest of this part of the MS in 1893; the second movement, the Andante, has no title on it at all, but this perhaps is not surprising, because Mahler was in a constant state of uncertainty at this time about the movement's status, whether it should be retained or discarded; the third movement bears only the inscription 'Scherzo', this appearing on the first page of that part of the movement that was revised in 1893 (it was the inscription in any case used for the Budapest première); the fourth movement's inscription reads 'Todten-marsch "in Callots Manier"/Ein Intermezzo à la Pompe funèbre', this appearing on the first page of a movement, the MS of which I believe formed part of the original score; and for the fifth and last movement, the title reads 'Dall' Inferno al Paradiso!'.

The titles cannot tell us anything significant about the pre-1893 chronology of the MS of the symphony where they have clearly been re-copied as part of the 1893 revisions on Hamburg paper, a consideration that automatically excludes the first and third movements. But where, which is the case of the fourth and fifth movements, the relevant MS pages are I believe part of the original score, it is of interest to note that the titles are squeezed into the available space in a manner that surely suggests—as does the colour of the ink—that they were *written into* the existing MS as a later addition, which was precisely the sequence of events: i.e. the programme and the titles followed after the initial launching of the work, and we can well imagine that at the stage that Mahler decided to issue a programme in the interests of comprehensibility, he scribbled the titles on to the MS he had before him. As for the second movement, the Andante, which again I believe in part to be the original MS, the absence of the title from the MS tends to confirm the probability of its authenticity as part of the 1889 score (in which the movement was untitled); and as I suggest above, Mahler's conspicuous *folie de doute* with regard to this movement is sufficient explanation of his leaving it uninscribed even when he was inscribing titles elsewhere in the MS. All this still cannot place the authenticity of what I suppose to be those parts of the original 1889 score beyond doubt, but one may say this: that in the case of the fourth movement and Finale, at least, this is how we would expect the first pages of the movements to look if we knew that Mahler had his original MS in front of him and was *adding* the titles that he had devised, at the urging of his friends, to improve the chances of an informed audience response to the forthcoming Hamburg performance.[85] Further than that one cannot go.

Until very recently the Yale MS was the only MS source for the symphony, but now (through the Stargardt sale catalogue mentioned in n. 52, p. 276) we know of the existence of a copyist's MS of the score that was in the possession of Bruno Walter (presumably a gift from the composer) and now belongs (?) to the Bruno Walter Foundation but—alas—is not accessible (at present, at least) for scrutiny. To have to rely on a necessarily very brief catalogue description is extremely frustrating, but there is something at least to be gleaned from it. (One wonders, incidentally, if this MS might be the '2nd copy' referred to by Mahler in his letter to Strauss? See p. 200.)

The copyist's MS still represents the five-movement version, though once again the second movement ('Blumine') has clearly been submitted to Mahler's customary dithering, e.g. the altered sequence of numbers at the head of each movement (Nos. 3–5 had originally read Nos. 2–4) indicates 'that the second movement was an insertion which was then removed again. The leaves of this movement are creased in the middle and were folded together so as to be skipped over in one turn.' It appears that this version of the movement is inscribed not 'Andante allegretto' as in the original MS, but 'Andante con moto' (a sensible clarification), to which Mahler has added a characteristic amplification: 'Das ganze Stück durchaus zart und fliessend! Kein *ff*!! Nicht schleppen!' ['The whole piece throughout tender and flowing! No *ff*!! No dragging!']

The other major item of information that the catalogue brings us concerns the first movement, the orchestration of which clearly received Mahler's continuous and detailed attention, for all the presumed total revision that was effected in 1893.[86] There are seven supplementary pages of orchestral revisions in Mahler's hand (which the copyist has entered into the MS)—these all in addition to the numerous autograph corrections made by Mahler throughout the MS—and, perhaps most interesting of all, what are no less than *two* versions of the introduction and the first seventeen bars of the exposition, i.e. from the opening of the symphony to nine bars after Fig. 5. As the catalogue records: 'The beginning of the first movement appears twice. Bars 1–79 were in the first place orchestrated more simply and were then written out afresh; the first ten pages were folded together in the middle and the pagination begun again at "1"'. It is a pity that we cannot compare these two versions, not only with the published version but with the 1893 revision; indeed, taking the 1893 version as the earliest to which we have access (but remembering that the EMS, so far as the introduction was concerned, already offered a replacement of the 1889 original), the introduction to the first movement has to our certain knowledge passed through at least four versions *en route* to final publication, and there may well have been further re-drafting between the time to which this copyist's score belongs and the materialization of the score which was sent for engraving. It is in the light of this manuscript evidence of the immense pains Mahler took to get his introduction right—and the final published version reveals the kind of highly organized and subtly differentiated acoustic experience that he was aiming to construct—that his sketching out in pencil on the published score of yet another possible instrumental permutation for the initial sequence of fourths catches one's attention (see n. 79, p. 288). Obviously, this was a passage that presented a perpetual challenge, and it seems as if Mahler only needed to have it before him momentarily for a new idea about its instrumentation to occur to him.

This copyist's MS would appear (if I interpret the catalogue's silence on these points correctly) not to be dated, nor to include the programmatic titles of the movements. We know that for the 1896 Berlin performance the titles were excluded and the Andante omitted, whereas the titles and the Andante were still current at Hamburg in 1893 and Weimar in 1894. Without a sight of this second MS, we cannot allot it a date more precise than post-August 1893 (which is the latest date on the EMS) and pre-March 1896 (by which date the work had emerged as a four-movement symphony without a programme). The copyist's MS clearly represents an important further stage in the evolution of the work and we must hope that it will soon become available for study. If we had to hand the EMS and the subsequent copyist's MS (heavily annotated by Mahler himself), we might still be missing several very vital steps in the progress of the work towards its final version, but nonetheless, the picture would be a good deal more complete.

Complete, that is to say, in so far as the history of the work's *orchestration* is concerned: one has to remind oneself that all the revisions, re-touchings and re-draftings of the symphony, certainly from 1893 onwards, were all confined to the instrumentation, and that the earliest MS source—Mahler's own autograph MS—already represents, compositionally speaking, the work we know today. It is just because the EMS contains evidence of Mahlerian practice outside the field of orchestration that a quite special interest attaches to it.

The re-structuring of the Finale, the movement in the MS that allows us a rare glimpse of a compositional revision of this nature, occurs at that critical formal point in the movement when (between Figs. 44 and 45) Mahler transides from the last statement of his big, passionate, string melody to the final bout of F minor music that precedes the triumphant culmination of the movement. This whole area of the Finale is of a recapitulatory character, in which Mahler, perhaps a shade too strenuously, laboured to leave no loose ends undone, and above all to tie together, both musically and dramatically, the Finale and the first movement, to spell out beyond doubt their inter-relationship, before bringing the symphony to an end. One may well feel that Mahler's enthusiasm for leaving nothing out—and I have in mind particularly the longish retrospective resurrection of the first movement's introduction—was somewhat too much of a presence in this part of the movement, and indeed I shall go on to suggest below that there is more than simply a local issue involved in this comprehensive recapitulatory process, which crops up again and again in Mahler's symphonies. However, the evidence of the MS goes to show that in this particular instance Mahler himself took remedial action, and for once deleted a substantial recapitulation: no less than a repeat of the Finale's stormy, noisy introduction, i.e. the passage from Figs. 1 to 6 which opens the movement with such a brilliant display of orchestral fireworks. The MS makes clear, surprisingly and intriguingly, that after the restatement of the big lyrical tune, which died away as Mahler has it dying away in the final version up to the audacious eruption of the violas (bar 519), Mahler initiated a recapitulation of the blazing, fiery introduction, including the cymbal clash (or bash, rather) which in bar 1 of the movement sets the whole drama in motion.[87]

It was a happy accident that the three completely cancelled pages formed part of a four-page signature. They provide us with the evidence of the return to the introduction which otherwise would never have been known. If readers care to consult Mr. Diether's Plate V, they will see how fortunate it is that we have the three continuing pages. Plate V *alone* would have led us to believe that the extent of Mahler's revision was confined to a handful of transitional bars, from bar 509 to Fig. 45. As Mr. Diether rightly remarks, if Mahler had taken the trouble to copy out afresh the seven extant bars illustrated in Plate V, i.e. bars 502–8, we should have had no clue to the fact that a major re-structuring had taken place.

After the three pages of cancelled recapitulation, the re-composed pages begin (on Hamburg paper), and continue for eight pages (across two signatures or folders). After the third bar on the last page of the interpolation, Mahler breaks off and leaves the rest of the page blank. On the succeeding page, which reverts to the earlier type of MS paper, the first six bars are cancelled—these are bars 582–7, a re-orchestration of which comprises the last bars of the preceding interpolation—and the original score is resumed (at Fig. 49) with bar 588. While the three extant cancellations indicate clearly enough the return of the introduction, we have no means of course of knowing what happened between bar 19 of the cancelled passage and bar 582 of the MS, by which point Mahler had as it were re-composed himself back into the main flow of the movement. It is my guess that the deleted passage probably represented a varied and compressed version of the intro- duction, *leading into* a version of the F minor march music from Fig. 6 onwards. (In this connection, it may be of some significance that where, in the deleted version, Mahler appears to unite the head-motive and continuation of the principal theme (see n. 87, p. 291), this results in the articulation of the theme that we have met for the first time at Fig. 6, and only after the intro- duction has been heard complete.) Thereafter, the music would presumably have continued, using of course the exposition as its model (as the exposition in turn had used as its model the parallel passages in the development of the first movement, e.g. six bars before Fig. 22 et seq.), until that passage was reached, bars 582–8 inclusive, that we know formed part of the discarded version because we have the cancellation, and which, with the preceding ten bars or so, have their parallel in the exposition (bars 84 et seq.). In sum, the actual gap in our knowledge is probably smaller[88] than we thought. With the benefit of the beginning and end of Mahler's cancellation, I doubt if we shall go far wrong in thinking of the discarded recapitulation as a modified version of music, the essential gestures of which we already know. Doubtless this was at least one of the reasons why Mahler himself revised his score at this point. In the programme, the fierce opening of the Finale was described as 'the sudden eruption of a heart wounded to the quick'. One really cannot do that sort of thing more than once without risking evoking the law of diminishing returns, and Mahler saw to it that the duplication was jettisoned before the second performance of the work was given at Hamburg towards the end of 1893.

*　　*　　*　　*

Mahler was certainly wise to make his revision of this recapitulatory enter- prise. Nonetheless, the recapitulatory habit of this particular kind stayed with him. It is a prominent feature of the First Symphony—one thinks of the recapitulation of the first movement's introduction at the onset of the develop- ment and its recapitulation in the Finale—and crops up prominently else- where in some of the succeeding symphonies, above all in the first movement of the Third Symphony. It would be out of place here to go through each work and assess the success of each recapitulatory gesture which involves the repeat of a movement's introduction, but as an independent investigation it would have something to commend it: first, the habit comprises a unique feature of Mahler's formal practice, and secondly, it manifests, in the most interesting way, the friction between the obligations of fulfilling a dramatic (or poetic) programme and the obligations of, as it were, pure, disinterested form—an inescapable Romantic inheritance this, not only for the composer but also for the listener (we are conditioned by history in the way we hear music, its forms no less than its styles, etc.). There is no doubt that for Mahler the slow introduction constituted a special attraction, permitting him to set the stage atmospherically and also, no less important, to set out his building materials. The tension begins to show, in my view, when, as is so often the case, Mahler brings back his introduction and, though one may see the programmatic intent of the recapitulation, formally one is bothered by it, sometimes on two grounds: first, such a recapitulation inevitably entails the reintroduction of a long stretch of (usually) very slow music, which—equally inevitably—interrupts the momentum and dramatic pace of the movement; and secondly, for all Mahler's skill at varying the recapitulations of his introductions, in substance this is music we have heard before, and there is the danger of impatience resulting from this practice of total recall. To take only one example: the huge first movement of the Third Symphony: there is no doubt about the brilliant quality of the invention in this most daring of Mahler's first movements, but I find it hard (as, I believe, may Deryck Cooke (see DC, pp. 28–9)) to take the return of the slow introduction (at Fig. 55 et seq.) in the midst of a movement that, by this stage, has accumulated a great deal of drive and energy. To be hauled back to the very slow tempo of the introduction, and to music *out* of which the great marching-on march has emerged, is in some sense an exasperating experience, but one that is attributable not to arbitrariness on Mahler's part but to a consistency of practice in which, for good or ill, he persisted well-nigh throughout his creative life. It is clear that where a symphony is intent on fulfilling or articulating a programme, there are bound to be crucial moments when a musical event occurs that will have a programmatic rather than a purely formal justification. The recapitulatory or retrospective component that, in Mahler, marks so many of these singular events, is surely due to the character of his programmes, of his inner dramas, so many of which depend on the idea of a continuing conflict, with victory for the most part hardly won. In order to keep the conflict, the basic dramatic idea—which may be projected in terms of Nature (as in the Third Symphony) or in terms of the innocent Hero, in tune with Nature, confronted by the world of Experience (as in the First Symphony)—in the foreground, and also to reinforce the impression made by the conquering moment when it comes, Mahler felt himself compelled to introduce these recapitulations as deliberate points of reference, reminding us of the initial point of departure and in some cases of the distance still to be travelled before resolution can be achieved. Some such reasoning as this, I think, was responsible for the eruption of the 'Winter' music in the midst of high Summer (in the first movement of the Third), or, to take a much more straightforward example in the First Symphony, for the resurrection in the Finale of the introduction to the first movement at Fig. 38, which constitutes a vital act of retrospection, of a return to the symphony's point of departure, before embarking on the stage that leads to the final and clinching resolution. Nonetheless, finding a perfectly intelligent and intelligible programmatic justification does not necessarily remove the sense of unease that these repetitions can still provoke; and it is my view that Mahler was not wholly successful in circumventing the formal problems to which they gave rise. In this one aspect of Mahler's work we encounter, as I have already suggested, a fascinating tension between the adoption of a traditional formal device, the slow introduction, which has a lot of symphonic history behind it, and the manipulation of it in a new programmatic or dramatic context. The truth is that the two concepts were fundamentally irreconcilable. Mahler, however, if he was aware of the problem, was certainly not discouraged by it, and even when he had put the explicitly programmatic world behind him and moved on, in his post-*Wunderhorn* symphonies, to inner dramas and, on occasion, to a more traditionally based concept of the symphony, it is highly significant that the old custom still persisted (though surely much more successfully and sophisticatedly handled), for instance in the Finale of the Sixth, or the first movement of the Seventh Symphony. All his slow introductions were governed by the same retrospective law. (Perhaps one should add that it was not just the slow introduction that was a problem for Mahler, for his Romantic predecessors and for some of his contemporaries. It was rather the total conflict, that emerged more and more sharply as the nineteenth century progressed, between the symmetries of the classical symphony, the forms of which (however diverse in practice as distinct from theory) relied heavily on the recapitulation principle; whereas the idea of recapitulation, of repetition, increasingly went against the newly developing dramatic or narrative symphonic forms, where recapitulation was no longer the point of the formal game. Indeed, the more dramatic and developing the 'programme', the less meaningful became the whole practice of recapitulation.)

*   *   *   *

If Mahler's discarding of the recapitulation of the introduction to the Finale of the First was in itself an act of prudence, the music that replaced the deletion was an example of Mahler's inspiration working in its best vein; indeed, he bridged the gap between the last gasp of the big lyrical melody and the onset of the F minor march music by writing one of his most brilliant transitions, using the head-motive of the march tune, in progressive augmentation, to lead into the F minor recapitulation (Ex. 86):

Ex. 86

This was a passage that Mahler himself apparently relished. When talking to Bauer-Lechner about the work (NBL, pp. 150–51), before the first Vienna performance of the symphony on 18 November 1900, he pointed out (in connection with the third movement, the Funeral March) that he often obtained the precise instrumental effect he wanted by using an instrument as it were *against* its predictable character. Hence his enjoyment of the violas in Ex. 86—'I could never have produced that powerful, forced tone if I had given the passage to the 'celli (the most plausible choice here)'. The continuation and extension of Ex. 86 (bar 540, et seq., Ex. 87) is again allotted to the violas, at which point one is reminded of a substantial likely influence in the shaping of Mahler's invention: Smetana's *Bartered Bride* overture.[89] The parallel is clear (see Ex. 88):

Ex. 87

Ex. 88

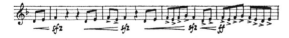

That remarkable passage not only offers parallels with Smetana but anticipates future developments in Mahler himself. In particular, the contrapuntal style we encounter in the Finale of the First Symphony—above all the energetic polyphonic continuations of pithy motives that are a feature of the F minor music—most vividly anticipates *one* of the pronounced contrapuntal styles that is characteristic of Mahler's technique in his maturity.[90]

We can see how prophetic he succeeded in being in his First Symphony, if
we compare the F minor music from the Finale with the Rondo-Burleske of
the Ninth. The actual contrapuntal technique in both cases is very similar,
and so in fact is the character of the ideas, cf. for example this leading idea
from the Rondo of the Ninth (Ex. 89) with the F minor march tune from the
First (Ex. 90). Small wonder that when these themes are broken down into
their constituent motives and treated polyphonically, the mosaic textures of
these chronologically widely separated movements seem so close in spirit

Ex. 89

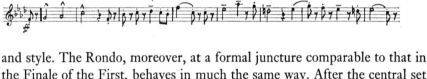

Ex. 90

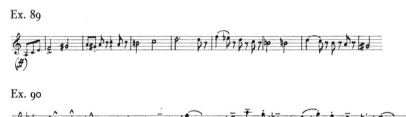

and style. The Rondo, moreover, at a formal juncture comparable to that in
the Finale of the First, behaves in much the same way. After the central set
of variations, the transition to Tempo I, during which principal motives
associated with the movement's main material gradually re-invade the texture
of the music, shows us very much the same kind of musical mind and
procedures at work as in the transition to the F minor music at Fig. 45 (and
beyond) in the last movement of the First. When Mahler got rid of his
redundant recapitulation and re-wrote the passage, he took, unknown to
himself, a step forward into his own future.

I think the fact that he recalled this spot in the symphony in the conversation with Bauer-Lechner cited above suggests that Mahler was conscious
of having brought off a particularly adroit compositional stroke. Another
passage of which he was proud, according to Bauer-Lechner (pp. 5–10), was
another transition (though of another kind) in the Finale of the First Symphony, but this time the passage from one bar before Fig. 33 to Fig. 34 (my
Ex. 91 quotes the bars in which the transition from C major to D major is
accomplished):

Ex. 91

Of this climactic passage, Mahler said: '[It] gave me a lot of trouble. Again and again, the music had fallen from brief glimpses of radiance into the darkest depths of despair. Now, an enduring, triumphal victory had to be won. As I discovered after considerable vain groping, this could be achieved by modulating from one key to the key a whole-step above (from C major to D major, the principal key of the movement). Now, this could have been managed very easily by using the intervening half-step and rising from C to C sharp, then to D. But then everyone would have known that D would be the next step. On the contrary, my D chord had to sound as though it had fallen from heaven, as though it came from another world. Then, I found my transition—through the most unconventional and daring of modulations, which I hesitated to accept for a long time and to which I finally surrendered much against my will. And if there is anything great in the whole symphony it is this very passage, which—I can safely say it—has yet to meet its match.' (It must have been Ex. 91 that Mahler had in mind. There are indeed ambiguities in the preceding text, but no other passage fits. It cannot have been the big transition that leads into the coda of the Finale, which certainly does not work in the context of Mahler's description and in any case was a passage that had already been composed as part of the first movement. It is hard to follow why, in HG¹, p. 757, M. de La Grange, in a baffling page of commentary, seems to argue that it is the pre-coda transition that Mahler was talking about.)

It is, I believe, of no little significance that Mahler seemed to retain particular memories of composing both this crucial passage—the modulation to D major—and the later return to F minor. Indeed, the MS confirms that these two passages were precisely those that Mahler subjected to revision in 1893, which would have meant that he had good reason to remember them. It is surely no accident that the two Hamburg interpolations in the MS of the Finale include the modulation to D (the first interpolation) and the return to F minor (the second). Moreover, it seems most likely that it was the fact of these two substantial revisions, which actually affected the substance of the music (i.e. involved re-composition, not re-touching of the instrumentation), which was responsible for Mahler's meticulously chosen inscription at the end of the Finale, 'umgearbeitet'—'remodelled' or 're-cast'—not, one notices 'Renovatum', which he wrote at the end of the Scherzo only a few days later (and was to use again at the end of the Andante in August), and which carries with it no implication of re-working but instead suggests making good or anew an existing edifice. 'Renovatum' surely indicates in this context the re-orchestration that Mahler carried out in 1893, whereas 'umgearbeitet' tells us that it was also re-composition that was involved in the Hamburg interpolations in the Finale. It is quite possibly the case, then, that the brilliant modulation to D, which is now such a climactic feature of the Finale, did not reach its final articulation, until 1893, and that a different version of the transition was heard at the first performance of the symphony.

*   *   *   *

What distinguishes the EMS from the published version of the First Symphony is not the substance of the invention—because this was established by 1893—but the orchestration. Mahler's orchestra in the EMS was smaller than the orchestra he finally settled on for publication in 1899. The dispositions of the two orchestras can be set out thus:

EMS	*Published Score*
3 flutes (incl. Picc.)	4 flutes (3 & 4 doubling Picc.)
3 oboes	4 oboes (3 doubling c.a.)
3 clarinets (incl. 1 E flat clarinet)	4 clarinets (3 doubling bass cl. and E flat cl., 4 E flat cl. throughout)*
3 bassoons	3 bassoons (3 doubling double bassoon)
4 horns	⎧ 7 horns
4 trumpets	†⎨ 4 trumpets
3 trombones	⎩ 3 trombones
Bass tuba	Bass tuba
Timpani	Timpani (2 players)
Percussion (Bass drum, cymbals, triangle, tam-tam)	Percussion (Bass drum, cymbals, triangle, tam-tam)
Harp	Harp
Strings	Strings

In comparing the published version of the *Gesellen* cycle with the earlier MS score, we discern a similar trend towards enlargement of the orchestra in the final version. But as I remark in connection with the Third Symphony (see pp. 326–7), Mahler's assembling of larger forces reflects not his predilection for overwhelming numbers,[91] but, rather, his need to have all the groups of the orchestra represented complete and in sufficient numbers (the woodwind especially) both to reinforce a line and make it tell, in however busy a texture—of special importance, this, in Mahler's busy contrapuntal

---

* See n. 18, p. 369f., for some detailed thoughts about Mahler's idiosyncratic use of this instrument.

† In the Finale (at Fig. 56), a 5th trumpet and 4th trombone are introduced to strengthen the horns. In the first published score, at least 3 extra horns were indicated to perform this role.

textures—and to have the range of instrumental colours available in sufficient numerical strength to serve the wealth of motivic articulation that is so remarkable a feature of Mahler's scoring. For we find, in fact, the 'colour' as such is only rarely Mahler's intention. His style of scoring was, rather, part and parcel of his method of composing, and nowhere is this seen more clearly than in his brilliant instrumental articulation of the motives out of which so many of his extended themes are actually compounded. Indeed, it is not too much to say that this is a kind of innovatory orchestration, that brings with it a built-in analysis of a work's thematic organization.[92] The shift from solo instrument to solo instrument, and from group to group, spells out—sounds out—the actual motivic architecture of the theme; and when, as frequently happens in Mahler, the motives become detached in the development and are re-ordered and combined in an unexpected polyphony (a mode of development at the centre of Mahler's composing method), a complementary polyphony in the field of timbre is obligatory if the motivic structure of the development is to be clarified.[93] Thus the need for maximum resources, for the maximum possibility of that selectivity which for Mahler was an indispensable aid to comprehensibility. Colour, ultimately, was not his aim, orchestrally speaking, except perhaps in magical moments like the introduction to the first movement of the First Symphony (and there colour, as I suggest below, is organized in an extraordinarily rigorous way). To enable us to comprehend his music by hearing precisely what was going on, this was the ambition that formed the rational basis of Mahler's orchestration. His scoring, one cannot too emphatically repeat, was not an 'aspect' of his composing: it was how he composed; and he was not able to realize his particular kind of clarity until he had the right numerical forces at his disposal. Hence, in Mahler's case, the evolution of the 'large' orchestra.

It would be impractical to carry out here a full-scale comparison of the orchestration of the 1893 revised score (the EMS) with the 1899 publication. That is an exercise which requires the scores to be surveyed side by side, if it is to be meaningful. Moreover, the 1893 stage was, as we know, only one of the stages in the history of the orchestration of the work. For a complete picture we should have to scrutinize (if we could locate them) other interim stages, like the copyist's MS described on pp. 203–4. But there are a few points to be made about the 1893 orchestration that are perhaps of general interest. For example, one might reasonably think that the kind of immensely elaborate dynamics we encounter in the Finale of the symphony between Figs. 12 and 14[94]—that remarkable series of short, powerful crescendi—was the result of the long refining process that the score underwent. The passage is there, however, in all essentials in the 1893 MS, including the elaborate dynamic specifications (and the same is true of the passage between Figs. 59–60: see

n. 94, p. 293). This is of particular interest because it shows that one of the most original sound-conceptions in the symphony, that certainly entailed some of the most sophisticated handling of the orchestra, was already established from the start. It is not even as if the crescendi formed part of the Hamburg revisions of 1893. On the contrary, these pages were left untouched.

In rather the same way we find—again perhaps to our surprise—that the Funeral March in almost every eccentric particular, was already established in the orchestral guise that we know today in the EMS. Indeed, as I have suggested elsewhere (see pp. 197–203), I believe the MS of this movement to represent what was heard at the Budapest first performance in 1889. If one compares the MS of this singular movement—unique in invention and unique in sound—with the published score, there are only a few passages where the later version alters, refines upon, or departs from, the MS. The amazing opening[95] is virtually as Mahler first conceived it, but for the presence in the MS version of a muted solo cello doubling the famous double bass solo (without mute). This duplication was of course dropped by Mahler, the double bass assuming the cello's mute, and the entry of the cellos, tutti and muted, reserved for bar 11. Apart from this minor modification, which only goes to increase the bizarre nature of the sound at this point (Mahler may also have found it difficult to keep the two soloists in tune), there is little in the way of significant variants to claim our attention here or elsewhere in the music. There are a few instrumental re-distributions, to be observed during the E flat minor reprise of the march, though nothing radical, and perhaps expectedly, the *col legno* in bars 135–7 (three bars before Fig. 16) is a later touch (in the MS, the violins are muted). The *col legno* in fact intensifies the atmosphere of a passage that Mahler seems to have thought of as pronouncedly grotesque in character. In the MS, above the staccato woodwind notes, he scribbled 'Wie Unkenrufe!' ['Like toad-calls!']. (Short, high-pitched croaks are the mating calls of male toads.) The inscription was deleted, but our knowing of it perhaps adds to our understanding of the peculiarity of timbre of these bars.

Apart from these slight variants, there is but one further prominent modification, and that is a prudent omission of the strings which, in the MS, presented a continuous texture between Figs. 17 and 18. Reference to the published score will show how Mahler cut short the strings at the return to Tempo 1 (Fig. 17) and picked them up again at Fig. 18, thus permitting the solo oboe (and its rubato) to make its full effect. If the original MS version of this movement were played today, we should be struck by the remarkable fact that one of Mahler's most innovatory sound-worlds did not, as it were, have to be fought for or attained as a result of continuous revision and refinement, but on the contrary was precisely imagined from the outset. But possibly it is not surprising, but is indeed eminently logical, that Mahler should have had from the start an absolutely clear idea of how to achieve his instrumental innovations, which in this case involved a highly personal and innovatory type of music, and was obliged to labour harder at more orthodox textures, which involved a more conventional use of the orchestra.

Convention, for the unconventional Mahler, clearly raised problems, especially when working, as he was in early performances of the symphony, with the resources of what was virtually the standard symphony orchestra. The paradoxical truth seems to be that what everyone would spontaneously imagine to be 'difficult' and the result of long cogitation, Mahler apparently found easy,[96] whereas he had to sweat to get right what one would have thought relatively simple and undemanding, e.g. the opening pages of the Ländler.

*   *   *   *

The last stretch of music I wish to consider is the evocative slow introduction to the first movement, which (in its published version) is undoubtedly an inspired piece of tone-painting ('like a sound of Nature', as Mahler himself inscribed the movement) and yet at the same time presents the basic building materials out of which the symphony is constructed. This was a passage that Mahler worked over continuously and seemingly subjected to continuous revision: I have already set out some of the documentary evidence for this on another page (pp. 203–4). But we may be sure that throughout Mahler's labours on this crucial part of the symphony he had two objects in mind: the precise delineation of atmosphere and the precise analysis by instrumental articulation of the motives and themes which form the unifying basis on which the work is erected.

The introduction, as it finally emerged in the published score, presents a kind of architectural impressionism, an original concept of acoustic space in which there is even an idea of directional sound involved. How rigorously and meticulously organized, for example, are the timbres and dynamics of the fanfares, one of the introduction's principal components. The table below sets out in the simplest way possible the progress towards the ideal sound-world at which Mahler was aiming, and eventually achieved in the published score, the 1893 revision of the MS representing only one of the many preliminary versions that Mahler attempted. In the 1893 score, of course, Mahler was obviously making the best he could of the forces available to him, which meant distributing the fanfares among the horns and trumpets (in independent groups and in combination) and making liberal use of the mute to achieve the kind of hushed atmosphere that was his objective. One sees at once from comparing the scoring of 1893 with the scoring of the 1899 publication the enormous advances Mahler made in the intervening years, advances that not only vastly intensified the colour and atmosphere of the introduction[97] but also defined even more sharply the motivic content of the passage in terms of brilliantly differentiated instrumentation. It is a progress and a process that once again underlines the rationale of Mahler's expansion of his resources, which enables him here to achieve a clarity of motivic texture and a delicacy and precision of effect which was simply not possible with a smaller orchestra. It would be superfluous to go through the introduction bar by bar but one cannot help but remark on Mahler's unconventional assignment of the first fanfare to a clarinet trio, which falls on the ear so unexpectedly (cf. the much more conventional idea of an opening horn fanfare in the 1893 MS), and thereafter his strict alternation of the pure colours of unmixed brass groups, with the horns, however, kept in reserve for their romantic song in bar 32 et seq. and removed from any obligations in the sphere of fanfares whatsoever. Note too the extraordinarily interesting acoustic effect that Mahler introduces along with the trumpet fanfares, with which, clearly, he wanted to create the impression of an acoustic space in which differentiated dynamics and direction of sound played a vital role. Hence the placing of trumpets 1 and 2

	1893 MS		1899 Score	
	Instrumental Group	Dynamics	Instrumental Group	Dynamics
Fanfare I (bar 9)	4 horns (in pairs)	*pp* (muted)	3 clarinets (incl. bass cl.)	*pp*
Fanfare II (bar 22)	2 trumpets, 2 horns (in pairs, the horns playing the role of the 3rd tpt. in the 1899 score)	*pp* (all muted)	3 trumpets (1st and 2nd off-stage and to sound 'in very far distance', 3rd 'in distance')	*ppp*
Horn Song I (bar 32)	1st, 2nd and 4th horns	*p* (muted)	1st, 2nd and 4th horns	*pp*
Fanfare III (bar 36)	1st and 2nd trumpets	[*pp*] (muted)	1st and 2nd trumpets (now 'in far [not 'very far'] distance')	[*ppp*]
Horn Song II (bar 39, continuation of I)	1st and 2nd horns	*p* (muted)	1st and 2nd horns	*pp*
Fanfare IV (bar 44)	1st and 2nd trumpets	[*pp*] (muted)	1st and 2nd trumpets (still in 'far distance'; after this fanfare, the 3 players take their places in the orchestra)	[*ppp*]

off-stage and 'in the very far distance'. Trumpet 3, however, which con-
tributes to the fanfare in bar 23 et seq., is placed nearer the main orchestra,
i.e. 'in the distance', not 'the very far distance', which in fact creates an
acoustic effect *within* the trumpet fanfare,[98] quite apart from the changing
spatial relationship between the group as a whole and the on-stage orchestra.
I think the table makes clear Mahler's plan that a *decreasing* impression of
distance should distinguish Fanfare III from Fanfare II. It is only when
Mahler's elaborate performing directions are scrupulously observed (which,
alas, they rarely are) that the introduction at which he laboured so hard over
such a long period makes its full impact. What we ought always to hear in
performance is a brilliantly articulated instrumental analysis of the work's
motivic components and a magical evocation of the sounds of Nature, in
which the sublest shadings of dynamics and variation of orchestral colour,
and a prophetic manipulation of directional sound, are brought into a highly
sophisticated and elaborately organized relationship. No wonder that it took
Mahler a very long time to get this passage to sound exactly as he wanted it.
Historically, it represents a pioneer exploration of the potentialities of
musical space.

The 'Blumine' Affair

A great deal—perhaps a great deal too much—has already been said and
written about this slender movement. It does not really constitute an 'issue',
and it is not (or ought not to be) controversial. There can be no question that
Mahler, after an initial and extended bout of uncertainty, dropped the movement (after the third performance of the work in its five-movement shape at
Weimar in June 1894) and never made any attempt to reinstate it. As Mr.
Diether correctly points out, Mahler's doubts about the movement are
already manifest in the 1893 MS, which shows that at a stage earlier than
August 1893 (when he revised the movement) Mahler had in fact thought of
omitting it:[99] and as I point out above, the later, copyist's MS again displays
evidence of the same *folie de doute*. I think it quite likely that Mahler was
never very certain about the wisdom of including the movement in the first
place, but it took a further two performances after the work's première to
convince him that he ought to heed his doubts and discard the movement
altogether.

It would seem to be most profitable, to begin with at any rate, not to
pursue one's own doubts about 'Blumine' but to attempt to uncover the
reason for Mahler's doubts, which, I believe, can be done reasonably briefly
and simply. Why was Mahler in such a protracted condition of two-minded-
ness about this particular movement?

I think the simple answer to that question, as I have already suggested
elsewhere (see AM[5], pp. xvii–xix), is that the Andante was an insertion, into

the body of the symphony, of music that had originated elsewhere, as part of the incidental music Mahler composed in 1884 for a dramatic presentation of scenes from Scheffel's *Der Trompeter von Säkkingen*.[100] This would also have been about the time when Mahler was composing the *Gesellen* cycle and when his thoughts may have been turning actively to the composition of the 'Symphonic Poem' that was to become the First Symphony. We know of the link between the Andante and the original *Trompeter* music (now presumed lost) because of the lucky chance that Max Steinitzer, in an article in 1920, quoted from memory—but in D major—the opening bars of the trumpet tune (cf. DM[1], p. 227, AM[5], p. xviii, and JD, p. 87). It was because I had made a point of including Steinitzer's music example in my earlier book on Mahler—at the time it seemed as if these six bars would be all we should ever know of the *Trompeter* music—that I recognized the opening contours of the tune when I was shown for the first time a photocopy of the autograph MS of the symphony. Naturally, I had turned eagerly to the hitherto unknown and long-missing second movement, and was astonished to find embodied there the complete trumpet melody, the *incipit* of which Steinitzer had, in the main, accurately recollected.

It was out of this encounter of mine with a photocopy of the MS that the first performance since 1894 of the Andante was given by the New Philharmonia Orchestra under Benjamin Britten on 18 June 1967, as part of the Aldeburgh Festival of that year, for which occasion I wrote in the programme book as follows:

> It has long been presumed that the Andante was lost or destroyed, and I was greatly surprised a few months ago, on having the opportunity to inspect the manuscript of the symphony's original version (which itself has only come to light quite recently), to find the "missing" movement still there and complete in every detail. One discovery often leads to another, and while the most important thing of all is the recovery of a complete symphonic movement by Mahler which has been lost sight of for something like seventy years or more, it is also my conviction that this Andante throws light on another early and lost work of Mahler's, some incidental music he wrote for the theatre. This was to accompany a series of "living pictures", after Scheffel's once famous poem, *Der Trompeter von Säkkingen*, composed and first performed in 1884. Hence, without doubt, the extensive and inspired melody for trumpet solo with which this beautiful movement begins.

The first modern performance of the Andante as part of the complete symphony, which also inconsistently mixed the 1893 ('original') and 1899 ('revised') orchestrations, was given by the New Haven Symphony Orchestra (Conn., U.S.A.) under Frank Brieff on 19 April 1968. The same performers played the symphony in its 1893 orchestration on 11 March 1969. The

1968 U.S. première was attended by a fair amount of publicity—e.g. programme notes, press notices, and newspaper interviews and articles galore—much of which, alas, was marred by ignorance and errors of fact. Mr. Diether (in JD) has done what he can to clear up the muddled and misleading account of the history of the MS issued by its original owners, though even he, at this stage (in his sleeve note for the Columbia Odyssey gramophone recording of the five-movement version of the symphony) was incautious enough to retail the obvious absurdity that it was the original publishers of the work (Weinberger) who insisted that a reluctant Mahler should discard the Andante (on the grounds of the symphony's undue length). Many nonsenses of many kinds were seriously aired at the time of the U.S. first performance. It would be tedious to try to correct them all, and one must hope that they will die a natural death and not become a future source of yet further misinformation. It is perhaps just worth gently restating the fact here that the retrieval of 'Blumine' dates from my recognition of it in 1966, and from the 1967 performance by Britten, to whose attention I drew the movement. As Mr. Gordon Emerson so revealingly remarked in the *New Haven Register* of 7 April 1968, the original MS had resided at New Haven 'for about nine years, for the most part unnoticed and unheralded until recently'. The Aldeburgh first performance, as it were, broke the long silence.

There can be no final proof (except in the unlikely event of the original *Trompeter* score turning up) that the Andante known as 'Blumine' was, in fact, a movement borrowed in its entirety from the incidental music, but I believe that to be the case. Mr. Diether, for one, thinks otherwise, but I find the musical evidence he adduces in support of his view of the Andante's integral relationship with the bulk of the symphony extremely thin. On the contrary, for me the Andante—just because of its particular charm and modest dimensions—sounds exactly like what indeed it probably was, a movement from the *Trompeter* score, in which case also, the singular instrumentation of the Andante (singular in the context of the symphony, that is: the movement is scored for a much reduced orchestra) makes perfect sense. Mahler would simply have taken over the original instrumentation of the music in its theatrical guise. Moreover it seems to me almost self-evident in terms of style alone that the Andante belongs to a world other than the symphony's. I do not for a moment doubt the authenticity of its voice; for example, I can see what 'Blumine' enthusiasts mean when they hear in the long solo trumpet melody[101] (Ex. 92) an anticipation of the famous, dreamy

Ex. 92

posthorn solo in the Scherzo of the Third Symphony. (I myself find a more interesting taste of things to come in the sinewy bit of two-part writing (Ex. 93) which develops one bar after Fig. 9, characteristically distributed between solo oboe and double-basses!):

Ex. 93

But fingerprints are not in dispute. My case for regarding the Andante as an 'alien' movement, quite properly ejected by Mahler after 1894, rests on what I can only describe as the total (if endearing) innocence of its content and its technique, which speaks volumes *for* its origins as a stretch of incidental music in the theatre, and as convincingly *against* the likelihood of its being a re-worked version, specially re-thought, for the symphony. Indeed, in so far as the latter proposition is concerned, I cannot see that any sort of a case can be made out for it. If Mahler had re-worked an earlier piece for the symphony, then one may be sure that it would show just those signs of an elaborateness of which the Andante is totally devoid. One may be equally sure that Mahler would have chosen some other piece, because the truth seems to me to be that the basic invention of the Andante, which is the big trumpet melody, would not in fact lend itself readily to development or elaboration in any very complex sense. What Mahler does with the tune in the way of variation is very simple and straightforward and was doubtless effective and appropriate in its original 'living picture' context, but one cannot imagine that this would have been the result of an extensively refurbished *Trompeter* movement; and it was surely just because the piece did not 'belong' to the symphony, and had not been—could not be—spontaneously re-formulated in any realistic sense to make it belong to the symphony, that Mahler felt unhappy about it. There was no compromise open to him. The nature of the piece meant that he had either to accept it as it was—which was as the Andante always had been—or drop it.

   In this connection, there is an extremely significant recollection of Bruno Walter's that was published as part of an article in *Der Tag*, Vienna, 17 November 1935: 'Personal Reminiscences of Gustav Mahler'. Walter writes: 'Mahler was tireless in polishing and improving his works, and did not spare himself in his work. Sometimes he destroyed whole piles of manuscript. Once I was present at just such an *auto-da-fé* and rescued what I could. In this way,

Mahler made me a present of an unpublished fifth movement of the First Symphony as a souvenir; it was a wonderful, idyllic piece with a trumpet theme, which he had found *insufficiently symphonic* [my italics].' Precisely.

We know that Mahler dropped the Andante. But why did he pick it up in the first place? First of all, one has to recognize the fact that Mahler, though he came to deplore the *Trompeter* enterprise as a whole, clearly liked this particular movement from it. One can see why he did; it is, in its own modest way, a genuine character piece, strong in atmosphere and certainly redolent of its composer.[102] It is wholly comprehensible why he did not want to chuck it away, and indeed his continuing affection for it is rather amusingly shown in later years by the fact that he drew the attention of his friends to it (and in more than one case made them a gift of the MS or of a MS containing the movement) while simultaneously 'denouncing' the piece, insisting on its destruction or enjoining them never to perform it. Bruno Walter, as we have just seen, was the recipient of a MS together with the appropriate interdiction. Max Steinitzer, a friend of Mahler's in the Leipzig years, fared less well. He records[103] that Mahler took with him to Leipzig in 1886 this one movement from the *Trompeter* score, in which Werner wafts his moonlight serenade across the Rhine to Margareta in her castle (see n. 100, p. 300). But Mahler came to find the piece too sentimental, was vexed by it, and made Steinitzer give his word that he would destroy the piano reduction he had made of it. (It was his valuable recollection of the opening six bars of his piano reduction that he then quotes in these reminiscences.) The decorated title-page of a contemporary edition (1888) of Scheffel's poem—Scheffel died in 1886 and thus could have known about Mahler's *Trompeter* success at Cassel in 1884—clearly takes as its subject matter this central episode in the narrative, which forms the climax of the fourth section of the poem, 'Jung Werner's Rheinfahrt':[104]

Vor dem traumumflorten Blicke
Lag ein neues reiches Leben,
Sonn 'nicht glänzt', nicht Sterne drinnen,
Nur das eine kleine Lichtlein,
Und vom Thurm, darin es brannte,
Kam mit leisem Flügelschlag die
Lieb' zu ihm herabgerauschet
Und sass bei ihm auf der Kiesbank,
Auf dem Acker Fridolini.
Und sie reicht' ihm die Trompete,
Die auch hierher ihn begleitet,
Und sprach: Blase, blase, blase!

Also blies er; und sein Blasen
Zog melodisch durch die Nacht hin.
Lauschend hört's der Rhein im Grunde,
Lauschend Hecht und Lachsforelle,
Lauschend auch die Wasserfrauen,
Und der Nordwind trug die Klänge
Sorgsam auf zum Herrenschloss.

[Before his dream-veiled gaze / lay a new rich life, / in it the sun did not shine, nor stars, / only the one small gleam, / and from the tower wherein it burnt / there came with a light beating of wings / love rustling down to him / and it sat by him on the gravelly bank / on Fridolini's field. / And it gave him the trumpet / which had also accompanied him hither / and it spake: Blow, blow, blow!

Thus he blew; and his blowing / went on melodiously through the night. / Hearkening, the deeps of the Rhine heard it, / Hearkening pike and salmon-trout, / Hearkening too the women of the water, / And the North Wind bore the sounds / Carefully up to the master's castle.]

In 1900–1, Mahler remarked to Bauer-Lechner (NBL, p. 149) that the discarded movement represented the 'love episode' in his First Symphony, that it was 'fulsomely sentimental' ['sentimentalschwärmerisch'] in character, reflecting the 'youthful asininity' of his Hero. Mahler was, we know, substantially the Hero of his own music, and there is little doubt that the *Gesellen* cycle—the narrative of which is continued and expanded in the First Symphony—was intimately associated with his passion for Johanna Richter, the singer, who was a member of the Cassel company[105] when Mahler was conductor there. It may well be that there was some personal association involved with the *Trompeter* movement which lent the piece an autobiographical significance for Mahler in the particular context of the First Symphony's inner drama. It also seems probable, however, that for a period at least the symphony offered a home to a piece for which he had a soft spot and, perhaps more interestingly, which he may have felt to provide a not invaluable extension of his programme, i.e. to supply what on the whole is absent elsewhere in the symphony, a note of pure, unalloyed romantic lyricism, neither tinged by irony nor contradicted by ensuing agitation. After all, the slow movement of the work (the Funeral March) is intendedly *anti-romantic*, and though the big lyrical melody in the Finale is romantic enough, it is a romanticism on which disillusioning experience has undeniably left an impression. Thus on this reckoning, the innocent, uncomplicated lyricism of the C major Andante, with the Hero portrayed in an arch-romantic posture, brought a touch of romance to Mahler's Symphonic Poem that was otherwise absent. We must remember that the Symphonic Poem concept was itself a somewhat loose one and therefore the interpolation of a movement—the addition of an episode in Mahler's life of an artist—would not have presented a major problem; and, moreover, there was a movement already in existence and one to which Mahler himself, without any doubt at all, had a sentimental attachment. I believe it was some such combination of reasons that

The title-page of a popular edition of Scheffel's *Der Trompeter von Säkkingen* (1888)

was responsible for the presence of the 'Blumine' Andante in the original version of the symphony. The reasons, I suggest, that made it possible for Mahler to incorporate the movement were those that ultimately (and rightly) led him to discard it. When the moment of truth arrived—'insufficiently symphonic' as he seems to have remarked to Bruno Walter (see p. 221)—then the fate of the Andante (which had, as it were, been promoted to a role above its station) was sealed. One is glad of course that the music, for all the vicissitudes to which it was subjected, survived. It gives us a real glimpse of what the *Trompeter* score was like and enables us to know what was, substantially, the five-movement version of the original Symphonic Poem of 1889.[106]

A clear historical gain has been made here. I can see no harm in an occasional performance of the symphony with the Andante installed as its second movement, simply on the grounds of historical interest: this, more or less, was the shape in which this familiar piece was launched at Budapest in 1889. There can be no grounds at all for attempting a *restoration* of the movement, which would be a demonstrably anti-musical act and fly in the face of everything we know of Mahler's wishes in this matter. Mahler enthusiasts pursuing this course only show that they rate their own opinions higher than the composer's, an evaluation the rest of the world is unlikely to follow. As for those who laboriously reconstruct a set of performing materials from the 1893 MS and then solemnly play an orchestration much of which Mahler spent years revising and refining—this seems to me to be musicology (if that's what it is) run mad. It is as if, in the study of lepidoptera, the chrysalis should be preferred to the butterfly. (In HG[1], p. 753, M. de La Grange quotes from the unpublished part of Bauer-Lechner's recollections a remark of Mahler's (made in 1900) that ostensibly gives a musical reason for the omission of the 'Blumine' movement from the symphony: 'It was mainly because of an excessive similarity of key that I eliminated the "Blumine" Andante from my First'. I cannot follow Mahler here, since the Andante in fact introduces a strongly contrasting stretch of tonality—C major—between the D major first movement and the A major Scherzo. The only explanation I can offer, which may throw light on Mahler's otherwise very odd remark, is that he may momentarily have thought himself back to the very first score of Werner's trumpet serenade which may, if Steinitzer's transcription was correct (see p. 218), have been in D major: in which case there would have been the lack of key contrast of which Mahler spoke. But I cannot think this speculation is a very convincing one. There is a puzzle here still be to solved.)

(A score of the Andante was published in 1967, under the title of 'Symphonic Movement/*Blumine*', by Theodore Presser, Pennsylvania. No editor's name appears, and it is a far from accurate text.)

The Literary and Pictorial Sources

There are a number of literary sources associated with Mahler's First Symphony. The most frequently quoted is a novel by Jean Paul (1763–1825), entitled *Titan* (1800–3). Jean Paul was undoubtedly a writer that Mahler much admired, but did he in fact take the overall title of his symphony from Jean Paul's novel? Bauer-Lechner writes for instance: '[People] connected [Mahler's] "Titan" with Jean Paul's. But all he had in mind was a powerfully heroic individual, his life and suffering, struggles and defeat at the hands of fate.' (NBL, p. 148).

Bauer-Lechner was certainly close to Mahler, and this is an area where one would expect to be able to rely on her accuracy. Her brief mention of the matter is more fully dealt with in a little-known article by Robert Holtzmann, which was drawn to my attention by Dr. Edward R. Reilly ('GMs Erste Symphonie', in *Der Kunstwart*, Munich, March 1918, pp. 113–17). Holtzmann writes as follows, relying one notices on the reminiscences of Bauer-Lechner, although these had not been published[107] at the time Holtzmann wrote his article (whose own footnotes I retain). He begins by asking: What does the title 'Titan' mean?

It is usually accepted that it indicates a connection, even if only a loose one, with Jean Paul's novel *Titan*. And indeed Mahler, at least later, had some inner affinity with the writings of Jean Paul. However, the title of the First Symphony ought not to be seen as referring to any connection whatsoever with Jean Paul. There is already a good reason for this in the fact that it is actually impossible to establish any such connection. I know of only one attempt to bring to light at least a small connection with Jean Paul in the symphony. From a Viennese note of 1901, which Ludwig Schiedermair was kind enough to pass on to me, I conclude that within the younger Mahler's circle of friends, the third movement of the First Symphony conjured up, or was thought to be supposed to conjure up, the image of Roquairol [a fantastic, extravagant character who appears in Jean Paul's novel]. A paragon of the art of strained interpretation! Mahler's own pronouncements lead to quite different conclusions. The explanatory remarks he provided for the Symphony in addition to the title contain not the slightest reference to Jean Paul's *Titan*. But Mahler also clearly explained that his 'Titan' Symphony had nothing to do with Jean Paul's novel.* The Titan Mahler's title referred to is much rather simply a titanic hero who appears on the scene as a glorious child of nature, is assailed by a hostile destiny, and must endure a fearful struggle with it in which all the strength in his soul is stirred up. In the last analysis this hero is the artist himself telling us of the joys and troubles of

---

* I am obliged for this statement (as also for other data which I have been able to use here) to the reminiscences of Frau Natalie Bauer-Lechner of Vienna, and in particular to a detailed letter of 1900 from her to L. Karpath.

his youth. Hence Mahler's words*: "On the whole, no one has yet understood the First Symphony except those who have shared my life." The struggle which the Titan had to fight through, however, was the struggle of a new culture of artistically abundant life against the short-sighted multitude with all its banalities, the struggle against the utterly impregnable philistinism of the commonplace. Here the title takes on its true meaning.

* To Ludwig Schiedermair, for the latter's commentary on Mahler's First Symphony (in Schlesinger's Musikführer No. 222, p. 18).

Holtzmann's explanation of the 'Titan' title is clearly modelled on Bauer-Lechner's; and perhaps this is the moment to recall that Ferdinand Pfohl, when giving his account of how the symphony acquired its title (see n. 45, p. 263), also made no mention of Jean Paul's novel. On the other hand, we know from Mr. Diether's investigations into the origins of the title of the discarded 'Blumine' movement (see pp. 217f. and JD, pp. 84–5) that there can be little doubt that Jean Paul *was* an influence on the constellation of titles that originally adorned the work. It is, after all, not just the case of the enigmatic 'Blumine' inscription (on which Mr. Diether has thrown some light); there is also the general sub-title for Part I of the symphony which, as we know, at one stage read: 'Aus den Tagen der Jugend, Blumen-, Frucht- und Dornstücke'. This singular construct surely reflects *another* title of Jean Paul's, i.e. his *Blumen-, Frucht- und Dornenstücke [oder Ehestand, Tod und Hochzeit des Armenadvokaten F. St. Siebenkäs]* (1796–7). If the subsidiary titles establish a pretty clear link with the world—and titles—of Jean Paul, then it seems more than likely to me that 'Titan' too, the overall title, must owe at least something of its origins to the same source. It would be positively outlandish if such were not the case. Would Mahler himself, who must have been aware of the trains of association involved in his scheme of titles, deliberately have perpetrated such an arbitrary and indeed somewhat meaningless confusion?[108] (M. de La Grange writes sensibly of this matter in HG[1], pp. 749–50.) Furthermore, although I generally rate Bauer-Lechner's testimony high, we should bear in mind in this context that the supposed link between the novel and the symphony's title was affirmed by many of those who were close to Mahler or close to his circle: one thinks, for example, of Stefan, Specht, Foerster, Bruno Walter and Alma Mahler.[109] It is difficult to imagine that the question of the work's early title and its relationship to Jean Paul's novel was not aired from time to time, in which case one would have expected, if the received view were indeed so emphatically the wrong one, i.e. that Mahler's 'Titan' was not in any sense related to Jean Paul's, a correction (or at least a corrective) to have emerged at a somewhat earlier date than Holtzmann's elaboration of Bauer-Lechner's brief recollection.

The truth, I believe, as in so many matters concerning Mahler, probably rests somewhere in the middle. It would not surprise me at all to learn that he maintained in later years what was his habitual ambiguity towards his texts and programmes and was characteristically reluctant to admit to any connection between his youthful masterpiece and Jean Paul's novel. Looked at from one point of view, of course, any denial he might have made would have been perfectly correct: it would certainly be absurd to look for any precise narrative correspondence between Mahler's music and Jean Paul's text.[110] But this is to seek a crude and literal relationship that could never have been part of Mahler's way of thinking. A much more worthwhile approach, which I think may well provide the correct answer, is to view the use of the 'Titan' title as an attempt to divulge a clue to the singular kind of world which the symphony inhabits; and I believe that if we look at the novel from this angle, we can find in its style and curious philosophy, in Jean Paul's handling of his materials, and in the nature of his imagery, a remarkably interesting and illuminating relationship between the world of the novel and the world of the symphony. This is a far cry from asserting that the music 'tells the story' of the novel (which Mahler would have been right to defend himself against), and indeed in no way excludes interpretations of the title such as Holtzmann's, e.g. Mahler's Titan is 'simply a titanic hero who appears on the scene as a glorious child of nature', etc., etc., or Bauer-Lechner's (and also Mahler's?) submission of a 'heroic individual, his life and suffering', etc. I do not doubt that in the symphony we do encounter a protagonist, and that the protagonist was in a very real sense Mahler himself. But the world in which the titanic hero plays out his role, the kind of experiences he undergoes, and the unique savour of those experiences, and the imagery which embodies them—these seem to me to owe a lot to the world of Jean Paul as revealed in his *Titan* novel; and it is at this level that the common title takes on real significance.

W. A. Coupe writes neatly of Jean Paul:[111]

> His prolific writings (6o volumes) are characterized by a highly developed sense of humour and an extreme formlessness—the plot is often slight and tends to be overlaid by a mass of digressions and interpolations. The mood of his works alternates between scepticism and emotionalism, between the "Turkish bath of sentimentality and the cold shower of satire"; similarly his style varies between over-ornamentation worthy of the Baroque and passages of great lyrical beauty. His great novels . . . all deal with the same central problem: the achievement of a harmonious personality, the dangers of one-sidedness and the conflict of the ideal and the real.

Even in that short assessment, one sees sketched out there certain contrasts and oppositions that call vividly to mind the temperament of Mahler and his characteristic mode of utterance in his music: the alternation of 'scepticism and emotionalism', 'the conflict of the ideal and the real', the implied contrast between complexity ('over-ornamentation') and direct lyricism ('passages of great lyrical beauty'), the juxtaposition of sentiment and satire—these are all conspicuous and familiar features of Mahler's art, and perhaps most flamboyantly expressed in his *Wunderhorn* period.

I think the existence of a relationship in style and spirit with Jean Paul has often been mentioned in Mahler studies, but rarely investigated; and thus it seems worth while to me to present to the reader some excerpts from the novel, *Titan*, so that he may judge for himself the significance (or otherwise) of the relationship. Jean Paul was a voluminous writer, hence even the offering of excerpts results in a bulky interpolation. But I think readers who are prepared to absorb themselves in Jean Paul's prose and at the same time hold in mind the untrammelled outpouring of music that was Mahler's Symphonic Poem of 1889 will find much of interest. I use the translation of Charles T. Brooks, published in London in 1863, and in each case follow up the translation with the original German.[112]

First, an example of Jean Paul's swooning, ecstatic nature lyricism (Albano's night-walk out to Lilar, from Chapter 23 of *Titan*):

He [Albano] fixed his eyes steadily on the western mountains, where the stars seemed to fall to *her* like white blossoms. Up on the distant height, the Hercules' cross-way, the right arm ran downward and wound along through groves and meadows to the blooming Lilar.

March on, drunk with joy, full of young, light images, through the Italian night, which glimmers and breathes its fragrance around thee, and which, as over Hespenotria, far from the warm moon, hangs out a golden evening star in the blue west, as if over the dwelling of the beloved soul! To thee and thy young eyes the stars as yet only shed down hopes, no remembrances; thou hast in thy hand a plucked, stiff apple-twig, full of *red* buds, which, like unhappy beings, become too *pale* when they bloom out; but thou makest not, as yet, any such applications thereof as we do.

Now he stood glowing and trembling in a dell before Lilar, which, however, a singular round wood, of walks lined with trees, still hid from his view. The wood grew up in the middle to a blooming mount, which was embosomed and encircled so curiously with broad sunflowers, festoons of cherries, and glancing silver-poplars and rose-trees, that it seemed, by the picturesque *ignes-fatui* of the moon, to be a single, enormous kettle-tree, full of fruits and blossoms. Albano was fain to ascend its summit, and be, as it were, on the observatory of the heaven or Lilar, spread out below; he found at last in the wood an open alley.

The foliage, with its spiral alleys, wound him round into a deeper and deeper night, through which not the moon, but only the heat lightnings, could break, with which the warm, cloudless heavens were overcharged. The magic circles of the mount rose ever smaller and smaller out of the leaves into the blossoms—two naked children, among myrtles, had twined their arms caressingly about each other's bent head—they were statues of Cupid and Psyche—rosy night-butterflies were licking, with their short tongues, the honeydew from the leaves, and the glow-worms, like sparks struck off from the glow of evening, went trailing like gold threads around the rose-bushes; he climbed amid summits and roots behind the aromatic balustrade toward heaven; but the little spiral alley running round with him hung before the stars purple night-violets, and hid the deep gardens with orange summits; at length he sprang from the highest round of his Jacob's ladder, with all his sense, out into an un-covered, living heaven; a light hilltop, only fringed with variegated flower-cups, received and cradled him under the stars, and a white altar gleamed brightly beside him in the moonlight.

But gaze down, fiery man, with thy fresh heart, full of youth, on the magnificent, immeasurable, enchanted Lilar! A second twilight-world, such as tender tones picture to us, an open morning-dream spreads out before thee, with high triumphal arches, with whispering labyrinthine walks, with islands of the blest; the pure snow of the sunken moon lingers now only on the gorges and triumphal gates, and on the silverdust of the fountain-water, and the night, flowing off from all waters and vales, swims over the Elysian fields of the heavenly realm of shadows, in which, to earthly memory, the unknown forms appear like Otaheite-shores, pastoral countries, Daphnian groves, and poplar-islands of our present world—wondrous lights glide through the dark foliage, and all is one lovely, magic confusion. What mean those high, open doors or arches, and the pierced groves and the ruddy splendour behind them, and a white child sleeping among orange-lilies and gold-flowers, from whose cups delicate flames trickle, as if angels had flown too near over them? The lightnings reveal swans, sleeping on the waves under clouds drunk with light, and their flaming trains blaze like gold after them in among the thick trees, as goldfishes turn their burning backs out of the water,—and even around thy summit, Albano, the great eyes of the sunflowers turn on thee their fiery looks, as if kindled by the sparks of the glow-worms.

. . . Er drückte das Auge an die westlichen Berge fest, wo die Sterne *Ihr* wie weiße Blüten zuzufallen schienen. Oben auf der weiten Höhe, dem Herkules-Scheidewege, lief der rechte Arm hinunter und wand sich dem blühenden Lilar durch Haine und Auren zu.

Schreite nur freudentrunken voll junger lichter Bilder durch die italienische Nacht, die um dich schimmert und duftet und die wie über Hesperien nicht weit vom warmen Monde einen vergoldeten Abendstern im blauen Westen aufhängt, gleichsam über der Wohnung der geliebten Seele. Dir und deinen jungen Augen werfen die Sterne nur Hoffnungen, noch keine Erinnerungen herunter, du hast einen abgebrochenen starren Apfelzweig voll *roter* Blütenknospen in der Hand, die wie Unglückliche zu *blassen* werden, wenn sie aufblühen, aber du machst noch nicht solche Anwendungen davon wie wir.

Jetzt stand er in einer Talrinne vor Lilar glühend und bange, das aber ein sonderbarer runder Wald aus Laubengängen noch versteckte. Der Wald wuchs in der Mitte zu einem blühenden Berge auf, den breite Sonnenblumen, Fruchtschnüre von Kirschen und blinkende Silberpappeln und Rosenbäume in so künstlicher Verschränkung einhüllten und umliefen, daß er vor den malerischen Irrlichtern des Mondes ein einziger ungeheurer Kesselbaum voll Früchte und Blüten zu sein schien. Albano wollte seinen Wipfel besteigen, gleichsam die Sternwarte des unten ausgebreiteten Himmels oder Lilars; er fand endlich am Walde einen offnen Laubengang.

Die Lauben drehten ihn in Schraubengängen in eine immer tiefere Nacht hinein, durch welche nicht der Mond, sondern nur die stummen Blitze brechen konnten, von denen der warme Himmel ohne Wolken überschwoll. Der Berg hob die Zauberkreise immer kleiner aus den Blättern in die Blüten hinauf — zwei nackte Kinder hatten unter Myrten die Arme liebkosend einander um die zugeneigten Köpfe gelegt, es waren die Statuen von Amor und Psyche — Rosennachtfalter leckten mit kurzen Zungen den Honigtau von den Blättern ab, und die Johanniswürmchen, gleichsam abgesprungene Funken der Abendglut, wehten wie Goldfaden um die Rosenbüsche — er stieg zwischen Gipfeln und Wurzeln hinter dem aromatischen Treppengeländer gen Himmel, aber die kleine, mit ihm herumlaufende Spiralallee verhing die Sterne mit purpurnen Nachtviolen und die tiefen Gärten mit Orangegipfeln — endlich sprang er von der obersten Sprosse seiner Jakobsleiter mit allen Sinnen in einen unbedeckten lebendigen Himmel hinaus; ein lichter Berggipfel, nur von Blumenkelchen bunt-gesäumt, empfing ihn und wiegte ihn unter den Sternen, und ein weißer Altar leuchtete hell neben ihm im Mondenlichte.——

Aber schaue hinunter, feuriger Mensch mit deinem frischen Herzen voll Jugend, auf das herrliche unermeßliche Zauber-Lilar! Eine dämmernde zweite Welt, wie leise Töne sie uns malen, ein offner Morgentraum dehnt sich vor dir mit hohen Triumphtoren, mit lispelnden Irrgängem, mit glückseligen Inseln aus — der helle Schnee des gesunknen Mondes liegt nur noch auf den Hainen und Triumphbogen und auf dem Silberstaube der Springwasser, und die aus allen Wassern und Tälern quellende Nacht schwimmt über die elysischen Felder des himmlischen Schattenreichs, in welchem dem irdischen Gedächtnisse die unbekannten Gestalten wie hiesige Otaheiti-Ufer, Hirtenländer, daphnische Haine und Pappelinseln erscheinen—seltsame Lichter schweifen durch das dunkle Laub, und alles ist zauberisch-verworren — was bedeuten jene hohen offnen Tore oder Bogen und die durchbrochnen Haine und der rötliche Glanz hinter ihnen und ein weißes Kind, unter Orangelilien und Goldblumen schlafend, aus deren Kelchen weiche Flammen perlen, gleichsam als wären Engel zu nahe über sie hingeflogen — die Blitze erleuchten Schwanen, die unter lichttrunkenen Nebeln auf den Wellen schlafen, und ihre Flammen lodern golden nach in den tiefen Bäumen, wie Goldfische den brennenden Rücken aus dem Wasser drehen — und selber und deine Bergspitze, Albano, schauen dich die großen Augen der Sonnenblumen feurig an, gleichsam von den Funken der Johanniswürmchen entzündet.—

Next, an example of Jean Paul introducing into his text, as he often does, in the sharpest and most deliberately grotesque contrast with the kind of exalted, lyrical evocation quoted above, vivid images which draw on the rites and ceremonies of death, and where one notices that he insists on the mixture of tragedy and comedy, that characteristic Mahlerian amalgam. The excerpt that follows comes from Chapter 47, where Albano sees Roquairol:

In Albano another spirit spoke than in Schoppe, but the two soon met. To the Count the night-like forms of crape, the still funeral banners, the dead-march, the creeping sick-man's-walk, and the tolling of the bells, opened wide all earth's charnel-houses, especially as before his blooming eyes these death plays came for the first time: but one thing more loudly than all—one will hardly guess what—proclaimed before him the partings of life,—namely, the beat of the drum stifled by the funeral cloth; a muffled drum was to him a broken reverberation of all earthly catacombs. He heard the dumb, strangled complainings of our hearts—he saw higher beings looking down from above on the lamentable three hours' comedy of our life, wherein the ruddy child of the first act fades in the fifth to the old man in jubilee, and then, grown up and bowed down, vanishes behind the falling curtain.

As, in spring, we think more of death, autumn and winter than in summer, so also does the most fiery and energetic youth paint out to himself in *his* season of life's year, the dark leafless one oftener and more vividly than the man in that stage which is nearest to it; for in both springs the wings of the ideal unfold widely and find room only in a future. But before the youth, Death comes in blooming, Greek form; before the tired, older man, in Gothic.

Schoppe generally began with *comic* humour, and ended with *tragic*; so also now did the empty mourning-chest, the crape of the horses, their emblazoned caparisons, the Prince's contempt of the heavy German Ceremonial; in short, the whole heartless mummery, lead him up to an eminence, to which the contemplation of a multitude of men at once always impelled him, and where, with an exaltation, indignation, and laughing bitterness hard to describe, he looked down upon the eternal, tyrannical, belittling, objectless and joyless, bewildered and oppressed frenzy of mankind, and his own too.

Suddenly a gay, shining knight broke the dark chain: it was Roquairol, on the parading gala-horse, who agitated our two men, and none besides. A pale, broken-down face, glazed over with long inward fire, stripped of

all youthful roses, lightening out of the diamond-pits of the eyes under
the dark, overhanging eyebrows, rode along in a tragic merriment. . . .

In Albano sprach ein andrer Geist als in Schoppe, aber beide begegneten
sich bald. Dem Grafen machten die Nachtgestalten aus Flor, die stillen
Trauerfahnen, der Totenmarsch, der schleichende Krankengang, das
Glockengetöse die Totenhäuser der Erde weit auf, zumal da vor seine
blühenden Augen zum ersten Male diese Totenspiele kamen; aber lauter
als alles rief vor ihm etwas — das man kaum erraten wird — die Schei-
dungen des Lebens aus, der vom Leichentuche erstickte Trommelschlag;
eine gedämpfte Trommel war ihm ein von allen irdischen Katakomben
gebrochener Widerhall. Er hörte die stummen erwürgten Klagen unsrer
Herzens; er sah höhere Wesen oben herunterschauen auf das dreistündige
weinerliche Lustspiel unsers Lebens, worin das rote Kind des ersten Akts
im fünften zum Jubelgreis ermattet und dann erwachsen und gebückt vor
dem herablaufenden Vorhange verschwindet.

Wie wir im Frühlinge mehr an Tod, Herbst und Winter denken als im
Sommer, so malt sich auch der feurigste kräftigste Jüngling öfter und
heller in seiner Jahreszeit die dunkle entblätterte vor als der Mann in seiner
nähern; denn in beiden Frühlingen schlagen sich die Flügel des Ideals
weit auf und haben nur in einer Zukunft Raum. Aber vor den Jüngling
tritt der Tod in blühender griechischer Gestalt, vor den müden ältern
Menschen in gotischer.

Mit *komischem* Humor fing Schoppe gewöhnlich an und endigte mit
tragischem; so führte auch jetzt der leere Trauerkasten, die Flöre der
Pferde, die Wappen-Schabaracken derselben, des Fürsten Verachtung
des schwerfälligen deutschen Zeremoniells und die ganze herzlose Mum-
merei, alles das führte ihn auf eine Anhöhe, wohin ihn immer das An-
schauen *vieler* Menschen auf einmal trieb und wo er mit einer schwer zu
malenden Erhebung, Ergimmung und lachenden Kümmernis ansah den
ewigen, zwingenden, kleinlichen, von Zwecken und Freuden verirrten,
betäubten schweren Wahnsinn des Menschengeschlechts;—und seinen
dazu.

Plötzlich durchbrach die schwarze Kette ein bunter glänzender Ritter,
Roquairol auf dem paradierenden Freudenpferde, und erschütterte unsre
zwei Menschen, und keinen weiter. Ein blasses eingestürztes Angesicht, vom
langen innern Feuer verglaset, von allen Jugendrosen entblößet, aus den
Demantgruben der Augen unter dem schwarzen Augenbraunen-Überhange
blitzend, ritt in einer tragischen Lustigkeit daher . . .

Now two further examples of Jean Paul's lyricism. I quote the first because I think, without pressing the parallel too far, that one immediately becomes aware in the excerpt of that pronounced conflict between man's
transitoriness and the enduring, blossoming earth that was so substantial a
presence in Mahler's art throughout his life. Most interesting of all, one
realizes that the Chinese texts of *Das Lied* reflect those very same preoccupa-

tions that Mahler had met with so much earlier in Jean Paul, and stayed with all his life. For Mahler, Bethge's versions of the Chinese originals (not to speak of the composer's own additions to the texts) merely refracted the old ideas at a fresh angle. But the character of the lyricism, and the anguished nature of the response to life, are identical. *Das Lied*, indeed, offers us a fascinating synthesis of Li-Tai-Po and (unexpectedly) Jean Paul. My excerpt comes from Albano's letter to Roquairol, again from Chapter 47:

> ... 'Stranger: if thou hast had no friend, hast thou deserved one? When spring kindled into life, and opened all her honey-cups, and her serene heaven, and all the hundred gates of her Paradise, hast thou, like me, bitterly looked up and begged of God a heart for thine? O when, at evening, the sun went down like a mountain, and his flames departed from the earth, and now only his red breath floated upward to the silvery stars, hast thou beheld the brotherly shadows of friendship which sank together on battle-fields, like stars of one constellation, stealing forth through the bloody clouds out of the old world, like giants; and didst thou think of *this*—how imperishably they loved each other, and thou, like me, wast alone? And, solitary one, when night—that season at which the spirit of man, as in torrid climes, *toils* and *travels*—reveals her cold suns above thee in a sparkling chain, and when, still, among all the distant forms of the ether there is no dear loved one, and immensity painfully draws thee up, and thou feelest, upon the cold earth, that thy heart beats against no breast but only thine—O beloved! weepest thou then, and most bitterly?
>
> 'Charles, often have I reckoned up, on my birthday, the increasing years—the feathers in the broad wing of time—and thought upon the sounding flight of youth: then I stretched my hand far out after a friend, who should stick by me in the Charon's skiff wherein we are born, when the seasons of life's year glide by along the shore before me, with their flowers and leaves and fruits, and when, on the long stream, the human race shoots downward in its thousand cradles and coffins.
>
> 'Ah, it is not the gay, variegated shore that flies by, but man and his stream: forever bloom the seasons in the gardens up and down along the shore; only *we* sweep by once for all before the garden, and never return.'

Fremder, wenn du keinen Freund hättest, hast du einen verdient?— Wenn der Frühling glühte und alle seine Honigkelche öffnete und seinen reinen Himmel und alle hundert Tore an seinem Paradiese: hast du da schmerzlich aufgeblickt wie ich und Gott um ein Herz gebeten für deines? —O wenn abends die Sonne einsank wie ein Berg und ihre Flammen aus der Erde fuhren und nur noch ihr roter Rauch hinanzog an den silbernen Sternen: sahest du aus der Vorwelt die verbrüderten Schatten der Freundschaft, die auf Schlachtfeldern wie Gestirne *eines* Sternbildes miteinander untergingen, durch die blutigen Wolken als Riesen ziehen, und dachtest du daran, wie sie sich unvergänglich liebten, und du warst allein wie ich? — Und, Einsamer, wenn die Nacht, wo der Geist des

Menschen, wie in heißen Ländern, *arbeitet* und *reiset*, ihre kalten Sonnen
verkettet und aufdeckt und wenn doch unter allen weiten Bildern des
Äthers kein geliebtes teures ist und die Unermeßlichkeit dich schmerzlich
aufzieht und du auf dem kalten Erdboden fühlest, daß dein Herz an keine
Brust anschlägt als nur an deine: o Geliebter, weinest du dann und recht
innig? —
— Karl, oft zählt' ich am Geburtstage die wachsenden Jahre ab, die
Federn im breiten Flügel der Zeit; und bedachte das Verrauschen der
Jugend; da streckt' ich weit die Hand nach einem Freunde aus, der bei
mir im Charons-Nachen, worin wir geboren werden, stehen bliebe, wenn
vor mir die Jahreszeiten des Lebens am Ufer vorüberlaufen mit Blumen
und Blättern und Früchten und wenn auf dem langen Strome das Men-
schengeschlecht in tausend Wiegen und Särgen hinunterschießet.

Ach nicht das bunte Ufer fliehet vorüber, sondern der Mensch und
sein Strom; ewig blühen die Jahreszeiten in den Gärten des Gestades
hinauf und hinab, aber nur wir rauschen einmal vor den Gärten vorbei
und kehren nicht um.

My second and final excerpt is Liana's poem of thanks, from Chapter 43,
the touching, expostulatory lyricism of which is again so close in manner,
one feels, to the form of lyrical address that Mahler often adopts in his music:

Do I then gaze again with blessed eyes into thy blooming world, thou
All-loving One, and weep again, because I am happy? Why did I then
fear? When I went under the earth in the darkness like the dead, and
caught only a distant sound of the loved ones and of spring above me, why
was my feeble heart in fear that there was no more hope for life and light?
For thou wast by me in the darkness, and didst lead me up out of the vault
into thy spring; and around me stood thy joyous children, and the serene
heavens, and all my smiling loved ones! O, I will now hope more stead-
fastly! Continue thou to break off from the sick plant all rank flowers, that
the rest may more fully ripen! Thou dost indeed lead thy human creatures
into thy heaven and to thyself over a long mountain; and they go through
the storms of life along the mountain, only overshadowed, not smitten,
by the clouds, and only our eye grows wet. But when I come to thee, when
Death again throws his dark cloud over me, and draws me away from
all that I love into the deeper cavern, and thou, All-gracious, settest me
free once more, and bearest me into thy spring,—into a still fairer one
than this, which is itself so magnificent,—will then my frail heart, near
thy judgment-seat, beat as gladly as to-day, and will the mortal bosom
dare to breathe in thy ethereal spring? O, make me pure in this earthly
one, and let me live here, as if I were already walking in thy heaven!

So schau' ich wieder mit seligen Augen in deine blühende Welt, du
Alliebender, und weine wieder, weil ich glücklich bin? Warum hab' ich denn
gezagt? Da ich unter der Erde ging in der Finsternis wie eine Tote und

nur von fern die Geliebten und den Frühling über mir vernahm: warum
war das schwache Herz in Furcht, es gebe keine Öffnung mehr zum Leben
und zum Lichte? — Denn du warst in der Finsternis bei mir und führtest
mich aus der Gruft in deinen Frühling herauf; und um mich standen deine
frohen Kinder und der helle Himmel und alle meine lächelnden Geliebten! —— O ich will nun fester hoffen; brich immer der siechen Pflanze
üppige Blumen ab, damit die andern voller reifen! Du führest ja deine
Menschen auf einem langen Berge in deinen Himmel und zu dir, und sie
gehen durch die Gewitter des Lebens am Berge nur verschattet, nicht
getroffen hindurch, und nur unser Auge wird naß. —— Aber, wenn ich zu
dir komme, wenn der Tod wieder seine dunkle Wolke auf mich wirft und
mich weg von allen Geliebten in die tiefere Höhle zieht und du mich,
Allgütiger, noch einmal freimachst und in deinen Frühling trägst, in den
noch schönern als diesen herrlichen: wird dann mein schwaches Herz
neben deinem Richterstuhle so freudig schlagen wie heute, und wird die
Menschenbrust in deinem ätherischen Frühlinge atmen dürfen? O mache
mich rein in diesem irdischen und lasse mich hier leben, als wenn ich
schon in deinem Himmel ginge!

*   *   *   *

Jean Paul, however, is not the only literary reference that one has to explore
in connection with the First Symphony. There is also the inscription that
belongs to the third movement, the Funeral March. Here (as my table shows,
see pp. 158–9), there exists a number of variants, but the hard core of the
programmatic information disseminated by Mahler resides in (1) the inscription 'in the manner of Callot' and (2) the title, 'The Hunter's Funeral Procession'. The reference to Callot was again perhaps less clear and clarifying
than Mahler imagined. As Foerster points out (GMB[2], p. 129): 'If the hearer
does not know the caricatures of Callot, if he does not know the lusty old-
world humour with which he speaks, he will not see what Mahler is driving
at in his music, either when the idea is—if one may so express it—positive, or
when, if you wish, negative; when he feels and speaks as Faust and when he
allows Mephisto to utter platitudes with a schoolmaster's leer'. Foerster, in
continuing, then makes the highly intelligent observation that what was novel
at the time was Mahler's extension of the principle of irony (or parody) to a
movement *in its entirety*. Berlioz, as Foerster mentions, had of course introduced parodistic elements into the *Symphonie Fantastique*, but these were
ironic episodes, not the totality of the music. One sees very clearly what
Foerster had in mind. Listeners can easily react to irony within a context
which is itself not ironic. But if the total conception is ironic, from first note
to last, then the listener can be at sea (and evidently was, in Mahler's day),
unless a hint of the overall ironization is vouchsafed (and even then, as

Mahler soon discovered, there was no guarantee that the hint would be taken). All this was doubtless responsible for his planting a programmatic clue here or there, in an attempt to clarify his intention.

But it was surely not on a possible familiarity with the work of the famous French etcher Jacques Callot (1592/3–1635) that Mahler was programmatically relying;[113] he must have been hoping, rather, to strike up a response in an audience that might be presumed to have some familiarity with a literary source, the *Phantasiestücke in Callots Manier* by E. T. A. Hoffman (1776–1822), like Jean Paul, another writer much admired by Mahler. An admirable front-page article in the *Times Literary Supplement*, 21 May 1970 ('Hoffmann: Where the fantastic meets the everyday'), describes the achievements of Hoffmann succinctly: 'His vivid evocation of vanished historical periods; his original blend of art-criticism and storytelling; his startling transitions from immersion in horror to ironic contemplation; his mingling of the tragic and the ridiculous, the grotesque and the sublime, the fantastic and the real—all these make up a genuine and recognizable style which should assure him of a permanent place in the European pantheon. No one has depicted more successfully than he that narrow border where the fantastic meets the everyday. . . . The central theme of Hoffmann's work is the inevitable conflict between the demands of the spirit and the exigencies of day-to-day living.' And so on. Once again, as we have seen in the case of Jean Paul, there was a remarkable identity of temperament and imagination between Mahler and Hoffmann. This is surely another literary association that would reward detailed investigation?

The pictorial source of the movement was identified in the programme issued by Mahler as a pictorial parody well known to all children in Austria, 'The Hunter's Funeral Procession'. (See p. 157, for his description of the influential picture.) In the Czech edition of Mahler's letters (GMB², p. 128) there is a reproduction of the woodcut by Moritz von Schwind (1850) which, it is claimed, was the source of inspiration of Mahler's Funeral March. I reproduce it here, because it must represent the kind of illustration from the old volume of fairy stories for children that Mahler evidently had in mind.[114] I am not wholly convinced that the Schwind woodcut *is* the illustration in question because it does not, as readers can check for themselves, quite correspond to the description of it in the programme note: Schwind's hares, for example, are carrying torches not flags, and where is the advance band of Bohemian musicians as distinct from the music-making animals? This last point is perhaps of some significance, for if it were a book of fairy tales that belonged to Mahler's own childhood, then the illustration might well have had a specifically Bohemian component in it. Moreover, if it had been the Schwind woodcut that Mahler was thinking of, I wonder, in view of the artist's eminence, if Mahler would not have been bound to mention him?

Though it may remain an open question whether or not it was the Schwind woodcut that Mahler had in mind in connection with the First Symphony's Funeral March, there can be very little doubt that Mahler would have been familar with Schwind's work. Schwind (1804–71), who as a very young man was a member of the circle of friends around Schubert, showed in his art a

Schwind's woodcut, 'The Hunter's Funeral Procession'

characteristically Romantic preoccupation with death (shades of Jean Paul and Hoffmann), and I was interested to note in a comparatively recent exhibition of his work[115] that he had illustrated with a series of woodcuts a book of 'Grotesken und Phantasmagorien' by Eduard von Duller entitled *Freund Hein* (1883): it is Freund Hein who plays the solo violin in the Scherzo of Mahler's Fourth Symphony.[116] As Redlich suggests (HFR, p. 194) the use of the solo violin—which Mahler directed to be played 'like a fiddle' ('Fiedel', a primitive ancestor of the violin)—evokes 'a Dance of Death as imagined by medieval German woodcutters'; and it was just this tradition that was revived by the Romantic Schwind in the first decades of the nineteenth century and seized on by Mahler in his own inimitable way as the century neared its end.[117] Mahler would have known about Freund Hein without the aid of Duller and Schwind, just as he could have known a version of 'The Hunter's Funeral Procession' other than Schwind's (and probably did). Schwind serves my purpose by typifying, with no little distinction, the kind of pictorial sources that here and there made a stimulating contribution to Mahler's stock of imagery. More profoundly—much more profoundly—Schwind's fantasies are graphic symbols of a whole imaginative world which Mahler inherited and which he made quite peculiarly his own. I have written a great deal in this section of the book about the relationship of Mahler's programmes to his music, but perhaps the deepest 'programme' of them all was the imaginative tradition of German Romanticism, a great tradition with a brilliant history, of which Mahler was one of the last exponents. There may be no direct relationship between Schwind and Mahler, but they undeniably breathed the same air.

Appendix

Hamburg Concert Hall

First Popular Concert

Friday 27 October [1893]

The first popular concert, which took place yesterday in the sumptuous great hall of the Ludwig Bros., enjoyed an extraordinarily full attendance, proof enough that as many as three concert-giving institutions can co-exist in present-day Hamburg. Since the artistic basis underlying these popular concerts in the Philharmonic style is the same as that of both the other societies, we believe we may safely assume that, provided that no experiments contrary to the laudable tendencies of the enterprise are undertaken, they too will firmly establish themselves with the public. We hope, therefore, that the one experiment that was made yesterday will be the last. This is the only word for it, when nothing but works by one modern composer are performed for two whole hours. This would be so, even were he another Brahms— though this most important and most gifted composer of our time has too modest an opinion of himself ever to consent to a programme consisting only of his own works. Once he did say himself that those conductors who performed only works by him throughout an entire evening were a source of displeasure to him. There is only one whose spiritual wings are so strong that we follow him everywhere with the same interest, the same enthusiasm, the same emotional participation, and this one is Beethoven, for whom all and everything became as Ariadne's thread leading into the holy sanctuary.

On the programme yesterday were six songs with orchestral accompaniment and a 'Tone Poem in the form of a Symphony' by *Gustav Mahler*, the length of which was in inverse proportion to its poetic and musical content. We have already often enough referred to the considerable abilities of Mr. Mahler as an operatic conductor, and we have always acknowledged his gift for getting what he wants out of an orchestral ensemble; today we must also make laudatory mention of his artistic conscientiousness and of the seriousness of his aspirations and endeavours. He is a musician with definite ideals of his own, and whether these be justified or not, he pursues them regardless. This is always a sign of an artistic personality which must be given acknowledgment even when it is on the wrong paths. But after yesterday's specimens neither we nor other serious and self-confident musicians for whom art is still something other than the product of an unbridled, undisciplined and not very aesthetically endowed subjectivity will be able to follow Mahler the composer. Beauty too has an important part to play in art, and it is idle talk when the moderns put forward the superficial view that only what is characteristic is valid in art; the characteristic, as such, is inconceivable without the fragrance of beauty. In a work of art, form and content, beauty of thought and character of expression have to be fused into a unified whole, and it is imagination, that divine gift of poets and artists, which holds everything together and forms everything out of a basic idea so that we can see, as Bettina wrote to Goethe, 'how energy rises and falls and goes to fetch the golden pails.'* We missed this kindling, creative power of imagination in every one of Mahler's compositions. We admired the motivic and instrumental artistry and the highly developed technical ability of the composer, but no human soul lives in his works. Everything is fabricated with ingenuity, but even the folksong could not but succumb to the blight of deadening reflection. In the songs from 'Des Knaben Wunderhorn' there is nothing of a naive impulse, and it is just this which is characteristic of folksong; they wander around on rude musical stilts and are completely deprived of their simple, thoughtful, touching, homely emotional content. They are nothing but interestingly embroidered studies in instrumentation, the words, serving merely as a foil. When, for example, in the song 'Das himmlische Leben', John the Apostle 'lets out the little lamb', we hear a lamb-like, child-like bleat in the orchestra, and when the Evangelist Luke 'doth slaughter the ox', some brass instrument in the orchestra bellows an indeterminable note so that we may know that it is a real ox bellowing; the roe tinkles its bell, for it seems to be the hunting season, and when all the fishes come swimming along so that the jovial St. Peter hastens 'to the celestial fishpond with his net and bait', the composer, completely misunderstanding this delicious detail, promptly strikes up pious organ-like sounds because St. Martha happens to be the cook. In folk-song, music must at the very least illustrate the meaning of each subject and predicate, and in lyrical song it has to fulfil a far more important and essential task, namely the reproduction of the general emotive content, rather than making a mere patchwork of bits of protoplasmic melodic material. In his songs Mahler works with monotonous motivic phrases, which he repeats endlessly in sequences in the most varied tonalities, and which become no more interesting by virtue of their distorted harmonies. We might call his lyricism a pseudo-Gothic lyricism; it is of about the same order as the literary pretentiousness of Ebers's *Gret* [*sic*].† Even though this lyricism may find the lame enthusiasm of obliging eulogists, such a composition as the symphonic poem 'Titan' can only repel a more finely organized aesthetic nature. The work has nothing at all in common with its title, nor is there in its long-winded musical perpetuum mobile the slightest hint of that spirit which, as Mephistopheles says, 'constantly presses forward unrestrainedly'.‡ There is no idea that seizes hold of us, but mere intellectual fragments that

* Bettina von Arnim, *Briefwechsel Goethes mit einem Kinde* (1835). [D.M.]
† *Die Gred*, a novel about Nuremberg life and customs by Georg Ebers (1837–98), novelist and dramatist. [D.M.]
‡ A reference to Goethe's *Faust*. [D.M.]

refuse to add up and come together in a mosaic; unceasingly repeated orchestral phrases which never get further than the mood of the opening; brutal noisiness which slaps every feeling for beauty rudely in the face.

We propose only a brief résumé of the individual movements. The first is entitled 'Spring without end'. If the composer had chosen the last two words as his superscription, then the character of this movement would have been best indicated. The violins sustain the note A for some five minutes; sometimes other sounds of life are added; muted horns and trumpets are heard in the distance. The earth begins to come truly alive; here and there the chaos is interrupted by the sound of an inquisitive bird, but the monotony of winter does not relinquish its dominion. Finally we hear a wealth of musical sounds of spring, yet the bare fifth of the triad, representing fierce winter, retains the upper hand, even though a bold snowdrop peeps out cautiously from time to time. We imagine we are in the ice age. Then finally it approaches—spring, with its timpani, drums and trumpets, with no chirruping, until the former bring the movement to a sudden end with a bad-tempered burst. This timpani passage at the end of the movement would seem to us the most interesting.

The second movement bears the unusual designation 'Blumine'. This Andante contains many an atmospheric moment, but here too there lacks a focal point, a basic idea to bind together all the parts, so that the mood flutters around in every wind, or rather in every tonality. The most original movement seemed to us to be the Scherzo 'In full sail'. Certainly the whole thing is maintained in a pretty uncultured style, but precisely in this does a certain characteristic trait find expression. The trio is based—of course freely, and perhaps also unintentionally—on the melody: 'Du, du liegst mir im Herzen'.* The fourth movement is called 'Aground', and the programme further gives the designation *Commedia humana* as a special heading. In order to be quite explicit, the composer also adds: 'A funeral march in the manner of Callot'. But since despite this the listener might still easily get the wrong idea, a

---

* This is the German folk-song to which Sittard refers, the reproduction of the incipit

Du, du liegst mir im Herz-en, Du, du liegst mir in Sinn,

of which I owe to the excellent musical memory of Professor Ronald Taylor. Readers may judge for themselves Sittard's confident assertion that there is a relationship between the delicate sentiment of Mahler's trio and the rather awful sentimentality of the folk-song. It

is hard to see much of a musical connection, unconscious or otherwise, except for the common waltz or Ländler time. [D.M.]

further annotation instructs us that the author was stimulated to write this tone painting by the parodistic picture 'The Hunter's Funeral Procession' from an old book of children's tales. 'The beasts of the forest bring the huntsman's coffin (?) to the grave. Hares carry a small banner, with a band of Bohemian musicians in front, accompanied by music-making cats, toads, crows', etc., which all 'escort the procession in comic postures'. In spite of this, we did not understand this *Commedia humana*. At first, we thought we had to understand the superscription 'Aground' as if it prepared us for a psychological impressionistic picture, perhaps like that produced by Raff in his symphony having the motto: 'Living, contending, aspiring, dying'. But this is not entirely how it has turned out here, and the contradictions the composer gets into with his titles and the commentary testify to the fact that he himself was not clear. Hares, toads, crows and other animals have their say in this 'human comedy'. However, despite its monotony, this is the movement which comes nearest to being likeable. Unfortunately the assembly of mourning takes on such an 'ironically merry' and 'weirdly brooding mood' (the commentary's own words), that it tears into the last movement, into hell—Inferno—with a tam-tam stroke* to convulse one to the very marrow. Compared with this musical bottomless pit, the 'Ride of the Valkyries' is a gentle zephyr that caresses our cheeks with a smile. The thunderous applause that was struck up at the end by one part of the audience concided most harmoniously with the character of this piece of music, the hearing of which is sure penance for a multitude of sins. However, no less did energetic opposition to such music assert itself through loud hissing.

Brief mention should also be made of the two soloists, Madame *Clementine Schuch-Prosska* from Dresden and Mr. *Paul Bulss* from Berlin. The former artist, with her excellently trained and agreeable voice, sang the great coloratura aria from Adam's charming comic opera: *The Doll of Nuremberg* ['La Poupée de Nuremberg'], in addition to three songs by Mahler, and Mr. *Bulss*, with his admirable vocal equipment, gave the aria: 'An jenem Tag' from *Hans Heiling* [Marschner] and likewise three songs by Mahler. We have once again cause to regret that the latter singer is more intent on displaying his phenomenal voice than on artistry in his delivery.

Finally we must express our warmest appreciation for the excellent orchestra of the concert hall, which, apart from the difficult compositions by Mahler, who again proved himself a distinguished conductor, yesterday also played the *Egmont* and the *Hebrides* Overtures.

J.[oseph] Sittard.

* There is no tam-tam stroke at this point in the published edition of the symphony, but there was in the early version of the work and it is still to be seen in the 1893 MS. I have no doubt that it was there in 1889, at the première, and survived until and including the Hamburg performance, as Sittard records. [D.M.]

Notes

1 The precise dates of the composition and publication of Mahler's works are by no means always easy to establish. The dates I give, for the most part, are the result of investigation of as many relevant sources as I have been able to consult, some dates emerging as the best calculations that can be made in often fragmentary or confused documentary situations. For dates of publication, I have used (though not exclusively) Hofmeister's invaluable *Verzeichnis*, the yearly catalogue of published music brought out (for the first time in 1829, as a monthly inventory) by the firm which initially was to publish Mahler's Second Symphony. (We learn from Ferdinand Pfohl, incidentally, that it was due to the generous financial intervention of two of Mahler's Hamburg friends, Hermann Behn and Wilhelm Berkhan, that the score and complete orchestral material of the Second Symphony were made available by Hofmeister. See FP, p. 39. Guido Adler too lent a generous helping hand when it came to securing funds for the publication of Mahler's early symphonies. For the details of this, see Edward R. Reilly's admirable article on Mahler and Adler in the *Musical Quarterly*, July 1972, pp. 445–8 and also HG[1], pp. 465–6 and 475–6.) The *Verzeichnis* is not wholly reliable as a source, some publications appearing in the catalogue probably a year late, owing to the dilatoriness of the publishers submitting them for registration, and some missing altogether, presumably when publishers forgot to take any action at all. But Hofmeister, for all that, is an indispensable and often illuminating source of information.

2 In February, according to HG[1], p. 738, who points out that 'the printing plates themselves prove that all three volumes were printed within a few weeks of each other early in 1892.' This fresh information means that the publication date (1885) given by GA, p. 58, and others, is incorrect. In the Library of the University of Stanford, California, there is a dedication copy of Vol. I of the *Lieder und Gesänge*, inscribed by Mahler and dated 8 February 1892. Advance copies of the volumes were doubtless ready before publication, but this very early date in February—which implies an even earlier date for the completion of the printing—lends further emphasis to the question I raise about the improbable speed of the publishing operation which M. de la Grange's chronology for these songs would necessitate. (See pp. 116–17.)

3 Now Kassel, but I retain the spelling as it was in Mahler's day.

4 The fact that there existed an earlier version of the *Gesellen* cycle in which

Neue Musikalien!

Gustav Mahler.
Lieder und Gesänge für eine Singstimme und Clavier.
Heft I.

No. 1. Frühlingsmorgen.
No. 2. Erinnerung.
No. 3. Hans und Grethe.   } Hoch u. tief 2 *M.* 50 *₰.*
No. 4. Serenade aus „Don Juan".
No. 5. Phantasie aus „Don Juan".

Heft II.

No. 1. Um schlimme Kinder artig zu machen.
No. 2. Ich ging mit Lust durch einen grünen
      Wald.   } Hoch u. tief 2 *M.* 50 *₰.*
No. 3. Aus! Aus!
No. 4. Starke Einbildungskraft.

Heft III.

No. 1. Zu Strassburg auf der Schanz.
No. 2. Ablösung im Sommer.
No. 3. Scheiden und Meiden.   } Hoch und tief 3 *M.*
No. 4. Nicht Wiedersehen!
No. 5. Selbstgefühl!

B. Schott's Söhne, Mainz.

Wiesbadener Männergesang-Verein.
Preis-Chöre.

Franz Abt, Willkommen! Begrüssungschor von Hermann Francke,
für Männerstimmen 3 *M.* Partitur 1 *M.* 20 *₰.* Stimmen à 45 *₰.*

C. Jos. Brambach, Im Frühling. Lied im Volkston von H. Weiser, für
Männerstimmen (Text deutsch und französisch). 1 *M.* 20 *₰.* Partitur
60 *M.* Stimmen à 15 *₰.*

Vinzenz Lachner, Op. 64b. Waldlied von Emil Engelmann, für
Männerchor 3 *M.* Partitur 1 *M.* 20 *₰.* Stimmen à 45 *₰.*

Ferdinand Möhring, Op. 101. Rheingauer Gruss! von F. Mäurer, für
Männerchor 3 *M.* Partitur 1 *M.* 20 *₰.* Stimmen à 45 *₰.*

Carl Reinecke, Sommerhymnus von Martin Greif, für Männerchor
2 *M.* 40 *₰.* Partitur 1 *M.* 20 *₰.* Stimmen à 30 *₰.*

Josef Rheinberger, Op. 173 No. 1. Germanenzug von August Silber-
stein, f. Männerchor 2 *M.* 40 *₰.* Part. 1 *M.* 20 *₰.* Stimmen à 30 *₰.*

Leonhard Wolff, Op. 12. Jung Werner von Victor Scheffel, für
Männerchor 3 *M.* Partitur 1 *M.* 20 *₰.* Stimmen à 45 *₰.*

J. B. Zerlett, Op. 112. Das Grab im Busento von Graf von Platen,
für Männerchor (Text deutsch und französisch) 2 *M.* 40 *₰.* Partitur
1 *M.* 20 *₰.* Stimmen à 30 *₰.*

befinden sich jetzt in meinem Verlage. Sendungen zur Ansicht stehen
zu Diensten.

Leipzig, im Juni 1892.   **F. E. C. Leuckart.**

Schott's 1892 advertisement for the publication of the *Lieder und Gesänge* the second and third songs were respectively in D flat and B minor was known to Paul Stefan, who included these significant details when describing 'the oldest manuscript score' of the work in the revised edition of his Mahler bio-graphy (PS[1], p. 101). It is curious that few of Stefan's successors followed up or even remarked upon his important disclosure. One might have expected H. F. Redlich to mention this significant fact in his foreword (1959) to the Eulenburg miniature score (No. 1053), but he does not touch on it. Perhaps this is not surprising, since he also fails to inform his readers that the poem of the first song is based on a *Wunderhorn* text, which, as it happens, was another fact conscientiously documented by Stefan (op. cit., pp. 100–1) and systema-tically ignored by later, though often more ambitious, critics.

5 See AM[5], p. 343, for further information on Behn, and HG[1] *passim*.

6 It is true that in the first $\frac{4}{8}$ bar of the VS, a bracketed $\frac{2}{4}$ is added (see opp.). The engraving in this bar—the spacing in particular—suggests to me that the insertion was dropped in at the last moment as a compromise gesture, per-haps because by then it was too late to bring the voice and piano text into line with the orchestral score. A clumsy further attempt to sort out this notational confusion must have been made by the publisher at a later stage in the life of the VS: hence the (literally) written-in amplification: sempre ♩ = ♩. e non ♪ = ♪

This inscription, of course, does not derive from Mahler (it is not to be found in the first printed edition of the VS) but stems from the inconsistencies revealed by a comparison of the VS and the PS. (♪♪♪ = ♪♪♪ at Fig. 24, on the other hand, *is* authentic. It introduces into the VS—though not into the first edition of the vocal score—Mahler's own ♪♪♪ wie vorher ♪♪♪ from the comparable spot in the PS.) The notation Mahler adopted in the PS solved the ritornello problem at a stroke, and was also doubtless the reason why he excluded from the PS the injunction that appears in the VS: 'Auf den fortwährenden Tempowechsel ist genau zu achten.' ['The continuous fluctua-tion of tempo is to be precisely observed.'] The only oddity is that still, after nearly seventy-five years, the VS and PS remain at notational odds. (As I indicate on p. 92, although Mr. Alfred Rosé was good enough to list the OV's variants for me, I have not had access to the MS, or a copy of it, myself. Dr. Zoltan Roman (Calgary), who is to edit Mahler's songs for the Critical Edition, has been able to scrutinize the OV (and the EV), as he makes clear in his important review of HG[1] in the *Musical Quarterly*, New York, Vol. LX No. 3, July, 1974, pp. 492–9. Students who want to follow up the textual history of the various MSS and printed editions of the *Gesellen* cycle should not fail to consult Dr. Roman's review.)

7 One should bear in mind that these last works of Mahler were drafted in circumstances of intense spiritual stress and turmoil, which doubtless added to the tentativeness of the preliminary sketches. Thus the Ninth might be

The first bars of the *Gesellen* cycle in the first printed edition (1897)

something of a special case. See Matthews entry in Supplementary Bibliography.

8 I am aware, naturally, that Mahler omitted the original Part I when revising the cantata for publication. Undoubtedly that was a revision of substance, but not of the kind that I have in mind. The interesting point for me, writing in 1958, was that the MSS of Parts II and III and the published versions were, in musical substance, virtually identical.

9 In the first printed editions of the VS, there appeared no rehearsal numbers. These were added at a later stage, again by hand (see also n. 6 above), to correspond with those in the PS, part of a general editorial attempt (a messy and unsuccessful one) to reconcile the two printed editions of the cycle. In misplacing Fig. 29, the copyist was following the location of the double bar instead of observing the notes!

10 I must take this opportunity to correct some gross errors of description in my commentary on the songs of Vol. I. In lines 13 and 14 of the text on the 'Serenade' (DM[1], p. 203), for 'an open end, on A major', read 'the dominant seventh'. In line 15 of the text on 'Erinnerung' (DM[1], p. 217), for 'the dominant and a warmer (major keys) climate' read 'the dominant seventh and move thence into a warmer (relative major) climate'. On p. 218 (DM[1]), the penultimate sentence of the second paragraph should read: 'The transition combines our return to the familiar melody (Ex. 11), with a mid-stream introduction, into the very flow of the transition, of a pedal E as the dominant of A minor, the key in which the old melody is to re-appear, entering on the dominant seventh (the voice-part is marked by the small notes within square brackets).' On p. 219, the first sentence should read: 'As Ex. 16 indicates,

Erinnerung, having set out in G minor, finally arrives in A minor, by way of the dominant seventh of E referred to in Ex. 15 above.'

11 In JW, pp. 83–4, Mr. Warrack writes neatly about the influence and importance of *Des Knaben Wunderhorn*, 'a mine of Romanticism that continued to give rich yields for many decades to come. . . . In 1808 there appeared the second edition of *Des Knaben Wunderhorn*, together with the short-lived journal, *Zeitung für Einsiedler*—a collection of poems, tales, legends and oddities of old German lore to which a wider group of poets than the Heidelberg Romantics contributed. . . . But the poetic glamour of the group attracted many contributors, among them the brothers Grimm (whose famous *Kinder und Hausmärchen* followed in 1812–15), not to mention Rückert, Lenau, Gottfried Keller, Hebbel and Eichendorff, many of whose best poems were written while he was studying at Heidelberg. The original movement was short-lived, for by 1808 the Heidelberg group had more or less disintegrated; but its influence on the younger writers, artists and composers was still potent by the time Weber arrived two years later and lasted far beyond his own lifetime'. As Mr. Warrack points out later (p. 251), it was Mahler's link with Weber and the Weber family that further confirmed and consolidated a tradition that was very much alive and kicking in the person of the twenty-seven-year-old composer: 'Mahler was already a great admirer of Weber: his *Das klagende Lied* of 1880 reflects this, and he had recently composed the first of his *Des Knaben Wunderhorn* songs from the copy of Arnim and Brentano owned by the Weber family.'

12 See Letter No. 47 in GMB[1], p. 63.

13 It is perhaps worth noting here that while there is no doubt that the First Symphony was completed in 1888, in a great burst of creative energy and exhilaration, some authorities (GA among them, p. 99) attribute the inception of the symphony to 1884 (see also n. 39, where this date crops up again in connection with the Budapest première of the work). If this were the case, and if also the *Gesellen* songs *were* composed principally in 1884, then we can speculate, perhaps not altogether unfruitfully, about a possible chronological simultaneity which lends support to the suggestion that the song-cycle was, as it were, overtaken and absorbed by the burgeoning symphonic project; and may explain—at least in part—why the song-cycle did not emerge in its own right until the symphony had at last materialized in a shape with which Mahler was satisfied (that there were other reasons too, I have no doubt: see, for example, pp. 111f.). If, moreover, the inception of the symphony and the creation of the cycle were virtually coterminous, this makes the more probable the idea that the cycle was orchestrated after the symphony had been written and that the cycle made its first *orchestral* appearance in the symphony. On the basis of this chronology (which I set out as clearly as I could in AM[5], p. xxiii, having raised the problem as long ago as 1958 in DM[1], pp. 254–5, n. 10), the symphony represented a creative interruption of the *Gesellen* cycle's history, postponing the songs' emergence in the guise which Mahler intended them to have by more than a decade.

14 Mahler was an accomplished and fertile versifier, and continued to be throughout his life. (See, for example, in AM¹, the many poems he addressed to his wife in his very last years.) He made in his youth, not surprisingly, MS copies of his verses—he expended a good deal of calligraphic artistry on a fair copy of the text of *Das klagende Lied*, for instance—and it is extremely interesting to find, as I mention above, that MS drafts of some of the *Gesellen* poems have survived and are at present in a private collection. These, I am convinced, are drafts of the type which Mahler would have sent to Löhr in January 1885, i.e. when Mahler writes that he is going to send his friend 'the closing song', it was a hand-written copy of his *poem* that he had in mind; and it is indeed a MS copy of the 'closing song'—'Die zwei blauen Augen'— that is among the MSS in question, a copy dated 15 December 1884. Also among these MS poems is a draft of 'Ich hab' ein glühend Messer', this text being dated a few days later, 19 December 1884. (One notes, too, that the discarded poem reproduced on p. 124 from the pages of *Der Merker* is also dated December 1884.)

That these particular MSS were never handed over or sent (if that was Mahler's intention) is probably due to the fact that as (or after) he wrote them out, he made fresh emendations, and thus the MSS were no longer serviceable as fair copies. A comparison of these MS versions with the texts of the songs leads to some not uninteresting conclusions. In the case of both texts, 'Die zwei blauen Augen' and 'Ich hab' ein glühend' Messer', we find differences between the texts as *set* and the texts as *copied*, and not only the differences one might expect, e.g. some repetitions omitted in the copies which, in the songs, are established for musical reasons, but some that one would not expect, on the assumption, that is, that Mahler was copying out the texts from the finished songs. The kinds of variant I have in mind here are illustrated by the following excerpt from 'Die zwei blauen Augen', where line 3 (in square brackets) does not appear in the song at all, nor do the words enclosed in brackets in line 2, while in line 4 the song reads 'niemand' for 'keiner':

> Ich bin ausgegangen in stiller Nacht
> wo[h]l [über Wald] mir die dunkle Heide!
> [fort niemand nach mir gefragt!]
> Hat mir keiner Ade gesagt!
> Mein Gesell war Lieb' und Leide!

On first consideration, these variants might lead one to suppose that the setting of the text could not have existed at this time, so different is the MS of the copied-out poem from the text that actually serves the music; in which case one would find oneself in the chronological quandary that I outline on pp. 119–21, i.e. with a draft text (for this song) dated 15 December 1884, and the music still to be composed before 1 January 1885, which would have led to the version of the text with which we are familiar today.

But I believe scrutiny of the amended MS texts of these poems suggests a different approach altogether. For example, we find that the new line (line 3) in the above excerpt is squeezed in between lines 2 and 4 and clearly represents an afterthought, an addition; and I believe, working from this clue, that for the major part the variants may represent attempted literary improvements of the already existing song texts. In other words, these drafts are evidence of Mahler trying to polish up the texts (by the addition and/or substitution of some lines and some words) in order to convert them into self-sufficient, self-justifying poems. This explanation not only fits the musical chronology, but also explains the otherwise bizarre numeration of the copies. 'Die zwei blauen Augen' (the last song!) is inscribed 'I' and 'Ich hab' . . .' (the third song), 'II'. The numeration would appear to be totally eccentric and inexplicable if we were obliged to think of the draft texts as studies for songs still to be composed; but of course if, as I am convinced is the case, the numeration refers to the order of the texts in some kind of literary exercise or project (was Mahler perhaps thinking of gathering together, in MS form, a small collection of his verse?), then the Roman numbers cease to be a puzzle. They had—and have—no relationship to the sequence of the songs as unfolded in the cycle. After all, we know that the work was essentially completed by 1 January 1885, and it is surely hard to conceive that as late as 15 December 1884, Mahler was still so uncertain about the shape of the *Gesellen* songs that he was able to think of the *Schlusslied*-to-be as No. I.

This fascinating MS source also reveals another poem in Mahler's hand, this time a copy inscribed 'for the 18th August 1884' and dated likewise, 18 August 1884. The poem includes in its last line a reference to a solitary 'fahrende Gesell', which tempts one to believe that this might be one of the missing texts, along with the other early poem (reproduced on p. 124), which also introduces the image of the 'fahrende Gesell' into its fifth line. (In HG¹, p. 114, there is mention of two poems written 'in August or September' which use the image of the 'fahrende Gesell', but the months to which these texts belong were, I think, August and December.) It may be that these two poems were among the texts that Mahler produced as part of the literary activity associated with the idea of the dramatically conceived, narrative song-cycle. That they were rejected, may, I believe, be due not only to their failure to contribute to the dramatic pattern but also—though this may be a different way of saying the same thing—to their style, which is much more in the vein of the conventionally lyrical and literary than the other texts, which are much more folk-ish, more *Wunderhorn*-like. Thus a desirable uniformity of poetic manner may have been a further reason why Mahler settled for the four songs rather than six.

Finally, there is a poem of Mahler's in his own hand, entitled 'In der Nacht' and dated September 1884 (another lyric). If nothing else, these drafts show that Mahler, towards the end of 1884, indulged in a bout of literary activity, writing and/or writing out those poems which were so intimately involved with both his life and the composition of his first song-cycle. (See also HG¹, pp. 824–37, Appendix 4, 'Mahler's Poems'.)

15 This, I think, is the basic confusion which effectively torpedoes Dr. Roman's gallant effort (in ZR¹, see n. 14, pp. 247f.) to prove that the 'missing' *Gesellen* songs might be 'Scheiden und Meiden' and 'Nicht wiedersehen!' (two of the *Wunderhorn* songs from Vol. III of the *Lieder und Gesänge*). Quite apart from the point I make on p. 123 above, however—which I believe to be crucial—I would in any event find it hard to understand how Mahler envisaged including in the same cycle two songs so close in musical character and formal type. Each song is, as it were, a 'Schlusslied', and there is scarcely room for two such songs in a cycle of the relatively modest proportions of the *Lieder eines fahrenden Gesellen*. Dr. Roman includes *both* songs in Part II of his projected reconstruction of a six-song version of the cycle, 'Nicht wiedersehen!' immediately preceding 'Die zwei blauen Augen'. Is it really likely that Mahler would have rounded off his cycle with two finales, i.e. with two slow marches for voice and orchestra which are virtually identical in musical character?! One is led into such remarkable contortions by misinterpreting Mahler's letter and by not realizing (which is surely the chronological case) that 'Nicht wiedersehen!' is itself modelled on the earlier 'Die zwei blauen Augen'. See also n. 14 above.

16 Actually, he did not quite discard it. Lines three and four lingered on in his mind, to be revived in the 'Abschied' of *Das Lied von der Erde*:

> ... die müden Menschen geh'n heimwärts,
> um im Schlaf vergess'nes Glück
> und Jugend neu zu lernen!
>
> [... Mankind, grown weary, turns homeward,
> That in sleep, forgotten joy and youth it may recapture.]

17 The songs were first published for voice and piano in three volumes of four songs each (or they could be bought complete in one volume), and included (as Nos. 11 and 12 in the overall sequence) 'Es sungen drei Engel' (from the Third Symphony) and 'Urlicht' (from the Second). Nos. 1–10 appeared in the order set out in the Summary on pp. 140f., i.e. in an order that corresponds with the ten songs as later issued by Universal Edition in miniature-score form in two volumes of five songs each. (Universal Edition also issued *Des Knaben Wunderhorn* in a two-volume edition of six songs each for voice and piano (edition number 1691a/1692a), the overall sequence of which followed the original Weinberger edition.) It should be noted, however, that the overall published order of the *Wunderhorn* songs does not correspond precisely with the numeration that Mahler himself indicated on some of his MSS of the songs. In the case of Vol. I, the published order of the first four songs, as shown in the table on p. 140, corresponds with the order of the Hamburg MS full scores; and when Mahler came to replace 'Das himmlische Leben' with 'Das irdische Leben', he replaced his original No. 5 with what seems to have been its planned successor, i.e. 'Das irdische Leben' was inscribed by Mahler on the MS as No. 6. The 'Fischpredigt' on the other hand was originally No. 8 (to become No. 6), and 'Rheinlegendchen'

No. 9 (to become No. 7). The 'Lied des Verfolgten im Turm' was also at one stage designated in MS as No. 8, and was published as such, and 'Wo die schönen Trompeten', likewise, retained in publication the number (No. 9) of its MS inscription. No doubt the discrepancies between the two sets of numbers—those on the MSS and those in the published edition—have their origin in Mahler transferring certain songs ('Das himmlische Leben' and 'Urlicht') out of the *Wunderhorn* series proper and into the symphonies, which would have upset the original MS numeration.

The orchestral full scores (with one exception) were issued by Weinberger as separate publications, in a numbered sequence that corresponds with the voice and piano volumes. The exception was No. 11, the orchestral score of 'Es sungen drei Engel', which was announced (and even listed with a price) but never published as part of the Weinberger series of *Wunderhorn* full scores. Readers should not be confused if they alight on a reference to a version of the song for solo voice and orchestra, as they will, for example, if they consult the catalogue of Mahler's works issued some years ago by the International Mahler Society. This is *not* Mahler's own version but an arrangement made long after his death by Josef Wöss (1863–1943), an editor for U.E. who was responsible for many of the piano editions of Mahler's symphonies, etc. As late as 1923, in a U.E. advertisement, the score of this arrangement of 'Es sungen drei Engel' for solo voice and orchestra was announced as being still 'in preparation', though the song was never actually published in this form but the score and parts made available only on hire (the full score, still available today, is in Wöss's (or a copyist's) hand). Thus was the gap in the series of twelve *Wunderhorn* full scores posthumously filled by editorial intervention. All this explains why the Österreichische Nationalbibliothek (Vienna) possesses no published score or set of parts, and why the British Museum similarly lacks a copy of this item (amusingly enough, though, the B.M. can show one the still extant official order for the missing No. 11, which of course was never fulfilled); and likewise, this is the explanation of why, in later advertisements from the publisher (for example, *c.* 1912), the full score of No. 11 is consistently and correctly omitted from the list, even while, rather confusingly, appearing on the series' uniform title page as a published item. I discuss the complex history of this song further on pp. 129–35 and in n. 21, p. 252.

18 Mahler, however, performed the song as an independent *Wunderhorn* setting until it was, as it were, digested by the Fourth Symphony and given a new status. We know, for instance, that 'Das himmlische Leben' was performed, along with 'Verlor'ne Müh' and 'Wer hat dies Liedlein erdacht?', in Hamburg on 27 October 1893, as part of the concert which included the first Hamburg performance of the First Symphony (the first performance to follow the Budapest première of the symphony in 1889). The soloist in these three songs (described in the programme as 'Humoresken' from *Des Knaben Wunderhorn*) was Clementine Schuch-Prosska, while Paul Bulss was the soloist in 'Der Schildwache Nachtlied', 'Trost im Unglück' and 'Rheinlegendchen' (which were not described as 'Humoresken', though attributed to *Des Knaben Wunderhorn*). 'Rheinlegendchen' had been composed in August 1893, and was the most recent of Mahler's *Wunderhorn* songs performed on this occasion. Ferdinand Pfohl, in his notice of 28 October (he was the music critic of the *Hamburger Nachrichten*), liked 'Das himmlische Leben': '... a real stroke of genius: a character piece of pungent wit, exceedingly delicate and enchantingly scored, in which magisterial humour wields the sceptre'. 'Rheinlegendchen', it seems, was such a success that it had to be repeated. (See the entries in the table on pp. 140–1, which distinguishes which songs on this occasion received their first performances.)

19 This is the date which appears on the MS fair draft of the song for voice and piano mentioned above. It is a complete, clean copy of the song, a MS which Mahler later gave to Arnold Rosé with the inscription 'a preliminary study for the Scherzo of the Second'. It seems probable to me that this MS (now in the Pierpont Morgan Library (Lehmann Deposit), New York) was the fair copy of the original voice and piano draft of the 'Fischpredigt'. The MS contains very detailed instrumental indications which, one suspects, may have been written in after the voice and piano fair copy was written out (perhaps after the orchestration of the Scherzo?). It is interesting to note that Mahler, in his inscription, uses the words 'preliminary study'. One has to remember, however, that the inscription would have been added after the Scherzo had become an accomplished fact. There is no reason to suppose that in the first instance the 'Fischpredigt' was thought of as anything but an independent *Wunderhorn* setting. Pamer suggests in the penultimate section ('The Songs and the Symphonies') of his pioneering study of Mahler's songs (FEP) that 'the symphonic elaboration may have originated at the same time as the composition of the song, possibly preceding it'. At the same time, yes; preceding it, no. (The voice and piano MS mentioned here (with the inscription) clears this point up decisively.) I outline the close chronological interpenetration of the song and symphonic movement on pp. 137–8. Pamer further suggests, presumably following Adler (GA, p. 101), that Mahler conjured a solo voice version of 'Es sungen drei Engel' out of the choral symphonic movement. (HG[1], p. 808, attributes the opposite statement to Pamer and Adler, but this must be based on a misunderstanding of what Pamer actually writes.) This reversal of Mahler's habitual procedure would seem to be supported by the evidence of the composition sketch for the fifth movement of the Third Symphony, which I discuss on p. 254. We find, in fact, Mahler's solo voice version of the movement, an *authentic* but later version (as distinct from the solo voice and piano arrangement or solo voice and orchestra arrangement mentioned on p. 131 and in n. 17, which are not Mahler's work), installed as No. 11 into the Weinberger *Wunderhorn* collection of 1899.

20 'First volume' means here (and henceforth) the five songs that make up Vol. I of the later miniature-score edition issued by Universal Edition. We have come to think of the *Wunderhorn* songs as a collection of ten rather than twelve songs—i.e. excluding the two excerpts from the symphonies—and it seems sensible to discuss them in this now established and familiar sequence which, in any case, still follows the original order of publication. This same qualification applies to any reference to the 'second volume'.

21 Most of Mahler's orchestral songs were drafted first in voice and piano versions. There is an interesting preliminary draft for voice and piano of one of the two late *Wunderhorn* songs, 'Der Tamboursg'sell', in the Pierpont Morgan Library, New York, a very sketchy affair indeed (see also pp. 139f. and the table on pp. 142–3); and there is a similarly sketchy and incomplete voice and piano draft of 'Trost im Unglück' (a MS in private hands), in which Mahler has written—appropriately enough, in all conscience!—'Trompeten-musik' above bars 3 and 4, precisely where the trumpets enter, in fact. An example of what was probably a typical draft may be found in E. Winternitz, *Musical Autographs: from Monteverdi to Hindemith*, Princeton, 1955, Vol. II, Plate 163, which reproduces a voice and piano draft of 'Der Schildwache Nachtlied' (now in the Library of Congress). This is clearly an early draft of the song, though not, it would seem, the earliest, which varies in many particulars from the published edition. (See Dr. Winternitz's own commentary on the MS in Vol. I of his anthology, pp. 130–1.) The sources for 'Der Schild-wache Nachtlied' conveniently offer us the opportunity to scrutinize the composition of a *Wunderhorn* song in some detail. These are represented by (1) the early voice and piano draft in the Library of Congress; (2) the fair copy of the voice and piano version in the Berlin Staatsbibliothek; (3) the MS of the orchestral full score (in the Library of the Gesellschaft der Musikfreunde, Vienna); and (4) the published editions of both versions. The MS items should be compared with each other and with the published editions. One can observe the same evolutionary process in the case of other *Wunderhorn* songs too, where the MS sources allow, e.g. the 'Fischpredigt' or 'Das himmlische Leben', for which we have access to complete voice and piano drafts and MS full scores.

The odd men out in this voice and piano context would appear to be two in number, both of them movements in the Third Symphony. The first is 'O Mensch! Gib Acht!', the song (words by Nietzsche, itself an unusual feature in this stressedly *Wunderhorn* period of Mahler's creativity) which forms the fourth movement of the symphony; and the second, the choral setting of 'Es sungen drei Engel' (another *Wunderhorn* poem), which forms the fifth movement of the work. In the case of 'O Mensch! Gib Acht!' there is an early (and significantly) *orchestral* draft of the song—perhaps the first draft in full score—which almost certainly belongs to the summer of 1895 (see n. 27, p. 257). This is inscribed No. 3 (!) in Mahler's hand, thus providing another splendid example of his chronic uncertainty about the sequence of the movements in the Third Symphony. In this connection, it is of some interest to note that the companion MS drafts of the Scherzo and 'Es sungen drei Engel' (entitled 'Was mir die Morgenglocken erzählen') are inscribed No. 5 (ink) *and* No. 4 (pencil) [the Scherzo], and No. 4 (ink) *and* No. 6 (pencil' ['Es sungen drei Engel']. (I refer also in n. 27, p. 257, to the missing

MS of the Minuet, entitled 'Was mir die Blumen auf der Wiese erzählen', which originally formed part of this draft MS full score: the movement was then inscribed No. 6! See, too, n. 73, p. 286.) The titles, too, undergo unceasing modification: for example, the Scherzo, where 'Was mir die Dämmerung erzählt' becomes 'Was mir die Thiere in Walde erzählen'. Yet another feature of these early draft scores is Mahler's indication of approximate durations: 12–14 min. for the Scherzo, 4 min. for 'Es sungen drei Engel', and 8 min. for 'O Mensch! Gib Acht!', which in this draft is entitled 'Was mir die Nacht erzählt!'. In a later MS of the song, dated Steinbach, summer 1896, the duration has been extended by Mahler to $11\frac{1}{2}$ min!

This 1896 version (which is partly reproduced in NBL, facing p. 112: the MS is now in the Library of Congress), combines, interestingly, the features of both a voice and piano version and a highly condensed orchestral score. It is certainly a kind of reduction, though it still falls far short of a voice and piano edition proper. Perhaps it was a practical version that Mahler made from his full score, for rehearsal purposes, or for a singer to try out? It could certainly be managed at the keyboard, while at the same time the orchestral lay-out and texture are usefully indicated. To sum up: the MS evidence that exists supports the view that 'O Mensch! Gib Acht!' was from the first conceived as an orchestral song and as an integral part of the symphony.

In connection with the last point, one must not forget, of course, at least to mention the complex of thematic links which exists between the song and the symphony's first movement and Finale, and which in this particular instance *can* be read as signs of a song which was custom-built rather than spontaneously ingested. As I point out on pp. 184–5 (see also n. 68, p. 283), the thematic link between 'Urlicht' and the Finale of the Second Symphony would promote on the face of it, a similar deduction—but there it would be the wrong one. It is not safe in Mahler to rely on overt thematic integration (think of 'Das himmlische Leben' and the Fourth Symphony!) as a guide to a song's status, i.e., to assess whether the song was born as part of a symphony or adopted. A more reliable indicator is the MS shape in which a song seems first to have materialized, hence the importance of the absence of a voice and piano draft in the case of 'O Mensch! Gib Acht!'.

The thematic relation of the song to the first movement (e.g. cf. the opening bars of the song with the first movement, Fig. 1), if viewed from a strictly chronological angle, produces its own kind of confusion, because we encounter a draft of the song made in the summer of 1895, whereas the first movement was composed (as Mahler saw it) in 1896. It is doubtful, however, whether we should interpret this to mean that the huge first movement was written, as it were, under the shadow of the song. As I point out in n. 27, p. 257, the amazing fluidity of Mahler's mode of composing probably meant that the ideas for both the song and the first movement were already fertile and blossoming in his mind in the summer of 1895, if not earlier. It was the conscious tying up of all the loose ends—the integrating—that was left to last.

I find that it is just this aspect of Mahler's creativity that is so fascinating,

partly because it runs counter to the conventional idea of integration as something virtually pre-planned and pre-set, a way of thinking that is further
confirmed by our habitual pattern of listening. We listen to a work, naturally
enough, in its established sequence, and tend to assume all too readily that it
was composed chronologically as we hear it, with its integration tidily developing step by step from beginning to end. If nothing else, Mahler's symphonies, and particularly the *Wunderhorn* group of symphonies, shatter this
mould of conventional musical thought. Time and time again, indeed, we
find that sequence and intermovement integration emerge at a very late stage
in the game, as the final means of disposing and ordering the masses of invention thrown up, almost arbitrarily, during the period of a work's gestation.

   In the case of 'Es sungen drei Engel', there is little doubt that this movement too, like 'O Mensch! Gib Acht!', was specifically drafted for inclusion
in the symphony. In the Pierpont Morgan Library (Lehmann Deposit), New
York, there is a composition sketch for the movement (dated 24 June 1895),
a setting of the *Wunderhorn* poem which in essence is the music with which
we are familiar today and which indicates the resources (women's chorus,
boys' chorus, etc.) that Mahler was ultimately to deploy, though in his final
version, as distinct from the sketch, he settled for one (contralto) soloist, not
soprano *and* contralto. This important sketch shows pretty clearly that the
movement was *from the start* envisaged as a choral setting of the *Wunderhorn*
text. As I have pointed out in n. 17, p. 249 and discuss in detail on pp. 130–5,
we have an authentic solo voice and piano version of the text published as
part of the 1899 publication of the *Wunderhorn* songs. I confess that I was
tempted at one stage to think that it must be the case that the symphonic
movement represented a *conversion* of what was originally a solo song in the
Wunderhorn series. But even a cursory glance at the MS of the choral/orches-
tral draft mentioned above precludes that possibility. Although the orchestral
reduction on two staves begins exactly as does Mahler's piano part in the solo
song, it later on turns into a typically sketchy outline, which could not
have been the case if Mahler had been working from a completed solo voice
version, e.g. something that would have been close to the version that Mahler
published as a solo voice 'arrangement' of the symphony's choral movement
in 1899. The composition sketch clearly demonstrates that the symphonic
movement *preceded* the solo voice version. It is fascinating to note that the
striking opening of the movement—boys' voices and bells—seems to have
been an afterthought, an imaginative, poetic little prelude which was scribbled
in after an altogether more conventional opening gesture had been conceived,
i.e. the boys delivering their first 'Bimm bamm' over the first bar of orchestral
accompaniment. The three bars of voices plus bells are laid out in their
familiar form in the draft full score of the movement that Mahler completed
in August 1895, a MS now in the Mary Flagler Cary Collection of the Pierpont Morgan Library and dated 'Sunday August 1895 [*sic*]. Holiday work
concluded.' (In the MS full score of the symphony, which forms part of the
Lehmann Deposit at the same library, the movement is dated Hamburg,

8 May 1896.) [We should not assume, I think, that the composition sketch I mention above was necessarily the *earliest* sketch for the movement, sketchy though indeed it becomes, particularly when we reach the later pages. At a very late moment in the writing of this book I alighted on the reproduction of the first page of a further MS of 'Es sungen drei Engel' (in Mahler's hand) that appeared as an illustration (p. 322) in a programme book of the Concertgebouw Orchestra, Amsterdam, of 12 January 1922, when Willem Mengelberg conducted a performance of the Third Symphony. This intriguing page (presumably the first page of a complete MS that was once in the possession of Alphons Jansen) shows a version (on four staves) for soprano and contralto soloists and chorus (with the orchestral part given as a piano reduction), in which there is no indication of the opening 'Bimm bamm' bells and in which the whole of the opening chorus as we are familiar with it today, i.e. from Fig. 1 to Fig. 3 in the published score, is laid out for the two solo voices and chorus: to begin with a simple alternation of soprano solo and chorus; then soprano and chorus; then contralto solo, followed by chorus with contralto solo; at which point the MS page comes to an end. What we have here, in fact, is a format that is close to the idea of *solo song with chorus*, whereas the final version is something different, *a choral movement*. There can be no doubt that this hitherto unexamined version represents an earlier stage in the evolution of the movement than the composition sketch. It was probable, in my view, that it was the very fact of this draft of the movement inclining in the direction of solo song that led Mahler to abandon it and devise a version in which the emphasis (*from the start*) was on the role of the chorus. One has to remember that a solo song, 'Das himmlische Leben', was the envisaged Finale, in which case a setting of 'Es sungen drei Engel' which was itself solo-song inflected (even though *with* chorus) would have offered too little contrast. It is teasing to have only one page of this sketch to scrutinize. What has happened to this important MS?]

22 It would seem that we owe the creation of 'Lob des hohen Verstandes' to Anna Bahr-Mildenburg (1872–1947). The following excerpt comes from the typescript of her lecture on Mahler, an English version of which was passed on to me many years ago by Erwin Stein. I have slightly mended Stein's English translation: 'I presented Mahler, shortly after I got to know him, with an early edition of *Des Knaben Wunderhorn* from my grandfather's library. At that time, he wrote to me: "Dear Mildenburgle [which means something like 'little Mildenburg'], You cannot realize how delighted I am with the charming book. It is so beautiful that its contents are almost new to me, and I am in danger of setting one or another Lied to music for the second time. This would then be your fault. I am only glad that I am not quite unworthy of this book, and thus, for once, have had a present which I have deserved a little bit beforehand. Immediately, I composed a merry little Lied which I shall call 'Lob des hohen Verstandes'. It deals with a competition between an old cuckoo and a nightingale, in which the donkey is to be the referee. Of course, he awards the prize to the cuckoo, with an air of great importance." ' Bauer-Lechner (NBL, p. 57) reports from Hamburg in September/October of the year in which 'Lob des hohen Verstandes' was composed (1896) that: 'With his coffee and cigarette, Mahler reads a bit. (*Des Knaben Wunderhorn*, Goethe and Nietzsche were on his programme when I was there . . .)'. There were, of course, two *Wunderhorn* songs still to be selected and composed before the collection that was published in 1899 was complete.

23 Mahler was correctly reported by Bauer-Lechner when she records his intention to base *two* song movements in the Third Symphony on *Wunderhorn* texts. In the summer of 1895 he was still contemplating using 'Das himmlische Leben' as the symphony's Finale. (See also GMB¹, p. 140.)

24 It is the independence of the voice and piano version that, until the composition sketch of June 1895 emerged, made it seem probable to me that the 'Morgenglocken' movement was a conversion of what had been originally a solo *Wunderhorn* song, i.e. that this was another instance of an existing *Wunderhorn* song being conscripted into symphonic service.

25 It was Wöss who was responsible for the piano-duet arrangement of the Third Symphony, published by U.E., and also for an arrangement for piano solo (!) of the so-called 'Glockenchor', i.e. 'Es sungen drei Engel' under yet another title. When preparing his version for solo voice and orchestra, Wöss of course followed the instrumental precedents set by the symphonic movement; and no doubt he also had to hand his (by then) published voice and piano arrangement. In the later arrangement, however—for orchestra—the textual discrepancy ('Bete zu Gott . . .') that I mention above on pp. 131f. has been corrected to 'Liebe nur Gott . . .', which no doubt reflects the fact that Wöss was working principally with the symphonic movement as his source and was no longer so closely in touch with Mahler's own voice and piano version. Thus Wöss's solo voice and orchestra version is closer to the symphony than to Mahler's solo voice setting. He could have made it a shade more authentic as a song for voice and orchestra if he had re-consulted Mahler's voice and piano version, especially with regard to the composer's disposition of the text in the closing section (from 'Hast du denn übertreten die zehen Gebot' onwards). This cunningly includes the complete concluding verse of the *Wunderhorn* poem, whereas Wöss omits part of it, i.e. 'Die himmlische Freud' ist eine selige Stadt' is included by Mahler but omitted by Wöss. It is the care Mahler took to preserve the integrity of the poem that also makes one speak of his voice and piano version as a setting in its own right.

26 How then *are* we to interpret Mahler's 1895 letter? Did he mean, I wonder, that he had a powerful intuition in the summer of 1893 that he was going to include the song in the symphony, and therefore completed its instrumentation, but—presumably because he was still uncertain, that summer, about the final details and shape of the symphony's last movement— confined himself in the first instance to an instrumentation that was appropriate to the song as an independent voice and orchestra item? (It also may have been the case that while Mahler foresaw that he might press the song into the symphony's service, he was still unsure about the precise placing of the song in the work's overall scheme.) The adjustment to bring the orchestration of 'Urlicht' into line with the resources of the symphony was made, as I point out on p. 136, at a surprisingly late stage, i.e. *after* December 1894, when the whole symphony already existed in MS, but with 'Urlicht' still in its orchestral song guise, so far as its instrumentation was concerned. All this suggests to me that it was possible that Mahler was thinking, when he wrote his letter, of the *final* revision of the instrumentation of the song, i.e. the modifications of the scoring that he introduced after 1894, doubtless in preparation for the first performance of the symphony in its entirety in 1895 (and eventual publication in 1897). Indeed, Mahler probably wrote the letter in question not long after he had been working on the retouching of the instrumentation. In n. 68, p. 283, I describe the Yale copyist's MS of the symphony, from which 'Urlicht' is missing. This was a copy made from Mahler's 1894 MS. That Mahler did not want 'Urlicht' copied from that MS, clearly shows that at this stage (in 1895) he had the orchestration of the song under review.

27 To be precise (which Mahler was not—quite): the MS fair copy of the full score of the second movement of the symphony is dated 11 April 1896; the third, 25 April; and the fifth, 8 May. So these three movements were certainly out of the way *before* Mahler's labours commenced in the summer of 1896. There is no date actually inscribed on the MS full score of the fourth movement, the Nietzsche setting, 'O Mensch! Gib Acht!', but we know (see also n. 21, p. 252) of an early draft of the movement in full score, entitled 'Was mir die Nacht erzählt [*sic*]!', which is one of three early orchestral drafts of the symphony's third, fourth and fifth movements in the possession of the Pierpont Morgan Library (Mary Flagler Cary Collection) New York. This orchestral draft of 'O Mensch! Gib Acht!' is undated, but the accompanying draft full score of the fifth movement ('Es sungen drei Engel') can be attributed, as we know, to [11] August 1895 (see n. 21 and the table on p. 142); and it seems safe to presume, since the MS drafts clearly belong together, that the Nietzsche song was drafted in the same period. (Incidentally, at one time a draft of the second movement, the Minuet, then entitled 'Was mir die Blumen auf der Wiese erzählen', formed part of this early MS full score, but has since become detached. Who has it?) Thus the Nietzsche setting, too, was substantially done before the summer of 1896. (As I point out in n. 21, p. 253, the condensed score of the movement dated Steinbach, summer 1896, was probably made for practical purposes.) The MS full score of the final Adagio is inscribed 22 November 1896, a month or so *after* the completion of the full score of the first movement on 17 October. The chronological contradiction, however, is more apparent than real. The date at the end of the Adagio undoubtedly records the date on which Mahler applied the finishing touches to the full score of the movement: it is not an indication of the date of composition (cf. the date at the end of the first movement, which is

a similar case). It is my guess that, for Mahler—particularly bearing in mind the remarkable fluidity of his compositional processes at this time—'already composed' would mean 'already drafted'; very probably sketched out in manuscript, but perhaps sometimes only sketched out in his mind. It is perfectly clear, for instance, as I point out in n. 21, p. 253, where I examine the complex chronology of the Third Symphony in greater detail, that a substantial amount of drafting and sketching of materials for the first movement must have been accomplished *before* the summer of 1896, even though we correctly attribute the 'composition' of the movement to that period; and Mahler would have been working during that summer, not only on earlier drafts and sketches (there are indeed dated sketches from 1895, while one of two leaves of sketches for the first movement in the Library of Stanford University, California, is dated Steinbach, 1893!, though according to HG¹ (p. 796), this sketch of the theme in the first movement at Fig. 11 is not in Mahler's hand), but also on ideas that he would have been carrying about in his head. We should also remember that the end date of the Adagio reflects what would logically have been the chronological case: i.e. the last touches to the Finale would have been made when all its predecessors were *in situ*.

28 I follow Bekker, who was presumably following Mahler, in allotting No. 5 both to the projected Scherzo and *Wunderhorn* Finale. As we know from the various sketch programmes that exist for the Third Symphony, Mahler was often uncertain not only about the order of the movements but about the actual number of movements a work was to contain. The duplication of No. 5 in this scheme for a fourth symphony most probably reflects the tentativeness and indecision characteristic of Mahler at an early planning stage. One may also note in passing Mahler's specification of E flat minor for No. 2, 'Das irdische Leben'. The song, in fact, is in a Phrygian B flat minor, and for clarity and convenience of notation Mahler wrote it out in six flats. One further notes that the 'real' key of the song is also the key of the 'Purgatorio' movement in the Tenth Symphony, with which the song is associated, though in the 'Purgatorio' the Phrygian inflection is absent.

29 When he was working on the Fourth Symphony, Mahler said to Bauer-Lechner in the summer of 1900: 'Actually I only wanted to write a symphonic Humoresque, and out of it came a symphony of the normal dimensions . . .' (NBL, p. 143). Perhaps Mahler was thinking of the abandoned draft programme?

30 The projected fifth movement clearly seems to be a reference to what we know now as the Scherzo (same key!) of the Fifth Symphony (see NBL, p. 165), and Bekker points out that at one stage Mahler's plans for the Eighth Symphony had included a 'Caritas' Adagio (see PB, p. 145). I think we can regard 'Die Welt als ewige Jetztzeit' ('The World as Eternal Present') as a suppressed title for the first movement of the Fourth, suppressed before the movement was even composed but retrospectively relevant in the light of the movement that Mahler *did* compose. There is no doubt that this draft programme must belong to the time when Mahler was engaged on the Third

Symphony and still uncertain as to the exact disposition of the wealth of invention and creative ideas available to him. Already, it seems, even before the final shape of one symphony was determined, the shape of another was materializing (see also my thoughts on this subject on pp. 41–2). For the almost day-by-day modifications of Mahler's schemes we only need to refer to his programme for the Third Symphony, which ran through any number of versions before the sequence of movements as we know it was finally adopted. All this, surely, is a manifestation of the kind of creativity that Boulez (PBZ) has in mind when describing (in the Preface to the Philharmonia pocket score of *Das klagende Lied*) Mahler's music *in toto* as an epic musical continuum. (What Mahler said to Bauer-Lechner in 1893 (NBL, p. 8) is peculiarly apt in this context: 'My two symphonies [I and II] contain my whole life; I have written down there everything I have experienced and endured—truth and poetry in notes. And if someone really understood how to read them, my life would be transparently revealed to him there. Creativity and experience are so intimately linked in me that, if my future existence were to flow onwards as peacefully as a meadow brook, I don't think that I would ever again be able to create anything worth while.') To return to the Fourth for a moment: whereas the Fourth Symphony that Mahler wrote progresses from its first movement to its last and plots a course that finally ascends to a vision of heaven, the Fourth he did not compose was to concentrate much more sharply on the *contrast* between the earthly and the heavenly life, with two of the *Wunderhorn* songs functioning as opposite poles within the total scheme. It was certainly an intriguing conception, though much obviously would have depended on the character of the central 'Caritas' Adagio, the one movement of which, musically speaking, we have no information outside Bekker. It remains a singular fact that the other four movements outlined in the programme are all to be found embedded in the Third, Fourth and Fifth Symphonies and *Wunderhorn* songs. Last point: one cannot but note that the Fourth that we know forgoes the rich mixtures and contrasts of the sketch programme in favour of a much more rigorous organization, one regulated in fact by just *one* aspect of 'Das himmlische Leben': the song's eventful progression from G major to E major. The programme of the symphony was narrowed down finally to the dramatic idea expressed symbolically in its most abbreviated form by the song's tonal organization.

31 All dates should be interpreted with caution, for the reasons I state on p. 158.

32 See n. 20, p. 251.

33 Some commentators, e.g., HFR, p. 275, and HG[1], p. 769, suggest that 'Der Schildwache Nachtlied' was initially drafted in Leipzig, *c.* 1888. There is a reference to the song, which would associate it with Mahler's Leipzig period, in Bauer-Lechner (pp. 162–3), which reads as follows: 'Mahler told me that, in Leipzig, after finishing the "Pintos" with Weber . . . he had wanted to write an opera of his own. He suggested the following subject to Weber for a libretto, outlining it in detail. [Bauer-Lechner includes here the outline of the plot, which involves the rescue of a soldier from the gallows by a young girl, whose compassion is excited by his plight. Though the soldier himself is beginning to love the girl, he is ashamed of owing his life to her pity, and thus rejects her offer of freedom and marriage and declares his preference for death. In the last act, the conflict is resolved, the girl ardently pleading and confessing her love.] Weber, however, had immediately altered this simple story. He introduced the young man's earlier love and sweetheart; this ran quite counter to Mahler's intentions and led him soon to abandon the whole idea.' Bauer-Lechner then remarks that the *Wunderhorn* song, 'Der Schildwache Nachtlied', survives as a 'first attempt' at this operatic subject, and adds that Mahler owes to this project his renewed acquaintance with the *Wunderhorn* anthology, which was to become so important to him.

The documentary 'evidence' produced in HG[1] is riddled with confusion, and for the reasons I give at some length in DM[3], pp. 1350-1, I see no sense in attributing the inception of the song to 1888. One wonders why, if the song was indeed composed at about the same time that Mahler was writing his first series of *Wunderhorn* songs (the *Lieder und Gesänge*), it was omitted from the 1892 publication? One notes also that Bauer-Lechner attributes Mahler's renewed acquaintance with the *Wunderhorn* anthology to this operatic project, thereby introducing a fresh strand into the already sufficiently complex texture of his relationship to that literary source. I must confess, too, that I find it difficult to envisage exactly what the proposed connection was between the song and the theatrical enterprise. Was 'Der Schildwache Nachtlied' to be a song in the opera—or what?

It is undoubtedly of interest in this connection that when Mahler conducted a performance of 'Der Schildwache Nachtlied' at Wiesbaden on 17 November 1893, the following description appeared in the programme in brackets after the song's title: 'eine Scene aus dem Lagerleben' ['a scene from camp life']. It may be that this relates in some way to Bauer-Lechner's reminiscence of the connection of this song with an earlier dramatic idea. See also HG[1], pp. 283-4, who, however, has the wrong date for the concert and offers contradictory information about the conductor of the songs in his main text and accompanying footnotes. It was, as I write above, Mahler himself.

34 I can see no justification at all for the modern practice of distributing the implied dialogue of certain *Wunderhorn* songs between *two* singers. Mahler, I am sure, did not have this possibility in mind. He would have expected a capable singer to have been able to characterize each role sufficiently, without recourse to a partner. The dialogue, in short, should be made explicit by the soloist's capacity for 'acting' with—and through—his (or her) voice (the kind of voice, in fact, in which Mahler himself was interested). A duet performance is alien to the songs' conception, damages their individual unities, and vulgarizes their contents.

35 The treadmill figuration of 'Das irdische Leben' seems to have returned to Mahler's mind when working on the 'Purgatorio' third movement of his Tenth Symphony—another case of the consistency of Mahler's imagery.

36 Mahler's original title—'Lob der Kritik'—confirms that he conceived this song, in part at least, as a hit at his critics. There is a clear recollection of it in the introductory flourish to the Finale of the Fifth Symphony (cf. the music example from the song which forms part of n. 95, p. 295):

It is possible, I think, that the reminiscence has a real point to it, i.e. it is a sardonic reference in the context of a highly sophisticated and artfully contrapuntal Finale to a song which was aimed at those with long ears, and of lofty intellectual equipment, who prefer the cuckoo's song to the nightingale's. Mahler was not free from sensitivity about his contrapuntal technique (he once lamented the fact that he had missed a 'thorough grounding' in counterpoint at the Vienna Conservatoire (NBL, p. 138)), and I fancy there was something of a deliberate gesture of defiance in his recollection of the *Wunderhorn* song in the Finale of the Fifth, as if he were daring the donkeys to fault his contrapuntal art—and half expecting them to do just that, at the same time. (See also n. 30, p. 374.)

37 It is exactly this dramatic tension between expectation and contradiction that we find in the orchestral songs of Kurt Weill, who was surely much influenced by this aspect of Mahler's highly original treatment of his materials, above all when deliberately 'popular' invention was involved. One feels that for Weill, the *Wunderhorn* songs must have had a special technical significance.

38 This was made up of members of the orchestra of the then Royal Opera House, Budapest, of which Mahler was Director.

39 'Five years ago', says Beer, which must have been information garnered at the time of the première from, as it were, 'inspired' sources (or sources 'close to the composer': from where else?). Five years ago would put us back to 1884! (See also n. 13, p. 246.) Could it really be that the First Symphony was already complete by 1884, as Beer suggests? It seems improbable to me. What is more probable is that Mahler launched out on the first movement of his projected symphonic poem, in which case the inextricably tangled chonology of the *Gesellen* cycle and the symphony's first movement becomes ever more likely and indeed meaningful. It also becomes clearer that we *do* have to think in terms of 1884 when locating the inception of the First Symphony.

40 This remark would tend to confirm the recapitulatory repeat in the original version of the symphony of the famous drum and cymbal din that initiates the Finale, a duplication Mahler sensibly subjected to later revision (see pp. 205–6).

41 Had Mahler followed up this idea of treating his first movement as an independent symphonic poem, then he would have left us an example of the genre which paid tribute, very consciously and deliberately so, I think, to the principles of symphonic first movement—i.e. sonata—form. After the free and unconventional forms of the First Symphony, it seems that Mahler went out of his way to demonstrate his command of traditional formal procedures. In many respects, the first movement of the Second Symphony, for all its huge romantic scale, is one of the most classical in principle of Mahler's first movements, anticipating the first movements of the Sixth and Seventh Symphonies. The independent symphonic poem idea in any event was surely in part *faut de mieux*, a consequence of the paralysing indecision that overtook Mahler after the first movement was done. (See pp. 165f.)

42 In the published score, the tempo indication is 'Immer sehr gemächlich', and there is no identification of the Introduction as such (no mention of 'Einleitung', that is). The EMS (earliest MS source) of the symphony is similarly blank in this respect. The indication that the first movement opened with an Introduction was probably something that Mahler thought might help his first audience, especially in view of the absence of a more detailed programme (for the Hamburg performance in 1893 (see pp. 158–9) Mahler made a programmatic distinction between the Introduction and the Allegro, by giving the Introduction its own explanation). Possibly for the same reason, he employed French when indicating the character of the fourth movement and Italian (rather than the elaborate and idiosyncratic German terminology which already abounds in the EMS) for his indications of tempi and musical character. At least the problem of finding adequate equivalents in Hungarian was thereby avoided!

43 At the Budapest performance, writes Löhr, in GMB¹ (pp. 481–2), in an annotation to Letter 67, '. . . a considerable part of the public, here as elsewhere uncharitably uncomprehending in the face of formal novelty, was disagreeably startled out of its customary thoughtlessness by the dynamic violence of tragic expression which here bursts forth. One elegant lady near me was so shocked by the Attacca leading into the last movement that she dropped a number of articles she had been holding in her hands.'

44 We must all be indebted to M. de La Grange for locating and reproducing a copy of the 1893 Hamburg programme, which allows us to see precisely what was the programmatic scaffolding that Mahler erected for this occasion. Many Mahler students will have had their first impression of the programme from Paul Stefan (pp. 113–14) or from Paul Bekker (p. 358), who was in fact following PS. If one compares Stefan's programme with the authentic Hamburg version, some interesting variants emerge, which one must attribute to the slight differences between the programmes for Hamburg and Weimar that Stefan himself mentions, though in a somewhat desultory and ill-organized manner. (Although Stefan made clear (p. 48) that at Budapest the First Symphony was launched as a Symphonic Poem, he omits to mention in connection with the Hamburg performance that the Symphonic Poem became 'A Tone-poem in the form of a Symphony' and contents himself with stating, after quoting the (Weimar?) programme, 'The whole is entitled "Titan".')

The differences between Stefan's account and the Hamburg programme cannot be entirely due to simple carelessness on Stefan's part. Indeed, it seems likely to me that Stefan was in fact transcribing the *later* Weimar programme in his book, not the first Hamburg version of it. If this supposition is correct, then the differences seem worth spelling out, for which reason I allot a column in the table on p. 158 to the 1894 Weimar performance. Stefan was wrong in attributing the Hamburg performance to 1892, which error in itself suggests that it was not the Hamburg programme that he had to hand when making his transcription. There may be something to be learned, then, from comparing Stefan's account with the authentic printed Hamburg version. I wonder, therefore, if HG[1], p. 748, is right in suggesting that for Weimar in 1894 'the same programme and the same titles were used' as for Hamburg in 1893. The evidence of Stefan would suggest that for Weimar some significant modifications were introduced, e.g. the introduction to the first movement was no longer evoking Nature's awakening from the sleep of winter but depicting the onset of early dawn, a minor modification of the programme, but one of real substance. (See also JBF, p. 410.)

45 Pfohl, in his characteristically voluminous review of the Hamburg performance in the *Hamburger Nachrichten*, 28 October 1893, refers to the work as 'this Titan-Symphony', and this sensible and economical mode of reference may have prompted Mahler towards the later formulation of the title that is to be found on the deleted title-page of the EMS (cf. the table, p. 159), in Mahler's own hand, and which clearly seems to me to represent a post-Hamburg performance stage and one that Mahler reached not long before the programme and the title were dropped altogether and the work reformulated as a four-movement symphony. This, in fact, is an *inside* title-page. (Mahler wrote it out on the inside cover of his bound copy of the MS.) M. de La Grange, in HG[1], p. 747, ascribes this title-page without reservation to the summer of 1893, but it would seem to me to be of later origin. The title-page is self-evidently a step or two closer to the stage when Mahler finally settled for 'Symphony' as the overall description of his work; and I think it improbable that he alighted on the more economic and factual inscription in the summer of 1893, only to reject it in favour of the much more cumbersome and elaborate title and programme which in fact accompanied the Hamburg performance a few months later. M. de La Grange makes the point that the title-page includes the 'Blumine' movement, which was finally discarded after the 1894 Weimar performance. It is true, too, that the Weimar programme (see the table, p. 158) is virtually identical with the Hamburg programme. But this does not mean, I think, that we are obliged to regard the EMS title-page as a draft *preceding* the formulation of the Hamburg and Weimar programme. (If this were the case, then perhaps the draft is related to the incident recounted by Pfohl, to which I refer at the end of this note.) It seems to me possible, because of the simplification of the programme and above all, as I mention on p. 160, because of the upgrading of Symphony as a component in the overall designation, that the EMS title-page might have been Mahler's last shot at reconciling the conflicting aims of 'Symphony' and programmatic 'Tone-poem', and one that may have been made and scribbled out *after* the Weimar performance. Soon after, maybe. For though we know that 'Blumine' was omitted after the Weimar performance, there may well have been an interim period, however brief, in which Mahler was still toying with the idea of a five-movement symphony, the shape of which (shades of Berlioz) would be clarified or justified by an accompanying programme. It was not to be; and along with 'Blumine', the programme was jettisoned for ever. The chronological point is scarcely of major importance. Of more significance, indeed, is the further proof the EMS title-page brings —no matter when it was formulated—of the dichotomy that persisted in Mahler's mind whenever he tried to find the right verbal formula to account for a symphony that was also a tone-poem (and vice versa). It may have been —indeed it probably was the case—that 'Titan' was performed at Weimar under the same overall title as at Hamburg, some months earlier. Nonetheless, it is striking that in correspondence dating from this period, and in particular the letters which refer to the Weimar event, Mahler refers consistently to 'my Symphony', not 'my Tone-poem'—which was perhaps an indication of the direction in which his mind was moving in the matter of finally settling the category to which the work belonged and was no less a sign of the ambivalence to which I have already referred.

Pfohl, in his laborious memoirs (FP, p. 17), claims to have had a hand in devising the symphony's literary framework, writing thus:

> When Gustav Mahler was working on his First Symphony, he repeatedly played me the essential parts from the sketches and from the movements as they were completed. He was frenziedly in search of an imposing and audacious title for this, his first symphony. 'I implore you, let me have a name for the symphony!' I told him: 'Call it the "Nature Symphony" or something similar, and give the third movement the designation: "Funeral march in the manner of Callot", for it is extremely singular: grotesque, bizarre, a fantastic spectacle . . .' But he hesitated, for he did not possess the 'Fantasy pieces in the manner of Callot' [by E. T. A. Hoffmann]. As chance would have it, that same day I saw a handsome edition of these famous fantasy pieces displayed in a bookshop window; I purchased it and brought it to him. A few days later Mahler informed me that he had now finally found a suitable title for his symphony. 'I am calling it: Titan . . .' The name had been suggested to him by one of the musical enthusiasts among his friends. But then, when the symphony, dressed up to kill in the hollow title, was performed in Hamburg and later in Weimar and was given a very disapproving, indeed almost annihilating notice in the press, Mahler erased the not very fortunate designation.

Those fustian reminiscences probably need to be taken with a fair pinch of salt ('I implore you . . .' etc.). Moreover, one has to remember that Mahler was not composing the symphony at Hamburg (which Pfohl seems to imply) but revising it. But there are one or two points of mild interest: for example, the description of the Funeral March, for which Pfohl claims he was responsible, and the absence of any mention of the Jean Paul novel in connection with the discovery of the overall title 'Titan' ('The name had been suggested to him by one of . . . his friends.') (See also pp. 225–35.)

46 The concert took place in Berlin on 16 March 1896, when Mahler conducted the First Symphony, the probable first performance of the *Lieder eines fahrenden Gesellen* and the first movement (still billed as 'Todtenfeier') of the C minor Symphony (though the programme ran in the reverse order). The details of the programme were as follows:

1. 'Todtenfeier' (I. Satz aus der Symphonie in C-moll für grosses Orchester.)

2. Lieder eines fahrenden Gesellen, für eine tiefe Stimme mit Orchesterbegleitung, gesungen von Herrn Anton Sistermans [the Dutch bass, 1865–1926].

3. Symphonie in D-dur für grosses Orchester.
   No. 1. Einleitung und Allegro comodo
   No. 2. Scherzo
   No. 3. Alla Marcia funebre; hierauf sogleich
   No. 4. Allegro furioso

It is curious that in this 1896 programme neither symphony is numbered, though a year *earlier*, when the first three movements of the Second were given their first performance, they were billed as such:

3 Sätze a.d. Symphonie No. 2 (z. I. Mal)
   I. Allegro maestoso   ⎫ Diese 3 Sätze bilden
  II. Andante con moto   ⎬ den I. Theil der
 III. (Scherzo) Allegro comodo ⎭ Symphonie.
     (Unter Leitung des Componisten.)

In the programme book of the same concert (notes by Dr. H. Reimann), however, this item was announced as 'Drei Sätze *aus einer Symphonie*' [my italics].

It is significant that on the occasion (1896) when Mahler renounced the programme for the D major symphony, he introduced at the same time alongside it the work—the song-cycle—out of which the symphony materialized, not only in a purely musical sense (i.e. a shared fund of invention) but also in a programmatic sense. Who can doubt that the hero of the *Gesellen* cycle continued his travels in the First Symphony, and only stopped when Mahler's own death put an end to his hero's epic chronicle? That Mahler was able in Berlin in 1896 to dispense with a programme for the First Symphony was surely due to the fact that the *Gesellen* cycle in itself provided the best of all programme notes for—the most penetrating of glosses on—the symphony. In the relationship of the first song-cycle and First Symphony we find the clue to the concept of the inner programme (or drama) which, implicitly or

The Berlin Philharmonic concert schedule (1894/5)

explicitly, played from the outset such an important role in Mahler's symphonic music.

47 Perhaps one of the 'past experiences' of which Mahler was ruefully thinking was the disagreeable experience (for such it must have been) of reading a hostile review, by Joseph Sittard, of the Hamburg performance of the 'Titan' Symphony. The programme certainly did nothing to aid Herr Sittard's comprehension of what Mahler was about. I reproduce his notice in its entirety as an Appendix (see pp. 238–41) because it documents very vividly the antipathies and resistances aroused by Mahler's music. Sittard (1846–1903) was appointed music critic of the *Hamburgischer Correspondent* in 1885.

48 On the other hand, in the same letter to Marschalk from which I have just quoted, Mahler confirms that, so far as the third movement was concerned, the programme actually disclosed the true source of the stimulus which led to the movement taking the shape, and having the character, it did: 'As regards the third movement (marcia funebre) it is certainly the case that I received the external stimulus for it from the well-known children's picture ('The Hunter's Funeral Procession'). In this case, however, what is represented is irrelevant—the main thing is the mood which is expressed, and from which, as suddenly as the lightning from a dark cloud, the fourth movement bursts. It is simply the outcry of a heart wounded to the quick, which is preceded by just that uncannily and ironically brooding oppressiveness of the funeral march. Ironically in the sense of the Aristotelian "eironeia".' It is interesting that Mahler, in attempting to explicate the symphony without a programmatic prop, in fact leans heavily on the programme that had been issued and then withdrawn. This suggests that the programme did, in some major respects at least, have a real bearing on the contents of the symphony. I think the truth was, for all Mahler's protestations (and see HG[1], p. 596, for further evidence of the *anti*-programmatic stance he was taking *c*. 1900), that he *needed* his programmes—they were a necessary adjunct to his composing process, as I hope to show in this book. (He observed to Bauer-Lechner, that Beethoven, after all, had his 'inner' (albeit unstated) programmes, with the clear implication that where Beethoven led, he might follow.) The teasing question for Mahler was to try to decide whether his audiences needed to know the programme that *he* knew (and had needed) himself. This was never satisfactorily resolved; and as I point out more than once elsewhere, the public reception of Mahler's early works cannot have encouraged him to have confidence in the illuminating powers of an inner programme made verbally (i.e. outwardly) explicit. Ferdinand Pfohl (see FP, p. 19) had the following observation to make on Mahler's ambiguous relationship with his programmes:

> He withheld indications of their poetic content from his symphonies after the less than cheering experiences with the 'Titan' Symphony. 'Programme?... meaning?... let them find it out for themselves...!' And when he said 'them', he meant the public. On top of the obstinacy with which he denies his symphonies programmatic indications from the

Third onwards, Mahler also forgets that the 'filter', that receiving organ of the imagination, works differently in every listener, and that his persistence in trying to ensure for his programme symphonies the deceptive appearance of 'absolute music' will result in his work being delivered over to arbitrary interpretation.

There can be no doubt that Mahler in later years was anxious to disentangle himself from his programmes, in which aim he was certainly encouraged by the development of his own music away from the explicitly programmatic area. (See also 'GM und die Programm-Musik' by Richard Braungart, *Musikalische Rundschau*, Munich, Jahrg. I, 6, 1906, pp. 83–6.) Nonetheless, even in 1900, when (as I mention above) HG[1] reminds us of the anti-programmatic platform on which he was prepared to stand in public, we find him still tacitly (if somewhat subterraneously) acknowledging the importance of the programme. In HG[1], pp. 748–9, there is set out the text of a programme that Natalie Bauer-Lechner sent the Viennese critic, Ludwig Karpath, the authenticity of which seems to be beyond doubt, since it coincides in many particulars with the programme she divulges in NBL, pp. 149–150. The interesting thing about the Karpath 'edition' of the programme is first, that it materialized in connection with the first Vienna performance of the symphony, for which occasion, at Mahler's special request, the customary programme-book analysis was *not* provided for the public; and second, that the quite lengthy descriptions of the Funeral March and Finale, which do not form part of the programme as it appears in NBL, are in themselves as revealing as anything in the 'official' programme that accompanied the Hamburg and Weimar performances (indeed, perhaps more revealing). That Karpath might be briefed by Natalie (one cannot but think with Mahler's sanction), while the public, programmatically speaking, was to be kept in the dark—this is a characteristic instance of the kind of ambiguity of decision that seemed to descend on Mahler when he was thinking about these sensitive areas of his art to which, in fact, clear-cut principles could not, and still cannot, be applied. With the right hand he did one thing; with the left quite another. It is an aspect of his personality that has to be kept in mind, especially when considering the statements he made at various times about his own music.

The amplifying commentaries on the third and fourth movements of the symphony in the Karpath text run as follows (as quoted by HG[1]):

'... Of the third, *Bruder Martin* movement, Mahler recently said: 'Now he (my hero) has found a hair in his soup and his entire meal is ruined.' ... The situation can be imagined thus: A funeral procession passes by; all the misery and all the sorrow of the world strikes our hero with its biting contrasts and its dreadful irony. The *Bruder Martin* funeral march must be imagined played by a cheap band, such as one hears at country funerals; it draws near, takes shape and disappears, thus finally becoming what it is. In the midst of this, all the coarseness, the mirth and the banality of the world are heard in the sound of a Bohemian village band, together with the hero's terrible cries of pain. In its biting irony and contrasting polyphony, it is the most moving moment! Particularly when, after a wonderful interlude, the funeral procession returns and a soul-piercing 'gay tune' is heard.

The last movement follows without pause, on a terrifying shriek. Our hero is now exposed to the most fearful combats and to all the sorrows of the world. He and his triumphant motifs are 'hit on the head again and again' by destiny. Once more he seems for a moment to get to his feet and become the master of his fate again. But only when he has triumphed over death, and when all the glorious memories of youth have returned with themes from the first movement, does he get the upper hand: and there is a great victorious chorale! . . .'

49 The MS is in the Mengelberg-Stiftung, Amsterdam. At some stage or other Mahler struck through the words 'Symphony in C minor'. Perhaps this was the moment when he was overtaken by the difficulties of continuing the symphony and decided to think (if only temporarily) of the movement as an entirely independent symphonic (or tone) poem, 'Todtenfeier'? (See also n. 41, p. 261, and n. 46, p. 265.) He was still using the title as late as March 1896, though by then 'Todtenfeier' was established as the first movement of his Second, C minor Symphony. It may be the fact that the movement was played alone in the programme in 1896 that caused Mahler to resurrect the old title once again in public print. It is instructive to compare the 1895 and 1896 billings of this movement, which I set out in n. 46 above.

An examination of the Amsterdam MS (Mengelberg-Stiftung) of the 'Todtenfeier' movement leaves one in very little doubt that the programmatic title was of a later origin than the descriptive title 'Symphonie in C-moll', etc. If one compares the ink and penmanship of this title with the inscription of the date and location at the end of the MS, it is clear that both sets of inscriptions were effected at about the same time, i.e. when the movement was first written out in full score. The programmatic title, a later addition, was substituted when Mahler crossed out his original symphonic designation. So it was as the first movement of a new Symphony in C minor (Mahler's First, at that time!) that the grand funeral march was launched. This first version of the Second Symphony's first movement is an outstandingly fascinating MS. At this stage in the evolution of the movement, the instrumentation was relatively modest. It is instructive to compare the constitution of the orchestra Mahler was writing for in 1888 with the orchestra that he required for the movement in the published version of the complete work:

ORCHESTRA

1888	**Published score (1897)**
3 flutes (incl. picc.)	2 flutes
	2 piccolos (1 doubling 3rd flute)
2 oboes	3 oboes (3 doubling c.a.)
1 cor anglais	

2 clarinets	3 clarinets in B flat (3 doubling bass clarinet)
1 bass clarinet	2 clarinets in E flat
3 bassoons	3 bassoons (incl. double bassoon)
4 horns	6 horns
3 trumpets	4 trumpets
3 trombones	4 trombones
1 bass tuba	1 bass tuba
Perc.	*Perc.*
Triangle	Triangle
Cymbals	2 Tam-tams (high and low)
Bass drum	Cymbals
Timpani	Bass drum
	Timpani (2 players)
1 harp	2 harps
Strings	Strings

It is true, as the late Erwin Ratz states in his Preface to the critical edition of the score of the Second Symphony, that in all almost all major respects, but for the instrumentation, the substance of the music did not vary between the draft of 1888 and the revision of 1894 (see also n. 50 below). But it is not quite correct, as Ratz suggested, that there was only one section of the movement that Mahler altered (i.e. abbreviated) in his renovation of the 1888 MS in 1894. In addition to the passage specified by Ratz, i.e. from four bars after Fig. 15 to the double bar, which Mahler tightened up to brilliant effect, there is also evidence in the 1888 MS of re-working, i.e. re-composing, at bar 220, after which bar Mahler made a significant excision (some nine bars or so, according to my calculation) and then continued with bar 221, virtually as we know it today. This first excision is to be found on pp. 17–19 of the Amsterdam MS and it clearly shows that Mahler had elaborated other compositional ideas on an appreciable scale before he settled for the modification that he adopted in the 1894 MS. This is an extensively crossed-out excerpt in the MS and it may well have been the case that it received revisionary attention from the composer when he was working on the score in 1888, and was then looked at and modified further during the course of the revision of 1894. Incidentally, the tempo indication at the start of the movement in the 1888 version was 'Maëstoso' [*sic*].

*　　*　　*　　*

50 The inscription at the end of the Finale reads: 'Finished on Tuesday, 18 December 1894, at Hamburg.' The MS full score of the symphony is in the Mengelberg-Stiftung, Amsterdam. Another MS full score of the Second Symphony (in a copyist's hand and lacking 'Urlicht') is at Yale University Library (Osborn Collection), while a copyist's MS of the first three movements was at one time in the possession of Bruno Walter (see n. 52, p. 274).

The complete Amsterdam MS of the Second Symphony unfolds all manner of absorbing musical information. There are, as we have already known, two dates only inscribed on the MS, one at the end of the first movement, 'Sunday, 29 April 1894, renovatum'—one recalls Mahler's use of this last word in connection with parts of the First Symphony (the first movement of the Second, one notices, was *not* 'umgearbeitet', as was the Finale of the First, which a comparison of the 1888 and 1894 MSS goes to confirm)—and at the end of the Finale, 'Tuesday, 18 December 1894'.

The first movement is written in black ink on Böhme paper, Hamburg, No. 20, with the first signature showing perhaps a finer penmanship distinct from the rest of the movement, though I do not know that any chronological significance can be attributed to this variation (if it be such). There are the customary blue pencil corrections in Mahler's hand, and a whole array of additional dynamics. The movement is marked Nro. I.

The Andante follows, written in the same ink (though the first page has faded somewhat), and is marked Nro. 2. An interesting feature of this MS is an additional bit of composition that Mahler evidently undertook after the original draft of the full score was completed. The passage in question, inscribed 'Einlage' by Mahler, can be identified by referring to the printed score, i.e. the bars between Figs. 9 and 10—the very beautiful expansion and extension of the flute and clarinets tune in the immediately preceding four bars—was an inspired afterthought.

We find a similar but more important expansion in the ensuing Scherzo, which is marked Nro. 3 (the last four signatures of this movement are written on paper with the imprint Böhme, No. 20). The expansion can again be clarified by reference to the printed score. In Mahler's original MS draft, the unique E major passage for a quartet of trumpets (beginning at Fig. 40) consisted of two statements of the tune, i.e. the first statement at Fig. 40 was originally followed by the second, again for trumpet quartet, at Fig. 42. Mahler clearly found this sequence lacking in contrast and thus introduced the intervening statement of the tune for woodwind which in the published edition is installed between Figs. 41 and 42. This whole passage (Figs. 40–43) has always been recognized as one of the movement's most striking moments (it is, after all, of crucial thematic and tonal significance), but the final shape and scale of it, we now realize, evolved at a very late stage in the composition of the Scherzo. (On the other hand, what turned out to be the movement's preview of the Finale, nine bars after Fig. 50 et seq., was there, one must presume, as part of the first draft of the movement.)

The unique trumpet music is not the only passage on which Mahler worked after the first MS draft of the Scherzo was done. Another, of equal interest and significance, is the 'call to attention' for drum solo that opens the Scherzo. In the first MS draft of the movement, this dramatic prelude for timpani did not exist at all: the movement began *precisely* as the orchestral *Wunderhorn* song begins, though with the song's double-bass pizzicato ostinato transferred to the timpani, i.e. the Scherzo began initially as at bar 5 of the published version (cf. with bar 1 et seq. of the 'Fischpredigt'). At a later stage Mahler introduced the idea of the dramatic prelude for solo drum, no doubt because he wished to make a much clearer interruption in mood after the serene end of the Andante than that first provided by the Scherzo, when it was based on a literal transcription of the opening of the song. The solo drum prelude certainly does perform that function; and there is an inserted page in the Amsterdam MS in which he carries through this important modification and expansion of the original draft. What is astonishing, however, is to find that the brilliant and highly dramatic re-introduction of the drum prelude at bar 482, just after the movement's climactic peak, was an even later inspiration on Mahler's part. It cannot have occurred to him at the same time as he conceived the idea of the drum prelude itself, because the Amsterdam MS shows no sign of the now familiar timpani intervention at this point: all we have in the MS is the sustained drum roll, across which the (second) drum erupts in the published version. So this startling but marvellously 'right' recapitulation of the new opening of the movement was generated as an afterthought by an inspiration that was itself an afterthought.

This is by no means the end of the story, so far as this particular passage is concerned. For a start, when Mahler first alighted on the idea of his timpani prelude, it was in a much more extended and elaborate version (a rhythmic and dynamic dialogue for two players; see Appendix F) than the four-bar version that we know today. It is a slightly abbreviated version of this extended version of the prelude in Mahler's MS that was initially followed by the copyist in the Yale MS mentioned above, and then further compressed by the composer (see n. 68, C., p. 283f.: the accuracy of Colin Matthews's 'reconstruction' is confirmed by the evidence of the Amsterdam MS). Mahler obviously worked extremely hard to get this passage right. This is not only clear from the inserted page on which the opening of the movement is written out afresh, but also—and even more emphatically—from the timpani part for the Scherzo and the first movement (in Mahler's own hand!) which luckily has been preserved as part of the Amsterdam MS (the first movement and Scherzo in sequence together because, as I explain elsewhere, at one stage in the evolution of the symphony, this was the envisaged order of the movements). That this instrumental part was preserved was doubtless due to the fact that it also contains an independent pencil version of the passage (in the copyist's hand?), which attempts to summarize neatly Mahler's intentions at this stage (see Appendix F).

The final point to be recorded about the MS of the Scherzo is an enigmatic blue pencil mark over the very last bar of the movement, where Mahler writes boldly the word 'Coda'. More than that, in the same blue pencil, he drew a vertical line that exactly coincides with the penultimate bar line, for almost the whole length of the page, thus isolating—detaching, as it were—the final bar itself. At what stage Mahler made these enigmatic marks we do not know; and we can only guess at what he had in mind. Did he think at one stage that the movement required an expansion, an extension, and that it was the final bar that should be filled out into a coda? We have seen how conscious Mahler was of the *proportions* of his middle movements by the expansions we have already noted in the Andante and Scherzo. It is as if Mahler, when he had the middle movements assembled in full score, scrutinized them carefully from just this point of view, extending a crucial passage here and there for the sake of a movement's individual proportions and perhaps also on account of the proportions of the middle movements in relation to the dimensions of the symphony as a whole. I wonder too—though this can only be speculation—if Mahler had these thoughts about a coda when (if such was the case) he was contemplating a scheme for the symphony in which the Scherzo was immediately succeeded by the Finale. (See also pp. 185–6 and n. 70, p. 285.) Was it the eventual placing of 'Urlicht' that displaced the need for a coda?

'Urlicht' itself presents its own set of enigmas (see pp. 184–7 and notes 26 and 68, pp. 256f. and 284), and we are confronted by a characteristic example in this Amsterdam MS of the symphony. As I have noted above, the copyist's MS of the work at Yale does *not* contain 'Urlicht', though we know (see pp. 136f.) of a MS full score of the orchestral song version dated Steinbach, 19 July 1893. The Amsterdam MS *does* contain the song. Indeed, it also contains the cover of the original brown paper folder in which the MS of the song was inserted. This still has its original label on it (in a copyist's hand?), which reads:

Urlicht—
aus den Knaben Wunderhorn No. 7
für eine Singstimme mit Orchester
von Gustav Mahler—
Partitur

This of course re-confirms everything we know about 'Urlicht': that it was first conceived as an independent song in 1892 (?), first orchestrated in 1893, and then incorporated into the symphony (in 1894). The Amsterdam MS enables us, as it were, to witness the act of physical incorporation.

There are, however, some puzzling aspects of the MS. While the label tells us that initially 'Urlicht' was designated as No. 7 in the series of *Wunderhorn* songs, the MS itself is quite clearly inscribed 'Nro. 4', in an ink consistent with the rest of the MS moreover, not the blue pencil that has been used for the numeration of the other movements in the MS; furthermore, the numeration on this page of the MS is entirely free of the usual signs of Mahler's inconstant numbering process, i.e. there are no numerical crossings out or substitutions. This is perfectly acceptable as evidence that *this* particular MS was intended to function as the fourth movement of the symphony (though one wonders, in that case, why the old brown paper folder is still about?); but what *is* confusing, if that is the case, is the fact that the instrumentation still represents the constitution of the independent song version of July 1893, not the instrumentation with which we are familiar from the published version of the symphony. It seems that it was not until a very late stage, when

Mahler was preparing his symphony for the première in 1895, that the final orchestral guise of 'Urlicht' was determined. The possibility that 'Nro. 4' might refer, not to this movement, but to an alternative placing of the song in the *Wunderhorn* series seems to me to be most unlikely. That 'Urlicht' was, as it were, inserted into the symphony in its authentic solo song version, even though Mahler seems to have gone to the trouble of writing out a fresh copy (the old paper folder notwithstanding), only goes to emphasize the random way in which the symphony's middle movements were assembled and perhaps lends further weight to my suggestion (see pp. 185f.) that the final decision about the placing of the song was itself made late in the game, i.e. when Mahler was approaching the completion of the Finale. He incorporated the song as it was in his MS, and did not re-think its instrumentation in the context of the resources of the symphony until later.

Finally, there is the last movement, with 'Nro. 5' marked in blue pencil on p. 1. In this Amsterdam MS, two indications of the movement's programme exist in the form of titles: at Fig. 3, Mahler writes 'Der Rufer in der Wüste!'; and at Fig. 29, 'Der grosse Appell'. Both these titles from 1894—which long preceded the actual formulation of a complete programme for the work (see pp. 179–84)—were included in the first edition (1897) of the score (so Mr. Knud Martner tells me), and indeed were used on occasion in a concert billing as part of the description of the Finale. The programme (for which I am grateful to Mr. Martner) was issued in connection with the performance of the Second Symphony in Basel Cathedral on 15 June 1903 (opp.).

It is clear from the Amsterdam MS that the concept of the off-stage band (introduced at Fig. 22) was at first simpler than the version with which we are now familiar. There is evidence in the MS of Mahler elaborating the idea, and we see too that the anxious note for the conductor (see also n. 68, E., p. 285) about the problems of performance implicit in the passage, was a later, scribbled-in addition.

When Mahler reaches the final chorus we encounter what appears to be a variety of MS papers and also a bout of purple ink (used for the last two signatures). The variation in the MS paper was probably due to the necessity to find a size and shape of paper that would accommodate the massive forces Mahler had assembled at this point in the movement. This whole section of the MS shows clear signs of the hard compositional labour that the choral appendix demanded.

51 It was a flood that also in time engulfed England. It is not only Elgar's *Falstaff* (1913) that I have in mind. To choose a rarer example, Parry's B minor Symphonic Fantasia of 1912—one year earlier than the Elgar—was subtitled 'A Symphony in four linked movements: Stress—Love—Play—Now', an inner programme (cf. the Raff symphony mentioned in Sittard, p. 241) that has a curiously modern resonance about it (though one cannot say that about the music).

52 This was a conversation that took place between Mahler and Bauer-Lechner in April 1899. In a footnote (p. 117), Bauer-Lechner's editor points

Symphoniekonzert
Montag den 15. Juni, Abends 7 Uhr
im Münster
(Hauptprobe Montag 15. Juni, Vormitt. 8 Uhr).

––––––––•••••––––––––

1. Das Sonnenlied
   nach Worten des « Sôlarliodh », von
   Max Bamberger, für Chorgesang,
   Einzelstimmen, Orchester und Orgel
   op. 26 No. I, III und IV . *Friedrich E. Koch.*

   > Sopran: Frau *Val. Riggenbach-Hegar,* Basel.
   > Mezzosopran: Fräulein *Frieda Hegar,* Zürich.
   > Alt: Fräulein *Anna Hindermann,* Basel.
   > Tenor: Herr *Richard Fischer,* Frankfurt a. M.
   > Bariton: Herr *Paul Boepple,* Basel.
   > Orgel: Herr *Karl Straube.*

2. Ew'ges Licht, Dichtung von Friedrich
   Rückert, für Tenorsolo mit Orchester
   op. 7 Manuscript   . *Hans Schilling-Ziemssen.*

   Herr *Richard Fischer,* Frankfurt a. M.

––––––––––––––

3. Symphonie in C-moll No. 2   . *Gustav Mahler.*

   I. Allegro maestoso. II. Andante con moto.
   III. In ruhig fliessender Bewegung. IV. „Urlicht"
   für Altsolo (aus „des Knaben Wunderhorn")
   sehr feierlich, aber schlicht. V. Allegro ener-
   gico — der Rufer in der Wüste — der grosse
   Appell.

   > Sopransolo: Frau *Maria Knüpfer-Egli.*
   > Altsolo: Fräulein *Hermine Kittel.*

   ––––––––––––

   Chor: Der Basler Gesangverein.

The Basel programme (1903) for the Second Symphony

out that at one early stage the Andante was actually designated as the *fourth*
movement (among Bauer-Lechner's papers were found early MS drafts and
sketches for the Second Symphony, given by Mahler to NBL). This chopping
and changing about of the sequence of movements was altogether characteristic of Mahler's practice at this time (we meet it again as the Third begins
to materialize), and in this particular instance, the footnoted information
seems to bear out Mahler's own statement about the lack of an integral,
scrupulously weighed relationship between the massive first movement and
the lyrical Andante (see also n. 58). As documented by Bauer-Lechner,
Mahler went on to say that, had other circumstances obtained he could at
least 'have begun the Andante with the song for the cellos, and only then
followed that with the present beginning. But now it's too late to recast it.'
It has never been clear to me what Mahler meant by this observation—if, of
course, Bauer-Lechner recalled this detail accurately. One does not see the
force of opening the Andante at Fig. 5 (is the added cello melody there (bar
92 et seq.) what he meant by the 'song for the cellos'?), if it were integration
that Mahler was seeking. There is no doubt, however, that he was bothered
about the Andante and its beginning. A copyist's MS score of the three movements (once in the possession of Bruno Walter) that was probably prepared for
the part-performance of the symphony in Berlin in March 1895 (see also n. 57,
p. 278) shows a deletion of the first sixteen bars of the Andante with a note
in Mahler's hand: '18 bars of prelude to be inserted'. The insertion which
might have solved the puzzle seems not to have survived. The sale catalogue
(J. A. Stargardt, Marburg, November 1971) in which this MS item appears
adds: '. . . if we compare the deleted bars with the printed score we find that
only the first 4 bars of the final version are missing, whilst the following 13
bars display differences in instrumentation', a description almost as obscure,
alas, as Mahler's reference to starting with 'the song for the cellos'. (There
are, incidentally, early sketches for the Second Symphony in the Nationalbibliothek, Vienna. Among them I recall a page (from the Leipzig years) on
which Mahler had sketched out, virtually in its entirety, the long, flowing
melody of the Andante. One would guess that this marvellous tune came to
him, as it were, fully shaped; and such seems to be the evidence of the sketch.
A sketch (from the same period and in the same library) of the complete
opening melody of the first movement would suggest that that great melodic
span too came to Mahler in one immense breath of inspiration, though in fact
the sketch (page 1) shows signs of the intensive labour he was obliged to
expend on this extended opening thought. There are in the Nationalbibliothek
six pages of sketches for the first movement on identical 16-stave paper
which must originate from the Leipzig period, as must two pages on 24-stave
paper. Pages 1–3 of the 16-stave paper run in sequence, page 3 including an
outline for the development. What is of particular interest in these composition sketches, which must be among the very earliest for the movement, is
the presence on them of scribbled-in references to a Finale—i.e. 'Schlussatz'
appears more than once in Mahler's hand, along with other verbal indications

of musical ideas he had in mind for the work. There is a need now for detailed investigation of these fascinating preliminary studies. They prove, however, that even at this very early stage, Mahler had no doubt that a Finale would, as it were, materialize. He was not to know how many years it was actually to be before his 'Schlussatz' was achieved. (On p. 3 there seems to be the word 'Gesang' scrawled in at the end of a section of the sketch. Can Mahler have had an inkling so early that the voice was eventually to have a prominent role in his new symphony?)

One page among these sketches includes a draft tune for a song, with a text that begins 'Ich hab' ein Schatz'. These are the words that open a *Wunderhorn* poem, but thereafter Mahler's text and the authentic poem do not coincide. This was a song that did not progress beyond the 10 bars or so of its incipit.

The sketches for the Andante (see above) are written on the same 16-stave paper (Leipzig) as the sketches for the first movement and inscribed '2. Satz'. If this title was written along with the draft of the melody, then doubt must be thrown on Mahler's claim that he did not know originally when he had the idea for the movement that the Andante was destined for the C minor Symphony (see n. 58 below). What is extraordinary about this particular pencil sketch is this: that under the opening melody, and obviously at a later stage (in ink), Mahler has added the cello counter-melody which appears at 7 bars after Fig. 5. This sketch, then—which has reached me late in the day—throws retrospective and revealing light on Mahler's expressed doubts about the opening of the Andante, which I touch on earlier in this note. At one stage, ironically, the very first sketch seems to have represented Mahler's last—though unrealized—thought on the subject!

This Vienna assembly of sketches includes finally a fine sketch (1 page) for the Scherzo, on Hamburg 18-stave paper (Böhme No. 11) and a pencil fragment (*verso*) that requires further analysis and accurate identification.

53 See NBL, p. 7.

54 *Die drei Pintos* was first performed on 20 January. If the Bauer-Lechner entry can be relied on, then Mahler must have been noting down musical ideas for other movements, or for unspecified future musical use, at the same time as he was working on, or thinking about, the completion of his 'Todtenfeier', which was finished in full score in September. The two sketches to which Mahler refers (NBL, p. 7) are now housed in the National-bibliothek, Vienna, and include the principal melody of the Andante (see n. 52 above) and also a draft of the first trio.

55 Foerster taught at the Hamburg Conservatoire and was also music critic of the *Hamburger Nachrichten*. When Mahler moved to Vienna, he engaged Berta Lauterer-Foerster for the Vienna company (where she sang from 1901–14), and Foerster took up an appointment there at the *Neues Konservatorium*. His long autobiography, *Der Pilger: Erinnerungen eines Musikers* (as it is known in its German version), Prague, 1955, contains some very important reminiscences of Mahler.

56 Hans von Bülow (1830–94) was resident in Hamburg from 1887 and was chief conductor of the Philharmonic Concerts there. When he became ill and was eventually obliged to resign, he recommended Mahler as his successor. The psychoanalyst Theodor Reik, in his fascinating book, *The Haunting Melody*, New York, 1953, offers a remarkably ingenious psychoanalytic interpretation of the Bülow-Mahler relationship, which also touches substantially on the mental block that seemed to afflict Mahler when it came to completing his Second Symphony.

57 There had been, pre-Berlin, a trial run-through ('behind closed doors', as Foerster puts it) of the three instrumental movements at Hamburg, with the orchestra of the opera house, in January 1895 (see HG¹, pp. 318–19 and JBF, pp. 406–7). What was the sequence of the movements at Hamburg? We know that at Berlin, in March 1895, the movements were performed in the order that we know today, i.e. Allegro—Andante—Scherzo (see the programme reproduced in HG¹, facing p. 670, that also tells us, interestingly, that at this stage, Mahler thought of these three movements as building 'the first part' of his symphony). We know, however, that the copyist's score that was probably connected with this Berlin preview has the movements placed as follows: Allegro—Scherzo—Andante. Mahler, then, must have had a final change of intention *before* the Berlin part-performance. But may it have been the case that for the semi-private run-through at Hamburg, the movements were played as they appear in the copyist's score, i.e. Allegro—Scherzo—Andante? One wonders indeed if this particular MS may not in the first instance have been associated with the Hamburg occasion. As Erwin Ratz points out in his Preface to the critical edition of the symphony, traces linger on in Mahler's MS full score of the complete work of his earlier intention to place the Scherzo second, i.e. the rehearsal numbers run without a break from the end of the first movement (Fig. 27) to the beginning of the Scherzo, which continues with Fig. 28. (This eccentric numeration, which entails the intervening Andante having its own independent set of rehearsal numbers, appears in all printed editions of the symphony, including—mysteriously—the critical edition, where one might have expected it to be corrected. The 'wrong' figures, of course, make an undeniably interesting and important musical point, but the point could have been made editorially. It seems needless to repeat in the score itself a confusion that had nothing to do with any logic but was the direct result of Mahler's uncertainty about the order of his middle movements, a state of indecision which persisted to a very late stage. Doubtless the real reason for this otherwise inexplicable show of pedantry was the necessity to produce a score that would match up with the existing sets of orchestral parts, the rehearsal numbers of which would correspond to early editions of the symphony. Thus do economics defeat editorial commonsense.) (See also n. 46, p. 265.)

58 See JBF, pp. 402–9, and also Mahler's letter to Julius Buths, written in 1903 (GMB¹, pp. 315–16), in which he writes as follows:

Dear Professor Buths,

I am in full agreement with everything you suggest and beg you to do just as you see fit in every respect.

Well then, this would mean that the main interval in the concert would come between the fourth and fifth movements. I marvel at the sensitive intuition with which you (in contrast with my own arrangement) have recognized the natural break in the work. I have long tended to this view, and all the performances I have hitherto conducted have reinforced the same impression.

Still, there really ought *also* to be a lengthy pause for recollection after the first movement, because the second movement does *not* have the effect of a *contrast*, but simply of a discrepancy after the first. This is my fault, not inadequate appreciation on the listener's part. Perhaps you have already felt this after rehearsing the two movements consecutively. The Andante was composed as a kind of intermezzo (as the echo of *long* past days in the life of the man borne to his grave in the first movement—'when the sun still smiled on him'—).

While the first, third, fourth and fifth movements are related in theme and mood, the second stands alone, in a certain sense interrupting the strict, austere sequence of events. Perhaps this is a weakness in the conception of the work, but you will certainly see my intention from the above indication.

It is quite logical to interpret the beginning of the fifth movement as a resumption of the first, and the long pause before the fifth will make the listener aware of this too.

(Translated by Eithne Wilkins: see entry for GMB[1] in the Bibliography.)

Hence, then, Mahler's establishment of a five-minute pause between the first and second movements. See also HG[1], pp. 782–3 and 788, and p. 508: '[Mahler] remembered [in 1899] that he had conceived two movements [the Funeral March and the Andante] separately in Leipzig, not intending to use them in the same symphony . . .'.

Quite apart from the interest of Mahler's own thoughts about the 'discrepant' A flat intermezzo, it is also fascinating to observe in the letter to Buths that he was evidently having a change of mind about the explicit direction in the published score of the Second Symphony that the Finale should follow the fourth movement *without* a break. Undeniably, were there a long pause *before* the second movement and again *after* the fourth, the middle movements would be blocked off, almost as an independent central unit, within the gigantic framework provided by the first movement and Finale. But it is odd to find Mahler commending the idea of emphasizing by this means the opening of the Finale as the resumption of the first movement, when after all he had taken some compositional pains to introduce here an explicit link with—an overt musical resumption of—the Scherzo, the *third* movement. But all this goes to show, I submit, that Mahler never entirely conquered his unease about the total shape of the symphony, a disquiet that would certainly have had its roots in the somewhat random manner of the work's assembly, and was reflected in his anxiety to find a mode of performance that would somehow place beyond doubt a unity or logic of conception that he felt (rightly or wrongly) not to be self-evident in the final plan of the symphony.

59 For a full account of the ceremony (including details of the music performed), see JBF, pp. 404–6, part of whose account is reproduced on pp. 168f., and HG¹, p. 293–7. It seems not to be known precisely which setting of the Klopstock it was that Mahler heard. There are many besides those mentioned in HG¹, p. 791. (See Appendix C, pp. 416–18.) It would be useful if the setting used at the service could be positively identified. The event is psychoanalytically interpreted by Reik in TR, p. 259 et seq. Mahler himself wrote a letter on the subject in 1897 to Arthur Seidl: see GMB¹, pp. 228–9.

60 KB¹, pp. 115–16. Herr Blaukopf refers to February 1894, in connection with Bülow's memorial service, but this was the month in which Bülow died. The service was held in March.

61 Cf. AM⁵, p. xxii, where I show a characteristic example of Mahler's conversion of a *Wunderhorn* poem to his own purpose. For more on Mahler's amending and amplifying of his texts, see FEP, and ZR¹ and ZR².

62 Elliott Carter, in *Flawed Words and Stubborn Sounds: A Conversation with Elliott Carter*, by Allen Edwards, New York, 1971, remarks that Mahler's attitude towards polyphony, towards simultaneity of different materials, is curiously like that of Ives and quotes in support of this view the now well-known passage on polyphony from Bauer-Lechner (NBL, p. 147, and see also pp. 339f.). A copyist's score (the so-called 'Tams' score) of Ives's Third Symphony was, it seems, taken by Mahler to Europe in 1911 (with an eventual performance in view?), shortly before he died. Ives himself gives an account of how this happened: 'When [the Third Symphony] was being copied in, I think, Tams' office, Gustav Mahler saw it and asked to have a copy—he was quite interested in it.' Ives may have heard Mahler conduct the New York Philharmonic (in 1910 or 1911?), but apparently recalled no details of the programme. See Charles Ives, *Memos*, ed. John Kirkpatrick, New York, 1972, pp. 55, n. 1, p. 121, and p. 137. See also David Wooldridge's study of Ives, *From the Steeples and the Mountains*, New York, 1974, pp. 150–1, where it is suggested that a performance of the symphony *was* given under Mahler in Munich in the summer of 1910.

63 TR, p. 241, et seq.

64 *Hamburger Fremdenblatt*, 5 October 1928. I would not have succeeded in tracing a copy of the newspaper without the kind help of Mr. Knud Martner (Copenhagen).

65 See NBL, pp. 7 and 8–11. The published version of Bauer-Lechner's reminiscences excludes some material; and for the summer of 1894 there are no entries at all: Natalie, in this year, did not make her customary summer visit. (See, however, p. 174.) Her only published reference to the Finale of the Second Symphony appears in an entry from 1897 (NBL, p. 81), when she remarks upon 'the cawing of ravens' that Mahler was eventually driven to incorporate into his Finale. (This must be the same incident that Mr. Rosé also refers to in his 1928 newspaper article, principally (N.B.) about the years 1893 and 1894, where it assumes the following guise: '. . . [Mahler] had for some time been trying to find what rhythmic shape to give a motive from the last movement of the Second Symphony. [On one of his regular afternoon walks at Steinbach] . . . a few crows flew up in front of him with a shriek, and in an instant the long-sought phrase came to him.') NBL locates this as a happening from 'two years ago', which would take us back to the summer of 1895, by which time, in fact, the fair copy of the Finale had already been completed (28 December 1894). However, this may well have been a simple slip of the memory, and a slip, moreover, that was at least in the right direction. It could well have been, of course, that the Second Symphony was a particular topic in the summer of 1895, when Mahler was almost bound to be reviewing his recently completed score in the light of the forthcoming first performance of the complete work in Berlin in December of the same year (13 December). (The first three movements, when performed at Berlin on 4 March 1895, were conducted by Mahler himself, not by Richard Strauss as has so often been stated. This error falls exactly into the same category as that occupied for years by the attribution of the première of the Fourth Symphony to Weingartner. It is a mistake (in both cases) which arises quite simply from crediting to the chief conductors of the orchestras involved all the performances within a series, for the general organization, execution and supervision of which the chief conductors were indeed responsible. But guest conductors, especially composer-conductors, could and did undertake programmes or part-programmes. It was in this role that Mahler himself conducted the first three movements of the Second Symphony in March 1895 (see illustration, p. 266). This long-standing error has continued to haunt references to the Second, despite the fact that the correct state of affairs was made known in 1924, in a footnote to a letter of Mahler's from February 1895: see GMB¹, p. 152.)

66 In the possession of Mrs. Charles F. Adler (Vienna) and reproduced by kind permission. It is interesting to note in this early sketch that Mahler apparently considered a cyclic quotation of material from the first movement after the first statement of the chorale. Another sketch of the same passage is in the Pierpont Morgan Library (Lehmann Deposit), New York. See also the frontispiece of the Philharmonia miniature score of the symphony, No. 395, which reproduces the opening of the final chorus from the Amsterdam MS that I describe in n. 50.

67 In this interesting letter at Yale University, Beinecke Library, Mahler refers to the fact that he has engaged for 'December 13 the *Stern* Choral Society, and as soloists *Götze* (Berlin) and *Artner* (Hamburg)'. The symphony was given its first (complete) performance on 13 December 1895, and thus this letter must belong to that year. It was written from Hamburg and includes a mention of Mahler's sisters, Justine and Emma ('still sleeping'), and his close Hamburg friend, the physicist Arnold Berliner (1862–1942). The letter asks for proofs to be sent 'so that I can start working on them for

you', an indication that Mahler was writing to Hermann Behn, who was preparing a two-piano version of the symphony for publication. The symphony was first brought out in Behn's arrangement by the Leipzig firm of Hofmeister in 1895 (together with the 'separate edition' of 'Urlicht', of which Mahler makes a special mention in his letter). The orchestral score was published in 1897, again by Hofmeister. The work was then transferred to Weinberger, who published a revision in 1903 (?), and was eventually incorporated in the catalogue of Universal Edition (1906).

Mahler's sketch for the 'Resurrection' Chorale in the Second Symphony
(By kind permission of Mrs F. Charles Adler. See n. 66)

68 The relevant passage in the Finale in the 1894 MS of the symphony shows the 'link' with the song (see Exx. 84 and 85, p. 185) already installed. There is certainly no indication that the passage was revised or was an afterthought; and this would suggest that the pre-existing and pre-selected song did influence the development of the very last part of the Finale. The same situation, expectedly, prevails in the copyist's MS of the Second Symphony (complete but for 'Urlicht': see (D) below) held at the Beinecke Library (Osborn Collection), Yale University. This was a copy made from the 1894 MS (possessed by the Mengelberg-Stiftung, Amsterdam) that is described in some detail in n. 50, p. 270. This Yale MS divulges some very interesting features. Among the most important are the following:

A. At the end of the first movement there is written in Mahler's (not the copyist's) hand: 'Hier folgt eine Pause von 5 Minuten!' ['Here follows a pause of 5 min.!'] This scribbled-in note suggests that it was at this MS stage that Mahler alighted on the idea of installing a substantial intermission after the first movement, to create an acoustic space in which the scale of the opening Allegro could diminish before the onset of the Andante. (See also n. 58, p. 278.)

B. In the Andante there is some re-touching of the instrumentation in Mahler's hand, e.g. we observe the customary deletion of superfluous doubling, etc. It was also at this stage that we evidently lost for good a tiny woodwind motive that played quite a prominent role in the movement's first trio section. (See Ex. A (the triplet motive), from the Yale MS.)

Ex. A

At Fig. 12, the delicious pizzicato passage, there is a fascinating note from Mahler (omitted in the published score) which instructs the violinists and viola players to hold their instruments like guitars and strum with the thumb. The conductor, says Mahler, is to insist on this. No doubt he was seeking to convey, in sound but also perhaps *visually*, the conspicuously serenade-like character of the movement, and at this moment wanted the string body to turn itself into a gigantic guitar. I dare say practical objections interposed (the reluctance of the players? the practicality of the suggestion?), for which reason the note was dropped. But it is worth bearing in mind, if only as a very clear indication of the atmosphere Mahler wanted to create at this moment and of the sonority that he wanted to embody it.

C. The Scherzo is headed '3 Satz.', very clearly. On the other hand, the first rehearsal number (Fig. 28) picks up from Fig. 27, which is the last rehearsal number in the first movement. The reason for this eccentric numeration I give in n. 57. Of great interest in this copyist's MS are the opening bars of the movement for the timpani alone (two players), which were first established in the Yale MS like this:

Ex. B

This longer version of the familiar drum prelude, which was probably the version heard when the three instrumental movements were first performed at Berlin in 1895, was abbreviated by Mahler (by cross-hatching) so that it came to read thus (Ex. C), which is, in fact, the terse, published version.

Ex. C

I describe the evolution of the drum prelude in the context of this MS in n. 50, pp. 270f., and Appendix F, pp. 427–9.

[The opening of the movement in the Yale MS in fact appears thus:

Ex. D

Ex. B is a reconstruction rather than a transcription. In addition to deleting four bars, Mahler changed the dynamics in bars 6 and 8, scratched out the notes in bar 7, and added ⎯⎯⎯⎯ *p* in bars 10–11. The hypothetical reconstruction (though there cannot be much doubt about it) is particularly fascinating as it shows Mahler experimenting with a simple form of serialism: not only do the dynamics decline by one degree for each phrase, but the pauses between each phrase similarly decline by one quaver each time up to the entry of the second timpani. Another striking innovation (evident in both versions) is the stereophonic effect of using two pairs of timpani to play the same notes. (C.M.)]

D. As I note above 'Urlicht' is missing from the MS. There is a note in the copyist's hand (at the end of the Scherzo) that the song is to follow. The absence of the song from this copyist's score makes clear, as I suggest in n. 26, p. 256, that it was at this stage that the independent song orchestration was undergoing its 'symphonic' revision.

E. One notes that there is no numerical inscription on the first page of the Finale in the copyist's hand. This has been supplied by Mahler himself—'V' in blue pencil. There are two places in which we alight on titles, evidence of the 'scenario' to which Mahler was working in the Finale. At Fig. 3 we have 'Der Rufer in der Wüste' ['The caller in the desert'] and at Fig. 29 'Der grosse Appell' ['The last trump'], titles which remind us of the detailed scenario for the first movement of the Third Symphony (see p. 194).

At Fig. 22, that prophetic passage for combined orchestras that I discuss later in detail (see pp. 337–8), Mahler included a note that (1) differs from the note that eventually appeared in the published score of the symphony at the same place and (2) reveals his anticipation of the difficulties of co-ordination that he expected (rightly) to emerge in the performance of it. In this copyist's score the note reads: 'Sollte die Ausführung dieser Stelle nicht ganz der Intention des Autors entsprechend erzielt werden können, so bleiben die Instrumente "in weitester Ferne aufgestellt" besser fort.' ['Should it prove impossible to obtain a performance of this passage entirely in keeping with the author's intention, it is better to omit the instruments "positioned at a very great distance off".'] (In the published score, the note about the off-stage band reads thus: 'Anmerkung für den Dirigenten: muss so schwach erklingen, dass es den Charakter der Gesangstelle, Celli und Fag. in keinerlei Weise tangiert. Der Autor denkt sich hier, ungefähr, vom Wind vereinzelnd herüber getragene Klänge einer kaum vernehmbaren Musik.' ['Note for conductors: this must sound so faintly that it in no way impinges on the character of the song of the cellos and bassoons. The composer here has in mind something in the nature of sounds of a barely audible music which are individually borne hither on the wind.'])

69 As we have seen (cf. table, p. 171), that the Scherzo was originally placed second in the overall scheme reflected the order of these movements' actual composition, i.e. the first orchestral score of the Scherzo was completed a fortnight or so before the first orchestral score of the Andante. See also pp. 137–8, where I touch on the complex chronological relationship between the Scherzo and its generative song, the 'Fischpredigt', and n. 57.

70 What is odd about Foerster's statement is the implication of a need for *binding*, when in fact the movements (if juxtaposed without the intervention of 'Urlicht') were already bound together, quite explicitly so, i.e. the opening bars of the Finale form the continuing link with the Scherzo; and what Mahler wanted, or what he came to effect through his interpolation of the song, was a clear *break* between the movements before the drama was resumed in the last movement.

71 It was probably this same reason, the need for contrast and relief, that caused Mahler to displace the C minor Scherzo as second movement and introduce instead the A flat Andante. One may be sure—despite the precedent of Beethoven's Ninth—that Mahler's uncertainty flowed from doubts about too sustained a concentration of C minor, which the original sequence presented. It was probably the same kind of consideration that led him to a bout of indecision long after, regarding the order of the inner movements of the Sixth Symphony. There too, initially, the A minor Scherzo followed the A minor first movement, a sequence which, for a time, he reversed.

72 PB, p. 106. Similar drafts are also reproduced in AM⁵, see pp. 38–9, and its Appendix, pp. 359–60. It seems to me now that the drafts quoted by Bekker and Alma Mahler did *not* derive from the same documentary sources but have independent status, though the second draft programme is virtually identical in either case.

73 This stimulates me to repeat here (see also pp. 252f.) the curious fact, which is quite as curious as the matter of the title, that at one stage Mahler seems to have contemplated placing the Minuet sixth in the sequence of movements, i.e. actually to fill the place occupied by the title 'Was mir das Kind erzählt', which, for a long stretch, was the symphony's projected final number. See also HG¹, p. 804, who suggests that Stanford University also possesses a complete sketch of the Minuet, entitled 'Was der Abend mir erzählt'. This is not the case, however, and the reference is wholly mysterious.

74 NBL, pp. 19–20. Readers will doubtless spot in the first paragraph the parallel with Mahler's famous and much-quoted remark to Sibelius, made in Helsinki in 1907: '... the symphony must be like the world. It must embrace everything.' As for Mahler's description of the first movement as 'prelude' [Vorspiel] or 'introduction' [Einleitung], one should remember that at this stage the huge first movement had not been fully composed (though the ideas for much of it must have been sketched). It was not completed until the following summer, by when it was of such dimensions that Mahler was seriously thinking of it as a two-part structure: an introduction, 'Pan erwacht' ['Pan awakes'], followed by the great march in celebration of summer, these two sections comprising Part I of the work and everything else Part II. I doubt if, in the summer of 1895, Mahler quite realized the size of the canvas on which he would find himself working in 1896. The composition schedule of the Third, by the way, exactly reverses that of the Second—in the new symphony, it was the *first* movement that was the last to be finished.

75 NBL, pp. 40–1, 41–2, and 45. If correctly reported in the final paragraph of the first excerpt from Bauer-Lechner, Mahler was exaggerating in claiming complete independence for each movement, which is certainly not the case. What he was thinking of, probably, was the compulsory abandonment of the interrelationships between movements which had depended on 'Das himmlische Leben' functioning as the Finale. When Mahler ditched the song he was left with a web of strategically executed interrelationships which was suddenly deprived of its logical fulfilment. If anything, then, it was the original Finale which came to nothing, not the interrelationships, which ironically are still there for all to hear.

This first excerpt is also of particular interest for the light it throws on the *evolutionary* character of the programme—I use the word in its biological sense. Much is always made of the opening contest between slumbering Winter (inert Nature) and the onset of Summer, rightly so; and of course the 'landscape' movements in Part II contribute powerfully to the evocation of Nature. But clearly Mahler envisaged the whole work as a planned, step-by-step progression, leading us on (in the manner of Ernst Haeckel?) from the inorganic and inarticulate to the peak of human consciousness and the articulation, in the last movement, of human love. This peculiar biological ground plan (see also Mahler's letter to Löhr quoted above, pp. 188–9, with its reference to 'the successive orders of beings') has perhaps not received its due. Dika Newlin, however, in DN, p. 164, wrote (in 1947) that 'the philosophical idea' informing the symphony became 'ever clearer to [Mahler] as the work progressed' and went on to quote Mahler's letter to Anna Bahr-Mildenburg of 1 July 1896. After setting out the inscription (see p. 189) for the slow movement, at this stage No. 7 in his programmatic scheme, Mahler writes: 'Do you know what this is about? It is supposed to symbolize the peak, the highest level from which one can view the world. I could almost call the movement "What God tells me!"—in the sense that God can only be comprehended as Love. And so my work is a musical poem embracing all stages of development in progressive order: It begins with inanimate Nature and rises to the love of God!' (See ABM, pp. 36–7.) Dr. Newlin suggests that the seventh movement was 'never composed'. But it was, of course. (See n. 6, p. 365.)

Mahler, moreover, if somewhat fancifully, seems to have extended the idea of lower and higher biological forms to musical forms. In July 1896, Bauer-Lechner reports him as claiming that in the Adagio of the symphony 'everything is resolved into peace and passive being; the Ixion-wheel of phenomena has at last been brought to a standstill. But in the fast movements . . . everything is flow, movement, a process of becoming. So, contrary to custom—and without knowing why at the time—I concluded my Second and Third Symphonies with Adagios: that is, with a higher form as opposed to a lower one.' An eccentric, romantic view, and by any reckoning a quaint appraisal of the Finale of the Second, which can be few people's idea of an Adagio (one supposes it was the choral conclusion that Mahler had in mind). Nonetheless, so far as the Third is concerned, one can see perhaps a little more clearly that the choice of an Adagio as the concluding movement was reinforced by an approach, however off-beat, that emerged quite naturally from the 'biological' conception that underpins the development of the programme.

76 When the First Symphony was performed for the first time in Vienna, under his own direction on 18 November 1900, a notice was printed in the programme saying that it was Mahler's own wish that there were no programme notes about the work. The only information for the audience was the bare list of tempo indications or expression marks found at the head of each movement—there was not a hint of the original programme, which on this occasion was conspicuous (if at all) by reason of its total suppression. The programme and Mahler's prohibition are reproduced in Wolfgang Schreiber's *Mahler*, Hamburg, 1971, pp. 94 and 96.

When Mahler's Second Symphony was first performed complete in Berlin on 13 December 1895, no programme accompanied the performance, not because Mahler had suppressed it, but because (at that time) it had not been formulated by the composer in verbal form. This was to happen after the Berlin première, in response no doubt to the kind of reaction made by Ferdinand Pfohl in his notice of the concert in the *Hamburger Nachrichten* of 13 December (see FP, pp. 67–72), where he expressed himself as follows: 'We are evidently in the presence of a work that belongs to the genre of programme music. This is established beyond all doubt. But how does the programme go? It is not at all easy to answer this question and to elucidate the poetic ground-plan of the work. Really only one person can do that—the composer himself. And unfortunately he has hidden himself away in impenetrable darkness and withheld from his instrumental movements the illuminating ray of any explanatory words. This reticence is all the more regrettable since the sequence of individual movements simply cannot be understood without further information and their relationships to the basic idea of the whole work cannot at all times be brought into clear, logical perspective.' Pfohl's quandary was a genuine one, which neatly illumines the problem: programmes are eminently dispensable and disposable—but one needs to know them first.

77 Some of these are set out in BW², p. 101. Walter must have known this score or had the details from Mahler.

78 We know the address at which Mahler wrote his First Symphony in Leipzig: Gustav-Adolf-Strasse Nr. 12. Max Steinitzer (1864–1936), the music critic and writer, and Mahler advocate, arranged for a memorial plaque to be placed on the house in 1911. (See PS¹, p. 46.) I wonder if the house still stands?

79 The score now forms part of the collection that was given to the University of Southampton by Anna Mahler, Mahler's younger daughter. This is only a very lightly marked score but interestingly enough there are attempts at re-distributing the woodwind in the two opening pages of the introduction, a passage that Mahler worked over again and again. It seems that he could not stop himself from tinkering about with his 'sounds of Nature'. The 1899 Weinberger publication of the score (along with a piano-duet arrangement) was followed by a revised edition (in which the repeat was incorporated), and then in 1906, Universal Edition brought out a final revision. According to Erwin Ratz (in his Preface to the critical edition of the score, Vienna, 1966), Boosey & Hawkes brought out a reprint of the score in London in 1943 but used as the basis for their offset edition the first Weinberger edition of 1899. But can this be so? The 1943 B. & H. edition contains the repeat mark, which was certainly not established in the original 1899 score. There is a discrepancy here that still has to be resolved. A miniature score of the symphony, edited (1963–4) by H. F. Redlich, is available in the Eulenburg series (No. 570).

80 III, 1, 1969, pp. 76–100.

81 One thing, I think, that cannot be deduced is what Mr. Diether claims in his *Chord and Discord* article (JD, p. 81), that the MS 'is obviously a completely re-copied score of the symphony dating from 1893'. Mr. Diether seems to have read too much into the fact that Mahler wrote the dates of the Hamburg revisions at the end of Parts I and II of the symphony (and also at the end of the Andante). But this did not imply that the MS was re-copied from the beginning to these last pages on which the dates are inscribed. The *dates* apply to the *interpolations* on Hamburg MS paper, and Mahler writes them perfectly sensibly at the *end* of the movements concerned because it would clearly have been eccentric and confusing to write them into the body of the movements, i.e. into the precise places where the interpolations had been made. Surely what happened was this: Mahler made his deletions from the original MS and then incorporated his substitutions (on Hamburg paper), and on the date that this process of renovation was completed—in the case of the Finale, for example, on 19 January 1893—he inscribed the date of the revision on the last page of the movement. It is not the case that the Finale was re-copied in its entirety in 1893, and the date at the end of the MS applies to the two Hamburg interpolations, one of which comprises the important re-working of the reprise. The same point applies to the third movement, where it is the *opening* pages that comprise the revision, and the date inscribed on the *last* page of the movement again must refer to the fact of the revision, and not be otherwise interpreted. There is no date at the end of the (completely) revised first movement, and it could well be that the date at the end of the third movement (and Part I)—27 January 1893—represents the date on which the revision of the whole of the first part of the symphony (excluding the Andante) was completed. One minor point: Mr. Diether (p. 81) misreads the heading of the Funeral March, which is 'à la *Pompe* [not 'Tempe'] funèbre'.

The chronological 'mix' of the original MS and later interpolations is of very real significance. Indeed, my interpretation of the provenance of the MS tends to support what the son (Mr. John Perrin) of the original owner of the MS has said about the complex history of the gift that Mahler made to his mother (Jenny Feld). It is true that much of what Mr. Perrin recounts as fact is demonstrably erroneous, and has been appropriately dismissed by Mr. Diether and M. de La Grange. Nonetheless, when Mr. Perrin recalls that his mother was asked to return the original MS to Mahler in 1893, so that he could get on with his revisions for the forthcoming Hamburg performance, this *cannot* be ruled out of court for the reason that Mr. Diether gives (JD, pp. 78–9), i.e. because the EMS is 'without question . . . a revised score of 1893'. On the contrary, it is, as I suggest, in part a revision of the Ur-MS; and thus supports rather than contradicts Mr. Perrin's assertion, though far be it from me to attribute more weight to Mr. Perrin's reminiscences than they properly deserve. They are, or so it seems to me, much open to doubt. But in this one detail at least, there might be some substance in what he says; and in any event, if his recollection is to be contradicted, the counter argument must itself be correctly based.

It must strike readers as odd in any case that Mahler was evidently willing
to be so free in his disposal of his MSS, especially in days when easy mechanical duplication was not available. M. de La Grange has something interesting
to say (in HG¹, pp. 465–6) when writing of Mahler's pleasure at hearing of
the arrangements for the publication of his first three symphonies in the late
1890s by Waldheim Eberle, Vienna: 'Mahler's relief upon receiving this
good news can be judged by the way he worried over his precious manuscripts; until then he had possessed only the original and one copy of each.
Because of this he had hardly ever dared to let them out of his possession . . .'
'The original and one copy . . .': if that were true of the First, then once
again, Mr. Perrin's story, despite all its faulty detail, rings true. It certainly
makes it credible that Mahler would want his original MS returned to him
on loan from time to time and also strengthens the point I make that the EMS
at Yale does indeed comprise substantial portions of the original, along with
the revisions from 1893. Also, does not all this make even more likely to be
true what I write on pp. 199–200 about the scores of the First that were the
subject of Mahler's correspondence with Strauss?

82 I am most grateful to Mr. Knud Martner (Copenhagen) for generously
supplying me with these details from the Hamburg Spielpläne.

83 See DM¹, pp. 141–96, for a discussion of the early MS sources of *Das
klagende Lied*, and pp. 91–112 of this book for a scrutiny of the MS sources of
the *Gesellen* cycle. Perhaps one might also add that, if any large-scale revising
were to be done on the First Symphony, it is not surprising that it became
necessary in the Finale, where one would expect almost as a matter of historical course that a young composer would run up against major problems,
particularly at critical formal junctures. One of these is the recapitulation,
which proved to be the very point at which Mahler in fact found himself in
trouble. The particular character of his Finale intensified the problem for
him, and I have attempted to show on pp. 206–8 how this was more than
a local issue: that it was in fact prophetic of later problems of a rather similar
kind.

84 Oddly enough, the only MS fragment associated with the First Symphony that is known to me is the opening of the Scherzo in a version for piano
duet (four hands, and only a handful of bars in length). This is obviously a
very early MS and one cannot be all that certain that in fact it had—or has—
anything to do with the symphony (except by way of retrospective association). In DM¹, p. 205 (the eleventh line of which, by the way, should be
deleted), I see I suggested that this sketch was evidence that it may have
been the Scherzo that was 'the first movement of the symphony to achieve a
clear shape in Mahler's mind, possibly at a date well in advance of the composition of the rest of the work.' I would not hold to that view now. It seems
to me more probable that the MS was evidence, rather, of Mahler playing
about with a musical idea that clearly haunted and fascinated him (cf. the
early song, 'Hans und Grethe'), and it is my guess that his abortive shot at a
piano duet was another sign of his tinkering about in this area, before the

symphony (or symphonic poem, strictly speaking) was a real presence on his musical horizon.

85 Mahler's hopes in this respect were disappointed, as the review by Sittard (see pp. 238–40) confirms. (For further documentation of the reception of the work at Hamburg, see HG¹, pp. 281–3.)

86 See also Mahler's letter to Richard Strauss quoted on p. 200.

87 The onset of the recapitulation, and the following page of MS, are reproduced (Plates V and VI) in Mr. Diether's 'Chord and Discord' article (JD). Mahler does not, in fact, quite repeat himself, although the substance of the music is unchanged. In bar 6 of the deleted version he introduces the descending triplet motive from bar 8 of the introduction and omits altogether, rather interestingly, the first motive (the head-motive) of the march tune which is given to the brass in the introduction in the published version. This variation, then, represents a slight overall compression. The march tune is restated in bar 17 of the deleted version, whereas in the published version it is at bar 19 that we pick up the continuation of the first motive from bar 6. It is just possible to discern in bar 19 in the deleted version (the last bar that remains to us!) the upbeat quaver of the continuation motive, which means that Mahler, characteristically, united at this point in his discarded recapitulation the two motives that had been separated in the introduction—hence, undoubtedly, the omission of the head-motive from the bar where one would have expected to hear it.

88 Possibly extending only to the stretch of music represented in the exposition by the passage from, say, Fig. 6 to bar 84, though of course there may have been a reprise of the introduction more substantial than nineteen bars or so. It is a real deprivation that the cancellation breaks off at such a critical moment.

89 This kind of cross-reference seems to me a good deal more interesting than the often made observation of the Tchaikovsky-like character of the big lyrical melody in the Finale. I am always conscious, on the contrary, of the peculiarly Mahlerian contours of the melody, though I concede a marvellous bit of mimicry in these bars, which are pure Tchaikovsky, the first three bars especially.

[The melody is perhaps closer to Chopin. Compare, for example, Chopin's E major Nocturne, op. 62, no. 2:

C.M.]

For the rest, the tune and Mahler's treatment of it surely anticipate substantially the style of the Adagios in the Third and the Fourth Symphonies, especially the Fourth. (Another interesting feature of the tune is this: that it introduces the kind of slow, lyrical music that one would have expected to encounter in a slow movement proper—if the symphony had one. Of course, it hasn't; it has instead the sardonic Funeral March. But Mahler found room in his episodic Finale for an insert of music without which the experience of his passionate Hero would be incompletely represented.) There is a good deal of work to be done, I believe, on what one might think of as 'local' influences on Mahler's music, not only folk or popular music but the music of those Bohemian composers like Smetana (he died when Mahler was twenty-four) who were struggling to achieve some kind of national identity for their country's music. One can scarcely think of Mahler as a Nationalist. On the other hand, there are occasions when one is very conscious of the fact that he owes something vital and memorable to Smetana and Dvořák, not only to Brahms, Wagner, Strauss, etc. Mahler, of course, knew Dvořák personally. He conducted the first performance of Dvořák's symphonic poem, *Heroic Song*, at Vienna on 4 December 1896, an occasion the composer attended; and Mahler was much interested in the idea of producing Dvořák's opera, *Rusalka*, at Vienna, a proposal which also gave rise to personal contact between the two men. I have found it interesting, the more so as I have become more familiar with Dvořák's symphonic poems and programme music, to hear a marginal but by no means insubstantial musical link between the two composers. It may be manifest in a patch of orchestral colour, a type of instrumental approach, or a melodic inflection, the latter perhaps emerging from a common source in popular Czech melody. As Mahler said himself to Bauer-Lechner (NBL, p. 11): 'The Bohemian music of my childhood found its way into many of my compositions. I've noticed it especially in the 'Fischpredigt'. The underlying national element can be heard, in its most crude and basic form in the tootling of the Bohemian pipers.' For whatever reason, and perhaps mainly for the reason Mahler himself gives, Dvořák and Mahler at times seem almost to rub shoulders, something that one would rarely suggest about Brahms and Mahler. Indeed, if there is a Brahms influence at all in Mahler, I wonder if it is not so much Brahms we encounter as, rather, Brahms transmuted through the medium of Dvořák. More than the central German tradition plays a role in Mahler's music. In this connection, his close friendship (from 1893, in Hamburg) with the veteran Czech composer J. B. Foerster may have been influential. (See JBF, pp. 373–6, a chapter entitled 'Smetana and Mahler', for an account of the famous Hamburg production of the *Bartered Bride* that Mahler conducted in 1894.)

90 I say *one*, because, though the distinction may be a crude one, Mahler developed two kinds of contrapuntal textures, one manipulating a texture predominantly composed of short, trenchant, often truncated motives, the other unfolding a contrapuntal texture, which may be of an intense elaboration or intense austerity, but which depends on the combination of long spans of melody. The Ninth Symphony presents both types of counterpoint and texture: long-breathed polyphony prevails almost throughout the first movement, for example, and again in the final Adagio; and the mosaics of short motives in the Rondo-Burleske. For the distinction between richness and austerity of texture, cf., say, the first movement, bar 211 et seq., and the Adagio, bar 28 et seq., textures that are worlds apart.

91 Though the swelling of the brass complement in the Finale of the First *is* a matter of sheer weight of numbers, providing at the appropriate moment the right dramatic effect of overwhelming triumph—almost literally so. But this was Mahler's deliberate aesthetic intention. A more elaborate and sophisticated example of the same kind of thing is found in the Eighth Symphony, where again, at particular moments, an enormous volume of sound is deliberately planned as a significant part of the aesthetic experience that Mahler aims to communicate. Vast numbers, when they are called for, are never accidental with Mahler nor simply an end-of-century habit. They are as precisely calculated as the most chamber-musical of his textures.

92 There can be no doubt that Schoenberg, and through him his pupil, Webern, were influenced by this practice of Mahler's. Cf. the latter's 'analytic' arrangement (1934–5) for orchestra of Bach's six-part Ricercare.

93 There are countless examples in Mahler's symphonies of his motivic method working hand in glove with his scoring. The development of the first movement of the First Symphony, for instance, is rich in passages in which the principal thematic material is fragmented into the varied instrumental articulation of reordered and freshly combined motives. See, for instance, seven bars before Fig. 16 to Fig. 18, a stretch of music which reveals a mosaic of detached motives, the map of which is drawn by the continuously changing instrumentation. See, too, in the first movement of the Fourth Symphony, not only the breaking down of the principal thematic material of the exposition into fresh patterns of motives in the development—a *locus classicus* this—but also the orchestration of the principal melody in the exposition, which represents most brilliantly what I have in mind when referring to the analysis of the motivic organization of a melody in terms of its own instrumentation.

94 This has always struck me as one of the most audacious passages in the whole work. It is built on a simple dynamic idea: p ━━━━ fff , repeated no less than nine times. This series of explosive crescendi, which erupts in a contracting musical space, forms the climax of the exposition of the F minor march music and also provides the transition to the D flat lyrical melody. It is among the most original of Mahler's transitions and in the extremeness of its expression, of which this nest of violent crescendi is a perfect image, the music crosses the borderline between expression and Expressionism. The crescendo, be it remarked, was to become an Expressionist imprint, and this passage in Mahler's First Symphony is already prophetic of the preoccupation with dynamics which is a distinguishing feature of Expressionist music. It is of interest to note that an emphatic use—even a consciously exaggerated use—of the crescendo is not confined by Mahler to this passage: cf. also Figs. 59–60. The movement as a whole is significantly coloured by this particular dynamic concept of the short but intense crescendo in frequent repetition. In Expressionist days still to come such a device would prove to comprise the total form and substance of a piece.

95 In talking about the evolution of the Funeral March to Bauer-Lechner (NBL, p. 149, see also n. 96 below) Mahler interestingly disclosed that 'even as a child he had never thought of "Bruder Martin" [Frère Jacques] as gay— the way it is always sung—but rather, as profoundly tragic. Even then he could hear in it what he developed from it later. Actually, when he was composing, it was the second part of this movement that occurred to him first. Only later, when he was looking for a beginning, was he continually haunted by the canon "Bruder Martin" over the pedal-point that he needed —until finally, with bold resolution, he adopted it'. (The 'second part'? This surely must mean that the idea of the Gypsy music (e.g. Fig. 5 et seq.) came to Mahler *first*. By pedal-point, I suppose Bauer-Lechner had the persistent drum bass in mind.)

But, in my estimation, it cannot only have been 'Bruder Martin' that was haunting Mahler when he was sorting out his thoughts about his Funeral March. I believe that he also had in mind—whether consciously or unconsciously scarcely matters, but we know he performed the work in Leipzig in October, 1886 (see HG[1], p. 155)—a much earlier (1843) parody funeral march, by Mendelssohn, the marvellous little melodrama that is part of his incidental music for the *Midsummer Night's Dream*, a virtually unknown part, one might add, because the complete music these days is rarely heard in the theatre and would make little sense in the concert hall without the words. The number I refer to is the Marcia Funebre that follows the death of Pyramus in the rustics' entertainment. Mendelssohn's notes speak more clearly than words, and I append below his funeral march complete but for the spoken texts. The ironical sound of the tiny wind-and-drums band is itself extraordinarily redolent of Mahler, but there is more to the parallel than that, of course. A soon as we hear the projection of the bassoon's lugubrious song over the drum fourth, we immediately encounter, in principle, Mahler's treatment of 'Bruder Martin' at the outset of *his* funeral march. It is true that he kicks off with his famous muted double-bass solo, but it is the bassoon to which he entrusts the next entry of the round. Furthermore, and more importantly, Mendelssohn's parody march tune not only *contains* the principal leading motive of 'Bruder Martin' but also the dotted rhythm of the continuation of the round, which Mahler was to detach from its melodic context and promote to independence (see Fig. 3, et seq., in his funeral march movement). It is true that in Mendelssohn's miniature the melodic and rhythmic motives appear in an order the reverse of Mahler's. But who can really resist the conclusion that it is Mendelssohn's brilliant invention that stands behind Mahler's, that at some stage was lodged immovably in his ear? There can be little doubt to my mind, indeed, that his *choice* of the 'Bruder Martin' idea was, as it were, pre-conditioned by his memory—conscious or unconscious—of Mendelssohn's melodrama. The anticipations in the Mendelssohn, moreover, extend beyond the significant melodic and rhythmic parallels into the area of 'tone' and character. The ironic tone of the clarinet's contribution, which emerges at its most explicit in the sarcastic, upwards-leaping, crescendo-ing octave with which the instrument makes its final thumb-to-nose farewell to the expiring Thisbe (5 bars from the end), is astonishingly close to the tone that we associate with Mahler in ironic mood, as is the brief but pungent shift to the relative major for the middle section, after the double bar. The abrupt move to the major, the swing back to the minor, and perhaps above all the sudden intrusion of the vein of quasi-rustic jollification that Mendelssohn introduces along with his E flat major—disrupting the funeral rite, so to speak—are all powerfully evocative of what we recognize as typical Mahlerian practice in the area of parody. Mendelssohn's miniature parodistic exercise, in fact, throws us forward, not only directly into the world of irony embodied in the Funeral March of the First Symphony of Mahler, but also previews that deceivingly 'rustic' manner of some of the 'Wunderhorn' songs, e.g. one surely cannot but think of the clarinet duo of the 'Lob des hohen Verstandes' (see below) when confronted with Mendelssohn's sardonically intended E flat invention. It seems to me that we must in future take into account Mendelssohn's vivid *Midsummer Night's Dream* parody when documenting the development of parody, of irony, in the history of music in the nineteenth century. This was a seed that grew, under Mahler's hands, into a tree of gigantic proportions; but the seed was Mendelssohn's—and it provides us with another instance, incidentally, of the fertilization and extension of the language of music—the extension of the images available to music—through the influence of the theatre. (I cannot avoid remarking, before I close, on the authentically Mahlerian re-shuffling of the order of the principal motives that make up the composition of Mendelssohn's Marcia Funebre, i.e., after the middle section, the opening march motives and subsequent clarinet continuation are presented in reverse sequence, allowing the march to end precisely as it begins.)

Mahler ('Lob des hohen Verstandes'):

Mendelssohn:

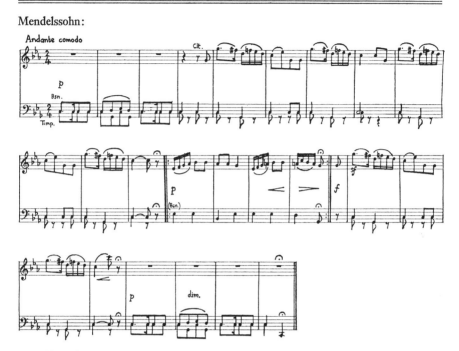

This brief account of Mendelssohn's little masterpiece of satire—which represents perhaps the recovery of a model, rather than the discovery of one: after all, we have read often enough of Mahler's 'debt' to Mendelssohn—only scratches at the surface of what is still a largely untouched, unexplored area, one that awaits vital research: the formation of Mahler's early style. There is much work to be done here, to establish in detail the extent and nature of the oft-stated 'debt' to composers like Mendelssohn and Weber. The time has come to cease repeating the platitude and actually to *look* at particular works where we might expect to find a precise relationship. Mendelssohn's *Midsummer Night's Dream* music was clearly a source worth specific investigation (and no doubt there is more to be uncovered than I have written about above). What about Weber? Even a cursory glance at, say, *Oberon* makes dramatically clear not just the predictably major extent of Mahler's indebtedness—of Weber's influence—but the depth and detail of it. For example, how fascinating it is to come across the Ballet (No. 8) in Act II of the opera, and to realize—with a start—that this tiny piece (shades of the Mendelssohn) must have inflected Mahler's inner ear and imagination when it came to the inventing—and above all the rhythmic formulation—of an important idea in the first movement of the Fourth Symphony. The realization comes when we compare my first example below (from *Oberon*) with the second (from the symphony); and it is not only that we recognize that the *Oberon* Ballet number served as the rhythmic model for Mahler in his symphony, but also that both ideas inhabit the same sonorous world, of the wind band, which surely confirms the relationship. (As John Warrack (JW, p. 325) observes about *Oberon*, the whole work 'might be taken as a primer of how to score for woodwind.' Small wonder that the decisively wind-oriented Mahler was so steeped in Weber or that his ear was mesmerized by Weber's miniature ballet!)

Weber:

Mahler:

There were, of course, much earlier models at work in Mahler than those we may investigate from the first half of the nineteenth century, immensely important and influential though these were. I have a good deal to say later (see pp. 345–62) about the influence Bach came to exert on Mahler, the more overtly, the more aware of and familiar with Bach's art Mahler became. As I point out later, there is a conspicuous Baroque, concertante element in Mahler's instrumental writing which seems to stem directly from his experience of Bach and which makes its presence felt at a comparatively early chronological stage in the development of the symphonies (e.g. in the Scherzo of the Second Symphony). But in fact it was not only in Mahler's handling of orchestral texture that Bach's influence was apparent. The orchestral *Knaben Wunderhorn* songs of the 1890s are not perhaps the works where one would first seek for 'Baroque' parallels in Mahler (though one must remember that the concertante Scherzo of the Second was derived from a *Wunderhorn* song), nor, in making the approach, would one necessarily turn first to one of the humorous songs. Nonetheless, is it not the case that the exuberant vocal cadenza which rounds off 'Wer hat dies Liedlein erdacht?'—the second of my two examples below—has its roots, not in any folkish yodelling, but in an 'instrumental' vocal style that Mahler would certainly have known from Bach? (My first example comes from a work as far removed from the *Wunderhorn* world as can be envisaged: the *St. Matthew Passion* (No. 19).)

Bach:

Mahler:

96 The use of all such concepts as 'easy' and 'difficult' can be terribly misleading, a caution that I am prompted to make by Mahler's own thoughts
about the Funeral March, as recorded by Bauer-Lechner (p. 151): 'To bring
out each new entry in the canon distinctly and in a startling colour—contrast
of sound—so that it calls attention to itself a little—caused me a great deal of
trouble in the instrumentation. Finally, I succeeded in getting the effect
which you find so strange and upsettingly uncanny.' I have no doubt that a
great deal of thought must have gone into the instrumentation of this movement, and perhaps Mahler had to work particularly hard at it in his sketches.
But the fact remains, as I have pointed out, that the unique orchestral conception which this movement represents, once it was established in the MS
full score, underwent scarcely any significant revision, unlike much of the
rest of the symphony. Perhaps it would be more accurate to suggest that
Mahler found it easier to arrive at a definitive version of the wholly singular
Funeral March than of music relatively less complex or exceptional in
character.

97 In speaking about the introduction to Bauer-Lechner (p. 152), Mahler
said: 'In Budapest, where I heard the A in all registers, it sounded far too
substantial for the shimmering and glimmering of the air that I had in mind.
It occurred to me there that I could have all the strings play harmonics . . .
Now I had the effect I wanted.' Mahler's 'there' means 'later', i.e. it was not
in Budapest that he used string harmonics in the *introduction*. We know this
because harmonics are not indicated, even in the Hamburg revision of the
first movement effected in 1893. Oddly enough, however, string harmonics
are already installed in the 1893 MS when the introduction is recapitulated at
the beginning of the development (i.e. at Fig. 12). Was this perhaps an idea
taken over from Budapest and then later—i.e. after the 1893 revisions had
been completed—extended to include the introduction (possibly in the first
instance Mahler wanted to vary the sound of the return of the introduction?).
We are unlikely to know for sure. But we can assume, I think, that the harmonics were established as we know them today by the time of the Weimar
performance in 1894, if not indeed by the time of the Hamburg performance
in 1893. Earlier in the same passage (NBL, pp. 148–52) Mahler makes a remark about the completion of the first movement in Leipzig that, if read
incautiously, might suggest that the harmonics in question were already
envisaged as early as 1888, but as the EMS shows, this cannot have been true,
at least of the introduction. Mahler talked a good deal to Bauer-Lechner about
the orchestration of the First Symphony (NBL, pp. 148–52). See also
Mahler's letter to Richard Strauss, pp. 199–200. There is an interesting letter
quoted in HG¹, pp. 635–6, in which Mahler makes clear how important
rehearsals were to him, for the purpose of assessing the success (or otherwise)
of his orchestration and for making any necessary modifications. In writing
about the arrangements for the first performance of his Fourth Symphony at
Munich, he says: '. . . the fact that I have never heard this work, that I am
anxious about the rehearsals because of the unusual orchestration, and that

I am not sure if I have really succeeded in expressing what I intended, all make me wish to be on the podium for the first performance, for I am the only one who knows my score by heart . . . I am not used to listening from the hall and making "apoplectic" changes. Up to now, I have always been able to go over my scores at least once with my own orchestra, and this gave me a certain sense of security. I have almost always had to make essential changes (during rehearsal)'. It is probable, as M. de La Grange suggests (HG[1], p. 751), that it was during the Hamburg rehearsals of the First Symphony that Mahler decided to use harmonics from the outset.

Mahler's rehearsals must have been fascinating affairs. There is an interesting account of one by Willibald Kaehler (in *150 Jahre Musikalische Akademie des Nationaltheater-Orchesters Mannheim 1779–1929*, Mannheim, 1929, pp. 63–6) of Mahler rehearsing his Third Symphony at Mannheim in 1904 (the work was performed at Heidelberg and Mannheim on 1 and 2 February, see also AM[5], pp. 231–4):

'At the first rehearsal the orchestra naturally had to get used to Mahler's way of conducting. In the first half hour the general nervousness reached such a pitch that no one was capable of blowing an untroubled note or of drawing the bow in a relaxed manner. Soon, however, he had the orchestra under control: the sharp instinct of good orchestral players told them that here was someone for whom the matter in hand was all that counted. Mahler rehearsed with incredible precision, fascinating each player with his glance. He did not rest until each phrase corresponded entirely with his intentions. He repeatedly called to the wind players: "In the long-held notes breathe where you like, but never at any price on a downbeat!" (A golden rule, moreover!) Even at the rehearsal stage he required everyone to give of his very best. On the other hand he was immediately prepared to exercise consideration when a horn player told him that in view of the opera that evening he would have to spare himself at times during the rehearsal. Mahler called out to him: "When you want to spare yourself, just give me a signal like so", and at that he tapped his lips rapidly a few times with the index finger of his left hand. A special word of praise was won by the "gentlemen choirboys" ("Herren Buben"), who managed their difficult entry brilliantly.

'There was a small incident with the first oboist L., an artist of distinction. Mahler demanded that he should play a certain passage "with the bell pointing upwards". L. declared this impossible. Irritated, Mahler burst out: "And I tell you, in ten years' time no one will play passages like this any other way! Just try it!" And lo!, it worked, and the effect Mahler intended came across extremely well. Whereas Mahler's stick technique in the rehearsals had been somewhat violent and often excessively vivacious, in the performance the great moderation of his gestures was surprising. It struck me that while conducting he almost continually gripped the left lapel of his dress-coat with his left hand. When asked the reason for this, he said that this was his means of compelling himself to relax as much as possible. (The trick might profitably be recommended to many of our younger conductors.)

The Sunday brought Mahler, Wolfrum and myself together for lunch in Heidelberg. Naturally we indulged in abundant shop talk about how things stood in the world of music. Mahler spoke of Richard Strauss appreciatively but with somewhat cautious restraint. He spoke little about his own works. I asked him whether he had intended to express anything of a specific kind with the characteristic trumpet theme at the beginning of the symphony's first movement (D minor triad rising in semiquavers). Mahler confessed himself an adversary of programme music, and only after a long hesitation he explained: In order to understand what he meant one must know a thing or two about Greek mythology. "Think of the tritons blowing on conch shells in the classical Walpurgisnacht."'

98 Mahler was probably already seeking such an effect in 1893, when allotting to the horns the part he eventually gave to a third trumpet.

99 JD, p. 83. Mr. Diether, like M. de Le Grange, suggests January as a probable date, when Mahler was revising the rest of the symphony.

100 See DM¹, pp. 225–9. Mr. Knud Martner (Copenhagen) tells me that the Cassel production of the *Trompeter* was announced as '7 lebende Bilder mit verbindende Dichtungen nach Viktor Scheffel von Wilhelm Benneck. Musik von Mahler.' For a complete list of the titles of the seven movements, see HG¹, p. 705. Surely the 'Blumine' movement was the first number in the theatrical suite, 'Ein Ständchen im Rhein'?

101 I am glad to have the opportunity to quote this lovely tune complete, if only to redress the harsh criticism I made of it in DM¹ (p. 228), based on Steinitzer's six-bar quotation.

102 To include a 'character piece' in a symphony was a practice that Mahler was to make his own, e.g. the Andante in the Second, the Minuet in the Third, even the nocturnes in the Seventh. From that point of view, the Andante of the First Symphony at least provides an historical precedent. But of course one only needs to compare the elaborate compositional character of, say, the Minuet from the Third Symphony with 'Blumine' to see at once the essential symphonic element—an indispensable *density* of musical thought—that is missing in the latter.

103 In 1920, a Mahler issue (April) of *Musikblätter des Anbruch*, Vienna, quoted in JD, p. 87. In 1910, Steinitzer had already told much the same story in his introduction to a Mahler Festschrift edited by Stefan (PS², 'Mahler in Leipzig', pp. 10–15) but on this earlier occasion interestingly added that Mahler had made use in the piece in question (i.e., the *Trompeter* movement) of a somewhat over-sweet melody taken from a lost composition of his youth. Clearly, the trumpet melody was meant; and if Steinitzer was correct in his 1910 recollection, then it would seem as if Mahler's attachment to the serenade may also have been influenced by the origins of its principal melodic idea in his own past. All this, to me, adds up to a convincing stylistic and psychological picture.

104 *Der Trompeter von Säkkingen: ein Sang vom Oberrhein*, by J. V. Scheffel, Stuttgart, 1888, p. 79. An indication of the contemporary popularity of this work is disclosed by the inscription from the publisher (Adolf Bonz): 'One hundred and sixty-eighth impression.'

105 Mr. Martner tells me that Johanna Richter made a guest appearance at Cassel in the spring of 1883, and was thereafter engaged by the theatre. She appears to have left Cassel at the end of the 1886–7 season. Mahler left Cassel for Prague in 1885 and moved on to Leipzig in 1886. See also HG¹, p. 753, where M. de La Grange suggests that it was unlikely (in his view) that Mahler's *Trompeter* serenade was addressed to Johanna Richter, and points out further that the First Symphony, despite the link with Johanna through its incorporation of *Gesellen* cycle elements, was in fact '"a declaration of love" . . . to Maria von Weber' rather than 'the Kassel soprano whom Mahler had probably all but forgotten by 1888'. There may indeed have been the transference from one love to another that M. de La Grange describes. Nonetheless, the experience of Mahler's painful affair with Johanna must still have been vivid for him and reflected in the history of his symphonic Hero. I find it more than probable, too, that Mahler had his current sweetheart in mind when he composed the *Trompeter* serenade. He may have scorned the poem but for quite a long while in fact this particular musical number retained his affection. In short, Johanna was still playing an active role musically speaking in the First Symphony, despite the switch in dedication.

106 It was culpable of the editors of the edition of the First Symphony published as Vol. I of a *critical* [*sic*] Collected Edition to give no information whatsoever about the Andante. The movement should at least have been fully described or, better still, included as an appendix. This unscholarly suppression of vital data has had the counter-productive effect, in my view, of attaching more importance to the 'missing' movement than otherwise would have been the case.

107 Bauer-Lechner's reminiscences were not published (and then still in an incomplete form) until 1923. Some excerpts from her diaries, however, had appeared anonymously in the Mahler issue of *Der Merker*, Vienna, March 1912, though this particular passage about the title of the First Symphony was not among them. The suppressed passages are now made known to us in HG¹.

108 If he *was* in fact trying to promote a meaningful association with Jean Paul, then he must have been disappointed—and probably perturbed—by the audience reaction described by Foerster (a description quoted in the Czech edition of GMB¹, p. 129: see Bibliography): 'Among the audience at the Hamburg and Weimar performances [1893 and 1894] there were probably very few readers of Jean Paul (at one time a favourite of the young Schumann), which was not to be wondered at; and so it appeared that, led astray by the title, "Titan", they expected a new "Eroica", instead of which Mahler presented them with the music of a young heart full of hope and despair with here and there satirical touches of parody and an ironical overlay of "folk comedy".' Doubtless, it was just this kind of grotesque

misunderstanding that encouraged Mahler to get rid of the whole programmatic apparatus.

109 It was Bruno Walter who wrote (in BW², p. 119): '[Mahler's] giving the
name "Titan" to his First Symphony signalized his love of Jean Paul; we
often talked about this great novel, and especially about the character of
Roquairol, whose influence is noticeable in the Funeral March. Mahler would
insist that an element of Roquairol, of his self-centred, self-tormenting,
scornful and imperilled spirit, exists in every gifted individual, and has to be
conquered before productive powers can come into play. He felt entirely at
home with the witty and complex humour of Schoppe. *Siebenkäs* was a
favourite work, and, he insisted, Jean Paul's masterpiece.' This is a strong
counter to the views of Holtzmann, Pfohl, Bauer-Lechner, et al. (See also
Bruno Walter's extremely interesting letter of 6 December 1901 to Ludwig
Schiedermair (BW³, p. 51), in which he makes the same point about
Roquairol.)

110 How absurd, only those who have attempted to follow Jean Paul's
mammoth, labyrinthine and shapeless narrative can know.

111 *Penguin Companion to Literature*, II: *European Literature*, 1969, p. 399.

112 *Titan. A Romance. From the German of Jean Paul Friedrich Richter.*
Translated by Charles T. Brooks. 2 vols. London, 1863. For the German
text of Jean Paul's novel I use the edition published in Munich in 1961:
Werke, III: *Titan*, pp. 122–4, 227–8, 231, and 211–12. I was interested to
read in J. W. Smeed's introduction to his edition of Jean Paul's *Des Feld-
predigers Schmelzle Reise nach Flätz*, Oxford, 1966, p. 10, that Jean Paul, at
the age of twenty-seven, 'recorded in his diary a vision of himself on his
deathbed.' One recalls, naturally enough, the similar vision that Mahler had
of himself, at the age of twenty-eight (in Leipzig), lying on his funeral bier.
This was surely an ironically appropriate experience for Jean Paul and Mahler
to share.

113 I must take the opportunity here to correct my reference to Callot in
DM¹, p. 135, as the author of a 'famous painting'. I am grateful to Dr. Dika
Newlin, who pointed out this slip in her review of my book in *Notes*, March
1959, pp. 248–9.

114 There must have been many versions by many artists of this particular
animal fantasy. A correspondent in Germany, Herr Heinz Kreutz, sent me
word of an old lithograph from Alsace, with the title, naturally, in two
languages: 'Le convoi funèbre du chasseur—Des Jägers Leichenzug'.
Clearly this was a favourite fairy-tale incident, with the illustration widely
dispersed throughout Europe.

115 At the Kunstmuseum, Basel, in 1971. The admirably informative catalogue was the work of Eva Maria Kraft. Schwind was also the illustrator
(1833) of a volume by Ludwig Bechstein, *Faustus*, in whose collection of
fairy tales Mahler found the story that he converted into his own text for
Das klagende Lied. Dr. Edward R. Reilly has also drawn my attention to the
fact that graphic representations of the legendary 'Rübezahl' and a luxuriantly

poetic evocation of 'Des Knaben Wunderhorn' (see jacket) are among Schwind's works.

116 'Freund Hein spielt auf', according to PB, p. 155, was originally inscribed by Mahler on the MS of this movement. (See also BW³, p. 52.) At one stage (see NBL, p. 171) Mahler seems to have invited Arnold Rosé (the leader of the Vienna Philharmonic) to play the solo violin part in the Scherzo on the viola (on which Rosé was also an accomplished performer). This, if Bauer-Lechner was correct, was suggested at Mahler's 'Leseprobe' with the Philharmonic in October 1901.

117 One could really elaborate a whole theory about the significance of the dark fiddler as an image in Romantic art—in music, painting and literature. One thinks in literature of such things as Grillparzer's remarkable short novel, *Der arme Spielmann* (1848), and there is also a rich and dazzling range of pictorial imagery. I was struck only recently in the Nationalgalerie, Berlin, by Arnold Böcklin's 'Selbstbildnis mit fiedelndem Tod', a brilliant document of late Romanticism from 1872 and a brilliant late pictorial development of the idea of Freund Hein: in Böcklin's painting, death plays the violin— a grinning skull, violin under the chin, the bow held by a skeletal hand—behind the artist, who turns as if half-hearing or only overhearing a distant music that he can neither locate nor identify. A Mahlerian canvas, if there ever were one. Chagall has sustained the image in more recent times, but perhaps more cosily than Böcklin. One wonders, incidentally, because of the conspicuous Jewish participation in, and wonderful talent for, string playing— violinists, especially, to the fore—whether the image of the fiddler might not be a particularly significant and resonant one for the Jewish composer, musician, or writer? Another classical high Romantic document which extends the tradition of Freund Hein is Delius's opera, *A Village Romeo and Juliet* (1907), after the story by Gottfried Keller, in which 'The Dark Fiddler' himself is among the dramatis personae.

Part IV

Contents: Part IV

CHRONICLE

IMPORTANT THOUGH THE *Gesellen* cycle and First Symphony are, for a demonstration of the cross-fertilization between song and symphony, it is the Third and Fourth Symphonies that confirm the altogether dominant influence of the *Wunderhorn* spirit at this period. As we have seen already, one of the *Wunderhorn* settings, 'Das himmlische Leben', composed in 1892 as an independent song, was not only intimately involved with the composition of the huge Third Symphony (1896) but was also the generating impulse behind the Fourth (1900). The role that 'Das himmlische Leben' was to play in the Third Symphony may be deduced from the thematic references and links that still remain. The first three movements of the Fourth Symphony were composed into a pre-determined, pre-existing Finale—'Das himmlische Leben'—and the total structure of the symphony, including its overall tonal organization (though its central tonality is G major, the work ends in the 'heavenly' key of E major, a tonal region already adumbrated in the Adagio and implied by the opening B minor bars of the first movement), is governed by the song.

If the First, Third and Fourth Symphonies may be said to be *Wunderhorn* symphonies, either because of their singular evocations of Nature (the vernal radiance of the First's first movement, the Ives-like documentary Pandemonium of the Third's vast first movement, 'Summer marches in') or because of their unique, varied fantasy (the grotesque Funeral March of the first, the childlike angelic bells of the Third's fifth movement, the total vision embodied in the Fourth), the Second Symphony (1894) would seem to stand a little apart from them in style and content (its chronology has been scrutinized earlier, see pp. 161–83). Though this symphony, too, includes major *Wunderhorn* components—an idyllic *Ländler*, satirical Scherzo, and song— 'Urlicht'—for contralto (functioning as a slow movement for voice and orchestra)—its underlying drama, i.e. the death, recollections and resurrection of its Hero, projected on an epic scale and yet convincingly contained within a simple, progressive tonal scheme, C minor→E flat major (from the C minor of the opening funeral march we progress to the resurrectory E flat of the concluding chorale), anticipates the content of Mahler's middle-period symphonies (particularly the Fifth and Sixth Symphonies and the metaphysics of the monumental Eighth).[I]

The *Wunderhorn* symphonies are marked above all by the fantastic qualities of their imagination, often verging on the bizarre; by their innovatory exploration of popular musical materials; by their no less innovatory exploration of instrumentation, of the wind particularly, which is often raised to a new status; by their intrepid exploration of acoustic space and multi-direction of sound (the Second and Third Symphonies especially); by their developing emphasis on polyphonic textures, often of very different kinds (Third and Fourth Symphonies); by their sometimes folk-inflected melody (as has been suggested in n. 89, pp. 291f., it is not always sufficiently appreciated that Mahler, musically speaking, was open to both Slav and Austro-German influences); and by their composer's exuberant ransacking of almost every available large-scale form. Thus in this first period the symphonies call on and variously re-interpret the resources of cantata, oratorio, orchestral suite, choral symphony (Beethoven, Liszt), symphonic poem, and dramatic or 'programme' symphony (Berlioz, Liszt, Tchaikovsky, and many others (see pp. 163–5)). Last, but not least, Mahler's own developing historical consciousness opened up his music to influences from a past other than the nineteenth century, e.g. Bach. Mahler's first four symphonies must be regarded as brilliantly diverse extensions of late Romantic 'symphony', a term which eventually came to embrace the most various and unorthodox of large-scale designs.[II] Indeed, these *Wunderhorn* symphonies may be regarded as eccentric and synthetic in the best sense of those words.

COMMENTARIES

I. The *Wunderhorn* Symphonies, particularly the Third and Fourth

WHEN TALKING TO Bauer-Lechner about his Fourth Symphony, Mahler remarked that the Fourth forms a conclusion to the preceding three, besides being closely connected with them. Indeed, it seems that Mahler regarded the four symphonies as 'a perfectly self-contained tetralogy' (NBL, pp. 145–6). If they are such—and perhaps 'perfectly self-contained' is something of an exaggeration—it is surely because they all in various ways employ song, and more particularly *Wunderhorn* songs, or songs in the *Wunderhorn* manner (i.e. the *Gesellen* cycle), as a principal compositional technique. If the Fourth Symphony 'forms a conclusion' to this, in some respects, unified period of *Wunderhorn* exploitation, it is because the work takes to a logical extreme the use of song material that in the preceding works had been less intensively, less rigorously organized, i.e. in the Fourth Symphony, the song ('Das himmlische Leben'), as I suggest in the Chronicle above, is the controlling presence which orders and determines the total conception of the work.

Whereas in the earlier symphonies song-sources had certainly played a vital role, but had not, as it were, regulated the shaping and development of the whole work, the Fourth was genuinely a 'song' symphony, not just because it had a *Wunderhorn* song-finale, but because the symphony in its entirety emerged from, and has its life in, the idea of the song (and by idea I have in mind both the programmatic and musical aspects of the song). Mahler was right, I think, to sense that the Fourth represented a terminal, summarizing peak in his symphonic development. In my view too, as I have said earlier, it is the Fourth that presents Mahler's neatest and most sophisticated solution to the problem of the programme, the success of which resides in the sheer single-mindedness and virtuosity of technique with which he carried through the project, not from beginning to end, but, rather, from end to beginning.

The Fourth, then, represents a quite special relationship in Mahler's output between a song and a symphony, with the idea of the symphony subordinate to the idea of the song. The song, as it were, was in the saddle, whereas before, for all their crucial importance, songs had in the main functioned as part (as vocal or instrumental movements) of the overall grand design. In the case of the Fourth, however, the song *was* the grand design.[1]

In the Third Symphony Mahler was already moving towards the concept of an overall unification in which a song would play the leading role. I have set out elsewhere some of the programmatic history of the Third Symphony (see pp. 187–94), which shows how at one stage 'Das himmlische Leben' was planned to function as the Finale of the work. But it was not just a matter of the song being planned as part of a programme, and then dropped. The song in fact was not dropped until it had substantially been built into the fabric of the music; and when one comes to examine the nature of the influence of the song on the symphony and to scrutinize the techniques by which Mahler intended to establish the song as the symphony's logical destination, one soon realizes that there was a process of thematic transformation, cross-reference and cross-fertilization planned for the Third that was almost as elaborate and sophisticated as that which finally emerged as the *raison d'être* of the Fourth Symphony. I write 'planned' but I mean planned *and* substantially executed. For the odd thing about the Third is that the grand design, as it were, was actually carried through almost to the very last step which would have been the song itself.[2] We have, indeed, in the Third Symphony an altogether singular case, a complicated set of relationships, evolving over an immense musical structure, that is denied the fulfilment— the Finale—that was its obvious evolutionary purpose. Small wonder that Mahler himself seemed somewhat confused when talking about the overall organization of the Third, and the interrelationships between its movements. He certainly never seems to have acknowledged the paradoxical situation that was created by diverting 'Das himmlische Leben' elsewhere. It is true that he lamented to Bauer-Lechner (NBL, p. 41) that nothing had come of his dreams for interrelating the movements in the Third, and that each movement constituted an independent whole (see also pp. 192–3). But this was a somewhat misleading way of looking at the work, which blandly ignores the interrelationships that *were* set up on the basis of the song-finale and excludes any mention of the omitted movement. Mahler was perhaps guilty of *suppressio veri* on this occasion. In any event, he seems to have found it necessary to make some sort of gesture towards the inter-movement relationships that he was prepared to acknowledge[3] and thus specifies the eruption of E flat minor in the Scherzo (Figs. 31–2) as a dramatic reminder of the symphony's point of departure, i.e. across the music falls the 'heavy shadow of lifeless nature, of yet uncrystallized inorganic matter'. One sees the particular point Mahler is making while noting that he says nothing at all of the explicit relationships between, say, 'O Mensch! Gib Acht!' (the fourth movement) and the first movement, or of the—again wholly explicit—return in the final Adagio of materials from the first movement (see, for example, two bars before Fig. 20, et seq.). In fact, Mahler neither hinted at the complex of inter-relationships that did not quite reach final materialization but was embodied in the symphony nonetheless, nor did he offer more than a very half-hearted and partial indication of the alternative interrelationships which came to constitute the unifying component in the work. The truth is that in the Third Symphony we have to deal with *two* sets of unifying elements, and to disentangle these we need to look in some detail at the mosaic of interrelationships that leads, as it were, a hidden life in the work, because the song which would have provided the 'key' to de-code the thematic complex was never added to complete the edifice.

If we remind ourselves of the main melody of 'Das himmlische Leben' (see Ex. 94) as first unfolded by the solo clarinet at the opening of the song, we

Ex. 94

see very clearly that it is none other than *x* in Ex. 94 that is shrilly, brilliantly outlined (see Ex. 95) by a quintet of clarinets at Fig. 12 in the midst of the

Ex. 95

introduction to the first movement of the Third Symphony (the grace-notes, which are themselves to play an important role in the movement as a whole, contain in compressed form the complete melody of Ex. 94). One notes at the same time that Ex. 95 introduces an onrush of flowing semiquavers in the lower strings (Ex. 96), figuration which not only has a special role to play in

Ex. 96

the Third, but also in the Fourth Symphony (cf. for example the passage at Fig. 12 and after with, say, Fig. 10 and after in the first movement of the Fourth Symphony). The generator of the flowing semiquavers was 'Das himmlische Leben', which is rich in this scurrying figuration.

At this stage in the unfolding of the vast first movement, the intimations of 'Das himmlische Leben' have not acquired a status more considerable than that of the many other influential subsidiary motives that make their appearance in the course of the introduction. But as the movement progresses— and this is the fascination of attempting to trace the history of Ex. 95—the song-associated motives do acquire (or at least, so I suggest) a quite *special* status, one moreover that has been very skilfully calculated by the composer. For instance we find that Exx. 95 and 96 are substantially involved in the crucial passage (two bars before Fig. 19 et seq.) in which the main march gets under way; and as the march evolves we find that Mahler detaches the repeated chords (with their grace-notes) from Ex. 95 (see *y*) and uses them continuously to punctuate the texture of the music. They are there as a constant presence, a continuous reminder. It would be pedantic to list all the occurrences of *y*: they are legion. But see, for example, Fig. 20 et seq.; two bars after Fig. 21, et seq.; Fig. 22 et seq.; and thereafter throughout the movement. The emphasis is continuous and deliberate, and as a result, within the context of this remarkable movement, with its great array of themes and motives, Ex. 95 begins to accumulate a quite particular weight. It does not emerge as rival to the principal march tune, but the persistence of it is striking and the idea itself unmistakable whenever it appears (the grace-note ornamentation, one sees, was an obligatory part of the invention, above all if it were to make an impact when projected as *y* alone).[4]

In the movement to this point, Ex. 95 has certainly been prominent, influential and inescapable, but it has just as certainly not been the regulating force behind the thematic organization of the music. One would not, at this stage, have assigned a principal thematic status to the motive, for all its powerful character. Thus the sense of surprise and excitement when, in the great central developmental section of the movement, Ex. 95 moves unambiguously into the foreground, holding the stage with a piercingly brilliant extension and ornamentation of the original motive (Ex. 97) and later

Ex. 97

(at Fig. 46, for instance) generating a new melodic expansion (Ex. 98)—an inversion of Ex. 95—which is combined in typically Mahlerian polyphony

Ex. 98

with a profusion of other motives. There is absolutely no question that in this
B flat minor part of the movement, Ex. 95 is as it were riding high, and indeed,
after the ensuing C major section (Fig. 49), it is significant that it is a straight
version of the clarinet signal that ushers in (two bars before Fig. 51) the
climax of the development, which is itself (see Fig. 51) based on the rushing
semiquaver figuration which, we remember, was associated with Ex. 95 on
its very first appearance (see Ex. 96 and cf. Figs. 12 and 51). There follows in
due time the recapitulation, and there, Ex. 95, after its assertiveness in the
development, reverts to that punctuation of the texture (by *y*) which was its
main function in the exposition. But there can be no doubt, when the huge
movement comes to rest, that Ex. 95 (whose contour, we must not forget, is
that of 'Das himmlische Leben') has, in a most skilful and indeed elaborate
way, performed a vital thematic role *within* the overall thematic organization
of the movement. The motive has, as it were, shown its power, its influence;
and one can see very clearly how Mahler, from this position, continued to
build up the sequence of interrelationships which would culminate in the
revelation of 'Das himmlische Leben'.

Thus in the Minuet we find that one of the alternating sections (see Fig. 5
and Ex. 99 below) introduces the rushing semiquaver figuration that was a
characteristic feature of the first movement in a form very close indeed to the
scurrying semiquavers in the song which were the origin of the idea.[5] Compare Ex. 99, for instance, with Ex. 100 (four bars before Fig. 9 in 'Das
himmlische Leben', et seq.), in which the relationship is clearly stated (note
too the ornamented triad):

Ex. 99

Ex. 100

In the fifth movement, the *Wunderhorn* setting 'Es sungen drei Engel', one
whole section of the movement—'Und sollt' ich nicht weinen, du gütiger
Gott' (four bars after Fig. 3 to Fig. 6)—is based on a parallel passage in 'Das
himmlische Leben' (Figs. 5 to 7). The clarinet scales and sobbing oboes are
common to both settings. In the Third Symphony, these graphically depict
sinful man and his weeping, whereas in the song, 'Das himmlische Leben', the
central image is that of the innocent lamb sacrificed for sinful man's sake.
The servicing of these linked images by the same music meant that in 'Es

sungen drei Engel' there was a literal anticipation of the heavenly life that the final song was to disclose. There could hardly have been a more direct way of binding together, musically, dramatically, and poetically, the two movements, the choral setting and the solo song.

The fifth movement brings us to the brink of the Adagio Finale, and this is an appropriate moment to look back at the ground which has been covered. If we add together the intimations of 'Das himmlische Leben' that are to be found in the first, second and fifth movements of the symphony, we uncover what was undoubtedly a whole complex of anticipations and interrelationships that would have culminated in the solo song, the child's vision of heaven; and the ultimate revelation of the fact that Ex. 95 above, and all the elaborate thematic and motivic events associated with it, could be attributed to the generative power of 'Wir geniessen die himmlischen Freuden' would certainly have counted as one of the work's glories. But the revelation never happened, and in so far as the symphony is unified by means of intermovement quotation and reminiscence, it is through the backward-looking references to the first movement that are made in the third, fourth and sixth movements of the symphony; though be it noted that none of this cycle of interrelationships attains anything like the degree of subtlety and complexity that we encounter in the cycle of developing relationships that was left hanging in the air.

I doubt now if we shall ever know the truth of the matter. I sometimes wonder if Mahler at one time had envisaged the projection of two programmatic ideas, each with its own resolution. First, a child's innocent vision of paradise emerging as the peak of man's destiny and summit of the symphony, and proving to emerge in musical truth from the non-human evolutionary stage with which the work opens. The long process of thematic transformation, whereby Ex. 95 was to become revealed as 'Das himmlische Leben', would have reflected Mahler's own 'evolutionary' programme (see pp. 188-9). Second, there was the contrast between inanimate Nature and the area of human love (in which man shows his divine aspect), and the possibility of an ultimate reconciliation, something Mahler attempts to effect in his fourth and sixth movements (in the second, the outburst of E flat minor is surely Pan giving the creatures of the forest a fright?). On the other hand, it might have been that this 'second' programme only came into being because of the abandonment of the song-finale that would have made sense of the first: in the light of this decision Mahler would at last have made certain, as he did, that the Adagio should reveal a clinching cyclic relationship with the first movement.

Undoubtedly this whole aspect of the internal organization of the symphony is of the greatest complexity, and as we have seen (pp. 188-94), the complication is intensified rather than clarified by what we know of the chronology of the work. We know that in the summer of 1895, Mahler was definitely thinking in terms of a seven-movement shape,[6] with the 'Love' movement (the Adagio) placed sixth and the child's vision of heaven ('Das himmlische Leben') placed seventh. In this scheme, both programmatic destinations were, so to say, juxtaposed, and possibly it is the trace of this original conception that is responsible for the curiosity of the twin sets of thematic interrelationhips, though, I believe, as I have already argued in some detail, that it was the solo-song set which for a long time was the governing factor in the composition of the work.

In this connection, it is of great importance to realize that it was by no means Mahler's first intention to place the Adagio at or towards the end of this symphony. On the contrary, earlier drafts of the programme (quoted by Paul Bekker (in PB, p. 106; see pp. 188–90) show that he had contemplated a precisely central position for the 'Love' Adagio, while still retaining 'Das himmlische Leben' as the Finale. I think that then there was a gradual process by which the Adagio, probably increasing in weight and scale as a concept in Mahler's mind, slid away from its central position towards the end of the symphony. I think it perfectly possible that it was quite a large-scale Adagio, to be followed by 'Das himmlische Leben', that Mahler still had in view when drafting the programmes of 1895 with the slow movement and song-finale juxtaposed. After all, and again interestingly enough, it was exactly this formal scheme that Mahler was to adopt in the Fourth Symphony (thus it was not only the Finale he took over from the Third, but also an important aspect of its original design).

It seems more than likely that the Adagio, as it were of its own volition— and one ought to remember that this was in fact Mahler's *first* real attempt at a slow movement—assumed the dimensions of a Finale (and in so doing created the precedent that Mahler was later to follow up in *Das Lied* and the Ninth Symphony). It may indeed have been the case that when Mahler set about the movement he was still thinking of it in relation to an ensuing song-finale, in the sequential manner of the Fourth Symphony. But once the Adagio was done (and perhaps the unexpected weight of it had something to do with a determination on Mahler's part to give birth to a slow movement that would not pass unnoticed), there can have been no doubt in his mind that the concluding vision of paradise would have to be jettisoned. The scale of the Adagio would have automatically excluded the possibility of anything succeeding it. (As M. de La Grange puts it, in HG[1], p. 809, 'Until the end of the summer of 1895, the Adagio was meant to be succeeded by the 1892 song "Das himmlische Leben", which was suppressed the following winter.')

This certainly will not have been the first time in the history of music that the shape of a work has radically altered during the making of it. However much detail may be planned in advance, in the actual business of creating, all manner of new emphases and vistas are uncovered. What, however, remains a strange aspect of the chronology of the composition of the Third Symphony is this: that although Mahler came to complete the first movement last (in 1896), i.e. after the Adagio (and the four preceding movements) had already been composed (by the summer of 1895), he still wrote the movement as if, thematically and programmatically speaking, 'Das himmlische Leben' were its—and the symphony's—goal; and yet if, as seems to be the case, the Adagio was already in existence, he must have known that the complex set of anticipations and intimations he was building into his first movement was, strictly considered, redundant.

All this, without doubt, is something of a puzzle.[7] I do not pretend to know all the answers to it (it is the kind of puzzle, one feels, which involves more than one answer) and have to remain content with stating the nature of the enigma rather than the solution to it. Much of the seeming confusion may have stemmed from an indecision about the Finale that Mahler may have sustained until the very last moment; and much seems attributable to the changes the work underwent in the actual process of composition and to the back-to-front chronology of its creation. But though the puzzle may go on teasing us, the fascinating clues are there to be read and interpreted; and there is at least one significant conclusion that can be drawn: that despite the singular fate that overtook Mahler's elaborate plan to evolve into a song-finale in his Third Symphony, sufficient evidence survives to show us that it was in this work—superficially the most loosely knit of all Mahler's symphonies—that the evolutionary form and concentrated thematic organization of the Fourth Symphony, and above all, the idea of a *Wunderhorn* song as a principal regulating feature, were all decisively adumbrated.

*   *   *   *

If nothing else, the preceding discussion of the Third Symphony at least demonstrates the wealth of subtleties to be explored in the music. Even the simplest of the movements, the Minuet, contains surprising refinements, one of which involves a technique and a principle that are encountered more than once in Mahler's art. As it happens, Mahler sketched out (for what reason I do not know) a brief thematic 'index' to the Minuet, including it as part of a document on which he sets out in full the titles of the movements.[8] This is the only programme note with music quotations by Mahler himself that I know of, and I reproduce it here as an amusing example of his trying his hand at a kind of potted musical analysis for which on the whole he had very few good words to say. A shame, though, that Mahler did not tabulate some of the other movements, besides the Minuet. His own thematic index to the first movement, for example, would have been of particular interest.

Symphony in F major: 'A Summer Morning's Dream'.

Introduction: *Pan awakes*
Nro. 1.: *Summer marches in*
Nro. 2.: '*What the flowers of the meadow tell me*' (Minuet).

Main theme unfolding itself in all the time richer variation:

In the course of this theme, there develops:

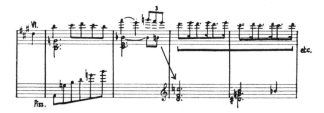

With this there develops a 2nd theme:

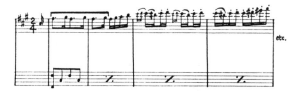

A 3rd theme:

A 4th theme:

There follow:

Nro. 3. *What the beasts of the forest tell me* (Rondo)
Nro. 4. *What man tells me* (Alto solo)
Nro. 5. *What the angels tell me* (Women's chorus and alto solo)
Nro. 6 (Final movement). *What love tells me* (Adagio)

> Father behold these wounds of mine
> Let no creature be unredeemed

Needless to add, there is nothing in Mahler's analysis about that prominent compositional technique to which I referred above and which I have already briefly outlined above (see p. 43) in connection with one of the *Kindertotenlieder*. I described the process there as 'telescoping'—the recapitulation is introduced while the lead-back to the recapitulation is still in motion—and it is a principle that in fact makes its first appearance in Mahler's music in the seemingly so simple-minded Minuet of the Third Symphony. (Mahler's 'flower piece' is really a brilliant instrumental study in the ornamental-exquisite style of the flower maidens' scene in Wagner's *Parsifal*.) The movement comprises the Minuet (the principal theme and its variations and extensions) and two trios (the first of which unfolds Mahler's themes Nos. 2, 3 and 4, though in the order 3/2/4 (!), the second built on an expanded version of the same pattern).[9] The crucial returns of the Minuet occur at Fig. 6 and Fig. 14. First, let us remind ourselves of the long opening span of the Minuet's melody (Ex. 101):

Ex. 101

In Ex. 102 below, Tempo I, A major (the principal key of the Minuet), and the main tune of the Minuet itself all seem to be resumed at Fig. 6. But in fact, it we examine the passage more closely we find that this traditional symmetry has been fascinatingly dislocated. The main tune is certainly felt to be resumed at Fig. 6, along with the return to Tempo I and the main key, but the tune, on inspection, proves to be already in mid-stream (at bar 3 of Ex. 101, indeed), the first two bars having already been resumed by the cellos as it were on the 'wrong' side of the double bar (see bars 1 and 2 of Ex. 102). What we encounter here, in short, is a characteristic example of Mahler's 'telescoping' procedures. At the conclusion of the F sharp minor→E minor first trio, the lead-back to the Minuet tune and the tonic combines a conventional transitional function with an unconventional recapitulatory one: the two events, normally spaced out as a step-by-step sequence in time, are rolled together, though this is not the only surprise embedded in this remarkable passage.

Ex. 102

It is not, first, a recapitulation of the original version of the main tune that we hear at Fig. 6 but the variation of it that Mahler introduces at Fig. 2 in order to round off the first statement of the Minuet; and second, if we scrutinize Fig. 2, which itself represents a transition from the middle section of the Minuet's exposition to the return of the (varied) principal tune, we find precisely the same dove-tailing principle already adumbrated; indeed, Ex. 102 is clearly a slightly more elaborate version of the transition at Fig. 2, and more prominent because of the more important formal juncture that Ex. 102 represents.

It is not only Mahler's 'telescoping' procedures that are a marked feature of this finely wrought movement. We also encounter his unceasing variation technique. This is already explicit, already heavily involved, even when we confine ourselves to a discussion of an isolated passage like Ex. 102. Mahler certainly remains true to his variational self in the return of the main tune after the second trio, i.e. the parallel passage to Ex. 102 (at Fig. 14), where, though the telescoping principle is the same, there are significant differences: this time the main tune at the double bar drops, not into the tonic, but into E major (the tonic is postponed), and Mahler sets off his recapitulation, again on the 'wrong' side of the double bar, not with the opening bars (1–2) of the main tune (as in Ex. 102) but with bar 3 of the main tune—the opening bars are omitted altogether. Bar 3, it will be remembered, was the bar with which the recapitulation proper began at Fig. 6. Thus Mahler at Fig. 14 effects a fresh dislocation by pushing the main tune further back across the double bar, decapitating it, and picking up the recapitulation proper at Fig. 14 in the wrong key and with bar 4 of the main tune (see Ex. 103).

Ex. 103

Another subtlety in this complex is that the resumption of the main tune grows out of one of the leading variation motives which was itself initially generated by a variation of the main tune, the very motive in fact that Mahler

took the trouble to mark up with brackets in his brief analysis of the movement (see his second and third examples).

One might think all this no more than a particular kind of intricacy associated with a particular movement, but in fact it betrays a quite specific turn
of mind that not only crops up again in the Fourth Symphony and the
Kindertotenlieder, but also in the slow movement of the Sixth Symphony,
again at a crucial moment of melodic recapitulation. Mahler's treatment of
his recapitulations was often unorthodox: a precedent was set in the first
movement of the First Symphony (to choose only one early example: see
pp. 30–1) and in his later music the traditional of unconventionality is
sustained, frequently in very elaborate formulations. The summing-up section of the Andante of the Sixth is no exception to the rule of the unpredictable. The tonic—E flat major—is clearly the goal to be achieved, but Mahler
sees no reason to synchronize the conclusive re-establishment of E flat and
the final re-statement of the movement's long-breathed melody. On the
contrary, E flat is largely re-affirmed in terms of a prominent motive initially
generated as a fresh continuation of the main tune, while the main tune itself
is in fact recapitulated as part of the strenuously developing and modulating
section of which E flat is the sought-after climax. Within that modulating
section, the main tune (or to be precise, a variation of it, cf. Fig. 55, et seq.—
see Ex. 104) is restated in B major, an interim tonal goal that is achieved at
Fig. 60. If we examine the music at this point (see Ex. 105) we find another
edition of the telescoping principle that was adumbrated in the Minuet of the
Third. The main tune of the Andante is already in full flow (violas and
cellos) at the moment that B major is decisively asserted, but the 'missing'
opening bars of the melody are in fact not missing at all. They are there,
though in slightly modified form, in the cellos and double-basses, but simultaneously combined with the strenuous transitional chromatic ascent that cul-
minates in B at Fig. 60: the parallel with the principle that we have observed
in the Third's Minuet is very striking. One has to keep one's ears open to
hear this subtle stroke in performance, particularly in view of the fact that the
cellos and basses have to assert their motivic rights at the same time as eight
horns are asserting theirs; and to add to the textural complexity, Mahler
re-introduces the counter-melody (see violins, Fig. 55) that originally
accompanied this variation of the principal melody. This may be another
way of saying that it is a sign of the first-rate performance if crucial events of
the order we are discussing here are made audible. If one does not hear the
density and intelligence of the musical thinking at Fig. 60—or at the critical
telescoping points in the Minuet—then one may be sure it is an inferior
interpretation.

But it is in the first movement of the Fourth Symphony that Mahler offers
us the most brilliant and sophisticated example of his telescoping technique,

Ex. 104

Ex. 105

rightly so, because in this case the technique is pressed into service at a highly important formal moment: the recapitulation in an elaborate sonata movement (Fig. 18). Because of the 'formality' of the movement, Mahler's treatment of it is all the more riveting. This is a well-known passage in the symphony and one of which Mahler himself was clearly proud. He remarked about it to Bauer-Lechner that the audience would only discover later 'how artful [kunstvoll] it is!' (NBL, pp. 176–7.) The artfulness rests in the ingenuity with which Mahler manipulates his telescoping principle. We recognize the principle involved just as soon as we hear the way in which Mahler recapitulates the principal theme (see Ex. 106). We drop into the tonic, G major, but

Ex. 106

the theme itself is picked up in mid-flow. In characteristic Mahler fashion, what he recapitulates is not in any case the first statement of the principal theme from the exposition but the varied repeat of it (see two bars after Fig. 1 et seq.), which, in the recapitulation, he surrounds with a whole nest of fresh motives (see, however, the lower strings, one bar after Fig. 18, where the principal tune persists). It is with bar 3 of the principal theme, in fact, that the recapitulation opens; and once again, and again precisely as in the Minuet,

the thematic recapitulation has started on the 'wrong' side of the double bar
at Fig. 18. If one looks back to the point of climax of the development (at
Fig. 17) and then at the ensuing lead-back to the recapitulation, one finds
not only the 'missing' opening bars of the principal theme in an augmented
version (bars 234–8) that carries one right up to the double bar and proves to
dovetail precisely with the continuation of the melody (bar 3) with which the
recapitulation so surprisingly opens, but also the introductory motives (cf.
bars 1–3) which in the exposition precede the main tune.[10] At bar 225, flutes
and sleighbells reintroduce the very opening idea of the symphony, and
thereafter, and before the double bar is reached, all the introductory motives
are recapitulated in a mosaic-like pattern of motivic combinations, as well as
the principal tune's opening bars; and to all this Mahler adds a nice touch of
symmetry by using the version of the introductory motives that actually
opens the development (Fig. 8) and now returns to close it (bars 233–8),
while at the same time serving in a recapitulatory role. This is altogether an
amazingly elaborate passage, the more so when one remembers that this
subtle recapitulatory process also has to work smoothly and effectively as
part of a transitional process, in which the development winds down and in
which we are finally led back through an ingenious modulatory scheme[11] to
the tonic and the recapitulation proper. 'Kunstvoll' indeed, and certainly a
more complicated compositional exercise than the Minuet in the Third Symphony. Nonetheless, it was in that 'simple' movement that the essential principle underpinning this complex construction in the Fourth Symphony was
first outlined.

Undoubtedly the complexity of this passage was part of the aesthetic game
that Mahler was playing in his Fourth Symphony: an outwardly simple-
minded, even backward-looking symphony (an early manifestation of neoclassicism?), that creates a peculiar world of its own by contradicting, in
developments of a demanding complexity and sophistication, the anticipations of simplicity and guilelessness that the very opening of the work seems
to arouse (though only momentarily). Of course, this was also part of the
programmatic concept, which implied a gradual reduction in complexity
throughout the work as preparation for the simplicity of the Finale, the true
innocence of a child's vision of paradise. Hence it was logical that the most
concentrated and intricate musical thinking should be assigned to the first
movement. It was undoubtedly this aspect of the Fourth that left its first
audiences bewildered, confused and hostile. Bauer-Lechner reports what she
was told by Mahler about the first performance of the work at Munich: 'In
the first movement, the audience was initially surprised by the seemingly
excessive simplicity of the themes (as they had expected something . . .
'outrageous' . . . from Mahler). But then, in the development section, they
were filled with consternation when they realized how little they could follow.

... The public was completely alienated by the second movement, of which it could make nothing at all. At this point, the hissing became so loud that Mahler's large youthful following in Munich ... was unable to drown the opposition by clapping. The last movement received the longest and least-dispirited applause ...' A subsequent performance at Frankfurt was no better received: '... the public', Bauer-Lechner was told by a friend, 'thought [Mahler] was merely trying to mystify them in his Fourth—in fact, that he was playing a practical joke on them!' He was further discouraged (at Munich) by a clamour on the part of the critics for 'verbal explanations of the meaning and content of the work'. This must have been particularly exasperating, all the more so because the song-finale, 'Das himmlische Leben', provided the key to the symphony's inner programme. The fact that the song did not, in the early life of the work at any rate, bring the illumination of the work's 'content' that one might have expected, is an indication of the depth of the incomprehension with which it was greeted. The critics, Mahler went on to say, 'are already so corrupted by programme music, they are no longer capable of understanding a work simply as a piece of music! This disastrously mistaken attitude emerged with Liszt and Berlioz. But they, at least, were talented, and gained new means of expression in this way. But now that we have these means at hand, who needs the crutches any more?' (NBL, pp. 176–8.) The truth is that Mahler had not thrown away the 'crutches' completely, even in his Fourth Symphony. But the work was certainly moving away from the kind of programme that could be spelled out, or required verbalization, and towards the inner programme, characteristic of the middle-period symphonies, that was to be wholly explicit in musical terms and musical images alone.

*   *   *   *

The Third Symphony, then, despite its great, sprawling length, already shows signs of the intense economy of organization that we encounter in the Fourth. There is yet another aspect in which the Third, in its own singular way, substantially anticipates the style of the Fourth, this time in the sphere of instrumentation. Again and again in the Fourth Symphony we find pages of scoring in which the wind predominate; and indeed the general impression left by the symphony is one of a sound-world to which the wind make the major contribution. Interested readers can check this impression for themselves by looking through Mahler's score, in which case I believe they can hardly come away without agreeing that in this work he has effected a radical shift away from the classical concept of the predominantly string-based orchestra.[12] (Good spots to look at in the first movement alone are: the first three bars of the symphony (!); Figs. 4–6; and the whole stretch, say, between Figs. 8 and 16, where, if anything, the strings are less hard-worked than the wind. (Incidentally, this last passage offers a marvellous illustration of how inextricably involved is the method of Mahler's scoring with his motivic method of development (see also pp. 28–32). One sees there how, to map out the mosaic of motives, a comparably intricate mosaic of instrumentation was imposed. It is an extraordinarily interesting example of how one cannot divorce a consideration of Mahler's orchestration from the character of his invention.)

This overriding trend to shove the orchestral balance in the direction of the wind is already powerfully established in the Third Symphony, although there, interestingly enough, the premises on which the shift is made, in some respects at least, are very different from those that accounted for the conspicuous wind-orientation of the Fourth Symphony. In the Third Symphony, and in the first movement in particular, there is again the same innovatory and voluminous writing for the wind, with the strings often relegated to a relatively subsidiary role; but here the move away from the traditional balance is not only conditioned by the same relationship that we find in the Fourth, between Mahler's scoring and his compositional method, but also by the programmatic concept of the great March to which Summer advances, of which Mahler himself remarked to Bauer-Lechner, '. . . I need a regimental band to give the rough and crude effect of my martial comrade's arrival. Such a mob is milling around you never saw anything like it!' (NBL, pp. 19–20.) And Mahler actually designated the appropriate section of the first movement 'Das Gesindel' (The Mob): see p. 194. He might have remarked with some truth: 'You will never have *heard* anything like it!', for there seems to be no precedent for the importation into symphonic music *on such a scale* of the authentic sonority of the military band, which is what the first movement of the Third Symphony brilliantly and daringly evokes and which colours virtually the total texture of the March itself. In the March, good spots to look at are: Figs. 23–6 and (in the development) the whole stretch of music between Figs. 44 and 55. Here we move substantially within the sound-world of the military band, which we know to have impressed Mahler in his formative years; and not only is the sonority of the wind band sometimes recreated with all the faithfulness of a replica, but the musical materials are themselves of a matching authenticity: the movement unfolds an elaborate thematic and motivic complex, almost exclusively built out of march tunes and rhythms, fanfares, and military flourishes and signals. The characteristic sonority of the March and the character of its invention are indissoluble, and if we note again Mahler's habitual re-shuffling of his motives into ever new patterns and combinations, then we are bound to be struck once more by the analytic contribution made by the continuously varied orchestration (see also pp. 212–13), and by the need for ample instrumental resources that this method of composition involves. Mahler makes good use of the very large orchestra that the Third Symphony demands, above all of the big battalions of wind: quadruple woodwind (but 5 clarinets, two of which are E flat clarinets, commonly found in military bands), 8 horns, 4 trumpets, 4 trombones, and tuba. With these resources to hand, he is able to bring to his busy motivic textures the maximum of clarifying instrumental colour. It is the same principle that we have already encountered in the First Symphony and meet again in the Fourth, but this time applied to a special category of motivic material, i.e. military signals and the like, territory in which the E flat clarinet, in particular, was thoroughly at home.

*   *   *   *

Mahler would certainly have first alighted on the shrill, penetrating voice of the E flat clarinet in the wind band, and, as I point out in n. 2, p. 80 and in n. 18, p. 369, he was quick to make use of the instrument in his own way and for his own special purposes in both *Das klagende Lied* and the First Symphony. But without doubt he was also influenced by Berlioz's arresting use of the instrument in the Finale of the *Symphonie Fantastique* (see NBL, p. 43), the impact of which on Mahler's Second Symphony is plain for all to hear (another work in which the E flat clarinet plays a substantial role). Perhaps it is to Mahler, indeed, that we owe the progressive change in the instrument's status, from its use for a special effect only to the possibility of its incorporation in the orchestra as a valuable extension of available timbres. In just the same way that ideas have changed about what music may accommodate (or express), so too have ideas changed about instruments and their status. The E flat clarinet was clearly thought to be an instrument of a not quite reputable character, because of its association with bands and popular music, and also because the cutting edge of its tone was, from an orthodox point of view, un-beautiful. Berlioz made a brilliant virtue of the instrument's disrepute by riding it into the orchestra on a broomstick and using it to colour his witches' sabbath. The satanic programme justified the instrument's presence in the conventional orchestra, though doubtless what appealed to Berlioz, as it must have done to Mahler, was the capacity of the instrument to penetrate however crowded a texture and articulate a sharp-edged line—truly, a *clarifying* instrument. This musicalization of the E flat clarinet—making it accessible to music in the widest sense—is akin to the musicalization of ideas that had hitherto not been considered 'proper' for music to accommodate, that could not, as it were, be 'felt' in music. Programme music, as Mahler recognized himself, did much to increase the range of areas and topics accessible to music, and in the process, as we can see in the case of the E flat clarinet, new programmatic or dramatic excursions brought with them comparable extensions in the sphere of the orchestrally possible. It is certainly no accident that the E flat clarinet won its symphonic legitimacy in one of the earliest and most famous of programme symphonies. (I do not forget, though, the debt that programme music owes in the first instance to opera. Indeed, a large portion of the history of music, and particularly that part of it concerned with the study of the expanding vocabulary of music, could be written in terms of the relationship between so-called 'absolute' music and music drama, in which the latter has continuously fertilized the former and fed it with new images, and often furnished the new techniques with which to express them.)

The concept of Berlioz's shrill, squawking witches required the piercing, high-pitched quality of the E flat clarinet, just as, in Mahler's case, the concept of the regimental band required the instruments that would make the band 'real'; and of course it was the basic programmatic idea behind the first movement of the Third Symphony—Summer marching in—that made it possible for Mahler to introduce into his symphony a style and a sonority that otherwise were totally alien to symphonic music. The programme enabled the transformation—the musicalization—to take place; and as a result of it, the vocabulary of music, its imagery, and the expressive means to realize it, were substantially expanded and enriched. But *without* the programme, without the quasi-dramatic justification, the transformation could never have happened. This was clearly what Mahler had in mind when appraising the advances made by Liszt and Berlioz. He was right to suggest that there came a time when the 'new means of expression' no longer required programmatic 'crutches', but was perhaps a shade ingenuous in not acknowledging the programmatic crutches that had been indispensable to him in the extension of his own armoury of expressive means.

There are many different forms of musicalization, and if one of them is the capacity to discover in an instrument a musical character (or characteristic) that is dramatically opposed to its established character, then in this field, too, Mahler showed remarkable powers of clairvoyance. Who would have imagined, for example, that from the piccolo—the jauntiest, most shrill of wind instruments—could be persuaded an ethereal thread of sublime poetry? But it is just this that Mahler achieves in one of his most extraordinary orchestral textures, the hushed transition in the second movement of the Eighth Symphony (Figs. 199–202 et seq.) that leads into the Chorus Mysticus. By any standards, this is a unique moment of instrumental imagination; and it is one to which the solo piccolo makes a distinctive contribution, and in which the instrument emerges in a new role. The metamorphosis that is enacted here, by means of which the most 'vulgar' of the woodwind (again with military band associations) participates in the creation of a profoundly mysterious, other-worldly sonority, is among Mahler's most fascinating achievements in opening up areas of feeling, the very opposite of those with which one normally associates a particular instrument. (Another example of a rather similar kind, involving this time the E flat clarinet, is found in the coda of the Ninth Symphony's first movement, bar 413 et seq.) In this field too, Mahler proved himself a master of paradox, from which flowed so many of his most creative and fruitful ideas.

I shall have more to say elsewhere about Mahler's use of popular materials in the first movement of the Third Symphony (see pp. 326f.). What still has to be mentioned here is the fact that it was not only the idea of the regimental band that accounts for the movement's emphatic wind-orientation. As Mahler observed to Bauer-Lechner (NBL, p. 20), Summer has to do battle with Winter, and it is Summer's opponent who is portrayed in the large-scale introduction to the movement (it will be remembered that until quite a late stage Mahler envisaged numbering the introduction as first in the over-all sequence of movements, as if it were to enjoy a completely independent status). What is interesting here is that Winter, like Summer, is conceived almost exclusively in terms of a large wind band (in some ways even more radically so than the ensuing March): but just as Summer represents a pole the opposite of Winter, so too is Winter's music not only wholly different from Summer's, but, despite the common preoccupation with wind sonorities, wholly different in sound and method of scoring. Mahler obviously wanted to convey in his introduction the idea of an ice-bound Nature gradually thawing into life; and this he ingeniously does from Fig. 2 onwards, by first exposing a texture composed of heaving, groaning motives (Figs. 1–5: note the dominance of wind and percussion, with only the lower strings inter-mittently (though importantly) engaged, a textural pattern that is much repeated), and then (around Fig. 5 and thereafter) expanding the motives outwards into long limbs of melody, scored for wind, and often for solo brass (see, for example, the trumpet solo at seven bars after Fig. 6, et seq., and the trombone solo at two bars after Fig. 13 to Fig. 17 (!)): perhaps the program: matic parallel here is the idea of a personified Winter stretching as he awakes from his slumber, his motives stretching into melodies.[13] These cavernous sounds of Nature introduce an emancipated style of solo brass writing that is remarkable for the 1890s, and must have sounded still very surprising in 1902, when the complete work was first performed. It also clearly pre-figures the solemn, reverberant introduction to the Seventh Symphony, not only in textural layout (tenor horn solo in the Seventh: cf., however, the long trom-bone solo at Fig. 13 in the Third) but in motivic and rhythmic character too (note the common trills!).

The long spans of melody for the brass, the main impression left by the introduction, contrast very sharply with the brilliant motivic detail of the March, which is continually fragmenting and as continually re-forming its prodigal fund of fanfares, signals, flourishes, snatches of march tunes and rhythms, etc. Two kinds of invention, in fact, serve the protagonists of the drama in the first movement of the Third, and no less discernibly, two radically different kinds of scoring; and yet both the introduction and the March exploit the wind as the prevailing sonority and both mark a radical shift away from a string-based orchestral texture. The sheer versatility of Mahler's scoring within his self-imposed constraints is no less than virtuosic, and one's admiration is increased when, in the fifth movement, the setting of the *Wunderhorn* poem 'Es sungen drei Engel', he shakes out of his sleeve yet another predominantly wind and percussion band to accompany the boys' and women's choirs, with the lower strings (no violins) only sparingly used (largely in a supportive role, though when required bringing a quite distinctive and calculated colour to the texture).

In sum, among all Mahler's symphonies the Third is unique, not only because of its highly idiosyncratic conception, but because of the wholly singular sound-world it inhabits, a monumental score that represents a drastic re-thinking of the traditional orchestral balance. It was not the first time that Mahler had shown signs of an innovating orchestral approach, nor was it the last; and there can be no doubt of a predilection for the wind, which manifests itself in some form or other in almost every Mahler symphony.

Everyone must have his own favourite page. One of mine is the remarkable passage in *Das Lied* where the world goes to sleep in the Finale (between Figs. 18 and 22) largely in terms of the wind. There is no doubt, I think, that Mahler's acute sensitivity to the sounds of Nature was also one of the prime reasons for his exploitation of wind instruments, which in general character stand closer to the sound-world of Nature than strings, which are more often associated (at any rate in Mahler's music) with human yearning and human passions; and indeed in *Das Lied* there is some emphatic and surely deliberate use of the wind as symbol of the remote and impersonal cosmos and of the strings as symbols of the impassioned, sentient human being placed at the centre of an uncaring world whose beauty can renew itself, whereas individual man must face extinction. Thus, in this particular work, Mahler's orchestration can itself be interpreted as part of the inner drama. It is no accident that one finds oneself writing about *Das Lied* and the Third Symphony in the same context. The Third was, in a very genuine sense, an earlier song of the earth in its own right (albeit a very different kind of song), and it is not surprising, in view of their common topic, that both the earlier work and the late attract attention for their lavish dependence on the wind.

It is the Third Symphony that embodies Mahler's most far-reaching and thoroughgoing upgrading of the wind and as such—and quite apart from whatever symbolic significance it might have in the framework of the piece itself—constitutes a major revision of the sound traditionally associated with the idea of symphony. It was a revolution that Mahler accomplished, and one that, possibly because of the oddity of the work, has not received the attention it properly deserves as both symbol and agent of the changing character of orchestral sound[14] that was in train at the turn of the nineteenth century.

* * * *

We know from various sources of authentic reminiscences of Mahler (his wife's and Bauer-Lechner's) that he was much given to the use of pocket sketchbooks in which he jotted down musical ideas—some of them very scrappy indeed—for possible future use. (It is mysterious that so few of these notebooks seem to have survived: one imagines that there must have been any number of them associated with each work.) Bauer-Lechner tells us, for example, that while working on the completion of the first movement of the Third Symphony, '... as usual he has filled a pile of sketch-sheets, and his pocket music notebooks, with a hundred variants of a motif or a modulation, until he has found exactly what he needs and exactly how it is to fit into the whole'. (NBL, p. 43.) I do not know of the survival of a pocket notebook from the time of the Third Symphony, but an old friend of mine, the late F. Charles Adler (1889–1959), a pioneer Mahler conductor of no little distinction, generously sent me photographs of a notebook in his possession that contained just such jottings as one imagines Mahler might have scribbled down when out walking.[15] Very many of the entries in the notebook in

Ex. 107

question are related to the Ninth Symphony (and some perhaps to the Tenth), but doubtless they are typical of the notebooks in general, above all in so far as they disclose the kind of evolutionary process mentioned by Bauer-Lechner in connection with the Third Symphony, hence my purpose in quoting them at this point. I am indebted to Mr. Colin Matthews who has allowed me to use his transcriptions of the material from the notebook (which form the substance of Ex. 107 (see p. 331)—the opening of the Ninth Symphony's Adagio) and has added an explanatory note. [Mahler frequently sketched in this way—'grafting' one idea on to another. The first idea, *a*, consists of three bars and the beginning of a fourth; *b* shows Mahler dissatisfied with bars 2–4 and writing a new second and third bar, the latter being superseded by a new third and fourth bar in *c*. Thus the sketch is to be read as a four-bar fragment using the first bars of *a* and *b* and the two bars of *c*. In the event Mahler didn't use *c* at all. Transposed into D flat major (in the sketch it is at the same pitch as the trio of the Rondo-Burleske, which is based on the same harmony) the passage appears thus in the Adagio:

C.M.]

II. Influences and Anticipations

Mahler and Berlioz

I suppose that one of the most profound influences on Mahler, and particularly on the music of his 'Wunderhorn' period, was that of Berlioz, and specifically that of the *Symphonie Fantastique*. There are few recorded remarks of Mahler's about Berlioz, but in this sphere actions—the sonorities—speak louder than words, even critical words. We know that he was an enthusiastic exponent of the work as a conductor, affirming its 'inspiration and originality', even though (in that perversely contradictory manner of Mahler's) he seems to have suggested in the same breath that it was perhaps not a work 'of the highest artistic achievement' (cf. HG[1], p. 491). For all that, it is significant that in his first season with the Vienna Philharmonic Orchestra after his appointment as chief conductor, he introduced the *Symphonie Fantastique* into his second programme (20 November 1898), along with Weber's *Oberon* overture and Schubert's B minor Symphony. In his programmes for 1900, he included two Berlioz overtures, *Carnaval Romain* (14 January) and *Rob Roy* (19 November), this last work a first performance with the orchestra. Again in 1900, when the orchestra visited Paris for the World Exhibition, Mahler performed the *Symphonie Fantastique* as part of the concert on 20 June (the rest of the programme was made up of Beethoven's *Egmont* overture and F major Romance (with Arnold Rosé, the leader of the orchestra, as soloist) and the Prelude and 'Liebestod' from Wagner's *Tristan*). It is scarcely possible to speculate very meaningfully about the probable quality of Mahler's Berlioz interpretations, but one feels confident that the extreme precision and intensity of Mahler's conducting must have resulted in outstanding performances of a composer to whom he owed a real creative debt and with whom he must have felt a certain kinship.[16]

It is improbable, for example, that Mahler's Second Symphony would have existed without the precedent set by Berlioz's innovatory programme symphony of 1830 (the year in which it was first performed). There are, certainly, other substantial influences at work in the Mahler, but the basic concept, and above all the idea of a dramatic, biographical narrative projected in a cumulative sequence of movements, clearly has its origins in Berlioz's radically original inspiration, his 'Episode de la vie d'un artiste'. This is not the place to dwell on the brilliance of Berlioz's achievement, but it must at least be said that of all the documents of the revolution generated by Romanticism, the *Symphonie Fantastique* proved to be one of the most influential and one of the most prophetic, exploring as it did the world of dreams, of the unconscious, which at a much later stage of Romanticism was to form the acknowledged inner programme of the Expressionists, that final flowering of an ultra-Romanticism to which Mahler, too, made a contribution, particularly in his group of last works. The development of Romanticism into Expressionism was a comparatively long and complex evolutionary process, with Berlioz (d. 1869) belonging to its early stages and Mahler (d. 1911) aiding the final convulsion that gave birth to Expressionist techniques. This fascinating stretch of musical history entails consideration of Mahler's last works, especially the Ninth and Tenth Symphonies, and thus any detailed discussion of it must await a later volume of the present study. Meanwhile, one recognizes the vital role in the evolution of Romanticism played by the idea of the 'programme' which, as the history of Romanticism progressed, gradually freed itself of exterior or pictorial associations and became increasingly interiorized—autobiographical, if you like. It was as an interior, almost purely autobiographical art that Expressionism, in some of its finest achievements, proved to be a logical culmination of the whole Romantic movement. A substantial part of the historic importance of Berlioz's amazing programmatic concept rests in the fact that, with uncanny prescience, it foreshadows this very development; because the programme of the *Symphonie Fantastique*, explicitly so, is the most innermost of dramas and narratives—none other than a dream. Berlioz's masterpiece is singular in this respect, perhaps; but if we view Mahler's development as a whole, it is significant that, within the scope of his symphonies, he methodically progresses *away* from the programme which can be exteriorized, until in his final masterpieces it is a type of inner drama with which we are confronted, and surely very often an autobiographical drama, nonetheless real for being beyond the reach of words. It is in these works, when one begins to feel that the form has been dictated by the flow of the inner programme, that Mahler seems to approach the borderlines of Expressionism. But this must be the subject of a future discussion.

It is the Second Symphony which must be our primary concern here, and the programme of the work (see pp. 179f. and 183f.)—itself episodes in the life and death of a Hero—is clearly indebted to Berlioz's elaborate scenario, whose brilliant 'March to the Scaffold' must have been in Mahler's mind when planning his own great March that is the centrepiece of his Finale— 'The last Trump sounds; the graves open. . . . Now they all come marching along in a mighty procession: beggars and rich men, common folk and kings, the Churches Militant, the Popes' (NBL, p. 23). I am not so much suggesting a direct musical relationship here but, rather, that for Mahler, Berlioz's March served as an influential *dramatic* model; in the same way, I believe that memories of Berlioz's glittering Valse would have encouraged Mahler to build his elegant Ländler (the A flat Andante) into his programmatic scheme as 'A blissful moment in the Hero's life'.

Indeed, if one wants to gain a quick impression of the different musical traditions represented by Berlioz and Mahler, for all their common pursuit of a programme, then compare Berlioz's Valse with Mahler's Ländler! It is as a dramatic model that the *Symphonie Fantastique* has its closest connection with Mahler's Second Symphony, though I have no doubt that it was from the Berlioz that Mahler took the idea of using the *Dies Irae* motive as part of his stock of Judgement Day imagery.[17] (The motive was also used by other nineteenth-century composers, by Liszt, for example, and Saint-Säens, but I am sure that for Mahler, Berlioz was the main source.)

I have already touched on Berlioz's use of the E flat clarinet in the *Symphonie Fantastique* (see pp. 327f.), which Mahler himself discussed in relation to his use of the instrument in the Third Symphony, but which he had in fact already incorporated in his First and Second Symphonies, most often either to strengthen the articulation of a line in a busy texture or to heighten the colour in a grotesque, bizarre or otherwise exceptional context.[18] Clearly, this is an example of Berlioz's influence in the sphere of instrumentation, though in fact Mahler must have learned a very great deal orchestrally from his study and performing experience of Berlioz's score. The remarkable adventurousness and emancipation of Berlioz's orchestration;[19] his theatrical sense of colour; the novelty of his textures—many pages in Berlioz's March are strikingly like those in Mahler's Third Symphony, where one is most aware of the shift towards a wind-dominated orchestra—his sheer exuberance as an orchestrator: all these qualities one finds in Mahler sixty or seventy years later, and one feels still, behind Mahler's orchestral gestures, his orchestral rhetoric, the glittering presence of the great Frenchman.[20] Moreover, it is interesting and wholly relevant to remember that both composers were greatly influenced by the sound-world of the military band, of the wind band, by the spatial acoustics of 'open-air' music; and this again means that both composers share a common source of inspiration and thus show some common characteristics. Berlioz's dramatic handling of brilliantly characterized instrumental sound, either massive or slender (and Mahler, with his ear for the musicalization of the sounds of Nature, must have found much to admire in the refined, solo landscaping of Berlioz's Adagio);[21] the precedent set by Berlioz's exploration of off-stage or multiple instrumental groups (Mahler would presumably have known of Berlioz's excursions into these territories): these, surely, were particular aspects of Berlioz's art that left a marked impression on the Second Symphony (see pp. 337–43 below), the very subject-matter of which seems to extend and amplify (and sometimes to parallel) the visionary programme of the *Symphonie Fantastique*. Indeed, if Berlioz's symphony may be said to have initiated a whole development within the history of the symphony, then Mahler's apocalyptic Second Symphony might be said to be the work in which the last chapter of that history came to be written. The general impact of the *Symphonie Fantastique* on Mahler, as I have suggested, was far-reaching, and perhaps has not received the detailed study it deserves. Meanwhile, a specific debt to Berlioz that I should like to point out does not involve the *Symphonie Fantastique* but the overture, *Benvenuto Cellini*, in which the characteristically Berliozian melodic shape (Ex. 108) clearly had a hand in shaping the contours of a long-spanned melody for strings in the Finale of Mahler's Second (Ex. 109):

Ex. 108

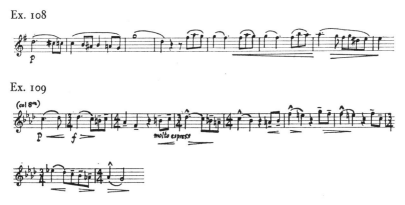

Ex. 109

The kind of relationship demonstrated above by Exx. 108 and 109 is a direct Berlioz/Mahler association. For much of the rest, and perhaps this is even more important than the pursuit of demonstrable influences, what one tends to attribute to the impact of one composer upon another may be due in fact to a similarity of mind and temperament. It is this which may bring two composers into a meaningful relationship, even when no direct influence is involved and when the composers may be separated by a substantial gap in time. In this sense, I think without doubt, Berlioz and Mahler can be usefully bracketed together, a juxtaposition that can be justified by their common *theatrical flair*. This feeling for the dramatic stroke, the telling theatrical gesture, was obviously a powerful component in the make-up of each composer, and thus it is not surprising that both should seek to utilize and develop these techniques and means of expression that flow from musical theatre. In Mahler's case, certainly, his innate sense of theatre manifested itself at an early stage. One thinks, for example, of the concluding part of *Das klagende Lied*, with its highly theatrical use of an off-stage band to depict the festivities that precede the final catastrophe. This was a concept—a prophetic concept, if ever there were one—that must have had its origin in the youthful composer's built-in theatrical imagination, which owed less to history than to his own personality, and proved to be a portent of things to come.[22] No doubt, as Mahler developed as a composer, so too did a complex of historical and contemporary influences come to bear on his music, Berlioz substantially among them. But it is probably true to say that it is the composition of a creator's personality that determines the influences to which he will creatively respond; and it is, I suggest, in this light that the Berlioz/Mahler 'dialogue' can be most profitably assessed. In the Second Symphony it is probably a synthesis of inner compulsion and outer influences that is responsible for some of the work's innovatory features.

New means of expression: the exploration of acoustic space (in Symphony II)

In the Finale of the Second Symphony one certainly encounters that flair for the theatrical gesture shared in common by Berlioz and Mahler; and in association with that theatricality we meet some of those 'new means of expression' (Mahler's words, see p. 325) to which the concept of the theatrical, the programmatic, gave birth. There is, for example, the remarkable passage from Fig. 20 to Fig. 25 in the Finale, in which one of the more complex of Mahler's excursions into the territory of directional sound (see also pp. 215–217) and multiple orchestral groups is revealed. Here, an off-stage band of trumpets and percussion, 'placed in the furthest distance', projects its military fanfares (see Ex. 110) into what develops to be primarily a string texture (an immense elaboration, in fact, of the music first heard at Fig. 7, et seq.). The fanfares are not only projected *into* but also, as it were, *across* the texture; and Mahler goes out of his way to spell out the character differences between the two kinds of music involved (the passionately lyrical and the quasi-military), and the two types of instrumental sonority involved, by making a clear *rhythmic* differentiation as well as a *spatial* separation.[23] In sum, this one passage contains a surprising number of sophisticated calculations, all of them aimed at achieving a precise acoustic effect at this juncture in the Finale; and it is a theatrical moment—a dramatic interplay, one may think, between the anguished introspection of the Hero and the fanfares that herald the approach of the 'Last Trump' (at Fig. 29)—in which are adumbrated more than one of the techniques that have become so prominent a feature of music in our own day. It is no accident that many of the 'new means of expression' we hear much of today in music that often allies itself to the idea of theatre— 'music theatre' is one of the slogans of the present time—should be related to those new expressive means ushered in by the theatricality of Berlioz and Mahler.

Ex. 110

The example I quote above is by no means the most elaborate spatial texture that Mahler devised for this movement; and, in fact, the exploitation of musical space is an important element throughout the movement. We find that many of the most overtly theatrical 'happenings' owe a good deal of their effect to a complex spatial conception. The dramatic interpolation of the 'Last Trump' is a case in point (see Fig. 29, et seq.), when the vast orchestra shrinks into two extraordinary instrumental groups, the off-stage group, 'in the far distance', comprising trumpets, horns and timpani, the on-stage group consisting of solo flute and piccolo; and it is an eerie dialogue that we hear between these spatially and instrumentally differentiated groups: slow horn calls and quick fluttering trumpet triplets (note too the reverberant sforzandi for the timpani) echo across the void, and are answered by, and finally enmeshed with, the spectral bird-song. The whole amazing passage—an audacious cadenza for wind and timpani, distributed between two spatially separated groups of instruments—sounds forth like the last, barely audible murmurs of a world which awaits the Creator's own *coup de théâtre*— Resurrection. A dramatic challenge this, for Mahler, which he brilliantly met by a simple yet very telling stroke of the imagination: the suppressed dynamics—*ppp*—of the entry of the chorus, which if scrupulously observed in performance, i.e. the volume must be sustained at a level scarcely above a whisper or a suppressed sigh, will unfold an acoustic phenomenon of a singularity to match the dramatic moment.

But all this by no means exhausts the complexity of this unique cadenza, and its choral sequel. Once again (as in the introduction to the first movement of the First Symphony) it is not just a crude spatial relationship between on-stage instrumental groups that we encounter here; on the contrary, within the brass group itself Mahler gives clear and detailed indications of significant acoustic discriminations. Scrutiny of the pages of score below, in which all the composer's detailed instructions are given in English, will reveal the dynamic differentiations that he wanted made in the off-stage band, i.e. there is a contrasting spatial relationship called for between the trumpets (nearer and stronger) and the horns (distant), not to speak of important dynamic differences indicated within the trumpet group alone. Even more remarkable, Mahler unequivocally exploits the possibilities of directional sound, with 'left' and 'right' clearly marked in the horn and trumpet parts. Thus the cadenza embodies an elaborate acoustic conception: it explores the rich possibilities of musical space—on-stage, off-stage, left, right, and multiple nuances within those broad distinctions, the whole framed within an overall dynamic scheme that starts from distance and near-silence, grows in dynamic strength and finally dies away again to silence—from which point, and only just above it, the chorus enters with the 'Aufersteh'n' chorale. The cadenza represents a genuine exercise in mobile sound, in which the only immobile factor (in the dynamic sense) is the on-stage bird song of the flute and piccolo. There is certainly nothing immobile about the bird song itself which, on the contrary, and in marked contrast to the measured trumpet and horn calls of the off-stage band, pursues extremely free, asymmetrical melodic shapes—hence the new notational device of vertical strokes that Mahler introduces in the last six bars of the cadenza, to indicate the points of rhythmic synchronization (cf. Britten's *Curlew River* of 1964, in which he uses a similar device for the same reason). In sum, this brief but crucial passage, theatrical in its inspiration, anticipates some of the major acoustical preoccupations of the most recent music of our time—one wonders what Mahler might have made of some of the technological facilities available today in this sphere—and provides an admirable instance of Mahler's foreshadowing of techniques that were not developed until long after his death.

In part, at least, Mahler's striking conception owed something to the acoustic of Nature and to natural sounds: the bird-song in the cadenza above is an obvious example of the debt (a nightingale is mentioned by Mahler in his programme note, but he also told Bauer-Lechner (see n. 65, p. 280) that the cawing of ravens crept into his Finale: where are they to be found?). Mahler himself remarked, again to Bauer-Lechner, 'Probably we derive all our basic rhythms and themes from Nature, which offers them to us, pregnant with meaning in the form of animal sounds. Indeed, man, and the artist in particular, takes all his materials and all his forms from the world around him—transforming and expanding them, of course. (NBL, p. 81.) But it is not only the transcription and transformation of animal sounds that we encounter in Mahler, though these do play an important role in his music. There is also the impression made on him by the acoustic experience of everyday life,[24] which also, one feels, must have contributed to his explicit interest in multidirectional sound. The following passage, once more from Bauer-Lechner (NBL, p. 147), is of particular note for more than one reason but perhaps especially because of the italicized phrase (Bauer-Lechner's italics, presumably in an attempt to register Mahler's own emphasis):

The 'Last Trump' in the Second Symphony

NB. The vertical strokes indicate the points where the various instruments should coincide.

31 Langsam. Misterioso.

Sopr. Solo (ohne im Geringsten hervorzutreten.)

Soprano-Solo.
ppp
Auf - er - steh'n, ja auf - er - steh'n wirst du, mein Staub, nach kur - zer Ruh!

Soprane.
ppp
Auf - er - steh'n, ja auf - er - steh'n wirst du, mein Staub, nach kur - zer Ruh!

Alte.
ppp
Auf - er - steh'n, ja auf - er - steh'n, wirst du, mein Staub, nach kur - zer Ruh!

Tenore.
ppp
Auf - er - steh'n, ja auf - er - steh'n wirst du, mein Staub, nach kur - zer Ruh!

Büsse.
31 *ppp*
Auf - er - steh'n, ja auf - er - steh'n wirst du, mein Staub, nach kur - zer Ruh!

*) Anmerkung für das Studium: Die 2 Bässe nicht eine Octave höher, sonst würde die vom Autor intendirte Wirkung ausbleiben; es kommt durchaus nicht darauf an, diese tiefen Töne zu hören, sondern durch diese Schreibart sollen nur die tiefen Bässe verhindert werden, etwa das obere B zu „nehmen", und so die obere Note zu verstärken.

Mahler told us at table [in 1900] that, on the woodland path at Klagenfurt
with W. (who had come to settle his repertoire) he was much disturbed by
a barrel-organ, whose noise seemed not to bother W. in the least. 'But when
a second one began to play, W. expressed horror at the caterwauling—
which now, however, was beginning to amuse me. And when, into the
bargain, a military band struck up in the distance, he covered up his ears,
protesting vigorously—whereas I was listening with such delight that I
wouldn't move from the spot.'

When Rosé expressed surprise at this, Mahler said, 'If you like my
symphonies, you must like that too!'

The following Sunday, we were going on the same walk with Mahler.
At the fête on the Kreuzberg, an even worse witches' sabbath was in progress. Not only were innumerable barrel-organs blaring out from merry-
go-rounds, see-saws, shooting galleries and puppet shows, but a military
band and a men's choral society had established themselves there as well.
All these groups, in the same forest clearing, were creating an incredible
musical pandemonium without paying the slightest attention to each
other. Mahler exclaimed: 'You hear? That's polyphony, and that's where
I get it from! Even when I was quite a small child, in the woods at Iglau,
this used to move me so strangely, and impressed itself upon me. For it's
all the same whether it resounds in a din like this or in a thousandfold
bird song, in the howling of the storm, the lapping of the waves, or the
crackling of the fire. Just so—*from quite different directions*—the themes
must enter; and they must be just as different from each other in rhythm
and melodic character. (Everything else is merely many-voiced writing,
homophony in disguise.) The only difference is that the artist orders and
unites them all into one concordant and harmonious whole.'

This is a particularly interesting excerpt from Bauer-Lechner's recollections in that it shows the appeal to Mahler of a random, everyday, open-air
polyphony,[25] and, even more significantly, suggests that the spontaneous
impression of multi-directional music was something that he wanted to re-
create in terms of his own music—which was something that he did, very
elaborately, as I have tried to demonstrate above. Thus we must bear in
mind that at least some of Mahler's theatrical gestures owe something to the
chance acoustic theatricality of the everyday world, not only to the established
tradition of the musical theatre in which he spent his working life.

Finally, the excerpt from Bauer-Lechner's text reveals an important
aspect of Mahler's use of popular musical imagery. This in general has been
much commented on, and there seems little to add to the already adequate
recognition of Mahler's symbolic or ironic or poetic or dramatic employ-
ment of everyday musical materials. The Finale of the Second Symphony,
in its central march section, which depicts the motley procession of the dead
after their resurrection, offers a splendid example of Mahler bending the

popular, vernacular style to his own unique purposes. (The movement also reveals the highly skilled practice of thematic metamorphosis, the systematic use of which shows how closely Mahler had studied Liszt, cf., for instance, the transformation of the jaunty trumpet tune at nine bars before Fig. 16 into the sublime Resurrection chorale at Fig. 31. As this particular example so clearly shows, the achievement of the latter depends on the presence of the former: in Mahler's music, at any rate, you cannot have the sublime without the vulgar, or attain the other world without experiencing the worldly. The unity of his philosophy finds perfect expression in the thematic unity that this example represents.) The march of the dead is certainly a brilliant and daring conception, and yet, for all its deliberate excursion into a flamboyantly popular vein, it remains very much a big symphonic march. It is certainly not in any actual sense the kind of music one would hear in the streets (except perhaps on Judgement Day). In the Third Symphony, however, it is quite another order of march that we hear, quite a different kind of popular music. I have already made the point (see pp. 326–7) that the wind-band march music of the Third Symphony's first movement is precisely *not* the kind of music that we would expect to hear in the context of a symphony, let alone forming the prime substance of a vast opening movement. It is, however, in style and sonority, very clearly and intendedly related to the musical sounds of the everyday world: that is the whole point of it; and in the sense that Mahler lifted this music from his environment (even if it was a remembered and, of course, re-imagined environment), he broke new ground, not only enlarging the boundaries of what might be embraced by 'symphony' but anticipating in his own way the impact on music of an everyday music that had hitherto been thought of as alien, if not indeed hostile, to 'art'. In so far as Mahler began, whether consciously or not, to blur this distinction, he was perforce making an early contribution to a radical development in our own time when, aurally speaking, the dividing line between 'art' and 'life' (or 'nature') has sometimes been entirely abolished.

Anticipations and prophecies

In the preceding section I have mentioned one or two of what strike me as the most interesting and prophetic aspects of Mahler's manipulation of sound and choice of materials. He was, undoubtedly, remarkable in foreshadowing so many of the techniques and trends that later generations of composers— and it is a long list of prominent names that would have to be mentioned in that connection—have assiduously developed.[26] It is not only techniques that Mahler anticipated but also styles; in the studied simplicity of his Fourth Symphony, for instance, we encounter for the first time on any scale a whiff of the neoclassicizing spirit[27] that was to become so prominent an aesthetic doctrine in the 1920s and 1930s. I write 'studied simplicity' because

I am sure that there was a good deal of highly conscious archaizing on Mahler's part,[28] and especially in the first movement, with its deliberately 'classical' gestures that the first audiences of the work found so misleading (see pp. 324–5).

Mahler himself referred to the 'childishly simple and quite unselfconscious' character of the first movement's principal melody, which it was undoubtedly his intention to achieve and which impression the long melody does momentarily make: it is only when one starts looking into the organization of the melody that one realizes how enormously elaborate and carefully thought out it all is. Interestingly enough, Mahler himself remarked at the same time that the actual scoring of the melody caused him 'untold trouble'. (NBL, pp. 153–4.) I think it probable that the difficulties Mahler encountered here were of his own making, i.e. the instrumentation problem was directly tied up with the complex motivic structure of the melody (as anyone can see by glancing at the opening pages of the symphony, from bar 3 onwards). Mahler, it seems wanted to stress at all costs the 'simplicity' of the main theme, because that was the end he had in view, however complex the means were by which he attained it: the labour pains that went into the scoring, on the other hand, could safely be acknowledged without compromising the reputation for unstudied innocence which Mahler was so anxious that his melody should enjoy. 'Childishly simple' may be what the melody pretends to be, but it is anything but that.

There were probably a number of factors involved in the forming of the Fourth Symphony's unique style, a style which is in some ways represented a reaction on Mahler's own part against the monumental edifices of the Second Symphony and biological evolutionary symbolism of the Third. The Fourth, of course, had the concept of 'innocence' at the dramatic centre of the symphony, hence a shift away from the vast dimensions and massive rhetoric of the preceding symphonies, a marked reduction in instrumental resources, and the cultivation of a more 'innocent' symphonic style, that meant, inevitably, calculated reference to the lost 'innocence' of classicism. Hence, the 'simplicity' at which Mahler's opening melody aimed and the quite deliberately classical cut of some of the rest of the tailoring in the first movement (figuration, rhythm, cadences, etc.). Thus in the style of the Fourth, the neoclassical component may be interpreted as both a symbol of the innocence that was the dramatic theme of the work and also as a form of 'classical' reaction, of a very sophisticated kind, against the elaborately programmatic symphonism of the Second and Third symphonies. I write 'sophisticated' because I believe that, without undue exaggeration, the Fourth in many respects can be claimed as the most perfect of Mahler's *programme* symphonies. I stand by that opinion; but because of the singular nature of the programmatic operation in this work (which I have touched on earlier in this book), because of its dramatic (or, if you prefer, poetic) theme,

which brought with it an association of classicism with innocence, and because, doubtless, Mahler felt that he wanted a change after working on the
huge canvases of the Second and Third Symphonies,[29] the style that gives
the Fourth Symphony its unique character represented a very substantial
shift in direction. It has been frequently observed that in the Fourth we
encounter Mahler on the move, away from the ultra-romantic, programmatic
symphonism of the first three *Wunderhorn* symphonies and towards the relatively concentrated and more 'abstract' forms and textures of the middle-
period instrumental symphonies. This, I think, is certainly true of the
Fourth, the first movement of which is undoubtedly one of the finest and
most complex examples of Mahler's large-scale instrumental thinking. It is
a closely worked, elaborately argued (not elaborately theatrical or pictorial)
movement, that clearly anticipates the 'classicism' of the ensuing purely
orchestral symphonies; and there is something very typically Mahlerian in
the paradox that the ushering in of what, for Mahler, was a more emphatically
classical style was accomplished by a work whose 'classicism' was initially
born out of a programmatic idea. The Fourth is so perfectly articulated a
work that it seems absurd to talk of it, or think of it, as a transitional piece.
Nonetheless, in the sense that it was the piece in which Mahler wrote himself out of his *Wunderhorn* period and into the next stage of his development
as a symphonist, the Fourth does function significantly as a bridge between
two contrasted styles of approach to the concept of symphony.

Counterpoint: Mahler and Bach

There can be little doubt that the very busy and prominent counterpoint of
the Fourth Symphony (again very much to the fore in the first movement) was
also part of Mahler's consciously classicizing intent. It was not only through
the character of his themes that he asserted his classical references in this
work but also through his polyphonic textures: after all, were not classicism
and counterpoint (perhaps especially for a composer of Mahler's period)
virtually synonymous? Here, then, we find the Fourth anticipating the
unequivocally contrapuntal style of the middle-period symphonies, and again
—in part at least—the stimulus to this fresh emphasis derived from the initial
programmatic idea: counterpoint was bound up with classicism, and classicism was one of the forms of the 'innocence' which the symphony was
'about' and another form of which was its eventual goal. It would be ridiculous to suggest that it was through the Fourth that Mahler discovered himself
as a contrapuntist. On the contrary, as I hope I have shown in connection
with the First Symphony onwards, Mahler was a naturally polyphonic
thinker of a most original and brilliantly endowed kind from the very start.[30]
But it was undeniably in the Fourth Symphony, in which persistently
polyphonic textures were raised to the status of a major stylistic feature, that

Mahler as it were declared his hand as a contrapuntist, a mode of musical thinking that was never to leave him and which he proceeded pertinaciously to exploit in his ensuing works.

It would be a fascinating independent study to take Mahler's counterpoint as a topic in itself and trace the development of it as a prime characteristic of his composing throughout his career. Mahler said himself, '. . . as far back as I can remember my musical thinking was never anything but polyphonic' (NBL, pp. 153–4), which is undoubtedly true in a general sense. But what a close scrutiny would reveal, I think, would be the changing nature of Mahler's contrapuntal technique, which altered in character though not in principle as the years—and works—passed. Between the mosaic-like counterpoint of motives with which we are confronted in the First Symphony and the long spans of polyphonically combined melody[31] we find in, say, the Ninth, a great distance was travelled by the composer; and at least one of the factors playing a role in this development was the music of J. S. Bach.

There is not a wealth of references to Bach by Mahler himself, or at any rate I have only been able to discover a few (one must suppose that Bach was among the 'Brothers in Apollo' to whom Mahler at one stage dedicated the fiercely contrapuntal Rondo-Burleske from the Ninth). (See PB, p. 348.) Mahler's admiration for Bach was certainly wide and deep, and, as Mahler grew older, came to mean more and more to him, and also (I believe) to have a progressively increasing influence on his own music, an influence that was surely reinforced by his possession of the Bach Collected Edition,[32] which, as Bauer-Lechner recounts, 'you always find him busy with when you go to his room'. Alma Mahler (AM[5], p. 45) tells us that in his summer house at Maiernigg, the only music that he had on his shelves was Bach; and in 1904, in a letter to his wife, Mahler writes, after a session studying Brahms ('I have gone all through Brahms pretty well by now. All I can say of him is that he's a puny little dwarf with a rather narrow chest'): 'And now to Bach (with two candles). I must clear the air a bit after Brahms.' (NBL, p. 157, AM[5], pp. 45 and 240. For a somewhat different view of Brahms from Mahler, see HG[1], p. 276.) As one might expect in the case of Mahler, who as man and artist was marked by such strong contradictions (for the most part fruitful ones), his approach to Bach was often remarkably forward-looking, though also clearly influenced by the taste and judgement of his own day. One of Mahler's great strengths was his sensitivity to the future of music, his feeling (which may have been only partly conscious) for the shape of things to come; and this prescience was not only a matter of his own music disclosing certain anticipations of style and techniques that were to be seized on by younger generations of composers but also extended to his activity as a performer, i.e. what he stood for as a conductor—'pedantic genius', was the description used in a lecture by Anna Bahr-Mildenburg,[33] by which she meant Mahler's fanatical respect for the notes, note-values and rests ('Accuracy', he said to her, 'was the soul of any artistic achievement')—and what he chose to perform. One thinks, for example, of his famous Mozart performances at Vienna, which played such an important role in the twentieth century's renaissance of Mozart. We tend now to take Mozart's impregnable position in our culture for granted, but it was not always so. Mahler not only foreshadowed the Mozart revival, but also helped to bring about one of the most significant shifts in musical taste and fashion of the twentieth century. His prescience here is as active and as recognizable as in those passages in his own music when he suddenly seems to open up vistas of the future; and of course at the other end of the historical scale, and again in the sphere of taste and judgement, there was his encouragement of, and sympathy for, the young Schoenberg.

For all this, Mahler was very much a man of his period, and a nineteenth-century man at that, who for all his insight could often discuss music as if it were immovably set on an evolutionary course of continuous progress and improvement, in which (at least in the field of resources) 'bigger' seems to be the equivalent of 'better'.[34] The fullest exposition of this point of view is set out by Mahler in his long letter to Fräulein Gisela Tolney-Witt, which for its intrinsic interest I reproduce in Appendix A (see p. 389). The translation of this letter appeared in the *Saturday Review*, New York, on 26 April 1958. The original (the German text of which was published in the *Neue Zürcher Zeitung*, 10 May 1958) was in the possession of the publisher, the late Walter Hinrichsen (New York). (See also HG[1], pp. 270–2.) This is a fascinating letter, written, it is useful to remember, in 1893, at a time when Mahler himself was in the habit of creating on the very largest scale, i.e. the Second and Third Symphonies: a letter on the same subject *after* the turn of the century, one guesses, might have read somewhat differently. But though some of the text now may read oddly to us—exactly three-quarters of the way through another century altogether—there are fascinating insights in it that show that Mahler was not simply an unthinking historical optimist (like many men of his time) but someone aware that the changing nature of music owed a good deal to the exploration of new areas of feeling. As Mahler puts it: hand in hand with the development of an elaborate notation for music went 'the acquisition of *new emotional elements* as subjects of expression through sound, i.e. the composer began to include more and more profound and complicated parts of his emotional life in his work—until the *new era* in music started with Beethoven.' We may smile at Mahler the historian, but embedded in that excerpt is a very interesting thought, one moreover that provides a rational and convincing basis for explaining the development and nature of Romanticism and for many subsequent developments in the music of our own immediate present.

Mahler's sometimes disconcertingly 'progressive' view of musical history manifests itself in a comment he made to Bauer-Lechner (NBL, p. 104) in 1898 about polyphony, a topic which also returns us to Bach. 'The master of polyphony, and of polyphony alone, is Bach,' Mahler said. 'The founder and creator of modern polyphony is Beethoven.' 'Haydn and Mozart', on the other hand, 'are not yet polyphonic.' Everything it seems has a new start with Beethoven, and Haydn and Mozart were born too early. But to do Mahler justice, he was quite capable of qualifying his evolutionary approach. 'Wagner', he said on the same occasion, 'is really polyphonic only in *Tristan* and *Die Meistersinger* (not in the *Ring*)'; and it was in responding to Bauer-Lechner's request for elucidation of this point, that Mahler made one of his most memorable observations on the nature of polyphony, a thought that quite cancels out the superficial historicizing. '... In true polyphony', Mahler explained, 'the themes run quite independently in parallel, each from its own source to its own particular goal, as strongly contrasted to one another as possible, so that they are heard quite separately.' A remarkable comment this, and also another example of Mahler's prescience, because his analysis of what constitutes 'true polyphony' not only precisely describes the concept of linear counterpoint,[35] which was a distinctively twentieth-century development, but also exactly foresees (in 1898!) the kind of contrapuntal texture he was to write himself in the late works from his last period, a development to which, as I have said, I believe 'the master of polyphony' made a contribution.

Mahler also had views about the performance of Bach, in which one meets the same disconcerting mixture of devotion, penetrating insight and the weirdest notions of, as it were, up-dating Bach in terms of turn-of-the-century resources and sonorities. He said, no doubt with considerable truth, to Bauer-Lechner in 1901 that 'bad Bach performances ... don't give us the remotest idea of how his music sounded when he played it on the harpsichord. Instead of the real Bach, they give us a wretched skeleton of him. The chords, which provide the wonderful rich fullness and body of the music, are, as a rule, simply left out, as if Bach had written the figured bass without aim or purpose. But it is meant to be realized—and then what a ringing sound those surging chords produce! That is how his violin sonatas—played so ridiculously by just *one* little fiddler—should be performed, and the cantatas too. Then, you'd be surprised how they sound! (NBL, p. 157.)

This is a passage that, in some respects at least, is somewhat obscure, though in so far as it suggests that a creative imagination and full-bloodedness must be brought to the realization of Bach's figured basses if the music is to live, then Mahler was decidedly right in principle and probably in spirit ahead of his time, which preferred a lifeless academicism to an authenticity generated by an attempt at re-creation. But what is one to make of his extraordinary reference to the violin sonatas? One presumes he must have meant here the solo violin sonatas and partitas of Bach ('*one* little fiddler'!) and was making the point (see also the Tolney-Witt letter which forms Appendix A, pp. 389–91) that the character and scope of the music implied ampler, richer resources than were historically possible for Bach to use.[36] A wrong point, in all conscience, but one perhaps born of the same sort of attitude that enabled Mahler to transcribe Beethoven's F minor string quartet (Op. 95)[37] for string orchestra, on the grounds that the orchestral scoring realized the orchestral implications embodied in the quartet. For Mahler, of course, and this again is made very apparent in the Tolney-Witt letter, it was the orchestra that was the supreme expressive medium, whereas chamber music was apparently somewhere lower down the evolutionary scale. See, however, n. 13, p. 367, where I stress the not infrequent chamber-musical implications of Mahler's scoring in his own works. At any rate, the 'chamber', as Mahler has it, receives none of the enthusiasm that he reserves for the orchestra and the concert hall.

On another occasion, Mahler remarked to Bauer-Lechner that he would like to perform the *St. Matthew Passion*, 'with two separate orchestras, one on the right, the other on the left. In like manner, there should be two separate choirs, as well as a third, which should actually be the congregation (the audience), who would have to be placed somewhere else. Then there's the boys' choir, which I would put high up in the organ loft, so that their voices would seem to come from heaven. You should hear the effect when question and answer are divided like this, instead of all being mixed up together as is always the case nowadays.' (NBL, p. 112.) If nothing else, this idea shows a characteristic feeling for the theatrically effective disposition of forces, a disposition moreover that explores the potentialities of acoustic space, with sound envisaged as coming from a multiplicity of directions.

I do not know if Mahler ever conducted a complete *St. Matthew Passion* (we know that he conducted the final chorus of the work in Hamburg in 1896 (HG[1], p. 360)), nor indeed how much Bach he performed in his lifetime.[38] During his brief period as conductor of the Vienna Philharmonic (1898–1901), only one work by Bach—the D minor concerto (with Carl Friedberg (1872–1955) as solo pianist)—was included in the programmes of the regular concert series, though this was probably a fact that registered more than anything else the unadventurous Viennese taste of the period. It is clear from Bauer-Lechner's recollections that Mahler's delighted plundering of the Bach-Gesellschaft led him to discoveries among Bach's cantatas[39] and motets. Bauer-Lechner recounts an occasion in 1901 when Mahler played through what was probably cantata No. 48, 'Ich elender [not 'sündiger'] Mensch, wer wird mich erlösen'. 'He called it a glorious work, perhaps even Bach's most glorious —one which opens up the widest perspectives. In this connection, he

mentioned Bach's tremendous freedom of expression, which has probably
never been equalled since, and which is founded on his incredible skill and
command over all resources. 'In Bach', said Mahler, 'all the seeds of music
are found, as the world is contained in God. It's the greatest polyphony that
ever existed!' Another work that excited Mahelr at about the same time was
Bach's third (?) motet (Gesellschaft edition): 'It's unbelievable, the way the
eight voices are carried through in a polyphony which he [Bach] alone
commands. I'm gradually learning to follow them with the eye (they literally
can't be played on the piano!). But some day I should like to, I *must* perform
this work—to the amazement of the world!' Mahler continued: 'It's beyond
words, how I am constantly learning more and more from Bach (sitting at his
feet like a child, of course); for my natural way of working is Bach-like. If
only I had time to do nothing but learn in this highest of all schools! Even
I can't visualize how much it would mean. But may my later days, when at
last I belong to myself, be dedicated to him!' (NBL, p. 157 and pp. 161–2.)[40]

There is more than one prophecy bound up in those words of Mahler. It
is surely significant, for example, that in 1905, when he came to conduct the
first performance in Vienna (with the Philharmonic) of his Fifth Symphony,
on 7 December 1905, the only other work on the programme was Bach's
Motet 'Singet dem Herrn ein neues Lied' (in which the Wiener Singverein
participated): and in the very last years of his life Mahler offered a practical
tribute to Bach in the shape of a Suite for orchestra, arranged by Mahler
himself, and consisting of movements from Bach's orchestral suites. I reproduce the title-page of this work—which was, ironically, Mahler's last
publication (it was published in 1910: Mahler signed the contract with his
publishers in New York on Christmas Eve 1909)—and have something to say
about the nature of the arrangement below. Here, what seems relevant to
emphasize is the evidence the Suite brings of Mahler's dedication to Bach in
his 'later days', and of the continuing stimulus provided by the study of his
precious Gesellschaft edition. I am sure that it was from Mahler's immersion
in that source that the idea came of putting together a string of movements.
Of course, the idea in itself must strike us in our time as very strange, when
we know Bach, as it were, in the round, and when it seems altogether surprising that Bach could not be left alone to speak for himself. But we have to
remember that Bach's orchestral works in Mahler's day were by no means the
staple diet of concert programmes, and were certainly not the familiar pieces
that they are for us today. Moreover, they were not the kind of music with
which a conductor of Mahler's rank would have been expected to concern
himself.[41] So, in assembling this Suite, Mahler was not just following up a
predilection of his own, but also breaking new ground. It is as something of
a pioneering effort to bring Bach's orchestral works to a wider public that
Mahler's Suite should be regarded.

Sale of Manuscript

This Agreement, made this

22nd   day of   December   19 09,

between   Gustav Mahler

of   New York   and G. SCHIRMER (INC.),

WITNESSETH: That said   Gustav Mahler

in consideration of the sum of

500.00   dollars, to   be   paid by said G. SCHIRMER (INC.),

has assigned, transferred and set over, and hereby does assign, transfer and set over

unto the said G. SCHIRMER (INC.) all   his   right, title and interest in and to the un-

published manuscript musical composition   entitled

Suite aus den Orchesterwerken

von J. S. Bach zum Concertvortrag

eingerichtet

and the copyright thereof in and for all countries, with the right to secure statutory

protection therefor, for such terms and renewals thereof as may be practicable.

Said   Gustav Mahler

hereby covenants with said G. SCHIRMER (INC.) that   he   has an unincumbered and

good title to the exclusive use of said manuscript and copyright therein, which title

he   hereby warrants to said G. SCHIRMER (INC.), their successors and assigns.

It is further understood and agreed by the parties hereto, for themselves, their heirs,

assigns and legal representatives, that the rights transferred by this assignment cover

also the author's right of renewal and the copyright for the second term as granted by

the United States copyright laws in force at this time, and for any further period of

copyright which may be granted hereafter.

The agreement with Schirmer for Mahler's Bach Suite

Said   Gustav Mahler

however, hereby reserves to   his self the exclusive right and license to reproduce or

cause to be reproduced said composition   in mechanical musical instruments, and agrees

that whenever he   may make use of such license,   he   and   his

sub-licensees will at all times attach to every copy of said mechanical reproduction of

said composition   the notice of copyright required or which may be required by any

copyright statute under which said composition   is   or may be protected.

IN WITNESS WHEREOF, the parties hereto have hereunto set their hands the

day and year first above written.

Signed in the presence of:

New York 24. Dezember 1909

Gustav Mahler

SUITE

AUS DEN ORCHESTERWERKEN

VON

JOH. SEB. BACH

MIT AUSGEFÜHRTEM CONTINUO

ZUM KONZERTVORTRAGE BEARBEITET

VON

GUSTAV MAHLER

I

OUVERTURE

II

RONDEAU UND BADINERIE

III

AIR

IV

GAVOTTE NO. 1 UND 2

ORCHESTER-PARTITUR   ORCHESTERSTIMMEN

NEW YORK : G. SCHIRMER

BOSTON : BOSTON MUSIC CO.

BERLIN : ALBERT STAHL   LEIPZIG : FRIEDR. HOFMEISTER   LONDON : SCHOTT & CO.

PARIS

A. DURAND & FILS   MAX ESCHIG

The title-page of the Bach Suite

This historical aspect of the enterprise has to be kept in mind if one is to understand why it was that Mahler presented a dressed-up anthology of movements rather than a straight performance of Bach's Suites.[42] Mahler was not that radical, in this sphere at least; and the 'dressing-up', for him, in any case, was not an enforced act of sacrilege, unwillingly undertaken, but a creative service that helped out the composer from the past who was less generously endowed with musical resources than Mahler and his contemporaries (see the Witt letter, Appendix A, for further documentation on this point). Yet, at the same time, Mahler was obviously conscious of the fact, and perhaps became increasingly so towards the end of his life, that some respect had to be paid to the sound-world inhabited by a composer at his particular point in history. He had already, in his famous new productions of Mozart at the Vienna Opera, accompanied all the recitatives at the harpsichord,[43] and when he performed *Don Giovanni* at the Metropolitan, New York, in January 1908, where it seems no appropriate instrument was available, he accompanied the recitatives 'on a pianoforte with an altered action so as to make it sound somehow like a harpsichord' (Krehbiel, in his obituary of Mahler, see Appendix B, p. 410). Thus there was a certain logic in the next step, which was to introduce into the concert hall, in his performances of his Bach Suite, a comparable manifestation of historical 'style'.

It would be going too far, I think, to suggest that Mahler suddenly discovered in himself an acute historical conscience, but there can be no doubt that it was an awareness of the music's need for some sort of authenticity of texture and sonority that was the reason for his being billed as 'Mr. Mahler at the harpsichord' in the performances he gave of his Bach Suite in the U.S.A.[44] Once again we must remember that the first decade of the century was not a time like our own, when the appropriate continuo instrument is a *sine qua non*. The great harpsichord revival, in Mahler's day, was still to come. What he seems to have used for performances of the Suite was a spinet, prepared for him by Steinway and strong in tone. (I daresay the piano-manufacturers' preparation had something to do with what must have been an amplified voice.) This is what Mahler wrote himself about the instrument in a letter to a friend from New York, postmarked 19 November 1909 (GMB[1], p. 407):

> ... I am highly satisfied with my position here. I have wished you were at many of these concerts. I particularly enjoyed a recent Bach concert, for which I arranged the *basso continuo* for organ, and I conducted and improvised—quite in the manner of the ancients—at a very full-toned spinet prepared for the purpose by Steinway. For me (and for the audience) some utterly surprising things emerged from this. This clogged-up literature was illuminated as if by a searchlight. It has a stronger effect (in its colours too) than any modern work. But I am a partisan as never before.[45]

His appearance at the keyboard of the instrument not unnaturally attracted a good deal of attention. The Suite was performed (though not for the first time) in New York on 16 January 1910, along with Rachmaninov's Third Piano Concerto, the Prelude and 'Liebestod' from *Tristan* and Smetana's *Bartered Bride* overture. Arthur Farwell (1872–1952) wrote of the Bach as follows, in *Musical America*: 'Mahler gave his audience a sensation by conducting the Bach Suite seated at a klavier [*sic*], such as was employed at the time of Bach, and playing upon it the continuo which is an integrated part of these early compositions. . . . The effect was both interesting and delightful although the orchestra was considerably impaired by the conductor's inability to use his hands except during passages when the klavier was silent or when he would disengage one or other from the klavier part.'[46] There is something fascinating, and also wholly characteristic, about Mahler appearing in this improbable role at the very end of his life, though, as we know, his accomplishment as a pianist was of very long standing. (See also DM[1], pp. 82–5.) It could, one feels, only be the paradoxical Mahler who, while appearing to us very much as a man of his time in his 'arrangement' of Bach, steps out of —or ahead of—his time by attempting to introduce an element of 'authenticity' into his performance, long before authenticity became the fashion. It seems as if once again we encounter here an example of that prescience which in Mahler's case extended to so many spheres of musical activity.

*   *   *   *

The Bach Suite consists of four movements:
   (1) Overture
   (2) Rondeau and Badinerie
   (3) Air
   (4) Gavotte No. 1 and 2

(1) is the Overture from the Suite No. 2 in B minor; (2) is the Rondeau from the same Suite (the second movement), which Mahler follows up with the Badinerie (the Finale of Bach's Suite); (3) is the second movement from the Suite No. 3 in D; and (4) is made up of Gavotte I and Gavotte II, the third movement from the same Suite. By selecting movements from the B minor and D major Suites, all of them in B minor and D major, Mahler of course automatically provided himself with a unifying as well as a progressively tonal relationship. (Minor to relative major, the overall key-scheme of the Second Symphony!) No doubt this was a factor that played a role in the choice of Suites from which Mahler selected his sequence of movements. Moreover, the D major Suite introduces three trumpets and drums, which enabled Mahler to build his Suite towards (in his terms) a brilliant, solid, dynamic conclusion.

There seems little point in laboriously giving a verbal description of every
page of the score. My reproduction (see pp. 358–9) of the first pages of the
Suite, which includes Mahler's performing notes, will provide some illumination of the character of the arrangement. The second footnote is entirely
characteristic. In the first, the reinforcement he had in mind was obligatory if the flute part was to hold its own in the pretty dense texture of the
tuttis. (Mahler, of course, observed the solo passages.) It is in this movement
—presumably to provide the Suite with an imposing opening gesture—that
Mahler uses both organ and harpsichord continuo (he drops the organ elsewhere); and when one adds to this the probable size of the string orchestra
involved, then one sees why Mahler would have needed a multi-manned flute
part. In this movement, certainly, we seem to be a long way removed from a
texture that we would recognize as Bach's.

However, it is unrealistic to search for revelations of Bach in Mahler's
Suite; it is rather what the Suite tells us about Mahler that must be our first
interest. When the Overture moves on from the slow introduction into the
quick part, we meet Mahler face to face. The theme, of course, is Bach's, but
the phrasing and articulation of it are Mahler's. Indeed, this is a fascinating
example of Mahler treating Bach's theme as if it were one of his own, and
attempting, through the meticulous notation of it (note the elaborate use of
staccato, dynamics, slurs and rests), to secure the precise characterization of
the theme that was his conception. This can be made very plain if we set side
by side Bach's notation and Mahler's (Exx. 111 and 112). Ex. 112, as one
immediately sees, might well have come straight out of one of Mahler's own
works, at least in so far as its notation is concerned. One of the side benefits
of the manic detail of Mahler's notation is that it gives us a very clear idea of
some aspects of his own performances (though *his* principal anxiety, naturally
enough, was to establish a notation by which others might be guided in the
future), and this example from the Bach certainly provides a clear picture of
Mahler's interpretative style:

Ex. 111

Ex. 112

To round off the record of this particular aspect of the score, here is Mahler's
idiosyncratic notation of the theme of the Gavotte No. 1 (Ex. 114), as compared with Bach's (Ex. 113):

Ex. 113

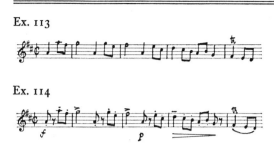

Ex. 114

One may properly question the notational fuss and the imposition of so vivid an interpretative personality on the shape of the music. Nonetheless, one cannot but feel that there must have been remarkably few dull bars in Mahler's performances, even if it was only a question of waiting to see what on earth was going to happen next.

There was no less of an unpredictable element, if of a somewhat different kind, in Mahler's realization of the continuo. He was not content to let this play a purely supportive or decorative role. On the contrary, his continuo either develops into a substantial keyboard part with a forceful, independent life of its own (see Ex. 115, from Gavotte No. 2) or ingeniously and with some delicacy embellishes Bach's counterpoint with fresh counterpoints of

Ex. 115

his own devising (see pp. 384–5). Once again, one may not be able to applaud Mahler's continuo for its stylishness. But life and a certain bold imagination it certainly has, as well as an undeniable historical interest for all students of Mahler. It is curious to think of him working at his continuo realization and preparing the Suite for publication while at the same time working at the Tenth Symphony and at revisions of the Ninth and *Das Lied*, which were already completed but never reached publication.

The Bach Suite, then, was the last publication that Mahler himself supervised, and it shows him, as I have tried to show, in an altogether characteristic light as very much a creature of his own time and a repository of many of its cultural attitudes, and also as a man with this mysterious sense

SUITE

aus den Orchesterwerken von
Johann Sebastian Bach

I

Ouverture

Bearbeitet von
Gustav Mahler

Flauto trav.*

Violino 1

Violino 2

Viola

Continuo

Clavicembalo**

Orgel**

Ped.

---

* Im Forte stark besetzt, eventuell durch eine Clarinette verstärkt.

** Sowohl die Klavier- als auch die Orgelstimme mögen als Skizze zu einer im Tutti möglichst vollgriffigen, im Piano sorgfältig abgetönten und im ganzen frei improvisatorischen Ausführung angesehen werden.

* In *forte* with additional flutes, reinforced by a Clarinet if needed.

** Both the piano-part and the organ-part are to be regarded as a sketch which should bear, in general, the character of a free improvisation, with as full harmonies as possible in the *tuttis* and most delicately shaded in the *piano* passages.

21792

Two pages from the first movement of the published full score of the Bach Suite

for what, musically, was just round the next historical corner. But, though
the Bach Suite makes its point, and for Mahler was a practical and public
means of declaring his devotion, it remains a curiosity. The profound debt
to Bach, less explicitly, perhaps, but all the deeper for that, we find in
Mahler's own music. No doubt, Mahler was always conscious of Bach, from
his early days onwards. I have already pointed to the Bach-like, concertante
textures of the Scherzos in the Second and Fourth Symphonies which it is
hard to envisage being written other than against a background of knowledge
of Bach's concerto techniques. But there is no doubt that Bach came increasingly into the foreground of Mahler's life at the turn of the century and after
it, reinforced, as I have suggested, by the companion that Mahler made of
the Bach Gesellschaft edition. That Bach became of increasing significance
to Mahler was perhaps inevitable; after all, his own music, from the Fourth
Symphony onwards, and as a result of compulsions exerted by the development of his own style, became increasingly contrapuntal, and thus it was
natural that he should turn to the greatest contrapuntist of them all. One
should not, I think, look for crude instances of influence, because these one is
unlikely to find. It is much more a case of perceiving behind Mahler's music
a model for a type of gesture that probably had its origin in a work by Bach.
An interesting example, I believe of this kind of subtle affinity, is to be found
in the Rondo-Burleske from the Ninth Symphony, a movement noted for its
intense contrapuntal activity. No doubt, as has often been remarked, Bach
had a hand in it. But though this is a true observation in a general sense, it
does not really take us very far. What strikes me as significantly Bachian in
this movement is not the obvious contrapuntal link but the way in which
Mahler twice in the reprise of the movement tries to dam with an interrupted
cadence the turbulent onward flow of the music, and twice the flow thrusts
on unimpeded until it reaches its final climactic bars. Compare Mahler's
gestures in this passage (see Ex. 116) with the comparable gestures made for
the same reasons and in the midst of the equally intense contrapuntal texture
which is the Finale of Bach's Fourth Brandenburg Concerto (see Ex. 117) and
I believe one uncovers a relationship with Bach, one of real compositional
principle, that speaks more for Mahler's identification with Bach than the
mere fact of common contrapuntal features.

Ex. 116

Ex. 117

In another sphere altogether, it has also seemed to me possible that it was Mahler's growing familiarity with Bach that may have led to his explicit use of the chorale in his middle-period studies. This is often attributed exclusively to the influence of Bruckner,[47] and I do not doubt the truth of this; but a comment of Mahler's to Bauer-Lechner in the summer of 1901 (NBL, p. 101), which touches on the subject of Bach's chorales, makes one wonder whether in fact there was not an additional stimulus from this source. Bruckner, in his use of chorales, was discharging his own debt to Bach—so either way, Bach was involved in Mahler's chorale technique. But this again might be an instance of the stimulus offered by the Bach Gesellschaft edition. One remembers that in 1901 Mahler was certainly busy with the Fifth Symphony, in which the concept of the chorale plays a prominent role.

One cannot of course leave the subject of Mahler's counterpoint *without* referring to Bach, though it is surely the case that when it comes to Mahler's late works, say the Ninth Symphony or *Das Lied*, there is nothing superficially Bach-like about Mahler's polyphony (no trace of pastiche or of an intentional neoclassicism: in this respect the counterpoint of the Fourth Symphony was singular in style). If one takes two remarkable examples, one from *Das Lied*[48] (see Ex. 118) and one from the Ninth Symphony (see Ex. 119), what one meets in principle is the purest form of that astoundingly

Ex. 118

Ex. 119

spare, long-limbed, linear polyphony that Mahler, with prophetic foresight, defined as the only 'true polyphony' in 1898 (see p.348), a decade or so before he actually wrote it himself in his final masterpieces. As any literate musical ear can hear, Mahler's counterpoint is not 'like' Bach's, except in ways which words cannot really describe; one is obliged to fall back on 'poise', 'economy', 'restraint', 'purity of line', and the rest, and it is better to jettison the words and leave the reader to study the music. What one can say is this: that given the direction in which Mahler's music was itself moving, the way in which his musical mind was developing, it is absolutely comprehensible why it was that he manifested a growing addiction to Bach, why he would have felt a quite special affinity to Bach and found his music a source of continuous technical inspiration. Not, I repeat, just in the immediately obvious area of contrapuntal thinking, but in many subtler spheres, where, I am convinced, Bach was the creatively influential model. It is my view that it was out of Mahler's study of Bach after the turn of the century, which must have included much music he had never known or heard or could hope to perform, that the unprecedentedly innovatory quasi-recitatives of 'Der Abschied' in *Das Lied*—with their amazing instrumental obbligati—emerged.

These remarkable examples of a flexible, asymmetrical, and intensely inspired musical prose, I submit, owe their existence not to Mahler's experience of recitative in the theatre (much though the theatre contributed technically to Mahler's music) but to his experience of Bach's recitative, an experience that was then transformed and transfigured by his own creativity. It was surely a foregone conclusion that Bach's mind and his music would come almost to obsess a composer, whose own works, now his great *Wunderhorn* period was behind him, progressed towards a music in which, as he said himself, 'There is no longer harmony, only counterpoint.'

Notes

1 The relationship between the song and the Fourth Symphony has been so thoroughly worked over now by so many commentators that it scarcely seems necessary to set it out again in detail here. Paul Bekker (in PB, p. 148) said most of what needed to be said, very adequately, in 1920, when illustrating his view—which is certainly the right one—that in these three opening bars of the vocal melody, the symphony is contained. The relationship between

Wir ge-nie-ssen die himm - - - -li-schen Freu-den

'Das himmlische Leben' and the Third Symphony is less familiar and therefore perhaps worth spelling out. (The actual chronology of the Fourth's composition is pretty straightforward, once allowance has been made for the composition of the song-finale in 1892. The only date inscribed in the complete MS fair copy of the symphony, which is in the possession of the Gesellschaft der Musikfreunde, Vienna, is 5 January 1901, at the end of the Scherzo. In the earlier MS orchestral score (which lacks the song-finale), the date Sunday, 6 August 1900, is inscribed at the end of the Adagio, which was undoubtedly an indication by Mahler of what he regarded as the termination of the composition of the whole work, for along with the date and a reference to the third movement he added the words, '. . . und somit die ganze Symphonie . . .' ['. . . and therefore the whole symphony . . .']. This means that the first three movements were composed between the summer of 1899 (when Mahler started work in the middle of July, after his completion of 'Revelge' (see HG¹, pp. 522–24)) and the summer of 1900, 'Das himmlische Leben' having been composed early in 1892. (As the orchestral song already existed in full score Mahler, naturally, did not need to copy it out again for his first MS full score of the symphony. The MS fair copy of the Fourth, of course, includes the song-finale.) The symphony was published in 1902.)

2 Which makes it all the odder that in the summer of 1900 Mahler talked so ingenuously (or so it seems) to Bauer-Lechner about the links between the Third and Fourth symphonies that derived from a common song-source, 'Das himmlische Leben'. Mahler, if Bauer-Lechner is correct (NBL, p. 146), expressed the relationship otherwise on this occasion: 'A particularly close relationship exists between the Third and Fourth; in fact, the latter even [*sic*] has themes in common with the movement of the Third called 'Was mir die Engel erzählen'. This is so unusual and remarkable [*sic*] that he even has misgivings about it.' Late in the day, one would have thought, for the composer to have misgivings about a unique aspect of the two symphonies that scarcely happened by accident; and strange that Mahler mentions the links of the Fourth with the Third through the agency of 'Was mir die Engel erzählen' rather than the elaborate relationship of the Third to the song that eventually became the Finale of the Fourth. (See also pp. 312–18.) This only goes to show that Mahler was not above giving eccentric (or even misleading) accounts of his own music—or to suggest that the faithful Bauer-Lechner may sometimes have faltered in her documentation of a particular exchange. There is certainly good reason not to accept every word of Mahler on his own music as if it were gospel. (Mahler once remarked that 'Das himmlische Leben' had given birth to *five* symphonic movements. M. de La Grange (HG¹, p. 820) thinks that Mahler may have meant the whole of the Fourth and the fifth movement of the Third, though that would entail counting the song itself as one of the movements to which it supposedly gave birth. M. de La Grange may well be right—it is certainly a tidy solution—but I wonder if perhaps Mahler may not have been thinking of the first movement of the Third Symphony, which, in a very real musical sense, was born out of the song and had the song in view as the eventual Finale.)

3 Mahler did, it seems, acknowledge (NBL, p. 146) the relationship between 'Das himmlische Leben', now installed in the Fourth, and the fifth movement of the Third Symphony, a relationship 'so unusual and remarkable that he even has misgivings about it himself.' If Bauer-Lechner is correct, Mahler made this relationship sound like an accident. But after all it was, in the first instance, calculated as part of the evolutionary progress towards the Third Symphony's goal. What was unusual was the dispersal across two symphonies of a system of cross-references that was originally destined for one.

4 As Romanticism progressed towards its late phase, a movement of which Mahler formed part, so did the ornament as such undergo a spectacular increase in importance (think of what the trill came to mean to Scriabin in his late piano sonatas, e.g. the tenth sonata). Ornamentation, which had been an expressive adornment, now began to assume a much more fundamental role, even to function (Scriabin again) as the very substance of the invention. We encounter nothing quite as radical as this in Mahler in the field of the trill or grace-note (what he did with the crescendo was another matter, as I have pointed out earlier (see n. 94, p. 293)), but even in this first movement of the Third Symphony one cannot but observe the pervasiveness of the grace-note and the trill that ultimately colours the texture of the music in a unique way (cf., for instance, the remarkable passage from Fig. 36 to Fig. 39, which is a self-contained study of the use of trills and grace-notes). It is indeed with the arrival of Ex. 95 at Fig. 12 that Mahler introduces grace-notes into the movement (trills have been established even earlier, two bars after Fig. 2, and are thereafter always with us). Here again, of course, the prime generating

source was the song, whose emphatic exploitation of the grace-note (cf. Fig. 3 in 'Das himmlische Leben') was also taken over by the Fourth Symphony, to function as its very opening gesture.

5 In a subsequent alternating section, the grace-note motive is also given prominence (cf. Fig. 12 of the Minuet with Fig. 3 of 'Das himmlische Leben').

6 See GMB¹, pp. 107–8 and p. 140, and my comments on pp. 187f. It is true that Mahler in a letter to Bahr-Mildenburg, dated 1 July 1896 (ABM, pp. 36–37) apparently refers to a seven-movement symphony, though with the 'Love' movement now installed as No. 7 (as the Finale, that is). But I think it is clear that this numeration arises because Mahler may still have been thinking of independently numbering the introduction to the first movement as No. 1 (see NBL, footnote to p. 42), which would automatically make the Adagio No. 7. By this time, however, 'Das himmlische Leben' was already out of the running. Dika Newlin seems to have misunderstood this point in her remarks on the letter to Bahr-Mildenburg (DN, p. 164). (Mahler's numeration of the movements in the Hamburg MS of the symphony, the MS mentioned on p. 194, supports my suggestion that the numerical confusion to which he was prone was mainly due to counting the first movement as *two* units.) See also n. 75, p. 286.

7 One has to keep on reminding oneself, however, of the formative influence of the song 'Das himmlische Leben', the symphony's *fons et origo*, which had been around since 1892. The song, in a very real sense, was part of the essential materials out of which the first movement of the Third Symphony was built, and *without* which Mahler would probably have found himself unable to proceed when turning to the completion of the movement in 1896, so integral a part of the conception of the movement had the song become. It would have been positively bizarre if, starting as it were from scratch in 1896, he had introduced the song relationships into the movement without any discernible justification. Last point: the remarkable scale of the first movement is less surprising if one bears in mind the obligation (of which Mahler must have been acutely conscious as he was composing it) to balance an Adagio that had itself turned out to be of unusually imposing dimensions. In this connection it is interesting to come across the following passage in HG¹ (pp. 808–9): 'After completing the initial [i.e. the first] movement the following summer [i.e. in 1896] [Mahler] simplified the conclusion of the Adagio: "It now ends the whole work with broad chords and in the one tonality of D major," he said to Natalie on 31 July of that year.' Undoubtedly, as I have just suggested, Mahler was aware of the scale of the completed Adagio when finally working on the first movement; and when that huge task was done, as this additional bit of information shows, and the decision taken that the Adagio was to be the Finale and not the song, Mahler turned to the coda of the Adagio, to ensure that the concluding bars of the movement were shaped so as to function as the concluding bars of the symphony. This was the final modification that had to be made, once Mahler had realized that, even though

unknowingly at first, in writing his great slow movement he had, in fact, also written his Finale. (See also HG¹, p. 377.)

8 This document appeared as the cover of a pamphlet issued by the Mahler Society of Berlin in 1967 [?].

9 Mahler's numeration of his themes reflects their thematic evolution, not their actual sequence in the movement.

10 So here we go again, with Mahler once more recapitulating his introduction, along with his recapitulation (see Ex. 22 and also my remarks on pp. 206–8). Old habits, it seems, died hard. Indeed, as a student of mine pointed out (Mr. David Gaster, to whom I am indebted for making this point), precisely the same thing happens in the Ninth Symphony, at the point of re-capitulation in the first movement. As Mahler makes the transition to this crucial juncture (bars 337–47) he knits into the texture the principal motives that form the few bars of prelude (bars 1–7) to the main theme, an obvious re-collection of this most pregnant of Mahler's introductions. (Interestingly, the facsimile of Mahler's draft score (Universal Edition, 1971, edited by Erwin Ratz) shows that these introductory bars, and the transitional bars preceding the recapitulation, had to be worked at by Mahler before he got them into the shape with which we are familiar today. There are indications, indeed, that it was a later revision of the pre-recapitulation transition that made explicit its relationship to the opening bars of the movement.)

11 Itself partly 'recapitulatory' in character, e.g. the B minor of the movement's very opening is re-evoked but this time in the context of the opening bars of the principal melody (cf. bar 234 et seq.). There is no end to the changes which Mahler rings; and there is certainly no guarantee that a calculated tonal reference will bring with it the theme or motive that was originally associated with it. This is yet another example of Mahler's characteristic and systematic method of displacement, which unpredictably unites what before was kept apart.

The B minor that is touched on here shows that this remarkable passage is not only thematically recapitulatory but tonally recapitulatory too, i.e. Mahler recapitulates keys of special significance along with his themes and motives (though, as I have pointed out, not necessarily in their established associations). It is in B minor, it will be remembered, that the movement is surprisingly launched—off-key, as it were—and it is with considerable ingenuity that Mahler plans for its re-emergence during this recapitulation-cum-transition. The pivotal chord that facilitates this materialization is projected, very forcefully, at Fig. 17, which bar represents the last dynamic peak of the development, after which the music begins to wind down and into the recapitulation (at Fig. 18). The chord at Fig. 17 is functionally ambiguous, i.e. it discloses a double face: we recognize it first as a German sixth on the flattened supertonic (a characteristic Mahlerian inflection) and then as the dominant seventh of F sharp minor, the key that emerges a few bars later (bar 231, et seq.) and which in turn leads to the recall of B minor (bar 234) in association with the return of the first limb of the main theme. The logic of this whole construct of dense musical thinking is faultless. The B minor must be got in, because it forms an essential part of the initiating materials that Mahler wants to recollect in their entirety (NB: introduction *and* (part) exposition (see pp. 323f.)). It must also be got out of the way before G major is dropped into at Fig. 18. Thus this vital bit of tonal recapitulation was effected too on the 'wrong' side of the double bar, which was chronologically the *right* place for it, along with the constellation of motives and themes that provide it with its proper thematic context.

12 It seems to me that this textbook-sanctioned concept may be largely true of some composers in the nineteenth century—Beethoven, Brahms, Schumann, Schubert—but that in the eighteenth, and particularly in Haydn and Mozart, one is much more conscious of an emancipated approach to the wind, one that allows the wind a status by no means always inferior to that of the strings. Thus for me Mahler's Fourth not only anticipates the twentieth century's upsurge of interest in wind sonority but also revives, as part of its 'classicizing', a pre-nineteenth-century orchestral texture.

13 It is hard to think of Mahler writing a concerto in any orthodox sense, but what one has to remember is that his highly developed concertante, soloistic style of orchestration very often approached the threshold of the concerto. Indeed, I would argue that, just as there are specific chamber-music aspects of Mahler's orchestration—which were his form of chamber music—so too are there distinctly concerto elements—his kind of concerto writing. It is not only the introduction to the Third Symphony of which I am thinking, that brings what is almost a trombone concerto within its scope. There are fine examples of Mahler's concertante technique in the Scherzo of the Fifth and in the Scherzo of the Fourth Symphony, where I have in mind not only the elaborate solo violin part but also the pronounced solo emphasis allotted to the first horn; and the Scherzo of the Second is sometimes positively Brandenburgian in texture and instrumental style.

14 It is naturally the tipping of the balance in favour of the wind that must engage most of our attention in the Third Symphony; but one ought also to take note of the striking handling of the percussion which, at two important junctures, bears the weight of a crucial transitional function. At eight bars before Fig. 13 what is virtually an independent percussion band (expanding on the bass drum precedents at four bars before Fig. 2 and six bars before Fig. 11) leads us back—the March, as it were, is not quite ready to get under way (cf. Fig. 12, et seq., with two bars before Fig. 19, et seq.)—to the heavy rhythms of the introduction (cf. Figs. 13 and 2), while at Fig. 54, in a transition that simultaneously relinquishes the tempo of the development and re-establishes the movement's tempo primo, the side-drum (placed in the distance) actually fades the central March section out—another fascinating example of Mahler exploiting the dramatic possibilities of directional sound (see also pp. 337f.). Here too, then, in this symphony, are signs of that growing preoccupation with percussion that was to become such a feature of the twentieth century. (A timely communication from the conductor, Mr.

Frederik Prausnitz, reminds me that another example of a two-tempi situation, if of a somewhat different kind, exists at the very beginning of the Fourth Symphony, where the regular tempo established by the opening sleigh-bell motive (bars 1–3) should be—but never has been, in my experience—strictly maintained for its total duration (see the note about the flutes in bar 3 (not bar 4 as stated) in the Preface to the Critical Edition of the symphony, p. 3) and *across* which, or *against* which, Mahler clearly wanted to introduce the poco rit. of the clarinets and the violins. In an authentic performance, then, one should hear in bar 3 a typically Mahlerian combination of regular and irregular tempi. The result of following Mahler's notation would be to 'detach' the introductory bars, to isolate them by, as it were, an unscheduled interruption, which then reveals itself to be the main business of the movement. All this, in my view, makes subtle musical sense, especially in view of the fact that the point of the enigmatic opening bars is not really wholly clarified until the whole symphony has been unfolded, to its very final note.)

15 'He's preoccupied with his work all the time, not just during the four hours in the summer-house. You can see this when you're walking or cycling with him. He's constantly losing himself in his thoughts, or else he lingers behind and pulls out his manuscript notebook to jot something down—only you mustn't notice this, or he becomes furious!' (NBL, p. 47). Alma Mahler wrote: 'Often and often he stood still, the sun on his bare head, he took out a small notebook, ruled for music, and wrote and reflected and wrote again, sometimes beating time in the air. This lasted very often for an hour or longer . . .' (AM⁵, pp. 46–7). What became of all these discarded notebooks? It may be that the answer to that question is found in an interesting passage in HG¹, p. 628, which includes the following: 'In August [1901], Mahler brought up the subject [with Bauer-Lechner] of [his] notebooks again, stating that he did not . . . want them to survive his death and that he would destroy everything he himself had not finished, for "such fragments only lead to misunderstandings". Beethoven's notebooks had revealed nothing except that he apparently worked on several different projects at once, whereas he was, in fact, constantly jotting down themes for future use. Musicologists had underlined the "progress accomplished" in the final version, but no one knew what he might have done with his first inspiration, nor indeed what any other idea might have become in his hands.' Perhaps, then, the notebooks were in the main destroyed, in which case the notebook discussed above is all the more rare and valuable. I know of only one other extant sketchbook, which is in the Nationalbibliothek, Vienna. According to Alma Mahler's inscription, this was Mahler's 'last sketchbook', a description that certainly requires investigation and may perhaps have to be modified when the sketches have been deciphered.

16 Excerpts from some reviews of Mahler's orchestral programmes in the U.S.A. were published in *Musical America*, February 1960, among them a reaction to one of Mahler's Berlioz performances. This at least gives one an indication of the probable quality of what seems to have been a memorable occasion—for composer, audience and conductor. The following appeared in the *New York Post* on 7 January 1910: 'The Philharmonic audience at Carnegie Hall last night enjoyed the equivalent of what in the opera house is called an all-star cast. One of the greatest living pianists played with a conductor who has no superior anywhere, in other words, Ferruccio Busoni played with Gustav Mahler [Busoni was soloist in Liszt's arrangement of Schubert's 'Wanderer' Fantasy]. . . . Equally stirring were the contributions made to the programme by Mr. Mahler and his orchestra—Berlioz's *Fantastic Symphony* and the final number, Wagner's *Meistersinger* Prelude. . . . The Berlioz symphony has been interpreted here by nearly every noted conductor of the time, but not one of them, not even Weingartner, who is a Berlioz specialist and apostle, succeeded in rousing a sober Philharmonic audience to such a state of frenzied excitement as [Mahler] did with the fourth and fifth movements. . . . Mr. Mahler has worked a miracle—no other word seems strong enough to describe what he has done in making his new organization the equivalent of the Boston Symphony Orchestra, if not its superior. No wonder the Mahlerites are growing so fast in numbers. . . . To hear him conduct the Berlioz symphony was like hearing Paderewski play a Liszt rhapsody. Everybody knows what that means.' In this same article, an interesting quotation is made from Rachmaninov's *Recollections* (Oskar von Rieseman: *Rachmaninov's Recollections*, New York, 1934, p. 160), in which Rachmaninov remembers the indelible impression made on him by hearing Mahler rehearse the *Symphonie Fantastique* in New York: 'He conducted it magnificently, especially the passage called "Procession to the High Court" [Rachmaninov is clearly referring to the 'March to the Scaffold' movement], where he obtained a crescendo of the brass instruments such as I have never before heard achieved in this passage: the windows shook, the very walls seemed to vibrate . . .' Mahler did not confine himself exclusively to performing the *Symphonie Fantastique*. He also played with the Philharmonic excerpts from the *Damnation of Faust* and three movements from the *Romeo and Juliet* symphony (both of these Berlioz items were included in his final 1910–11 season in the U.S.A.). For excerpts from some reviews of Mahler's performance of the *Symphonie Fantastique* in Hamburg, see HG[1], p. 322. These also make clear that battle had to be done in Germany on behalf of Berlioz. It was not only Mahler who had a rough ride with the critics. The same was true of Vienna, where the *Symphonie Fantastique* in 1898 still met with entrenched opposition (HG[1], p. 491). For the reception (or dismissal, rather) of Mahler's performance of the *Rob Roy* overture there, see HG[1], p. 604. In Paris in 1900, however, his 'brilliant' interpretation of the *Symphonie Fantastique* was ecstatically acclaimed (HG[1], p. 576).

17 See eight bars before Fig. 17, et seq., in Mahler's first movement, where the *Dies Irae* motive is introduced for the first time as part of the symphony's thematic complex.

18 It is of no small interest to look at the use Mahler makes of the E flat clarinet in his first four symphonies. As one would expect, it is in the first movement of the Third Symphony, much of which is based on the sonority of the regimental band, that the instrument is most generously employed; however, it is also present elsewhere in the symphony, conspicuously so in the third and fifth movements. The instrument is least prominent in his Fourth Symphony, but its voice is heard frequently in the Second, especially in the satirical Scherzo, to which a solo E flat clarinet brings its own pungent tone (e.g., five bars before Fig. 30). In the First Symphony, as one might predict, the instrument is found prominently in the grotesque Funeral March. What is fascinating here is to locate the precise spot at which Mahler introduced the E flat clarinet in the MS (1893) version of the symphony. This appears to happen at one bar after Fig. 16 in the Funeral March, at the very moment when Mahler splits off his woodwind and treats them as an independent wind band, within the total texture; and along with this formation of a small wind band (with its music in the popular vein) Mahler introduces the E flat clarinet, the instrument so closely associated with wind bands and popular music. If nothing else, this indicates how intimately for Mahler the E flat clarinet was involved with his memories and experience of wind bands. When he came to use the image in his own music, the right instrument accompanied it. (No doubt, too, Mahler remembered, and was following, the innovatory precedent of the wind band in his youthful cantata, *Das klagende Lied*, in which he had used E flat clarinets as part of the ensemble. See n. 2, p. 80). Thereafter in the MS, i.e. in the Finale, he continues to use the E flat clarinet, though it is noticeable that the instrument was only brought into the last movement in 1893, as a result of the Hamburg revisions of the MS (see, for example, three bars after Fig. 29 in the EMS). This would seem to suggest that in the earliest versions of the symphony, the E flat clarinet was only used in the bizarre context of the Funeral March, with its wind band associations. It was some little while before the instrument was legitimized and incorporated into the symphony as a whole. There is no doubt that the E flat clarinet not only fascinated Mahler but also actually coloured the image of his music and his music-making in the public ear. M. de la Grange quotes a vicious Viennese attack on Mahler (HG[1], p. 487), of which the following forms part: '. . . Beethoven's talent for orchestration must have been very imperfect, for he failed to use an E flat clarinet in the "Coriolan" overture. How lucky you are, Beethoven, to have found an epigone to immortalize your work; without him "Coriolan" would have been eternally deprived of the E flat clarinet. . . . But let him leave our Beethoven in peace, since he already impresses and pleases us, even without an E flat clarinet and without Mahler! . . . Yes, Mr. Mahler has E flat clarinets on the brain.'

19 How amazing, in 1830, to find a composer writing for the double-basses as Berlioz does in the introduction to the Finale of the *Symphonie Fantastique* (bars 5 and 16), where he persuades the instrument to yield an entirely new sonority. It is a passage that confronts us with the emancipation of the double-bass.

20 Mahler would probably have known Berlioz's influential *Treatise on Instrumentation* (1844) long before Richard Strauss made a present to him in 1905 of his own newly published translation of the *Traité*. (See AM⁵, letter of 8 November 1905.)

21 The meticulousness and complexity of the dynamic markings of the close of the movement, from bar 175 onwards, interestingly prefigure Mahler's super-elaborate dynamic schemes, themselves manifestations of late Romanticism.

22 I have discussed this dramatic event in *Das klagende Lied* at some length in DM¹, pp. 187–90 and 195–6. There is an interesting passage in Bauer-Lechner (pp. 106–7) which shows how Mahler himself, after some doubts about the practicality of it, was rightly convinced that the theatrical effect he was after could only be achieved by the resources he originally deployed. He said, when working on the revised score for publication: 'I shall have to alter a whole passage, that is restore it to its original form from which I once changed it in Hamburg. Unfortunately, in the meantime I've lost the original version! It is the part where I use two orchestras, one of them in the distance outside the hall. I knew no one would ever perform *that*! In order to make performance possible, I cut out the second orchestra and gave its part to the first. When I saw the passage again, however, I immediately realized that this change had been detrimental to the work, which I must now restore to its original form—whether they play it or not!'

23 Klemperer, as a young conductor, conducted the off-stage orchestra in a performance under Oskar Fried (1871–1941) at which Mahler was present. Klemperer writes (in *Minor Recollections*, London, 1964, pp. 12–13), 'The passage in question is an extremely difficult one involving constant changes in tempo which have to be handled with the utmost care. Mahler was present in person at the full rehearsal. When I went over to him and asked if the off-stage orchestra had been satisfactory, he said: "No, it was frightful—much too loud." I ventured to point out that the score said 'fortissimo'. "Yes," he replied, "but in the far distance". I took this to heart and prevailed on my musicians (who were much too close) to play very softly during the actual performance. It was, as I have said, an unqualified success. After taking innumerable bows, Mahler came down to the green-room. When he caught sight of me he promptly shook my hand and said, "Very good." ' This memory is of some interest, illustrating as it does that Mahler was keenly conscious of the separation effect that he wanted to achieve. Once again (as in the First Symphony, see pp. 215f.) he not only wants the effect of distance but also the reduction of distance (by an increase in volume) as the off-stage band music progresses (see his instructions in bar 7 after Fig. 23 and again in bar 4 before Fig. 25). If the band is not correctly sited in the first instance, the effect of mobile, approaching sound cannot be realized. Actually, Klemperer is not quite correct in claiming that the score is marked fortissimo. There are no dynamics marked for the off-stage band, which is clearly intended to find its own dynamic level in relation to the marked dynamics of the on-stage orchestra. (As we have already seen (p. 285), Mahler addresses a special note on the topic of balance to his performers at this very point in his score (at Fig. 22).) Klemperer is right, however, in pointing to the 'constant changes in tempo'. These are largely conditioned by the extreme flexibility and asymmetry of the string melody, as distinct from the symmetry of the fanfares. The notation of this passage is, in fact, extremely ingenious, and above all *practical*, i.e. it is designed specifically to enable the two orchestras (and conductors) to keep together in performance. The notation may seem to the eye to smooth over the rhythmic differentiation between the two groups, but in performance one hears—or should hear—a regular and an irregular pattern in simultaneous combination, i.e. the passage should sound freer than it looks.

24 Ferdinand Pfohl, in his recollections of Mahler from the Hamburg period (FP, pp. 18–19), describes a trip to the harbour in the composer's company which itself proved to be something of an 'acoustic experience': 'We were standing on the Sandtorkai [Sandgate Quay] and looking out over the river, over its yellowish-grey waves, furrowed by steam ferry boats: the waves lapped against the bulwark and rocked the moorings from which we looked out over the Elbe, that tradesman's river apparently void of poetry, as far as the docks on the other side. The sirens were wailing like bad contraltos, and the winches were grinding, whining, groaning. Somewhere chains were rattling. Everywhere there was a moaning, a pounding, a clattering, a rattling and a rumbling. We both stood in silence, listening to the chords of this new music, the coming music of the machine: fascinated by the rhythms, by noises apparently irregular, but yet subject to a measure, to an irrational beat. Around us pealed a paean of rhythms. . . . All at once a hooter wailed out a clear D minor triad: vigorous and deafening, it was like a trombone chord. There followed in the far distance a G major triad like a suspended horn note vanishing on the horizon. One of those moments in which space, consciousness and emotion expand towards the cosmic. I said to Mahler: "Just look at that!" and I pointed to the commotion of the harbour scene, "That would make a symphony." "Why?" Mahler asked, and I answered: "Yes, a symphony of industry—not a nature symphony, but a symphony of the rhythms, the rhythmicality, of labour." Quick as a flash he gave me a peculiarly piercing look, and was silent. I was reminded very vividly of this soon-forgotten scene many years later when in Essen, that town of smoke, of steam hammers, gigantic foundries and smelting shops, in that town of logically ordered industry, I heard a new symphony of Mahler's: that in A minor [the Sixth Symphony], an austere work built on brusque rhythms, in which a gigantic kettledrum and a hammer seem called upon to play a particularly germinal role in this work's secret programme. The symphony began. The first movement unfurled itself. Suddenly I recognized in a muted trombone chord the questioning hoot of that minor triad in the harbour at Hamburg, and again in a Dorian major triad the distant answer as a soothing complement.

'When we were going home from the harbour that day, we met labourers laying street-pavings: remarkably exactly in the rhythm and sequence of the "Smithing motive" of Wagner's Nibelungs. We stood still and listened absorbedly. Mahler said: "Now if a composer were to use this motif of the streets as, so to speak, a naturalistic industry-motif, would he not be reproached for plagiarizing Wagner? So why do we not now reproach these street-pavers for plagiarizing Wagner?" I answered: "Because these workmen are not artists and would make not the least out of anyone's reproach. Surely reproaches are only made with a view to something being made out of them." Mahler grinned and pulled a face: "We musicians ought to follow suit . . ." He is right.'

25 See also my earlier remarks on Mahler and Ives, pp. 169f. I had noted in my first book on Mahler (DM¹, p. 77) the resemblance between Mahler's experience, as quoted by Bauer-Lechner, and the kind of polyphony we meet in Ives—which identical point I was glad to find made again by Mr. Elliott Carter in 1971 (see n. 62, p. 280)—but would now think (having got to know more about Ives since then) that the relationship has to be studied a good deal more seriously than I implied in 1958. There is, as I suggest on p. 170, a very real dividing line between what was acceptable to Mahler's ear and what was acceptable to Ives's, but I think that in both cases the two composers' approach to popular materials was governed in fact by their consciousness of tradition. Mahler's exploitation of the popular was one way of refreshing and extending the language and vocabulary of an established musical tradition. Ives's quotations 'from life' were a way of asserting a genuine culture and cultural independence in an historical context where 'culture' meant European culture, and where, if an indigenous culture was to be created, then the characteristic sound of it had to be, as it were, taken out of the air in which Ives breathed: which was precisely what Ives did. If Mahler was an end-of-a-tradition man, which was also the reason for *his* explorations, then Ives was a start-of-a-tradition man, which was also the reason for *his* explorations; and just as Ives up to a point can be said to exhibit, if in a wholly singular way, some of the signs of a musical nationalism, because there is a sense in which his choice of materials makes him peculiarly and identifiably American, Mahler too, in responding to *his* local music (as described by Bauer-Lechner above) and embodying it on a large scale in, for instance, the first movement of the Third Symphony, declared himself as something of a nationalist, or at least as a composer more musically sensitive than is often imagined to his Bohemian origins and early environment. (I touch on this point on pp. 292f.; see also DM¹, pp. 94–5. Incidentally, a maddening misprint crept into the published text of that RMA paper. See p. 84, line 6, where '23 November 1901' should read '25 November 1901'.)

26 The fruitful *influence* of Mahler on succeeding generations of composers is a complete subject in itself. A detailed study of it would involve a surprising number of the most distinguished twentieth-century composers in and outside Europe: Berg, Britten, Copland, and Shostakovich immediately come to

mind, and there would be many other names from a more recent generation, e.g. Peter Maxwell Davies and Luciano Berio. To make a general point, Britten's four orchestral song-cycles, which span the period 1936–1958, are brilliant extensions and developments of the great tradition initiated by Mahler in his *Gesellen* cycle in the 1880s. He would have relished them! And more specifically, the marvellously keen, spare and independent writing for the wind in, say, the first movement of the Cello Symphony (1963) clearly belongs to that order of dazzling transparency and instrumental emancipation which Mahler did so much to establish. Even were his own music not to survive, Mahler would still enjoy a substantial immortality in the music of those pre-eminent successors who have embraced his art and assimilated his techniques.

27 I suppose, though, that there is a deliberate feeling of 'in the old style' about the Minuet of the Third Symphony, or at least about its main tune. (See also p. 320, when I suggest that this movement stands in a special stylistic relationship to Wagner's *Parsifal*.) It is in his Third that Mahler juxtaposes a Minuet (the second movement) with a Scherzo (the third), thus unfolding in chronological succession the Scherzo and the dance out of which the Scherzo grew. (I believe Hans Keller was the first to point this out.) In the Scherzo of the Ninth, Mahler mingles Ländler and Minuet characteristics, thus juxtaposing—this time in the same movement—the Minuet with *its* historical predecessor. In view of the claim made in the sentence to which this note is attached I must add that I am aware of neoclassicizing precedents like Wagner's *Meistersinger* or the Finale of Brahms's Fourth Symphony. But in those celebrated precedents the evocation/manipulation of the past seems to me to be quite different in kind from Mahler's, where, I believe, we encounter a particular type of conscious reference to the past as a prime component in the *deliberate* fabrication of a style; and it is thus, precisely, that Mahler unmistakably anticipates the neoclassical practice of composers in later decades in the twentieth century.

28 I think one gets the feeling of that in a remark of Mahler's to Bauer-Lechner (p. 145): 'This [first] movement, in spite of its freedom, was, he said, built up with the greatest well-nigh pedantic correctitude'.

29 ['The Fourth Symphony] is in G major, and takes 45 [*sic*] min. (that is, not longer than the first movement of his Third!). "Actually," [Mahler] had told me before, "I only wanted to write a symphonic Humoresque, and out of it came a symphony of the normal dimensions—whereas, earlier, what I imagined would be a symphony turned out, in my Second and Third, to be three times the normal length."' (Bauer-Lechner, p. 143. See also p. 139, where the title 'Humoresque' is again referred to. The actual duration of the work is nearer to 55 min. than 45.)

30 Which makes it all the more odd that he himself had a sensitive spot when it came to discussing his contrapuntal technique. For example, even when talking about music as skilfully polyphonic as the first movement of the Fourth, Mahler felt obliged to attribute some of his compositional difficulties to his 'still suffering from lack of strict counterpoint, which every student who has been trained in it would use at this point [Mahler is commenting on the opening melody] with the greatest of ease [*sic*].' (NBL, pp. 153–4.) It is strange that he thought in this defensive way about an aspect of his technique which, to us, is conspicuously masterful, but it was an attitude that he displayed on more than one occasion. There was clearly some experience from Mahler's student years involved here that was at the root of this seemingly wholly irrational sensitivity in his maturity. I touched on some matters relating to Mahler's youthful study of counterpoint in DM[1], pp. 36–7, but was mistaken there in suggesting (p. 36) that Mahler did not give voice himself to any regrets at a deficiency of training in strict counterpoint. As the quotation above shows, he did. Ferdinand Pfohl (in FP, p. 39) also has something to contribute in this context:

'Before the impending performance of his C minor Symphony, the Second, in Berlin, Mahler came to me and played the symphony, which made a strong impression on me, though without being able to convince me completely, as Mahler's eclecticism emerged unmistakably throughout the first movement. He seems to have been reminded by a counterpoint of the violins in the first movement of the fact that during his time as a student at the Vienna Conservatoire he had failed his examination through a contrapuntal exercise [which was not, in fact, the case]. He triumphantly pointed out this line in his orchestral score and called out: "What do you say to that counterpoint!? That really is counterpoint!" He was quite justified in finding this passage excellent.' (For further observations and information, see also HG[1], pp. 38–9, p. 580, pp. 606–7.)

31 See also p. 293, where I mention some of the different types of contrapuntal invention that we find in Mahler.

32 This was published in fifty volumes between 1851 and 1900. Perhaps it was the completion of the great edition that prompted Mahler to acquire it?

33 The text of this lecture, in an English translation, was given to me many years ago by the late Erwin Stein. It is clearly based on the recollections of Mahler that Bahr-Mildenburg published in her (1921) volume of reminiscences (ABM). She speaks vividly in her lecture of his 'dedication to the *work* . . . his objectivity and his wonderful mixture of pedantry and genius', through which she found her own discipline as an artist. She continues: 'In his farewell letter before he left the Vienna Opera, he impressed on me always to remain "on top", by which he meant that I should serve the *work* in the smallest details, in order to live up to its greatness and make others live up to it, too. His conducting was a result of his pedantic genius. Nothing was unimportant or inessential to him: the smallest notes served as a means of expression, every rest was imbued with his spirit and had its own life.' There was some resistance among the singers to Mahler's ferocious insistence on precision, but 'all of them, more or less, were subject to the compulsion of his personality. He was stronger than those who opposed him; in the end, they sang as he wanted them to sing. He forced them to think and feel as they had never thought or felt before.' (Bahr-Mildenburg (b. 1872), the Austrian soprano, sang under Mahler in both Hamburg and Vienna and was a close friend. It has been suggested (see KB², pp. 116–19) that at one period she and Mahler were unofficially engaged. She died in Vienna in 1947. An immensely full account of the Mahler/Bahr-Mildenburg affair is given throughout HG¹.)

34 That, of course, is putting it very crudely. Perhaps it might be better expressed as an ungovernable itch on Mahler's part to re-compose, to substitute himself for the composer he was supposedly interpreting. (One remembers Mahler on Smetana's *Dalibor* (NBL, p. 174): 'Whenever I conduct it, I am always in a rage, I would like to cut a passage here, change the orchestration there, and sometimes even entirely re-compose a passage . . .'). This had its good side, if only because of the passionate self-identification involved, which clearly lent Mahler's performances a quite exceptional quality. Perhaps it was rather disconcerting, however, when this boundless re-creative energy led him to introduce (as it did at Hamburg) 'fresh recitative, composed by himself, forming a curious foreign body in the organism of Haydn's oratorio [*Die Schöpfung*]'—'foreign', evidently because the recitatives were 'new, very modern', according to Pfohl, from whom all these comments derive (see FP, p. 36, and also HG¹, pp. 385–6): I wonder if a copy of the oratorio with Mahler's additions still survives?

35 The term 'linear counterpoint' was introduced by Ernst Kurth in 1917 in his *Grundlagen des linearen Kontrapunkts* (significantly subtitled 'Bachs melodische Polyphonie')—seven years after Mahler's death—'in order to emphasize the "linear", i.e. horizontal aspect of counterpoint, as opposed to the harmonic (or vertical) point of view which prevailed at the time the book was published' (*Harvard Dictionary of Music*).

36 Mahler, one feels—fears—might have approved of the full-blooded transcription for piano solo by Busoni of the Chaconne from Bach's D minor solo violin Partita, a transcription which, as it were, realizes in terms of keyboard harmony the harmonic implications of Bach's solo instrumental writing. But how horribly wrong the realization sounds! It has the merit of throwing into sharp relief the conspicuous self-sufficiency of Bach's linear conception. The realization, the spelling out, of the implied harmony translates Bach's invention into quite another language. M. de La Grange interestingly points out (HG¹, n. 21, p. 938), that 'throughout his life Mahler had a pronounced aversion to the violin' as a solo instrument, though one notes that this did not prevent him from occasionally introducing the violin in a solo capacity into his symphonies (and I am not thinking only of the Scherzo of the Fourth Symphony).

37 The first performance was given at Vienna by the Vienna Philharmonic, Mahler conducting, on 15 January 1899. Stefan (PS², pp. 66–7) tells us that the purpose of Mahler's enterprise was to 'enhance the effect of the "miserable" instruments [Mahler's adjective: "elend"] and to make it possible to perform the work in a large hall.' When discussing the idea of these Beethoven transcriptions with Bauer-Lechner (NBL, pp. 107–8), Mahler used the same sort of dismissive numerical image that we have encountered in his response to Bach (see above): this time, however, the inadequacy was not manifest in 'just *one* little fiddler' (as in the Bach) but in the 'four pathetic little players' who were struggling to achieve in Beethoven what could only be achieved (according to Mahler) by a small string orchestra. For a detailed account of the critical reception given to this event, see HG¹, pp. 498–9.

38 An analysis of Mahler's concert programmes throughout his career might be very revealing. There is room here for a systematic study. In a letter to the leader of the New York Philharmonic, Theodor Spiering, dated 15 September 1909, Mahler invites him to play 'the Bach violin concerto' in the first 'historical concert' of the series of programmes he was evidently planning (GMB¹, pp. 458–9). 'A piano part (continuo) must surely be worked out for this, for I find that when Bach's and Handel's works are performed without a continuo realization they are decidedly violated. Do you perhaps know whether such a realization exists?'

The Bach concerto to which Mahler refers was the E major concerto, performed, with Spiering as soloist, on 10 November 1909.

39 There is firm evidence that Mahler not only knew some of Bach's cantatas but performed some of them, though it is not quite clear to me what were the circumstances of the performances. Among the collection of printed scores, used by Mahler himself, which Anna Mahler presented to the University of Southampton in 1973, are two bound-up volumes of vocal scores of Bach's cantatas in the Peters Edition. One of these is rubber-stamped 'Wiener Konzert-Verein', and most of them bear the rubber stamp of the music shop from which they were acquired—Albert J. Guttmann, whose address in fact was 'Wien, K. K. Hofopernhaus'. Three of the cantatas (Nos. 19, 65 and 78) are heavily marked by Mahler in blue pencil: these marks include his customarily intense dynamics (see the reproduction of the closing chorale from No. 78 (the opening *ppppp* surely sets up a record even for Mahler?)), some cuts and (p. 30 of vocal score) indications as to how the accompaniment is to be distributed between organ (there are some written-in hints about registration) and piano, and how in certain places doubling of the chorus at the keyboard is to be omitted (here Mahler writes 'nur Harmonie spielen!'). All this suggests that these performances (when and where did they take place?) were conducted with keyboard accompaniment only, not with orchestra. Whatever the circumstances, there can be no doubt that church cantatas by Bach were at times part of Mahler's active musical life, a somewhat unexpected offshoot of the opera conductor's activities. To what precise period of Mahler's life these scores belong, I am still uncertain. We know, however, that Bach's cantatas were among his prominent musical interests in Hamburg in the 1890s (see also HG¹, p. 248 and p. 287). Did this continue, in any active sense, in Vienna? (See also BW³, p. 18, where Bruno Walter writes to his parents from Hamburg (!) in 1896 that Mahler made an Easter gift to him of the scores of the *Matthew* and *John* Passions and

Choral.

(Str. 12 des Liedes: „Jesu, der du meine Seele")

Herr! ich glaube, hilf mir Schwachen, lass'mich ja ver-zagen nicht; du, du kannst mich

stär-ker machen, wenn mich Sünd' und Tod anficht. Dei-ner Gü-te will ich trau-en,

bis ich fröhlich wer-de schau-en dich, Herr Je-su, nach dem Streit in der süssen E-wigkeit.

Edition Peters.   8904

The vocal score of Bach's Cantata No. 78, with Mahler's dynamics (see n. 39)

the Christmas Oratorio, 'the possession of which gives me great joy'.)
40 Bach's motet No. 3 in the old Gesellschaft edition is 'Jesu, meine Freude', and this in fact is a five-part motet. Both the remaining motets in Vol. I are in eight parts: No. 1, 'Singet dem Herrn', and No. 2, 'Der Geist hilft unsre Schwachheit auf'. (Nos. 4 and 5 in Vol. II are also in eight parts.) Either the number of the motet or the number of parts is wrong in Bauer-Lechner's account. We should note, however, that it was 'Singet dem Herrn' that Mahler conducted in Vienna in 1905 at a Philharmonic Concert (see p. 350).
41 It is interesting to note that when Mahler was conductor of the New York Philharmonic (1909–11), and for the first time had the opportunity to influence in a major way an orchestra's repertory, the programmes were conspicuous for their enterprise and originality. Some of the new music Mahler conducted in these years makes enlightening reading now. He was clearly anxious to promote contemporary work. It is not possible here completely to list the works that show the range of his programmes or the scope of his inquisitiveness, but I think even this brief résumé speaks for itself:

Works	Performed
Busoni: *Turandot Suite* (1904)	(10/11 March 1910)
Berceuse élégiaque (1909)	(21/24 February 1911)
Debussy: *Nocturnes* (1892–9)	(17/18 February 1910)
Prélude à l'après-midi d'un faune (1892–94)	(10/11 March 1910)
Rondes de printemps (1908–9)	(15/18 November 1910)
Ibéria (1906–8)	(3/6 January 1911)
Elgar: 'Enigma' Variations (1899)	(29 November/2 December 1910)
*Sea Pictures (1897–99)	(14/17 February 1911)
Enesco: Suite (No. 1) (1904)	(3/6 January 1911)
MacDowell: Piano Concerto No. 2 (1889)	(5 February 1911)
Rachmaninov: Piano Concerto No. 3 (1909)	(16 January 1910)
Stanford (!): 'Irish' Symphony (1887)	(14/17 February 1911)
Strauss: *Tod und Verklärung* (1889)	(10/11 March 1910)
Also sprach Zarathustra (1896)	(1/4 November 1910)
Ein Heldenleben (1898)	(17/20 January 1911)

One notices at once that Mahler was astonishingly quick off the mark where Debussy was concerned. The first performance of *Rondes de printemps*, for

* Excluding 'The Swimmer', Mr. Michael Kennedy tells us in his book on Mahler, p. 63. He adds that Sibelius's violin concerto was 'among the works Mahler had scheduled but did not conduct' and that 'he intended in his third season to include a symphony by Charles Ives' (see also n. 62, p. 280).

example, was not given until 2 March 1910, and yet Mahler had the work in his programme only a few months later. *Ibéria* was a similar case, the first performance of which took place on 20 February 1910, and which in less than a year was installed in one of Mahler's concerts. His attitude to 'modern music' was clearly one of the matters about which he was questioned in an interview conducted for the *New York Daily Tribune* (3 April 1910). In the light of his programmes, it is interesting that the two living composers Mahler mentions in this context are Strauss and Debussy:

> 'I am absolutely opposed to dogma in criticism,' he said. 'You cannot limit anything absolutely. The radical of today is the conservative of tomorrow. What really counts is genuine self-expression. It is this that interests me. If a man writes a composition that is sincere, no matter if it breaks the old rules, that man must be admired.'
>
> In this connection Mr. Mahler shows little patience with those who call much modern music, notably that of Richard Strauss, decadent.
>
> 'How can we tell what is decadent?' he said, rather heatedly. 'When a man produces something new, something that surprises the conservatives, it is immediately branded as decadent. I admire Strauss, I admire Debussy. They have done something original. Fifty years from now perhaps we can tell whether or not they are decadent. But we are too near to them to tell now.
>
> 'In the case of Mozart or of Beethoven we see the whole field; they are far enough away for us to judge them as a whole and in an unbiased manner. But when our contemporaries produce something original we are not able to get the right perspective. We pick out solitary spots that seem to us flaws, without realizing that if we were able to see the whole work these flaws might disappear.
>
> After all, what a transitory world we live in! How true is the saying of the Greeks, "Everything flows." A work of art, the name of a musician, may last one, fifty, or five hundred years; what matter? Nothing is immortal, and the critic should be enough of a philosopher to realize this. Dogmatic standards must crumble like everything else.'

At the other end of the historical scale, Mahler doubtless thought that there was much magnificent and neglected Bach that ought to be brought to the attention of audiences fed on a surfeit of nineteenth-century music. It was, I am convinced, out of this spirit that his Bach Suite was born and the concept of the 'historical concert' (see n. 38, p. 377). Needless to add, Mahler's pioneering programmes were only accomplished in the teeth of strenuous opposition from the conservatives among the Philharmonic's board. For a taste of the kind of hostility Mahler aroused in the U.S.A., (though of course it must be remembered that he was also passionately admired by the more discerning of musicians and music-lovers), see the obituary by H. E. Krehbiel (1854–1923), which appeared in the *New York Daily Tribune* on 21 May 1911 (see Appendix B, pp. 407–13). This gives one the authentically bitter taste of the controversy which surrounded Mahler's years in New York. (I also include for comparison in the same Appendix obituaries of Mahler from Vienna and London.)

42 Apart from the question of Mahler's own taste, the fact that it was probably only in this guise that Mahler could have got an orchestral work by Bach into his programmes tells us something about the prevailing taste of audiences at that time.

43 See Erwin Stein, 'Mahler and the Vienna Opera', *The Opera Bedside Book*, London, 1965, p. 305. Stein, for some reason, writes 'clavicembalo'. He adds, almost unbelievably, that formerly the *secco* recitative in *Figaro* and *Don Giovanni* had been spoken, as dialogue. This alone is an indication of the kind of tradition and taste against which Mahler had to battle. (Stein adds: 'Mahler had already abolished the extra top notes and cadenzas which singers used to insert, but he maintained those appoggiaturas which he felt to be in the style of the music.' See KB[2], pp. 173–74, who comments on what he suggests was Stein's 'very tactful' account of Mahler's approach to—or neglect of?—the 'correct' vocal ornamentation in Mozart.) I sometimes wonder whether the stirrings of the feeling for authenticity of performance that Mahler seemed to show in his late years may have been encouraged, if only indirectly, by his long friendship with the Viennese scholar and musicologist, Guido Adler (1855–1941). In a highly interesting paper on Adler, by Edward R. Reilly, 'Mahler and Guido Adler', which is based on the Adler collection in the University of Georgia Library, Dr. Reilly writes: '. . . it was during the year 1898 that Mahler, undoubtedly through Adler's efforts [he was editor of the series], became a member of the Board of Directors of the *Denkmäler der Tonkunst in Oesterreich*, perhaps filling the vacancy created by the death of Brahms in the preceding year. How seriously Mahler took this position is uncertain. Adler says only that he was an 'effective member' of the board. . . . That he later actually possessed copies of the volumes in both the Austrian and German *Denkmäler* series is confirmed by letters of Alma Mahler in which she asks Adler to dispose of them after her husband's death.' (See also HG[1], p. 465 and p. 544. Mahler appears to have commented at one stage that the series comprised 'mediocrities of the last century' and to have deplored the spending of money on them.)

For all Mahler's scepticism, might it not have been that this connection, slender though it was, with the world of musicology—which was then beginning to make an impact on performing practice—stimulated his own thinking in this area? He would at least have been made aware of the issues involved. One wonders what on earth Adler made of the Bach suite. We know, on the other hand, what another celebrated musicologist made of Mahler. Through the mediation of Ferdinand Pfohl, Mahler was put in touch with the eminent Handel scholar and editor, Friedrich Chrysander (1826–1901). But the efforts of Chrysander to engage Mahler's interest in the Handel revival were not, it seems, successful, as Pfohl recounts in his memoirs (FP, pp. 36–7). The two men, as appears below, did not hit it off at a personal level at their meeting in Hamburg. But that failure apart, it would seem that the Handel renaissance, which was to represent such a pronounced shift in twentieth-century taste, was not an area that greatly excited Mahler's curiosity, at any rate not to the degree that his curiosity was excited by Bach. (See however the mention of Handel in Mahler's letter quoted in n. 38, p. 377, and the programme of his 'first historical concert' (n. 45, below.)) Pfhol's record of the Mahler-Chrysander encounter runs as follows:

> ... a renaissance of the Handelian oratorio was already in the air; its founder and the leading light of all the endeavours to revive Handel's music was Dr. Friedrich Chrysander, a researcher of the highest merit, who lived in nearby Bergedorf. I enjoyed his frequent visits. One day he asked me to arrange for him to make the acquaintance of Gustav Mahler; he wished to try to get Mahler interested in Handel's oratorios and to persuade him to perform a Handel oratorio at one of the Good Friday concerts instead of the works that were repeated *ad nauseam*. The idea was an excellent one and I felt it my duty to give the old gentleman due warning of Mahler's peculiarly difficult character. Mahler readily agreed to the meeting I proposed between him and Chrysander. The interview took place in a Viennese coffee-house on the Neue Jungfernstieg; there two exceptional people came together: the idiosyncratic, unfathomable Gustav Mahler and Chrysander, who, for all his amiability, was not entirely immune from a certain irritability in his nature. I myself was prevented from taking part in the conversation; it sufficed me to have brought the two men together there in that coffee-house. On the same evening I chanced to meet Mahler, and asked: "How did you like old Chrysander, then?" Mahler put on an impenetrable expression and contented himself with saying: "That Chrysander, he's a sly old fox, I tell you." He used a Viennese term ('Schlauherl') intended to convey the artfulness of one who is always looking to his own benefit. This term, used in the sense described, could never be appropriate however, since it was not his own needs as an editorial worker but a disinterested sympathy with the work of Handel that prompted Chrysander to campaign for the revival and historically authentic performance of the great art of the eighteenth century. Unfortunately the conversation was entirely fruitless, for Mahler never seriously, if at all, considered performing an oratorio of Handel, and as an operatic conductor one would moreover scarcely expect him to. When I saw Dr. Chrysander again and asked him: "How did you like Mahler?" he hesitatingly answered: "Mahler? ... he is not at all straightforward ..." Thus, in plain language: he had not liked Mahler.

44 See the reproduction of the Carnegie Hall poster (1910) in AM[5], p. 155, and also Alma Mahler's comments on the work, pp. 154–5. She tells us that 'He altered his continuo realization according to his fancy every time' and that the 'cry of sacrilege' was not raised by critics in the U.S.A. but by the 'pundits of Europe', which presumably means that Mahler performed the Suite in Europe. But when or where I do not know. (See also the Schoenberg entry in the Supplementary Bibliography, pp. 437f.)

45 In this letter Mahler clearly refers to a concert that he had given a few days earlier, on 10 November 1909, a concert about the planning of which he had already written on 15 September 1909, to Theodore Spiering, the leader of the New York Philharmonic Orchestra (see n. 38, p. 377). The 'first historical concert' to which Mahler refers in his letter to Spiering was in fact the concert of 10 November, about which he writes in the letter posted on 19 November, the complete programme of which consisted of the following:

Bach/Mahler: Suite for Orchestra (See pp. 350f.)
Handel: 'Quanto dolci' from *Flavio*
Bach: Violin Concerto in E major
Rameau: 'Rigaudon' from *Dardanus*
Grétry: Recitative and Air from *Céphale et Procris*
Haydn: Symphony in D (B. & H. No. 2: i.e., No. 2 in the Breitkopf
              & Härtel edition. This was Haydn's Symphony No. 104.)

Soloists: Theodore Spiering (violin): Corinne Rider-Kelsey (soprano)

The very concept of an 'historical concert' is in itself extraordinarily interesting. In this field, too, Mahler made an early entry. It is fascinating to observe him developing in his programme planning a peculiarly modern historical consciousness and conscience, while at the same time (as we see from the programme details in n. 41, p. 379) exploring some of the newest of the new music of his day. (Incidentally, according to Hanslick, Mahler performed Haydn's Symphony No. 104 'in an unforgettable manner, perhaps never equalled anywhere in the world'. HG[1], p. 509.)

46 See the Mahler centenary issue of *Musical America*, February 1960, p. 162.

47 See, for example, AM[5], pp. 47–8.

48 I wonder how many other students of Mahler have been struck, as I have been, by the relationship between the passage from *Das Lied* I quote on p. 361 (Ex. 118) and the uncannily close, well-nigh parallel texture that we find in the music associated with Pimen in Mussorgsky's *Boris Godunov* (Act I, Scene 1). This is a characteristic example from Mussorgsky's opera:

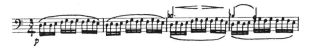

Was this a mere chance, mere coincidence? I know of no mention of Mussorgsky by Mahler. But *Boris* was first performed in 1874, in which year a vocal score was also published. The work was then not revived until 1896, and again in 1901 and 1904, though only in productions inside Russia. There is nothing to suggest that Mahler may have witnessed one of the later productions outside Russia. It is more than possible, however, that he would have known of the work by repute, and not impossible that he may have seen a score of the work, of some kind. If so, and however cursory his inspection, it is difficult not to believe that Mussorgsky's inspiration left its impress on Mahler.

Two pages from the second movement of the Bach Suite

Appendices and Bibliographies

A Letter to Fräulein Tolney-Witt

Dear Fräulein Tolney-Witt,

Although I am not easily prevailed upon to start a 'correspondence' and even my best friends have reason for complaints about me in this respect, I nevertheless feel the urge to answer a question in your last letter. 'Why does it require such a large apparatus as an orchestra to express a great thought?' But I must be somewhat lengthy in order to make you realize how I look at the matter.

You seem to have browsed around in musical literature and I assume that even the older and old music, as far back as Bach, is not quite unknown to you. Haven't you been struck by two facts there?

First, the farther you go back in time, the more primitive are the marks for the performance, i.e. the more do the authors leave the explanation of their thoughts to the interpreters. For example, in Bach you find only in very rare instances a designation of tempo, or any other indication as to how he thinks the work should be presented; even the crudest differentiations, like *p* or *ff*, etc. are missing. (Wherever you do find them they have usually been added by the publishers, sometimes even quite incorrectly.)

Secondly, the more music develops, the more complicated becomes the apparatus which the composer uses to express his ideas. Just compare the orchestra Haydn uses in his symphonies (i.e. it was not the way we see it at the 'Redoute',* in Philharmonic concerts, because more than half the number of instruments has been added later) with the orchestra Beethoven requires in his Ninth. Not to mention Wagner and the newer composers. Why is this so? Do you believe that this is accidental or, even, a composer's unnecessary extravagance brought on by some unfathomable whim?

Now let me tell you my view of this matter: In its beginnings, music was merely 'chamber music', i.e. meant to sound in a small room, before a small audience (often consisting only of the performers). The feelings on which it was based reflecting, in accordance with the period, simply, naively, and only sketchily the sentiments of the soul: joy, sadness, etc.

The 'musicantes' were sure of themselves; they moved in a circle of ideas

* Mahler refers to the Redoutensaal in the Hofburg, Vienna, where concerts were given. [D.M.]

familiar to them, based on a definitely circumscribed and, within these limits, well-founded artistic skill. Therefore, the composers did not give any instructions; it was a foregone conclusion that everything would be correctly seen, felt, and heard.

There was hardly any 'dilettantism' (instances like Frederick the Great and such were presumably rare); rather did the noble, wealthy class pay trained musicians to play in their chambers for their enjoyment, and therefore the compositions were not mistreated by ignorance. Usually the composers and 'musicians' may even have been identical.

In the church which, naturally, was the chief domain of this art, where it also originated, everything was strictly defined by the ritual. Briefly, the composers were not afraid of being misunderstood, and were satisfied with sketchy notes for their own use—without giving much thought to the fact that others would have to interpret them, or that they might even misinterpret them.

As time passed, however, they probably had unpleasant experiences and now aimed to convey their intentions to the performer by decipherable signs. Thus resulted, gradually, a wide system of sign language which—like the musical notes indicating the musical pitch—gave definite indications of tempo or dynamics.

Hand in hand with this went also the acquisition of *new emotional elements* as subjects of expression through sound, i.e. the composer began to include more and more profound and complicated parts of his emotional life in his work—until the *new era* in music started with Beethoven. From then on there are not just the fundamental sentiments, such as mere joy or sadness, etc. which are the subject of musical creation, but also the transition from one to the other: conflict, its nature and its effects upon us; also, humour and poetic thoughts.

Now even the most complicated signs were insufficient. So, instead of imposing upon one individual instrument such an abundant palette of colours (as Mr. August Beer would put it), the composer used a separate instrument for each colour. (The analogy is retained in the expression *Klangfarbe* ['timbre'].)* So, gradually, out of this necessity, grew the modern, the 'Wagnerian' orchestra.

Thirdly, I would finally like to mention the external necessity for enlargement of the musical apparatus: music became more and more common property—audience and performers increased steadily. Instead of the chamber there now was the concert hall; instead of the church, with its *new* instrument, the organ, there was the opera house. Thus you see, if I sum up

---

* These thoughts of Mahler's in 1893 make one realize how lively his discussions with Schoenberg of just these kinds of technical matters and possibilities must have been in later years. See AM⁵, pp. 77–8 and p. 182, for example.

once more: we moderns need such a large apparatus to express *our* thoughts, be they large or small. First, because we are forced to distribute our numerous prismatic colours upon various palettes, to protect ourselves against mis-interpretation; secondly, because our eyes learn to see more and more colours and even finer and more delicate modulations in the rainbow; thirdly, because, in order to be heard by the multitudes in huge concert halls and opera houses, we have to make a big noise.

Perhaps since women are rarely convinced—at best sometimes persuaded —you will now object 'Well, but was Bach less great than Beethoven, or is Wagner greater than he?' Here I must reply, my little 'tormentor' (tor-mentor indeed—here I am tormenting myself for almost an hour, writing this letter!), to get an answer to this question you will have to ask someone who can take in, at a glance, the entire spiritual development of humanity. We are what we are! We 'moderns'. Even you are that way. Can I prove to you now that you, little nuisance, require a more complex apparatus for your living than did the Queen of England in the seventeenth century who—as I read recently—had a pound of bacon and a mug of beer for breakfast, and spent her evenings in her chamber, spinning by the light of one tallow candle to combat her boredom? What do you say to that?

So—away with the piano! away with the violin!† They are all right for the 'chamber', when you, by yourself or with a good friend, want to recall the works of the great masters—like an echo—just as an etching may bring back memories of the colourful paintings by Raphael or Böcklin. I hope I make myself understood, and, in this case, I do not mind having devoted an hour of my life to you who has put such charming trust in a stranger.

Since this epistle has become so long I would like to know that I have not written it in vain and ask you to please let me know if it has reached you.

With my best wishes,

GUSTAV MAHLER

Hamburg, 4 February 1893.

† Poor old solo violin, about which Mahler, as we have seen, was distinctly unenthusi-astic. See also notes 36 and 37, pp. 376–7. [D.M.]

Obituaries: Vienna, New York, London

I reproduce the Obituaries exactly as they appeared at the time, with only minimal editorial additions and *no* editorial amendments. Much of the factual information is wrong, some of it at the most elementary level. But the Obituaries are included here, not for factual consultation, but as vivid and fascinating documents in their own right, i.e. they register, very colourfully, diversely, and sometimes very movingly, the impact of Mahler's death. Their many inaccuracies are in a sense part of their immediacy; and it would have been a mistake, I think—as well as extremely time-consuming—to have attempted their methodical correction.

I. Vienna
1. *Illustrirtes Wiener Extrablatt*, Nr. 136. Friday, 19 May 1911

GUSTAV MAHLER IS DEAD

At 7 minutes past 11 last night in the Loew Sanatorium Gustav Mahler departed this life.

Gustav Mahler has died, in the city where he worked for ten years. As the shadow of death closed over him, he began to long for Vienna, the cradle of his fame. For Vienna made him what he was. Prague, Leipzig, Budapest and Hamburg knew him simply as a competent musical director. Here in Vienna, Mahler the composer was honoured no less than Mahler the conductor. Here in Vienna, Gustav Mahler's international reputation was made. While he lived, it was often impossible to take his side: one could only acknowledge his gifts as a conductor. Indeed respect was often all one could allow him, for during the last years of his work with the Vienna Opera his violent disposition would brook no opposition, and in the end he even lost the respect due to him as a composer. Yet those who sought to reproach him were often undermined by the keenness of his personality, his temperament and his honest enthusiasm for everything that he represented. Gustav Mahler was an artist of his time. Among the many followers of Wagner, Liszt and Bruckner he was one of the few who stood out: he was never one of the crowd. His life was devoted to the ideals of Wagnerian theatre—to the precarious marriage of music with the speaking arts. He identified himself with the

Art-Work of the Future, which now holds sway as the Art-Work of the Present. In Wagner, he never allowed the use of bel canto, which would have given undue importance to the singers. Instead, the producer and the designer came into prominence. The care taken over scenery often exceeded theatrical necessity: it was important to be as realistic as possible. This systematic over-refinement and excessive enthusiasm for realism was the current theatrical trend, which manifested itself in Reinhardt-like efforts towards a monumental naturalism. One cannot deny that this exuberance nevertheless bore some fruit, for out of such profusion came original and interesting ideas. But on the whole the music gained very little thereby: it became a mere component part of the whole artistic apparatus, instead of being the controlling factor—which is what, for innumerable reasons, it should have been.

But let us return to the man who is now dead. Whoever is in sympathy with modern trends cannot praise Gustav Mahler enough. The great conductor stimulated the composer: yet it is remarkable that this artist, whole-heartedly devoted to the stage, should have composed music that had nothing to do with the theatre. Nine symphonies exist, created in his free time. All are utterly different one from another, but all mirror his love of the fantastic. They are written with the desire to seek eternity: every sound betrays the composer's longing for the freedom of immortality. The dazzling exotic flower of Mahler's music grew in the deep shadow of Beethoven's Ninth. The colour may be vivid, but the fine and complex instrumentation is, nevertheless, a deceptively beautiful artificial flower—late-born music, that always wanders and tries to escape, yet does not realize to what extent it is caught in the labyrinth of the German *avant-garde*. There is a difference in music between the mystical and the mystic. Schumann is mystical, so are Wagner, Liszt and Bruckner; but the mystic in Mahler is too open, his intentions lie just beneath the surface. The darkness of Mahler's creativity comes incessantly to light.

For all that, the symphonies express Mahler's whole being. He was a modern Jakob Boehme, obsessed with the metaphysical. For men of higher intellect fulfilment comes through coping with the problems of life. For one, temporal existence is illusory: it is merely something to barter for life on a higher plane; for another, material things are not to be cast off and overcome as if one were a 'pure fool'; the third relies on his senses as far as he can: the ego is for him the first and last reality. Gustav Mahler manifested characteristics of all three groups. He was unsure of his philosophy when he went to America. It seems strange that Mahler should have allowed himself to be billed as a 'star' conductor; that he could have adapted himself to the land of superficiality. It is as if, at the end of his life, doubts had destroyed all his convictions. We know that after five [*sic*] years of intense and successful activity at the Vienna Opera he suddenly became disillusioned. No longer did he have any faith in the theatre, in the possibility of a lasting ideal theatre. He walked out. He had had enough. Not only is this quite understandable, it is also artistically consistent; but if the disillusionment was genuine it should have continued: the man who renounces the theatre* loses his public, and the rejected public only see the concert hall as a theatre without wings or backdrop. In this context, it is astounding that the Eighth Symphony should have been performed at the Munich Music Festival— Munich, a city whose highest ideal is to cater to the tourist trade. A hymn to the Holy Ghost serves as introduction to fragments from the second part of *Faust*. Positive belief is dissipated in a mystical pantheism. So he departed from us, leaving behind these symbols of unfulfilled artistic expression and personal disquiet. Perhaps this is what will indict the symphonies at the moment that their creator had died; while he lived, one could respectfully say 'He strives', but now that he is dead, the history of music may well say 'He failed.'

LIFE OF MAHLER

Gustav Mahler was born in Kalischt in Bohemia on 7 July 1860. His musical gifts became apparent in early childhood, through his appreciation and understanding of folk-songs and soldiers' ballads. His first instrument was an accordion, from which he was able to produce exciting notes and chords. At six he started learning the piano, and by the time he was eight, he was trying to give piano lessons himself. When the family moved to Iglau, he became a pupil at the local Gymnasium, and later studied at the Gymnasium at Prague. His love of music finally drove him to Vienna. Thanks to a recommendation from Professor Julius Epstein, he became a student at the Conservatoire when he was barely fifteen years old. Epstein taught him piano, Robert Fuchs harmony, and Theodor [Franz] Krenn composition and form. He was at the Conservatoire for three years, and during this time completed his studies for the Gymnasium as a private pupil, matriculated in Iglau, and then enrolled in the Philosophy faculty at Vienna University.

When he was twenty he became conductor at Hall (Upper Austria), carrying out all the drudgery of the spa orchestra and the summer theatre. In 1881 and 1882 he was conductor in Laibach, in 1883 in Olmütz, and the following year he was second conductor in Cassel. In 1885 Angelo Neumann invited the young musician to Prague, where he worked intensively with Arthur Seidl, and Karl Muck, and soon acquired a name for himself.

A previous commitment forced Mahler to leave his activities in Prague,

* 'Wer dem Theater abhanden gekommen ist', an obvious allusion to one of the best known of Mahler's Rückert songs. [Trans.]

and take up an engagement at the Stadttheater in Leipzig, where he worked
with Arthur Nikisch. Meanwhile Mahler's lively creative urge was beginning to become apparent. A violin sonata, a symphony, an opera fragment,
Die Argonauten, the inception of *Das klagende Lied*, a fairy-tale, *Rübezahl*,
and a few songs comprise what may be called Mahler's first period of
composition. His arrangement of Weber's opera *Die drei Pintos* marks the
end of this period.

In the summer of 1888 Mahler accepted an invitation to Budapest. He
became Director of the Royal Opera, which he took over in a disgraceful
state; in less than three years he had brought the opera up to an excellent
standard. But continual battles with the new Intendant, Count Zichy, led to
Mahler's resignation; his contract still had eight years to run, so Mahler
waived his rights in return for a considerable sum of money. Pollini, who
was always on the lookout for young talent, immediately invited him to the
Hamburg Stadttheater as first conductor, with an unlimited sphere of
activity. He worked there for six years, and produced some splendid achievements. A series of performances of Wagner and *Fidelio* conducted by
Mahler in London in the summer of 1891 so increased his reputation that it
finally reached Vienna. Just at the right moment. Wilhelm Jahn, the unforgettable Director of the Opera, was gradually going blind, and had to be
replaced. The Master of the Royal Household, Prince Liechtenstein, asked
Mahler to be first conductor of the Opera. On 11 May 1897, Mahler conducted in Vienna for the first time. Wagner's *Lohengrin* received a breath-
takingly splendid rendering. A few months later Jahn left, and Mahler
became his successor. He threw himself into the opera whirl with all his
energy and, to begin with, artistic recklessness. That Hans Richter, himself a
high individualistic person could not hold his own against Mahler's equally
strong temperament, was only to be foreseen. His departure, for which indeed
Mahler could not have been held responsible, meant a sad loss to the musical
life of Vienna which has never been replaced.

Mahler's activities as Director in Vienna are still fresh in our memory.
The dazzling rise of the first five years was followed by a crushing setback;
and although there were still many beautiful evenings of music, the decline
of the establishment could not be checked. The Mozart renaissance, performances of *Tristan*, *Fidelio*, Gluck's *Iphigénie*, revivals of operas by Weber
and Lortzing, as well as a few premières, formed the high points of the Mahler
era. The increasing nervousness of the brilliant musician, as well as the
change in his artistic ideas brought on by his surroundings, began to have an
effect on his system. Mahler said farewell to the Vienna Opera in 1907, and
accepted an invitation to New York. And it was there that the malignant
disease overtook him, to which at the age of fifty he finally succumbed.

Mahler's symphonies were composed during his second creative period.

Of these seven are already well-known in Vienna, the Eighth had its first performance in Munich last autumn, and the Ninth is being printed at the moment. The Tenth Symphony is already completed in manuscript [*sic*]. Apart from the symphonies, Mahler has written innumerable Lieder and songs with orchestral accompaniment, all of which display his lyrical talents.

Mahler at the Vienna Opera

It was Privy Councillor Wlassack, after Bezecny the most influential director on the Board, who brought Mahler to the Vienna Opera. At the beginning, he was a conductor. But his position as head of the orchestra was very soon changed. He took over the organization of the whole Opera. The establishment had become totally disorganized during the last years of Jahn's directorship, and desperately needed a forceful influence. Mahler was a messenger of hope. He put the house in order, built up the repertory, and attracted a series of prominent artists to the Opera stage. But Mahler's golden era was followed by a period of conflict. Peace was made, and Mahler regained his popularity. He had great charm and could inspire great faith in the people around him. They carried out his instructions with great enthusiasm. But his excitability once again took possession of him, and it was impossible to prevent clashes with the artists.

As conductor of the Philharmonic Concerts Mahler came into conflict with the orchestra. People objected to the excessive rehearsals, and the caustic criticisms he would often hand out after concerts. In the end the Philharmonic chose another conductor, Josef Hellmesberger, and Mahler was, naturally, very offended. When attempts at reconciliation were made, Mahler stipulated that the choice of conductor should be his and his alone. Well might he impose such a condition, since under his leadership the Philharmonic Concerts improved out of all recognition. There were violent battles of opinion after every concert, particularly when Beethoven had been played . . . but even Mahler's most implacable opponents had to admit that the Philharmonic Orchestra was led by one man, who, as conductor of the orchestra, knew how to attract and bewitch his audience.

Mahler, in the directing of new works, had no equal. In rehearsal, he amazed and enthralled people by his brilliant arrangements of the scenery, and by his ability to draw out the composers' most secret ideas. If he produced a revival of an older work, previously unknown depths would be brought to the surface. Evenings devoted to Wagner and Mozart became gala performances, and even Weber and Gluck became great triumphs for the Opera.

Mahler, who earlier had held sway in the office of the Master of the Royal Household, especially when Prince Rudolf Liechtenstein had the deciding word, lost his influence when Prince Montenuovo began to negotiate directly with dissatisfied members of the company. Mahler had not recommended the re-engagement of [Fritz] Schrödter, unless he received a lower salary. In spite of the conductor's protests the singer Schrödter was given a new, favourable contract . . . Mahler wanted to put on a new production of *Götterdämmerung*—he was refused the money and complaints were made about Roller's methods, with whose artistic principles Mahler identified himself. He repeatedly sought for his own dismissal, but they would not let him go. But when the Director heard that Mottl had been invited to Vienna without his knowledge, nothing could hold him. The negotiations with Mottl, concerning his take-over of the directorship of the Vienna Opera so embittered Mahler, that he refused to stay at any price. He gave up his office, and left Vienna in a sulk.

After Weingartner's resignation, attempts were made to bring Mahler back to the Opera. He was offered the job of guest director by mediators—Mahler refused, and thereby burnt his bridges . . .

Memories of my Pupil Gustav Mahler by Professor Julius Epstein
It was 1875. I was giving lectures at the Conservatoire, when a visitor was announced. A man came to me, and asked for my advice. He was accompanied by a boy of fourteen or fifteen. 'My name is Mahler, and I have a spirit factory [distillery] in Iglau', began the elderly man. He gestured towards the boy. 'This is my son Gustav—he is absolutely set on being a musician. I would prefer him to study at the technical college and the university; so that eventually he can take over my factory, but the boy does not want to . . .'

The man's voice became troubled . . . unwillingly I examined his son . . . there was something unusual, and special about his appearance. I replied: 'I decide on his future? That is a very difficult request. But I shall try. Play something for me!' This addressed to the young man. 'What?', he asked, quite undeterred. On the contrary, he gave the impression that he was perfectly capable of forging his own destiny, and removing any obstacles.

'It doesn't matter. Just begin,' I urged.

I cannot even remember what he played, and at most it lasted five minutes. My judgement was firm. I put it in these words: 'Mr. Mahler, your son is a born musician!'

Mr. Mahler looked at me surprised, and even somewhat dismayed, and said: 'Forgive me, Professor, but just now you said it was difficult to decide on a person's future. You have barely listened for five minutes, and you have already made up your mind . . .'

'I am not being unreasonable,' I explained. '*In this case I could not be wrong. This young man has spirit, but he will never take over his father's spirit factory . . .*'

I remember clearly the grateful look that these words aroused in the young man's eyes.

Mahler entered the Conservatoire. I taught him the piano, and Krenn gave him lessons in theory. At this point I must mention the fact that *Mahler was never a pupil of Bruckner*, an error that is always included in biographical notes. As soon as the young Mahler entered the Conservatoire, I saw, to my own delight, that I had not overestimated him at his audition. I was thrilled with his progress, in spite of the fact that he rarely bothered to practise the piano. I was very patient with him about this, as I did not really visualize him as a pianist.

I took a special interest in Gustav Mahler from the beginning, and, unlike everybody else, prophesied a glowing artistic future for him.

One day my pupil came to me for some advice. He had been offered the job of conductor in Hall. His parents and colleagues were against the idea of his accepting a job with a so-called 'troupe of strolling players'. But I decided: 'Accept immediately! You are beginning to make your own way. You will improve your circumstances very quickly.'

Mahler followed my advice. He went from Hall to Laibach, and then to other provincial engagements, quickly gaining the necessary experience, so that very soon he had reached the pinnacle of his art.

One episode from his time at the Conservatoire is very typical of Mahler. He was not only a brilliant musician, but an amusing young man, and distinguished himself in his personal contacts by his ready wit. One day, as I entered a class, he called out to me: 'Professor! Hellmesberger would like to see you in the office after the class.'

I could hardly believe my ears; I said pointedly: 'I beg your pardon! I didn't quite hear!'

Gustav Mahler repeated: 'Hellmesberger would like ...'

Somewhat annoyed, I snapped at him: 'That is bad manners. You should say Director Hellmesberger.'

Mahler replied, without a pause: 'But Professor! I have often heard you say that Director Hellmesberger is a genius! ...'

I interrupted: 'Certainly I have said that! And so he is!'

'Now', said Mahler with a grin, 'Do we speak of a genius in this way ... Mr. Beethoven, Mr. Mozart or Mr. Schubert? If these great masters do not need to be called Mister, nor does Hellmesberger.'

I had to admit that my pupil was right ...

My Director by the Court Singer Lucie Weidt

The news of Gustav Mahler's death filled me with great distress, and an indefinable sadness is in my heart at the passing of this unusual man. I owe him my place in the Vienna Opera, for it was he who brought me to the stage, he who employed me in this centre of the arts. This is how it happened:

The year was 1902. Fräulein von Mildenburg heard me sing at the

Conservatoire. I sang an aria from *Aida*, and it appears that I pleased her so much that she mentioned me to Mahler. Mahler gave me the opportunity of singing for him. I chose the Nile aria from *Aida*, and I must confess that I went to the audition in fear and trembling, as it really was a tremendous experience for me to have the opportunity of showing my modest talent to the highly critical Gustav Mahler. While I sang the aria, Mahler sat without moving, like a bronze statue, and gazed at me as though he was trying to guess my innermost thoughts. When I finished the aria, there was a short pause. Suddenly, Mahler got up, came towards me, and said:

'Fräulein Weidt, you are engaged!'

Anyone else would have been overcome with joy at this news, but I went pale, and stammered:

'I thank you from the bottom of my heart, Director ... I am delighted, only I cannot accept your kind offer, as I am ... contracted to the Opera in Leipzig.'

It is hard to describe what followed my revelation. Mahler stamped on the ground with both feet, and shouted furiously: 'How can one be so careless! Forgive me, Miss Weidt, I should have said, how can anyone be so stupid as to want to leave Vienna. What have you to lose in Leipzig? Your place is in Vienna!'

I was utterly bewildered, and could not say a word.

Mahler went on shouting, and his voice became more and more high-pitched, so that at times he was screeching: 'Of course I should not and will not persuade you into a breach of contract. So, for all I care, go back to Leipzig, but promise me that you will come back to Vienna soon. See to it that you come back as soon as possible, and when you get here, come and see me. Goodbye, and learn a lot in Leipzig!'

Deeply moved, I wanted to shake his hand, but he brushed me aside. Then he became more pleasant, and said: 'Forgive me for shouting, but I always get very angry when I cannot draw talent to the Opera. So, again: Goodbye!'

A year and a half went by. I came back from Leipzig, and went to see Mahler. He gave me a very friendly welcome, and asked, 'Are you free?'

I said: 'Yes.'

'Then I engage you. When do you want to start?'

We agreed on a date, and the roles that I would sing for my début. They were Elisabeth in *Tannhäuser*, and Aida. For obvious reasons, I will not say any more about my career at the Vienna Opera. I simply want to say this:

Gustav Mahler was one of the greatest musicians, and one of the most outstanding men of all time. He was a colossal artistic soul, who electrified everyone who came into contact with him. He was a fiery and firing person-ality, who demanded the highest standards from the singers, and stimulated their talents to ever greater achievements. He was single-minded, and for him the important issue was the unity of the whole, which partly explains why he could rarely be persuaded to promote a single artist. As I have already pointed out, he was concerned with the unity of the whole, and therefore he tended to overlook individual talent. Like all great people of violent temperament, he often disregarded convention and abandoned tradition, so that he acquired many enemies. I shall never forget his performances of Mozart at the Vienna Opera, or the quality of his revival of Beethoven's *Fidelio*. With the Mozart-cycle and with Beethoven, Mahler gave the Viennese an exquisite experience. The Vienna Opera has had nothing comparable to these productions. When Mahler directed Mozart, the singers reached heights of expression that had never been known before, and will never be reached again.

Just one short reminiscence from America. In January this year I was in New York, and spent a free evening at a Philharmonic concert, where his Fourth Symphony was performed—a triumph for Mahler. In the interval I went to the artist's room to see Mahler, and blurted out the following words: 'Dear, unforgettable Director, allow me to bring a little Viennese air into the room.' Mahler received me with great friendliness, and we talked for a long time about Vienna. Yet again, I felt that Mahler was a phenomenal person, with outstanding attributes. If he also had failings, we should not forget that he was a character, who loved to go his own way. In the pursuit of many goals he sometimes overlooked the fact that the means he employed might not only enchant and intoxicate but also scandalize. . . . We shall not see his like in Vienna again.*

Anecdotes about Mahler
While Mahler was Director at the Vienna Opera, many stories were circulated about him.

Mahler had a quarrel with the tenor [Leo] Slezak. A very stormy discussion took place in the Director's office, and the noise of the dispute could even be heard in the corridor. The voices sounded so angry, that people were afraid that the two men would come to blows at any moment. While this wild scene was going on in the room, the bass singer Willy Hesch was wandering peacefully up and down the corridor, looking as though he was quite unaware of the noise. Suddenly there was a crack . . . as though a chair had been smashed . . . then an unnatural silence fell on the field of battle. . . . Not a sound could be heard from Mahler and Slezak, who seconds before had been quarrelling bitterly . . . At last the door opened, and Slezak rushed into the

---

* Another celebrated singer, Elisabeth Schumann, recalled Richard Strauss's astonishment that Mahler's influence survived so long at the Vienna Opera. Once, it appears, when Strauss gave an order to a subordinate, the latter replied in some evident confusion: 'Very well, Herr Dr. Strauss, but Director Mahler did it differently.' [D.M.]

anteroom, in a state of high indigation. He fell on his friend Hesch, who with perfect composure said: 'Tell us, Slezak . . . is he dead?'

A guest star was engaged to sing Wotan in *Valkyrie*. After the performance, he went up to the Director, when he came backstage, and begged Mahler to pronounce his judgement. The Director had only this observation to make: 'Stay a salesman!' By this, he alluded to the singer's former career.

This incident took place at a rehearsal for *Fidelio*. Weidemann was singing Pizarro. In the first act, he had to come on stage, pass the gateway to the citadel, and move towards the front of the stage. Weidemann made a terrible face. Mahler, who was conducting the orchestra, shouted up at the stage: 'Dear Mr. Weidemann! Why do you look so cross and worried? Are you the Director of the Opera, that you have to look like a Prophet of Doom?'

A singer went to Mahler and complained that she did not have enough to do. 'You made me come to Vienna, and promised me important roles. Now you neglect me. Is this the way you keep your promise, by trying to make me leave?'

Mahler sat motionless in his armchair. Then with a wicked smile he said: 'Yes, I do keep my promise—about your departure . . .'

History of His Illness
The fatal illness of the sorely tried artist dates back many months, and from a medical point of view represents a very rare case. A bad throat inflammation probably marked the beginning; an illness whose dangerous nature, like that of influenza, especially with regard to ominous complications, has been known to doctors for several years.

Mahler had several times suffered from severe angina in the previous summer when he was in Toblach. At the same time there were signs of a grumbling appendix, a well-known side-effect of angina. Mahler's wife became ill herself while looking after him, and took some time to recover. He left for America before he was completely fit.

In December last year, Mahler became ill with an inflammation of the throat. At first it was not serious, and Mahler devoted himself to his work with his customary impetuous enthusiasm. But on 20 February he caught a chill, and had to retire to bed. He soon had a temperature of 100 and even at that time his life was in danger. At first, it was difficult to decide exactly what was the nature of his illness. The first blood test, taken by Professor Dr. Fränkel, a personal friend of Mahler's, who was attending the case, revealed blood poisoning from streptococci.

When other means failed, Professor Fränkel suggested serum injections to combat the illness. Still seriously ill, in April Mahler made the journey back to Europe, to seek out the doctors in Paris who had been recommended by Professor Fränkel, in particular a Dr. Vidal. But neither he, nor any of the other doctors were in Paris, and Vidal's assistant, Professor Chantemesse, took over the case, and Mahler was taken to Dr. Desfours' Sanatorium in Neuilly. The serum treatment begun by Professor Fränkel was continued, but with very unsatisfactory results. At the same time a worse complication arose when it was discovered that Mahler had had a bad heart for years. The treatment was changed, the serum injections were replaced by a vaccine produced from the patient's own blood, and he was given radium compresses.

Eight days earlier, Professor Chvostek had been called to the sick-bed from Vienna. As soon as Mahler saw him, he was seized with a longing for his homeland. He wanted desperately to be taken to Vienna, and Professor Chvostek gave his consent to the journey, providing that it was undertaken immediately.

On Friday, 12 May, Mahler returned to Vienna on the Orient Express. He had survived the journey comparatively well, and was taken to the Loew Sanatorium. A lost man. Professor Chvostek had never held out any hope that the sick man could be saved.

According to the present state of medical knowledge, there had only been one possible means of recovery; self-regeneration of the organism. But there was little hope of that happening, in Mahler's weakened state and with his bad heart. The only possible treatment consisted in making every effort to increase the patient's strength, and to regulate the heartbeat. All efforts were made to follow this course. But to no avail.

The final hours

Gustav Mahler's illness became critical yesterday, after he had passed a comparatively quiet night, and reached its final stages in the early evening.

Mahler lay apathetically in bed all day, and could only with difficulty be persuaded to take a spoonful of milk, egg or tea. His consciousness was cloudy, he no longer answered questions, and only responded to loud calls. Also he was not able to move without help.

In the evening he gradually became completely unconscious. His breast rose and fell in short sharp breaths, his respiration rate, which until then, with the help of oxygen had been almost normal, fell to 40, a sign that the lungs could no longer fulfil their function in spite of the artificial oxygen supply.

The patient no longer had the strength to clear his throat and get rid of the aggravating mucus which had collected in the throat and windpipe.

His pulse was very fast, and he was feverish. Attempts to give him his food in liquid form failed because he kept his teeth firmly clamped together.

Medical aid was reduced to the injection of caffeine, and the oxygen supply.

Later he was given injections of ether and camphor to combat the encroaching lung paralysis.

At eight o'clock, Professor Chvostek appeared at the sick-bed. He reported that there was little hope of keeping the sick man alive. 'He is very ill. All the symptoms of lung paralysis—of edema—are beginning to appear. The patient is totally unconscious. His pulse is 160. His temperature is too high to measure, and his breathing is very fast. The illness has reached its last stages.'

Death came at seven minutes past eleven in the evening, and there was no noticeable struggle. The patient, who had been semi-conscious for the last two days with only a few isolated moments of clarity, slipped into total unconsciousness, at 6.30 p.m. In an effort to make the candle of life flicker one more time, a camphor injection was given at 7.30 p.m., and the oxygen supply continued. In spite of his unconsciousness, it was possible to give him a spoonful of soup and some caviare. But the relentless progress of the lung-edema, the immediate cause of death, could not be halted.

At Mahler's death-bed were Professor Chvostek, the resident physician Dr. Michalik, the grief-stricken wife, Frau Alma Mahler, and her parents, and the orchestra leader [Arnold] Rosé and his wife, who was Mahler's sister [Justine].

Mahler's body spent the night in the death-chamber.

Gustav Mahler was married to a stepdaughter of the painter Carl Moll. There is a small son [sic] from the marriage, who is now five years old. One of Mahler's sisters is married to the orchestra leader Rosé.

[Translated by Ruth Ludgate.]

2. Extracts from Obituary in *Fremden-Blatt*, Vienna, Friday, 19 May 1911

Mahler and the Vienna Opera

Mahler's first appearance as conductor for the Vienna Opera took place on 11 May 1897. He conducted *Lohengrin* and Ludwig Speidel wrote at the time: 'Mr. Mahler is short, slim and energetic, with intelligent, sharply defined features, which remind one very much of Heinrich Effer. His appearance is not belied by his personality as a conductor: full of energy and sensitivity. . . . His method of conducting *Lohengrin* was extrovert, but he still brought out the spiritual character of the work. He treated the dreaminess of the Prelude with great delicacy, but at the climax of the piece, where the brass enter in full force, he swept the whole orchestra into a dramatic change of mood. The effect was tremendous . . . he showed an awareness for every detail. He had a lively relationship with the orchestra, the choir, and their component parts; not a single person would miss his signs . . . . There could be no better way of caring for the ailing Director, and supporting him and his work, than by placing such an artist at his side. Mr. Mahler will certainly have a lively effect on the Opera, when he is allowed to work on his own.' His second triumph was *The Flying Dutchman*. On 1 August, Mahler became deputy to the Director; within a month he was provisionally Director, and a month later became Director. He had already freed the *Ring* from its conventional interpretation. Now work began in earnest. The claque disappeared, late-comers were not allowed in during the performance; the Wagnerian spirit was brought to bear on the older operas, especially those of the great German masters. *The Marriage of Figaro* was worked over again and again, the revolving stage was used for the first time in *Così fan tutte*. Marie Gutheil-Schoder starred in the first performance of [Nicolai's] *Merry Wives of Windsor*, and then [Offenbach's] *Tales of Hoffmann*; there followed Haydn's *Il Dottore*; Lortzing's *The Opera Rehearsal*; Siegfried Wagner's *Bärenhäuter*; Rubinstein's *Dämon*; Tchaikovsky's *Iolanthe* and *Queen of Spades*; Smetana's *Dalibor*; Bizet's *Djamileh*; Zemlinsky's fairy-tale opera, *Once Upon a Time*; [Strauss's] *Feuersnot*; Reiter's* *Bundschuh*; Thuille's† *Lobetanz*; Forster's‡ *Dot mon* ['The Dead Man']; *Un Ballo in Maschera*, *Ernani*, and *Aida*; [Meyerbeer's] *Les Huguenots*; Mozart's *Zaïde*; *Fidelio*; and *Rienzi*. These were the most noteworthy productions in the first year. Mahler brought a host of distinguished artists to the Opera: Mildenburg, Gutheil-Schoder, Kurz, Foerster-Lauterer, Weidt, Forst, Weidemann, Slezak, Mayr, to name only a few. In 1899, he also took over the Philharmonic Orchestra, which achieved great success under his direction. His performance of Beethoven's Ninth will remain memorable for many. Like Wagner, Mahler tried to improve the instrumentation of Beethoven's Ninth Symphony, in order to achieve greater clarity and directness in performance. The first performance, with modifications which had once been suggested by Wagner, had to be repeated. Mahler replied to the outcry of some of the critics with a printed explanation, which was distributed in the foyer:

> As a result of certain derogatory statements by members of the public, the general opinion could emerge that tonight's conductor has been making arbitrary alterations to Beethoven's works, and in particular to the Ninth Symphony; therefore it seems necessary to give some explanation on this point.

* Josef Reiter (1862–1939).
† Ludwig Thuille (1861–1907).
‡ Josef Forster (1845–1917).

Because of his deafness, Beethoven had lost his essentially close contact with reality and the physical world of sound, just at that period of his creativity when an enormous heightening of conception had led to the discovery of new means of expression and to totally innovatory ways of handling an orchestra. This is well known, as is also the fact that the design of brass instruments at that time precluded their playing those melodies which were necessary to the texture of the music. With the passage of time, this defect has been made good; and not to use this improvement to achieve the most accomplished performance possible of Beethoven's works seems nothing short of sacrilege.

Richard Wagner, who, throughout his life, strove by every means in his power to save Beethoven's works from ever-increasing neglect, has outlined in his essay 'On the Performance of Beethoven's Ninth' (Collected Writings, Vol. IX) the way to perform this symphony, so that it expresses the composer's intentions in the best possible manner, and since then all conductors have followed this line. Tonight's conductor has done the same, out of the strongest conviction from his own experience of the work, and without in any way going beyond the limits indicated by Wagner.

Re-orchestration, alteration or even improvement of Beethoven's works are naturally out of the question. The now traditional increase in the size of the string section—which has been accepted for some time—has led to an increase in the number of wind instruments, which is necessary for greater volume, but in no way implies an additional orchestral role. On this, as on the former point, as far as the interpretation of the work is concerned, both as a whole and in its component parts, the authority of the score is absolute (and the more one studies it, the more compelling it becomes). All that any conductor should do, far from being arbitrary and wilful, and in no way diverging from any 'tradition', is feel for Beethoven's intentions even in the tiniest details, and, in performance, make certain that none of his ideas is sacrificed, or allowed to become submerged in a bewildering maze of sound.

According to Mahler's devoted and painstaking biographer, Paul Stefan, he conducted twenty-five works by Beethoven, and fifty-two by other composers. Among these, the new works were: Bruckner's Fifth and Sixth Symphonies, Liszt's *Festklänge*, Berlioz's *Rob Roy*, Goetz's Symphony in F, César Franck's Symphonic Variations, *Aus Italien* by Richard Strauss, and works by Bizet, Tchaikovsky, Dvořák and Smetana. Of Mahler's own works the following were performed: Second Symphony (1899), *Lieder eines fahrenden Gesellen*, orchestral *Wunderhorn* songs and the First Symphony (1900). In 1902, when he was no longer conductor of the Philharmonic, Mahler was invited to conduct the first performance in Vienna of his Fourth Symphony. In 1900, the conductor gave five concerts with the Philharmonic Orchestra in Paris at the World Fair; in 1901 his *Klagende Lied* was performed for the first time at a concert at the Singakademie. In 1902, there was another performance of the *Klagende Lied* at the Singakademie with the Philharmonic Orchestra conducted by Mahler, and eight days later the Fourth Symphony was performed. In 1905 the orchestra took part in a concert for a new 'Society for Composers', and, as honorary president, Mahler conducted his *Wunderhorn* songs, the *Kindertotenlieder*, and the rest of the Rückert songs.* The programme had to be repeated a week later: also, not long before, the (first) performance of Mahler's Third Symphony at a subscription concert under his direction had to have a second performance (end of 1904). The Philharmonic Orchestra conducted by Mahler gave the first performance of the Fifth Symphony at a subscription concert in December 1905; in 1906, the Concert Society gave the first performance of the Sixth Symphony, with Mahler as conductor, and in 1907 he bade farewell to the Philharmonic and Vienna with a performance of the Second Symphony. In all his time in Vienna, there were only six performances of Mahler's symphonies by other conductors in any form of concert; and his songs have been hardly heard of again. His connection with the Philharmonic Orchestra was severed in 1901.

Mahler set to work in conjunction with Roller to renew the repertory not only from a musical point of view but from that of design. The first example was *Tristan und Isolde*, which was followed by a Mozart cycle, *Fidelio*, Gluck's *Iphigénie*, *Euryanthe*, *Rheingold* and *Walküre*, *Lohengrin*, Goetz's *Die Widerspenstige*. There were also new productions of Wolf's *Corregidor*, Charpentier's *Louise*, Pfitzner's *Rose vom Liebesgarten*, and Verdi's *Falstaff*.

It was inevitable, because of Mahler's energy and his inability to delegate in his work of managing the theatre, that he should make many enemies, and it may well have been because of these that he submitted his resignation in the summer of 1907. A Viennese address, signed by all the leaders of society, assured him of the highest possible evaluation but he did not wish to stay. Mahler's farewell letter to the artists at the Opera is thoroughly characteristic:

> To the honoured members of the Vienna Opera. The time has come to put an end to our mutual activity. I must take my leave of this work place, which has become so dear to me, and say farewell to all of you.
>
> I had dreamed of leaving something that was complete and integrated; instead I leave behind a patchwork, full of loose ends, as seems to be man's fate.
>
> It is not my business to pass judgement on what has been the effect of my work on those to whom my efforts have been devoted. But, may I, at

* The reference is to the 'Society of Contemporary Musicians' founded by Schoenberg and Zemlinsky in 1904. See AM[5], pp. 81 and 84.

this point, be allowed to say this about myself: Everything I have done has come from the heart, and my goal has always been set very high. My efforts could not always be crowned with success. The resistance of the material with which he has to deal, the malice of objects—these are burdens peculiar to the interpretative artist. But I have always tried my utmost to subordinate myself to the goal, my inclination to my duty. I have never spared myself, and could therefore demand the greatest exertions from others. In the heat of battle, and the anger of the moment, no wounds or differences of opinion were spared either to you or me. But if a work was successful, a task well performed, then we forgot all trouble and pain, and felt richly rewarded—even if there were no outward signs of success. We have all made great progress, and with us, the establishment which we sought to serve.

Now I send my heartfelt thanks to all those who have encouraged me in my difficult and often thankless task, those who have helped and striven with me. I send you my most sincere good wishes for your future, and for the prosperity of the Opera House, whose fate I shall always follow with the greatest sympathy and interest.

Gustav Mahler

In America, over a period of some months, Mahler twice conducted performances of Mozart and Wagner. Later, he formed a New Philharmonic Society in New York. He then had a new orchestra to work with, and together they gave forty-six concerts during the last winter. But he only gave very few performances in the theatre.

In Europe, he conducted performances of his symphonies in Munich, Amsterdam, and Paris. Finally, he conducted his Eighth Symphony in Munich, in June last year. We have not yet heard this symphony in Vienna; and now we shall never hear it conducted by Mahler. . . .

[Translated by Ruth Ludgate.]

II. New York
New York Daily Tribune 21 May 1911

DEATH OF MR. MAHLER
HIS INFLUENCE ON MUSIC IN NEW YORK

Conductor at the Opera House and of the Philharmonic Society Gustav Mahler is dead, and his death was made to appear in some newspaper accounts as the tragic conclusion of unhappy experiences in New York. As a matter of fact, though his American career, which endured three years, was more productive of disappointment to him, and also to others, than of delight, there was nothing that happened to him here which could by any stretch of the imagination be considered as even a remote cause of the disease which brought about his death. He was a sick man when he came to New York three years ago. His troubles with the administration of the Philharmonic were of his own creation, for he might have had the absolute power which he enjoyed for a space in Vienna had he desired it. He was paid a sum of money which ought to have seemed to him fabulous from the day on which he came till the day when his labours ended, and the money was given to him un-grudgingly, though the investment was a poor one for the opera company which brought him to America and the concert organizations which kept him here. He was looked upon as a great artist, and possibly he was one, but he failed to convince the people of New York of the fact, and therefore his American career was not a success. His influence was not helpful but pre-judicial to good taste. It is unpleasant to say such things, but a sense of duty demands that they be said.

Gustav Mahler was born at Kalischt, in Bohemia, on July 7, 1860. His parents were Jews, but when he went to Vienna in an official capacity he, like so many Austrians, thought it expedient to embrace Christianity. Concerning this incident in his career a characteristic anecdote is told. Some of his friends expressed their surprise that he should have been baptized into the Roman Catholic Church when there remained what they thought a middle course in some form of Protestantism. 'Wenn schon, denn schon!' is said to have been Mahler's sententious reply. The spirit of the familiar phrase is not to be expressed in English. As a lad he studied at the Gymnasia of Iglau and Prague and later matriculated at the University of Vienna. There, too, he entered the Conservatory when he decided to become a musician. This was in 1877. Three years later he began conducting in some of the smaller Austrian towns, and in 1883 he received an appointment as second chapelmaster [*sic*] at Cassel. In 1885 he followed the late Anton Seidl as first chapelmaster at Prague and a year later he succeeded him at the Munici-pal Theatre in Leipsic, where he was associated with Arthur Nikisch. It was eminently characteristic of the man that in New York, where Seidl's memory was revered, he seldom, if ever, mentioned him. His next appointments were at Budapest and at the Stadt Theatre in Hamburg. Thence his reputation as a conductor grew and spread rapidly until in May 1897, he was called to Vienna, first as conductor and five months later as director of the Court Opera, as successor to Wilhelm Jahn. He was elected to conduct the Phil-harmonic concerts in the Austrian capital and also the Gesellschaft concerts. In spite of a great deal of friction in all his activities, he made himself the autocrat of musical Vienna, and so remained till shortly before he came to New York in December 1907.

When he first went to Vienna Mahler introduced many changes, some of which were not looked upon in the light of reforms, but he adhered to them and built up a party which has made itself troublesome to all his successors since. He was prodigal in the expenditure of money and in experimenting with singers who came on trial engagements—as 'guests', to use the German phrase. When he was accused of breaking traditions he said: 'Traditions mean slothfulness.' There are many stories current of the independence with which he enforced his will and pursued the course which he had marked out for himself. Thus it was said that even the Emperor's wish had no weight with him. Once the Emperor had it notified to him that he wanted to have an opera produced which had been composed by one of the archdukes. Having a poor opinion of the work, Mahler replied: 'I recognize the Emperor's command, but not his wish.' The speech having been reported to the Emperor, he smilingly observed: 'In matters artistic I do not give any command.' And the archduke's opera fell by the wayside. Many stories were current as to the causes which finally led to his resignation, one of them having more or less of a parallel with one in some degree associated with his departure from New York at the close of the season lately ended. An ardent patroness of Herr Mahler a decade ago was the Princess Pauline Metternich, who arranged the Philharmonic Concerts given under his direction in Paris at the time of the international exposition eleven years ago and was also the projector of the musical and dramatic exposition held in Vienna a few years before. Mahler exacted more obedience from the musicians of the orchestra at the Philharmonic concerts than they felt inclined to yield to a conductor whom they had themselves elected. The sympathies and influence of the Princess Metternich were given to the musicians and, so the story goes, she complained of his want of consideration of them to the Princess Montenuovo, wife of the Emperor's representative in musical and theatrical affairs. She also objected to Mahler's persistent efforts to bring about a representation of *Salome*, which had been frowned upon by the court. When Mahler finally handed in his resignation the princess is said promptly to have telegraphed to Mottl to apply for the post.

Under his administration the expenses of the Court Opera are said to have been trebled. 'Like few others,' said a writer in the *Tageblatt*, of Berlin, at the time, 'Mahler has demonstrated that it is necessary to throw money out of the window in theatrical management in order to see it stream in at the door.' Yet it has been urged in behalf of Mahler's administration that he never wrought a deficit of alarming dimensions, as did his more economical predecessors. The experience of the New York enterprises which Herr Mahler directed were different. He was brought here as one of the conductors of the Metropolitan Opera House by Heinrich Conried in the season of 1907–8, arriving in the city on 21 December 1907, and effecting his first appearance as a conductor on 1 January 1908, in Wagner's *Tristan und Isolde*, a performance also made notable by the debut of Mme. Fremstad in the role of the heroine. Mahler's work was greatly admired by the reviewers for the newspapers and the public, but it was in no sense revolutionary, and there was even disappointment in the circumstance that there was nothing except things with which the cognoscenti were only too familiar in the stage management—a department which needed reformation. Three weeks later Mr. Mahler, after many rehearsals, brought forward Mozart's *Don Giovanni*. Here some novel elements were noticeable, most of them generally conceded to be excellent, some of them of a kind that caused more than a little head-shaking. There were changes of tempo which ran counter not only to long accepted tradition the world over, but which could not be reconciled with a conviction that Mr. Mahler was familiar with the original text, which is Italian, or its spirit. An innovation on which he seemed to pride himself not a little, as was disclosed later, when he came to figure in the concert life of New York, was his own playing on a pianoforte with an altered action so as to make it sound somewhat like a harpsichord (which was the instrument used in its day for such a purpose) of the accompaniment to the dialogue of the opera, the so-called *secco recitative*.

On 7 February 1908, he brought out Wagner's *Die Walküre*, and on 19 February, *Siegfried*, both with admirable musical effect. In fact, from a critical point of view, these Wagnerian performances were Mr. Mahler's principal contributions to the art life of New York. Much ado was made over other things, as, for instance, his production of *Fidelio*, with the scenic outfit and the changes which he had introduced in the score in Vienna, but they were not accepted here as inspired revelations, because it was recognized that the personal equation in them was so large as to compel the raising of aesthetic questions which every honest and intelligent musician felt went to the heart of artistic purity. Thus, he did not scruple to change the orchestration of the introduction to the second act, and gave it a distinctly latter-day cast, simply because he thought, or professed to think, that Beethoven would have orchestrated the number in a different manner if he had had his perfect hearing—meaning, if it meant anything, if he heard and desired as Mr. Mahler heard and desired, nearly a hundred years later. This disposition to meddle with the classics grew upon him later and had much to do with the disappointment which he brought as a conductor of the Philharmonic Society.

It was not long before the local musical authorities, those of the operatic and concert field, found that Mr. Mahler was an expensive and unprofitable proposition. He had a large reputation, and the directors of the Symphony Society thought it wise to engage him to give three of their concerts for the season of 1908–9. They found that not only was he quite as prodigal with their money as he had been with that of the Austrian Court Opera, but that he had strange notions about legal and moral obligations; for while still under contract to the Symphony Society he entered into an arrangement with a committee of women to give three concerts with the orchestra of the Philharmonic Society. He was prevented from thus violating his contract, but after the season was over he gave two concerts with the Philharmonic Society's orchestra and completely reversed the rule illustrated in the story of the wisdom of large expenditure set forth in the story of his administration of the Vienna Court Opera, as he had already done in the cases of the opera and the extra concerts of the Symphony Society; it was in each instance a large outlay and a small income. This fact did not prevent a committee of women composed of Mrs. William H. Draper, Mrs. John Jay Knox, Mrs. Samuel Untermeyer, Mrs. Ernest Schelling and Mrs. George R. Sheldon from carrying out a plan for the reorganization of the Philharmonic Society so that Mr. Mahler might be secured permanently for the musical evangelization of New York. A similar effort had been made a few years before by some of the same people, but had been frustrated, partly by the objections of the veteran members of the society to a radical change of its internal economy, partly by dissensions among the women who had undertaken to raise the guarantee fund. But in the spring of 1909 it was known that Mr. Mahler had been engaged to conduct the concerts of the Philharmonic Society (at first it was announced for three seasons, afterward for two) and that he was to have absolute authority in the engagement of the orchestra and the choice of programmes during his period. Meanwhile, as a forecast of joys that were to come, Mr. Mahler was permitted to give two concerts with the orchestra of the Philharmonic Society after the regular season, conducted by Mr. Safonoff, was over. He gave the concerts, and also, under special arrangement with Mr. Dippel, a few performances of Smetana's opera, *The Bartered Bride*, a work which turned out to be a distinctly valuable acquisition to the Metropolitan repertory.

Later he also produced Tchaikovsky's *Pique Dame*, but this opera did not hold a place in the repertory. To pursue an orderly course in the story of Mr. Mahler's life, something ought now to be said about his compositions, because it was as a composer as well as a conductor that his friends, a well-defined party, or clique, sought to impress the world with a sense of his greatness. In his youthful years his thoughts leaned toward the opera, and he composed two works in this field entitled *Die Argonauten* and *Rübezahl*, but nothing came of them. In 1888 he completed the opera which Carl Maria von Weber had let fall, *Die drei Pintos*, but nothing lasting either for his reputation or that of Weber came of the experiment. In 1891 he produced his First Symphony, four years later a second one. Afterward, though he wrote songs with orchestral and pianoforte accompaniment, and added six symphonies to his list—No. 3 in 1896, No. 4 in 1901, No. 5, which created a sensation because of its unexampled demand for performers (the 'Riesensymphonie' was what the Germans called it): No. 6 in 1906, No. 7 a year or two later (the score is not dated), and No. 8, which was produced with a large noise in more than one sense at Munich last summer. In this work he demanded an extraordinary orchestra, besides choirs of mixed mature voices and boys, and in a way that was not attempted before and has not been attempted since he tried to establish a connection between the ancient church hymn 'Veni creator spiritus' and the finale of the second part of Goethe's *Faust*. It is eminently characteristic of German criticism that it never even undertook to find out whether or not the composer had any connecting link in his mind: one thing only was sure—criticism could find none. This needed to astound nobody who knew that after Mr. Mahler began to attract attention as a composer, as was plainly proved in an article printed in this journal after the performance of his Fourth Symphony, he professed to cut loose from the programmatic school, and though his early symphonies are utterly inexplicable without the titles, mottoes and sub-titles which he gave them, he insisted on their acceptance as absolute music. It is a harsh thing to say of a dead man, but the truth demands that it be said that in one instance he denied in a letter to this writer that he had even written a letter quoted in an analysis of one of his symphonies written by a warm admirer and friend, and made believe that he could not understand it at all, though the symphony demanded some such a programme as was suggested. In other cases he insisted that he had written as freely and unconstrainedly as Mozart and Schubert, though his symphonies bore titles and sub-titles. It needs no argument to prove that by his choice of a medieval hymn in one portion and a selection from *Faust* in another in his last symphony he put himself in line with the musicians who demand that their hearers go outside their art in order to be understood.

It was a singular paradox in Mahler's artistic nature that while his melodic ideas were of the folksong order his treatment of them was of the most extravagant kind, harmonically and orchestrally. He attempted in argument to reconcile the extremes by insisting that folksong was the vital spark of artistic music, but in his treatment of the simple melodies of his symphonies (some of them borrowed without acknowledgement) he was utterly inconsiderate of their essence, robbing them of their characteristics and elaborating them to death. He should have been an ingenuous musician—a musician, had he had that genius, like Dvořák. Instead, he tried to out-Strauss Strauss and out-Reger Reger, and not having the native force of either of them he failed. We cannot see how any of his music can long survive him. There is no place for it between the old and the new schools.

There remains much to be said about his activity for two years in connection with the Philharmonic Society. A very large endeavour was made by the management, especially during the season which has just closed, to arouse popular interest in the concerts of the venerable society. It failed. Not only did the general public fail to respond to the loud appeal, but the subscription list grew steadily smaller. For this no one was to blame except Mr. Mahler. It is a fatuous notion of foreigners that Americans know nothing about music in its highest forms. Only of late years have the European newspapers begun to inform their readers that the opera in New York has some significance. Had their writers on music been students they would have known that for nearly a century New Yorkers have listened to singers of the highest class—singers that the people of the musical centres of the European continent were never permitted to hear. Mr. Mahler early learned a valuable lesson at the opera, but he never learned it in the concert room. He never discovered that there were Philharmonic subscribers who had inherited not only their seats from their parents and grandparents, but also their appreciation of good music. He never knew, or if he knew he was never willing to acknowledge, that the Philharmonic audience would be as quick to resent an outrage on the musical classics as a corruption of the Bible or Shakespeare. He did not know that he was doing it, or if he did he was willing wantonly to insult their intelligence and taste by such things as multiplying the voices in a Beethoven symphony (an additional kettledrum in the 'Pastoral', for instance), by cutting down the strings and doubling the flutes in Mozart's G minor, by fortifying the brass in Schubert's C major until the sweet Vienna singer of nearly a century ago seemed a modern Malay running amuck, and—most monstrous of all his doings—starting the most poetical and introspective of all of Schumann's overtures—that to 'Manfred'—with a cymbal clash like that which sets Mazeppa's horse on his wild gallop in Liszt's symphonic poem. And who can ever forget the treatment of the kettledrums which he demanded of his players? Wooden-headed sticks, not only in Beethoven's Ninth symphony, but even in Weber's 'Oberon' overture! But the man is dead and the catalogue might as well be closed. Of the unhappy relations which existed between him and the Philharmonic Society's promoters it would seem to be a duty to speak: but the subject is unpleasant; those most interested know the facts; the injury that has been done cannot be undone, and when it becomes necessary the history may be unfolded in its entirety. It were best if it could be forgotten.

H. E. K.

[H. E. Krehbiel]

III. London
The Times 20 May 1911

OBITUARY

HERR GUSTAV MAHLER

The death of Gustav Mahler, one of the most distinguished musical conductors of the world, is announced as having taken place in Vienna on Thursday night.

He was a Bohemian, of Jewish origin, and was born on 7th July, 1860; he received his general education at Iglau, Prague, and Vienna, and from 1877 was a pupil of the Conservatorium in the last-named city. In 1883 he received his first regular theatre appointment as the second *Capellmeister* at Cassel, and in 1885 succeeded Anton Seidl as chief conductor at Prague. After two years as Nikisch's coadjutor at Leipzig he began an important engagement at Pesth. From 1891 to 1897 he filled the chief conductor's place at Hamburg, and in the latter year was appointed *Hofcapellmeister* at the Vienna Opera, succeeding Richter as conductor of the Philharmonic concerts there. It was in 1892 that he made his first appearance in England, conducting a memorable series of German operas at Covent Garden. In the autumn of 1907, having resigned his Vienna appointments, he went to New York as chief conductor of the Metropolitan Opera House, and was re-engaged for the two following seasons.

His work as a conductor was of great importance, being entirely free from exaggeration and in some ways more restrained, complete, and accomplished than that of any man save Richter; he made a considerable mark as a composer, mainly of symphonies, of which there exist no fewer than eight. He made various experiments in the way of extending the scope of the symphony, as, for example, when he introduced a soprano solo in the Finale of the Fourth and a choral Finale into the Eighth, which was produced in Vienna last autumn. Two of the symphonies, the First and Fourth, have been played at Promenade Concerts and elsewhere in London; the operatic works of Mahler are few and unimportant, but he finished Weber's opera *Die drei Pintos*, which was produced in 1888 at Leipzig. It is too early to guess at the place which his symphonic works will ultimately take, for while they are undoubtedly interesting in their union of modern orchestral richness with a melodic simplicity that often approached banality, they are obviously sincere in expression and original in design.

A correspondent writes:

The appointment of Herr Mahler to the directorship of the Vienna Imperial Opera closed the period of decadence associated with the names of Jahn and Richter. A strong personality, Mahler displayed a vigour approximating to ruthlessness. Any public personage who essays a policy of reform, be it political, economic, or musical, in the atmosphere of the Austrian capital exposes himself to the fate reserved for those who try to 'bustle the East', and Mahler's untimely death is in part an after-effect of his constant and largely successful struggle against the semi-Oriental atmosphere of Vienna. His title to fame as Director rests mainly upon his introduction to Vienna of what is now regarded as the orthodox interpretation of Wagner's operas, and particularly of *Tristan*, and upon his resolute return to the spirit of Mozart in the production of *Don Giovanni*. Although his innovations and resuscitations gained for him warm support and enthusiastic admiration among the greater part of the Viennese public, they failed to disarm his opponents, among whom were members of the Imperial Family and high Court officials. Financial deficit afforded them at last an opportunity of giving practical shape to their opposition, and Mahler indignantly resigned the position in which he had rendered signal services to the Imperial Institute.

After his retirement from the Opera he devoted himself principally to the completion of his Eighth Symphony, which was performed with marked success at Munich in September 1910. Partly upon the advice of Richard Strauss he accepted a call from New York to conduct a series of performances, and during his first stay in America made so favourable an impression that he was permanently engaged as one of the four conductors of the Metropolitan Opera. It was during his recent visit to New York in this capacity that he contracted the malady that has now proved fatal.

A man of Mahler's directness and force of character naturally aroused opposition as fierce as the devotion which he inspired in other quarters was intense. He spared no feelings, but went straight to his object, believing that recognition of the exalted character of his aims would ensure acquiescence, if not approval. In speech he was curt and often peremptory, rarely troubling to find a euphemistic form for disagreeable truths. Some years since, when invited to witness a performance at the Paris Opera, he was asked to express an opinion on the qualities of the house. 'Very dirty' was his only rejoinder. Struck by his blunt remark the directors of the Paris Opera ordered a general cleaning, in the course of which more than a ton of dust was removed.

The Text of Klopstock's 'Auferstehung'

In almost every reference made to Klopstock's 'Auferstehung' text, the hymn is described as an 'Ode'. (See, for example, HG[1], pp. 791–2, or KB[1], p. 115, to name only two of the more recent studies of Mahler.) But if one looks for 'Auferstehung' among Klopstock's Collected Odes (the best edition is that edited by Muncker and Pawel, Vols. I & II, Stuttgart, 1889), one does not find it there, for the good reason that an Ode (metrically) it is not. The verses appear in fact in another place altogether, among the poet's 'Geistliche Lieder' (this, M. de La Grange correctly points out). I quote the complete Klopstock text below, from the 'Geistliche Lieder', and use as my source Vol. VII of his Collected Works, Leipzig, 1804, pp. 133–4. I follow up the authentic Klopstock text with Mahler's version, where the composer uses only the first two of Klopstock's verses (very slightly re-modelled) as his point of departure, but invents the rest of the text for himself, for his own use, though returning, one notices, in his final verse to Klopstock's first as a basic model (thus neatly rounding off his own poetic excursion). This is a wholly typical instance of Mahler's intensive re-modelling and vast expansion of a text. It is interesting that the principle unfolded in his treatment of Klopstock's text is *identical* with his re-modelling of the *Wunderhorn* poem in the first of the *Gesellen* songs (cf. AM[5], pp. xxiii–iv).

DIE AUFERSTEHUNG

Mel. Jesus Christus unser Heiland, der den Tod überwand.

> Auferstehn, ja auferstehn wirst du,
> Mein Staub, nach kurzer Ruh!
> Unsterblichs Leben
> Wird, der dich schuf, dir geben!
> Halleluja!
>
> Wieder aufzublühn werd ich gesät!
> Der Herr der Erndte geht,
> Und sammelt Garben
> Uns ein, uns ein, die starben!
> Halleluja!

Tag des Danks! der Freudenthränen Tag!
Du meines Gottes Tag!
Wenn ich im Grabe
Genug geschlummert habe,
Erweckst du mich!

Wie den Träumenden wirds dann uns seyn!
Mit Jesu gehn wir ein
Zu seinen Freuden!
Der müden Pilger Leiden
Sind dann nicht mehr!

Ach ins Allerheiligste führt mich
Mein Mittler dann; lebt' ich
Im Heiligthume,
Zu seines Nahmens Ruhme!
Halleluja!

*   *   *   *

Mahler's version

Aufersteh'n, ja aufersteh'n wirst du,
Mein Staub, nach kurzer Ruh!
Unsterblich Leben!
Wird, der dich rief, dir geben!

Wieder aufzublüh'n, wirst du gesät!
Der Herr der Ernte geht
Und sammelt Garben
Uns ein, die starben!
O glaube, mein Herz, o glaube:
Es geht dir nichts verloren!
Dein ist, dein, ja dein, was du gesehnt!
Dein, was du geliebt, was du gestritten!
O glaube: du wardst nicht um sonst geboren!
Hast nicht um sonst gelebt, gelitten!

Was entstanden ist, das muss vergehen!
Was vergangen, auferstehen!
Hör' auf, zu beben!
Bereite dich! Bereite dich, zu leben!

O Schmerz! Du Alldurchdringer!
Dir bin ich entrungen!

O Tod! Du Allbezwinger!
Nun bist du bezwungen!

Mit Flügeln, die ich mir errungen,
In heissem Liebesstreben
Werd' ich entschweben
Zum Licht, zu dem kein Aug' gedrungen!

Mit Flügeln, die ich mir errungen,
Werde ich entschweben!
Sterben werd' ich, um zu leben!

Aufersteh'n, ja aufersteh'n wirst du,
Mein Herz, in einem Nu!
Was du geschlagen,
Zu Gott wird es dich tragen!

Herr Blaukopf, in KB[1], pp. 115–16, quotes Klopstock's 'Ode' [*sic*] from the programme of the Bülow memorial service on 29 March 1894, and if this quotation is correct, it indicates that only *three* of Klopstock's five verses were sung at the service.

The reference above the text of Klopstock's hymn to 'Jesus Christus, unser Heiland' refers to the melody to which the words were intoned, it would seem during Klopstock's lifetime, since the Collected Edition I use as a source was published only one year after the poet's death, in 1803. If this custom did not persist, it must have been because, as a note informs us in Johannes Zahn's *Die Melodien der deutschen evangelischen Kirchenlieder*, Gütersloh, 1889, Vol. I, p. 540, the 'old' melody of 'Jesus Christus, unser Heiland' did not fit the metre of Klopstock's text. Incidentally, this same source gathers together the incipits of no less than 25 settings of the Klopstock words for church use. They include melodies by Graun, C. P. E. Bach, Glaser, Kühnau, Telemann, Rinck, Kittel, etc., etc. None of them, I think, could have had an influence on the melodic shape of Mahler's choral Finale. I am grateful to Dr. Edward R. Reilly and Professor Ronald Taylor, both of whom valuably assisted me in pursuing this topic, though we still have to determine the setting that Mahler actually heard in Hamburg on 29 March 1894. It was unlikely to have been 'Jesus Christus, unser Heiland', for the reason given above.

Mahler's Edition of
Mozart's *Figaro* (1906)

On p. 22 of AM[5], reference is made to a recitative that Mahler specially composed for his new production of *Figaro* in Vienna in 1906. Alma Mahler writes:

> Mahler went so far as to emend the libretto of *Figaro*, to clarify the action of the comedy. He used motifs of Mozart's for the recitatives he had to compose. He did all this to make the work more living.

Later, on p. 96, she writes of the year 1906:

> *The Marriage of Figaro* was given on 30th March, in Mahler's edition. It was one of his finest productions and, with *Don Giovanni*, *Fidelio* and *Tristan*, one of the sacred few he kept under his own hand and eye.

The recitative is also mentioned by Erwin Stein in his important articles, 'Mahler and the Vienna Opera', reprinted in *The Opera Bedside Book*, London, 1965, p. 308, where he writes:

> There was an extension of da Ponte's libretto in the *secco* recitative that precedes the sextet of the third act: in order to make the story more easily understandable, a court scene from Beaumarchais's original play *Le Mariage de Figaro* was inserted, with the Count presiding, Don Curzio as judge and Marcellina as plaintiff. The scene was a short *secco* recitative and led directly to Don Curzio's *È decisa la lite, o pagarla, o sposarla*. Purists complained of the insertion, as they would today, but artistically no harm had been done to the opera.

Mahler's extra recitative appears in the vocal score of *Figaro* published by C. F. Peters under the title 'Bearbeitung der Wiener Hofoper' (Edition No. 9332). The edition I have consulted uses a German translation by Max Kalbeck (1850–1921) and between pp. 186–93 may be found what I presume to be Mahler's recitative, which in fact is not as Stein suggests, an exclusively *secco* recitative but also *accompagnato*, for which reason this vocal score also includes the relevant two pages of orchestral score for the conductor's use, pp. 190–91. I reproduce these pages overleaf, see pp. 420f., constituting as they do an item of some historical interest and importance. They give us all

Two pages from Mahler's edition of *The Marriage of Figaro*

Bartolo. Ich Endesgefertigter bescheinige hiemit von der Dame Marzelline die Summe von zweitausend Piastern empfangen zu haben. Diese Summe werde ich ihr auf ihr Verlangen jederzeit zurückzahlen oder sie aus Erkenntlichkeit heiraten. Gezeichnet Figaro!

Figaro. Aber wenn ich das Geld nicht habe? **Curzio.** Unsre Sache ist spruchreif, du bezahlst oder nimmst sie. Hast du verstanden? **Marzelline. Figaro.** Ich lebe wieder. Und ich sterbe. **Marzelline.** Ich Glückliche, mir fällt ein Stein vom Herzen. **Figaro (bei Seite).** (Und mir fällt er auf den Kopf.) **(laut)** Exzellenz, ich appelliere. **Graf.** Da gibt es keinen Einwand! Bezahlen oder heiraten! **Curzio.** Sehr gut, Herr Richter. **Graf.** Gar zu gütig, Exzellenz. **Curzio.** Die Verhandlung ist geschlossen. Hoch lebe unser gnädiger Herr Graf! **Chor.** Hoch! Hoch! Hoch! — **Bartolo.** Ein voll-

(Die Gerichtsdiener, Dienerschaft und Landleute ab durch die Mitte.)

but the opening thirteen (*secco*) bars of Mahler's recitative. Altogether, this new recitative is quite an elaborate affair, making brief use of the chorus as well as the principals. Stein seems not to be strictly correct in writing that Mahler's recitative 'led directly to Don Curzio's *È decisa la lite*'. The Mahler expansion in fact leads directly to Bartolo's 'Che superba sentenza!', which means that for the first nine bars of Mozart's recitative Mahler substitutes forty-eight bars or so of his own devising.

One notes, however, how ingeniously he stitches into the flow of his recitative the 'missing' nine bars of Mozart (i.e. see bars 36–44 (p. 189) in the piano reduction or bars 3–11 on the second page of the orchestral score below (p. 191), where Mahler incorporates —or absorbs— bars 1–9 of the original Mozart, which of course is *secco* throughout). It is this, I think, that Alma Mahler means when she writes, loosely, that Mahler 'used motifs of Mozart's for the recitatives he had to compose'; and Stein, too, is accurate in his description in so far as Don Curzio's 'È decisa la lite' is certainly there, motivically speaking, embedded in Mahler's re-composition of the recitative. The trial scene in Beaumarchais, on which the dramatically clarifying recitative is based, occurs in Act III of the play. There is no attribution of the recitative to Mahler in the Peters edition of the vocal score, but *Figaro* in this Hofoper edition was listed among Mahler's 'arrangements' by Paul Stefan, his early biographer (see PS¹, p. 165) and Mahler himself refers to the edition in a letter to Karl Hörwitz from Toblach, 27 June 1908 (GMB¹, p. 427): '"Figaro" was published by Peters, simply described as "Vienna Arrangement" [*sic*], without any rights reserved, and is therefore free.'

The MS Voice and Piano Versions of Mahler's *Wunderhorn* Songs

In the music collection of the Berlin Staatsbibliothek (MS Mahler 1), there is a highly interesting MS of the voice and piano versions of some of the best known of the *Wunderhornlieder*, in Mahler's own hand.

After a title page, which is inscribed 'Des Knaben Wunderhorn', the songs appear in the following order:

1. *Der Schildwache Nachtlied*
   [Ink, 5 pages, upright 16-stave paper, imprint B.C. No. 6, with the device of a lyre.]
2. *Verlorene Müh*
   [Ink, 5 pages; p. 1 of the song follows on the verso of the last page of the preceding song. With p. 2, the paper changes to 14-stave paper.]
3. *Wer hat dies Liedlein erdacht?!*
   [Ink, 4 pages, continuing with the same 14-stave paper.]
4. *Das himmlische Leben* (See Plates between pp. 136 and 137.)
   [Ink, 10 pages, continuing with similar 14-stave paper. At p. 11 (the page number on the MS), the paper changes to a 16-stave paper, and again for the last page, which is an 18-stave paper, with the verso blank.]
5. *Trost im Unglück*
   [Ink, 3 pages, 18-stave paper, though a different paper from the preceding (see 4 above).]
6. *Rheinlegendchen*
   [Ink, 4 pages, 18-stave paper, but again a different kind from the preceding (see 5 above).]

Though the dates on these MSS are given in the appropriate places elsewhere in this book, perhaps it may be thought useful to state them precisely as they appear at the end of each MS:

1. Hamburg, 28. Januar 92.
2. Hamburg, 1. Feber 92.

3. Samstag, 6. Februar 92, Hamburg.
4. Mitwoch [sic], 10. Feber 92.
5. 22. Feber.
6. Steinbach, Mitwoch [sic], 9. August, 1893.

The MS of the songs presents many interesting features, not least the odd assortment of papers, with the type of paper not only changing between songs but even *within* individual songs. Although Nos. 1–5 share a common period, i.e. the dates of completion fall between 28 January and 22 February, the songs do not share a paper in common. As might be expected, the penmanship too varies from song to song.

These MSS were clearly fair copies made by Mahler and used by him for performance or, possibly, rehearsal purposes (the MS of 'Das himmlische Leben', for example, is much thumbed). Here and there, there are pencil corrections—for example, missing accidentals have been added—and, most important of all, Mahler has written in metronome marks for some songs, and sometimes *throughout* the songs, in very great detail, indications of tempi which are of both musicological and great practical significance. The metronome, of course, must be treated as a guide rather than a law, but it is much to be hoped that singers, accompanists and conductors will at least heed these authentic suggestions from the composer himself. I list the metronome marks in sequence from those songs where Mahler has provided us with an indication of the tempi that he probably adopted himself in his own performances (at the keyboard, or as conductor):

1. No metronome marks given by Mahler.

2. ♪ = 132

3. At beginning: ♪ = 160
   After end of first vocal 'cadenza', i.e. at bar 47 ('Wieder gemächlich'):
   ♪ = 152

4. At beginning: ♩ = 96
   Bar 25 [Fig. 2]   ♩ = 108
   Bar 36 [4 bars
      before Fig. 3]   ♩ = 92
   Bar 40 [Fig. 3]   ♩ = 116
   Bar 57 [Fig. 5]   ♩ = 104
   Bar 76 [Fig. 7]   ♩ = 116
   Bar 80 [Tempo I]   ♩ = 96
   Bar 95   ♩ = 126
   Bar 106 [Fig. 10]   ♩ = 92
   Bar 115 [Fig. 11]   ♩ = 116
   Bar 122 [Fig. 12]   ♩ = 96

5. At beginning: ♩ = 100
6. At beginning: ♪ = 132

All the metronome marks are of interest, but none more so than the elaborate scheme of tempi Mahler worked out for 'Das himmlische Leben', a pattern of related and recurrent tempi which is suggestive of the kind of fluctuating yet always formally clarifying tempi which would have been characteristic of Mahler's performance (not only of this song but probably also of his performances in general). (Another guide, of course, and one worth referring to comparatively in this context, is Mahler's own (piano-roll) performance of the song, which was issued on disc. His companion performance of the first movement of the Fifth Symphony has also been issued on disc in the U.S.A. Perhaps I might add, finally, a reference to Mengelberg's conducting scores, in the possession of the Mengelberg-Stiftung, Amsterdam, on at least one of which, the score of Symphony IV, there are marks by Mengelberg and Mahler, and detailed indications of what are claimed to be authentic metronome marks. (A recording of the Fourth, under Mengelberg, made from a live performance in 1939/40, was issued by Philips as part of their 'Documenta Musicae' series, the sleeve of which recording reproduces, among other fascinating illustrations, the first page of Mengelberg's heavily annotated score that I refer to above.) There is a whole fund of information here about probable performing practice in Mahler's own time—and perhaps about his own performing practice—which calls for thorough investigation.)

Another conspicuous feature of these MS fair copies is the elaborate detail of the instrumentation which is written into the piano part. The degree of detail varies a little between one song and another. Among the most detailed MSS in this respect are 'Der Schildwache Nachtlied', and 'Das himmlische Leben': it is fascinating to observe in the orchestral *ritornello*, for example, that Mahler even goes so far as to indicate the detail of the percussion, e.g. triangle, tambourine, etc.

Points of interest in some of the songs are as follows:

1. A meticulously corrected copy, from which one cannot doubt that Mahler performed. The note for the singer at the end of the song (the final verse) already exists in the MS.
2. One bar has been scratched out in this copy.
3. There are some ink and pencil additions in this MS.
4. This most evocative of all Mahler's *Wunderhornlieder* in MS shows signs of having been intensively worked over, i.e. scratching out, pencil additions, variants, etc. Perhaps one might add here that Mahler's metronome marks for this song also help to indicate the tempi he may have had in mind for the first movement of the symphony. (See Mahler's own footnote to Fig. 3 of the

song in the published score of the Fourth Symphony. We now have from the Berlin MS of 'Das himmlische Leben' a metronome mark for this passage— ♩ = 116—which could serve as a basis for the tempo of the 'corresponding places', as Mahler puts it, in the first movement.)

5. The fairest copy among the six songs, written in a particularly neat, fine hand.

6. The MS of 'Rheinlegendchen' is inscribed 'für hohe Stimmlage'. The song's first title 'Tanzreime' is crossed through. The MS shows some amendments, amplifications, corrections and crossings out in ink, among them an adjustment of the transition to the final verse, 'Mein Schätzlein tät springen . . .', which brings it into line with the original lead-in (cf. bars 12–16) and the comparable preceding transitions, and a re-drafting of six bars of the subsequent voice part (bars 96–101).

APPENDIX F

The 'Drum Prelude' (Original Version) to the Scherzo of the Second Symphony

A study of *all* the variants of the drum prelude embodied in the Amsterdam and Yale MSS of the symphony offers a fascinating exercise in following the evolution of one compositional idea through its many stages.

It seems worth while setting out here (see Ex. X below) Mahler's formulation of the opening bars for solo timpani precisely as they appear in the handwritten percussion part that I mention in n. 50, p. 270. From this it will be clearly seen how meticulously organized was the dynamic detail—*ff* diminishing to *ppp* and then growing again to a climax through a carefully planned and graded crescendo in which both players are involved, though not in immediate synchronization—and how integral, initially, was the stereophonic effect to which Mr. Matthews refers on p. 284. Altogether, a remarkable idea for the onset of the movement, but one supposes that Mahler, in a fit of typical economical thinking, decided that less, ultimately, would prove to be more, and so drastically reduced the scale of the passage.

Ex. X

Ex. X above is not amended in the part but boldly crossed out. The version that appears on the inserted first page of the Scherzo in the MS full score does not, interestingly, exactly correspond with the part. It is written out on one stave, not two, and the alternation of the drums is far less complex, i.e. the second player is not marked to enter until the equivalent of bar 9 in Ex. X. Mahler worked out his ideas for the revision of the passage in his score, not on the part, and it is not possible to reproduce his original conception and at the same time show all the amendments and deletions that adorn it. However, Ex. B, p. 284, in fact *precisely* corresponds to the original form of the drum prelude in the Amsterdam full score, while the various crossings-out and amendments (alterations of note-values, etc., if carefully analysed, give us the picture of what emerged as Mahler's final solution, i.e. Ex. C (p. 284).

It is not absolutely clear to me at what chronological moment the copyist's (presumably) pencil *explication* that I mention in n. 50 was prepared. This was self-evidently an effort to bring the shape and sequence of the opening bars into line with Mahler's evolving ideas about it. As will be seen from my reproduction of this version below (Ex. Y), the copyist in fact documents the final published solution, providing one ignores the insert of 3 bars which is mapped out as an alternative to the one bar's rest (bar 4). This one remaining uncertainty is related directly to one of the scribbled-in amendments to the stave in Mahler's full score, but oddly enough the first and third bars of the insertion do not follow the pattern established in the full score (cf. Ex. B, bars 6–7) but reinstate 3 bars (bars 6–8) from the original timpani part (see Ex. X above). Keen-eyed scrutineers will notice that the empty bar in Ex. D (p. 284) corresponds to the spot to which the insertion is attached in Ex. Y.

Ex. Y

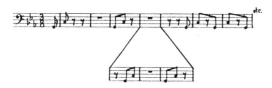

Mahler's metronome marks
Certain metronome marks in Mahler's hand appear on the Amsterdam MS of the symphony as listed below:

Second movement, at start: ♪ = 92
   Third movement, at start: ♩. = 52   Mahler indicates that by the time
                                          bar 14 is reached ♩. should = 58.

          At Fig. 40: ♩. = 54   (This is the trio for trumpet
                                          quartet.)

None of these marks was included in the published edition, though Mahler did include in a footnote for the conductor some metronomic suggestions about the tempi at which the main theme of the first movement should unfold.

Hanslick on the 'Wunderhorn' Songs (1900)

On 14 January 1900, Mahler conducted the Vienna Philharmonic in a programme that included five of his orchestral songs (these were first performances in Vienna). The group was made up of two songs from the *Gesellen* cycle (Nos. 2 and 4), and three from the *Wunderhorn* orchestral settings, 'Das irdische Leben', 'Wo die schönen Trompeten blasen', and 'Wer hat dies Liedlein erdacht' (the rest of the programme comprised Schumann's Fourth Symphony and Berlioz's overture, 'Carnaval Romain'). Hanslick's notice of this concert (see also the Supplementary Bibliography, the entry for Nicolas Powell) was reprinted in his collected writings, in the volume 'Aus neuer und neuester Zeit', Berlin, 1900. His comments on Mahler's songs (pp. 76–7) seem to me to be of such intrinsic interest that I think it worthwhile to set them out here in their entirety. Perhaps one ought to add that Hanslick's orchestral list must have been intended as an indication of the richness of Mahler's orchestral resources. It does not, of course, attempt to be a comprehensive account of the actual orchestra(s) involved. One notes, by the way, that Mahler must have used 2 harps in the *Gesellen* songs on this occasion. (For further press reactions to this event, see also HG[1], pp. 552–54.)

Philharmonic Concert
FIVE SONGS BY G. MAHLER

What most especially aroused the public's curiosity, were the five songs with orchestral accompaniment by G. Mahler, sung by Fräulein Selma Kurz. Some of the poems are from 'Des Knaben Wunderhorn', some from a cycle, 'Lieder eines fahrenden Gesellen', for which we are told the composer himself was poet. Until now, Director Mahler has shown a modesty bordering on self-denial in holding back his own compositions from performance in Vienna, however favourably they may have been received in other towns. Something new and individual has come to be expected of him. In his Second Symphony (which unfortunately I know only from report), he proved to be an innovator in the grand manner, vastly enlarging both symphonic form and the performing medium. In the songs we heard yesterday, too, he proclaims himself an enemy of the conventional and the customary, a 'chercheur', as the French would say, without implying any derogatory criticism by the use of this term. The new 'songs' are difficult to classify: neither Lied nor aria, nor dramatic scene, they possess something of all these forms. More than anything, their form recalls that of Berlioz's songs with orchestral accompaniment, 'La captive', 'Le chasseur danois', and 'Le [jeune] pâtre breton'. Mahler has taken most of his texts from the folksong collection 'Des Knaben Wunderhorn'. Although this contains things of peculiar beauty, it has become somewhat less admired than in previous times, since when German lyric poetry reached such a high level of inspiration in Goethe. It is well known that Goethe criticized at length the 'Wunderhorn' that was dedicated to him by Arnim and Brentano: he praised the 'woodcut style' of the folk song, but assigned the book to a place 'by the window, under the mirror, or wherever else songbooks and cookery books are usually to be found.' Mahler, one in the forefront of modernism, shows a desire, as so often happens, to seek refuge in the opposite extreme in naivety, in unremitting sentiment, in the terse, even awkward language of the old folk song. However, it would have been contrary to his nature to have treated these poems in the simple, undemanding manner of earlier composers. Although a folk-like character is retained in the vocal line, this is underlaid by a sumptuous accompaniment, alert in its sprightliness and vivid in modulation, which Mahler gives, not to the piano, but to the orchestra. For folk songs, this is an uncommonly large and indeed refined ensemble: three flutes, piccolo, three clarinets, bass clarinet, cor anglais, four horns, two harps. It is impossible to ignore the fact that there is a contradiction, a dichotomy, between the concept of the 'folk song' and this artful, superabundant orchestral accompaniment. Yet Mahler has pursued this venture with extraordinary delicacy and masterly technique. As we stand at the beginning of a new century, we are well advised to say of each new work produced by the musical 'Sezession' (Mahler, Richard Strauss, Hugo Wolf, etc.): 'It may very well be that the future lies with them.' Fräulein Selma Kurz performed these extremely difficult Mahler songs from memory, completely mastering the words and the notes, and displaying both sonorous tone and warm, absolutely natural expression.

Bibliography

AM¹   Mahler, Alma: *GM: Erinnerungen und Briefe*, Amsterdam, 1949.

AM²   ———: *GM: Memories and Letters*, translated by Basil Creighton, London, 1946.

AM³   ———: *GM: Memories and Letters*, translated by Basil Creighton, enlarged edition, revised and edited and with an Introduction by DM, London, 1968.

AM⁴   ———: As for AM³, but with an Editor's Note for the American Edition, New York, 1969.

AM⁵   ———: As for AM⁴ but with new Preface and new Appendix and Chronology by Knud Martner and DM, London, 1973.

AM⁶   ———: *GM: Erinnerungen an GM*, Herausgegeben von DM, Frankfurt M.—Berlin, 1971. [This edition purports to be a re-issue of AM¹, with editorial matter and modifications adopted from AM³ and AM⁴. The result is a publisher's muddle, with old errors repeated and new ones created. It is unfortunate that this recent German edition would seem to present the most unreliable of available texts. Mr. Knud Martner (Copenhagen) generously sent me a list of corrections to this edition, which I shall be happy to make available on request.]

AM⁷   American edition of AM⁵, with substantial additional material by DM and Knud Martner, University of Washington Press, Seattle, 1975. [This Washington paperback represents, in fact, the most recent and up-to-date revision of AM. As I write, I learn from Dr. Edward R. Reilly that transcripts of the letters from Mahler that are included in AM—transcripts of the German originals, that is—are in the possession of the University of Pennsylvania. If the transcripts are accurate and complete, they will enable future editors of AM to check the authenticity (or otherwise) of AM's editing of her husband's correspondence and restore, if necessary, any expurgated or editorially modified passages. This is clearly an important task, and I hope it will soon be undertaken.]

AM⁸   Mahler Werfel, Alma: *And the Bridge is Love: Memories of a Lifetime*, London, 1959.

ABM   Bahr-Mildenburg, Anna: *Erinnerungen*, Vienna, 1921.

BW¹   Walter, Bruno: *GM*, trans. James Galston, London, 1937.

BW² ——: *GM*, new edition of BW¹, translation supervised by Lotte Walter Lindt, London, 1958. [See also EK.]

BW³ ——: *Briefe* 1894–1962, Frankfurt, 1969.

DC Cooke, Deryck: *GM 1860–1911* [BBC publication], London, n.d. [1960].

DM¹ Mitchell, Donald, *GM: The Early Years*, London, 1958.

DM² ——: *GM: Prospect and Retrospect*, Proceedings of the Royal Musical Association, 1960–1, pp. 83–97.

DM³ ——: 'Mahler under the microscope', *Times Literary Supplement*, 29 November 1974, pp. 1349–51 [a review, principally, of HG¹].

DN Newlin, Dika: *Bruckner/Mahler/Schoenberg*, New York, 1947.

EK Křenek, Ernst: *GM*, a Biographical Essay, contributed to an edition of BW¹ published by the Greystone Press, New York, 1941.

ER GM: *IX Symphonie*, Partiturentwurf der ersten drei Sätze, Faksimile nach der Handschrift, edited by Erwin Ratz, Vienna, 1971.

ES Stein, Erwin: *Orpheus in New Guises*, London, 1953.

FEP Pamer, Fritz Egon: *GMs Lieder, Studien zur Musikwissenschaft*, Vienna, 1929 and 1930, XVI, pp. 116–38; XVII, pp. 105–27.

FP Pfohl, Ferdinand: *GM: Eindrücke und Erinnerungen aus den Hamburger Jahren*, ed. Knud Martner, Hamburg, 1973.

GA Adler, Guido: *GM*, Vienna-Leipzig, 1916. [I should like to acknowledge here an admirable English translation of Adler's monograph, translated, edited, and annotated by Dr. Edward R. Reilly of Vassar College, who was kind enough to send me a typescript of his work.]

GE Engel, Gabriel: *GM, Song-Symphonist*, New York, 1932.

GMB¹ *GM: Briefe, 1879–1911*, edited by Alma Maria Mahler, with notes by Friedrich Löhr, Berlin-Vienna-Leipzig, 1924. [An English translation (by Eithne Wilkins and Ernst Kaiser) of an expanded and annotated edition of this volume, edited by Knud Martner, is in preparation by Faber & Faber, London.]

GMB² As for GMB¹, a Czech edition (*M: Dopisy*), trans. Marie and Frantisek Bartoš, and edited and extensively annotated by Frantisek Bartoš, Prague, 1962, with letters included from AM¹.

GMSZ *GM und seine Zeit*, Vienna, 1960. Catalogue of the Mahler Exhibition assembled in Vienna to mark the centenary of Mahler's birth.

HG¹ de La Grange, Henry-Louis: *M*, I, New York, 1973.

HG² ——: 'Mistakes about Mahler', in *Music and Musicians*, London, August 1972, pp. 16–22. [A shorter version of this contribution was published earlier in the *Saturday Review*, New York, 29 March 1969.]

HFR   Redlich, H. F.: *Bruckner and Mahler* ('The Master Musicians' series), revised edition, London, 1963.

JBF   Foerster, Josef Bohuslav: *Der Pilger: Erinnerungen eines Musikers*, translated from the Czech by Pavel Eisner and with an introduction by František Pala, Prague, 1955.

JD   Diether, Jack: 'Notes on Some Mahler Juvenilia' in *Chord and Discord*, Iowa, III, 1, 1969, pp. 3–100.

JW   Warrack, John: *Carl Maria von Weber*, London, 1968. [This Weber study includes an admirable chapter on Mahler's reconstruction of *Die drei Pintos.*]

KB¹   Blaukopf, Kurt: *GM oder Der Zeitgenosse der Zukunft*, Vienna, 1969.

KB²   ——: *GM*, translated by Inge Goodwin, London, 1973. (English edition of KB¹.)

MT   Tibbe, Monika: *Lieder und Liedelemente in instrumentalen Symphoniesätzen GMs*, Berliner Musikwissenschaftliche Arbeiten, Band I, Munich, 1971.

NBL   Bauer-Lechner, Natalie: *Erinnerungen an GM*, Leipzig-Vienna-Zürich, 1923. [For the most part I make use here of an English translation of Bauer-Lechner by Dika Newlin which is to be published by Faber & Faber, London, to whom—and to the translator—I make grateful acknowledgement. The page references, however, are to the original German text, published in 1923.]

NDM   Del Mar, Norman: *Richard Strauss*, A Critical Commentary on his Life and Works, I–III, London, 1962, 1968, and 1972.

PB   Bekker, Paul: *GMs Sinfonien*, Berlin, 1921.

PBZ   Boulez, Pierre: Preface to GM, *Das klagende Lied*, Philharmonia Pocket Score No. 392, Vienna-London, 1971, pp. iv–v.

PS¹   Stefan, Paul: *GM: Eine studie über Persönlichkeit und Werk*, revised edition, Munich, 1920.

PS²   Stefan, Paul (ed.): *GM: ein Bild seiner Persönlichkeit in Widmungen*, Munich, 1910.

RS   Specht, Richard: *GM*, Berlin, 1913.

RSW   *Die Welt um Richard Strauss in Briefen*, edited by Franz Grasberger in association with Franz and Alice Strauss, Tutzing, 1967.

TR   Reik, Theodor: *The Haunting Melody*, New York, 1953.

ZR¹   Roman, Zoltan: 'M's *Lieder eines fahrenden Gesellen*—a cycle of six songs?' Paper read before the annual meeting of the American Musicological Society, Toronto, November 1970.

ZR²   ——: 'Mahler's songs and their influence on his symphonic thought'. Thesis submitted to the University of Toronto, 1970.

Supplementary Bibliography

Adorno, Theodor W.: 'Zu einer imaginären Auswahl von Liedern GMs', in *Impromptus*, Frankfurt M., 1973, pp. 30–8.

Franklin, Peter: ' "Funeral Rites"—Mahler and Mickiewicz', *Music and Letters*, Vol. 55, No. 2, April, 1974, pp. 203–8.

Kennedy, Michael: *M* ('The Master Musicians' series), London, 1974.

Matter, Jean: *Connaissance de M*, Lausanne, 1974.

Matthews, Colin: 'Mahler at Work: Some Observations on the Ninth and Tenth Symphony Sketches', *Soundings* (University College, Cardiff), No. 4, 1974, pp. 76–86.

McGrath, William J.: *Dionysian Art and Populist Politics in Austria*, New Haven, Conn., 1974. [This is a highly original and important study of the aesthetics and politics of Mahler's time and their interaction. The book is rich in references to literary friends and acquaintances of Mahler—Richard von Kralik, for instance, and Siegfried Lipiner—and includes a long and interesting chapter on his Third Symphony ('The Metamusical Cosmos of *GM*') which, in part at least, touches on some of the same philosophical ideas that I discuss on pp. 286–7, though the author presents an elaborate theory of his own about this particular work. In a concluding chapter, Dr. McGrath quotes the famous comment of Richard Strauss (see RS, pp. 248–9) that, whenever he conducted the first movement of Symphony III, he had a vision of 'uncountable battalions of workers marching to the May Day celebration in the Prater'; and one of the many bits of illuminating information unfolded in this book is the fact that the great May Day rallies, organized by the leader of Austria's Social Democrats, Victor Adler, a symbolic political demonstration of mass aspirations, began in 1890 and increased in influence. They were certainly a prominent part of the Vienna scene and undoubtedly were well known to Mahler in his later Vienna period (see AM[5], p. 82, for example, where we learn of his enthusiastic response to the rally of 1905 and of Pfitzner's characteristic antagonism to the same event).

The first movement of the Third Symphony was
actually completed in 1896, i.e. before Mahler's move
to Vienna in 1897, though it is not impossible that
he may have witnessed a May Day celebration in the
city before taking up his post at the Opera (he would
certainly have heard of these massive gatherings). It is
tempting to think that one of Adler's rallies may have
made a direct contribution to the first movement of
the symphony, but I think cause and effect here is
less interesting, less significant, than the fact that the
May Day rally and Mahler's great symphonic march
(aptly described by Dr. McGrath as 'communitarian
music': I think it *does* have that stressedly 'demo-
cratic' quality about it) belong to the same period and
emerge, in some respects at least, from a common
philosophy. In those circumstances, it is context
rather than chronology that matters, though I think
Dr. McGrath is over-stretching a good point when
he suggests (p. 245) that 'In a very real sense one
could invert Richard Strauss's image and argue
that Adler's workers marched to the rhythm of
Mahler's music.' It would be fascinating, by the way,
to know precisely what music, if any, was played,
and how it was performed on these great socialist
occasions.]

O'Brien, Sally: 'The "Programme" Paradox in Romantic Music as
Epitomized in the Works of *GM*', *Studies in Music*,
University of Western Australia Press, No. 5, 1971,
pp. 54–65.

Powell, Nicolas: *The Sacred Spring*, The Arts in Vienna 1898–1918.
[A useful survey of architecture, painting and the
applied arts in Vienna during the Mahler period,
with a chapter on '*M* and the Vienna School', in
which Mr. Powell reminds us (p. 207) of Hanslick's
(1825–1904) response in 1900 to some of Mahler's
songs with orchestra (two from the *Gesellen* cycle and
three from the *Knaben Wunderhorn*). See also
Appendix G.]

Raynor, Henry: *M*, London, 1975.

Roman, Zoltan: 'Structure as a Factor in the Genesis of M's Songs',
Music Review, Cambridge, Vol. 35, No. 2, August,
1974, pp. 157–66.

Sams, Eric:	'Notes on a Magic Horn', *Musical Times*, July, 1974, pp. 556–9.
——:	'Footnotes on a Magic Horn' (Letter), *Musical Times*, February, 1975, p. 140.
Schoenberg, Arnold:	*Berliner Tagebuch*, edited by Josef Rufer, Berlin, 1974. [This is a fascinating document, of course, in its own right: a diary of Schoenberg's second domicile in Berlin, which ran from 1911 to 1915 (the diary, in the main, was kept during the early months of 1912). There are several references to Mahler, two of which concern his late arrangement of a Bach Suite (see pp. 350f.). This had been published by Schirmer's in 1910, and clearly the Suite, quite apart from Mahler's own performances of it at the end of his life, had aroused interest among leading musicians of the day, and no doubt especially among those who had been closely associated with Mahler. The first excerpt comes from the entry for 2 February 1912 (p. 16), and it surely must be [Henri] Hinrichsen (not Henrichsen), the publisher (C. F. Peters) about whom Schoenberg writes. Peters had published Mahler's Fifth Symphony in 1904, and it is presumably the plates of their edition of the work which were under discussion. Small wonder that Schoenberg was incensed. That the suggestion could even be made, tells us something about the state of Mahler's reputation as a composer, less than a year after his death; which makes Schoenberg's prophecy about the future all the more interesting (and percipient).

. . . Henrichsen [sic] asked me about Mahler, and when I expressed enthusiasm he asked whether he ought, then, not to have the plates melted down. Horrifying!! This is scandalous indeed. It is high time that I wrote something on Mahler! This is truly a terrible fate. I answered him: 'For God's sake, not that of all things! Young people today worship Mahler as a god. His time will come in five to ten years at the most!' But here we must act before it is too late. If only I had the authority! – Before that I had a rehearsal of the new piano pieces with Closson. He will certainly play them very well. Somewhat dry, to be sure. – On Monday evening I was at Busoni's Schirmer concert, already mentioned. Heard Mahler's arrangement of Bach which I am to conduct [in Prague]. Sounds very well, except organ too loud. The other things not very interesting (violin concerto), and a symphonic thing by [name omitted] actually unbearable.

The second excerpt comes from the entry for 15 September (p. 23):

. . . Decided to add a continuo part to the third movement (Andante, 'Trio') of the Bach–Mahler Suite. Mahler considered it superfluous, I find it necessary. Indeed Bach wrote it down too, and I see that it follows naturally from everything. Besides this I also find that in Mahler's arrangement the first movement has too little of the character of the organ. And moreover I do not find the idea of such a Suite a good one. One can sense that it is not a piece that was conceived as a whole. It lacks 'consequence', inner coherence. Moreover I have the feeling that Mahler perhaps sensed this himself. Originally had the present second movement as the final movement and then decided to change its position. Of course that could make no difference, since good taste can never be a substitute for intuition.]

Addenda

p. 17 I want to add to my list of acknowledgements: the late Walter Hinrichsen (New York), Miss Annie Steiner, Miss Ruth Ludgate, and the Music Library of Stanford University, Calif. (Edward E. Colby and Florian J. Shasky); and to salute, though posthumously alas, my old friends Eithne Wilkins and Ernst Kaiser, some excerpts from whose as yet unpublished translation of GMB[1] I use in my text with the kind agreement of Faber and Faber. I should also like to thank *High Fidelity* (Mr. Warren B. Syer) for permission to reprint the article by Paul Stefan which appears on pp. 51ff.; and *Saturday Review-World Magazine* for permission to use the material quoted on p. 347 and in Appendix A.

p. 35 A MS title page among Alma Mahler's papers lists the following titles (which I abbreviate) in Mahler's hand: *Kindertotenlieder*; 'Blicke mir nicht . . .'; 'Um Mitternacht'; 'Der Tamboursg'sell'; 'Ich atmet . . .'; and 'Ich bin der Welt . . .'. It is hard not to conclude that this page was once wrapped round the harvest of Mahler's song-writing activities in the summer of 1901, in which case there would not have been more than three completed *Kindertotenlieder* in the folder. One notices that the song 'Liebst du . . .', which was not composed until 1902, is not listed; nor does 'Revelge' appear, already composed in 1899. It seems possible then that this title page belongs to 1901, and that the *Kindertotenlieder* were so called even before the full array of songs existed. Teasingly, along with this same title page, there is a further page on which are inscribed the opening 11 bars for piano of the *last* song, No. 5, 'In diesem Wetter'. This sketch, draft, incipit, or fair copy—which is it?—abruptly breaks off, and there are no other marks on the MS. What does this mean? Does the fragment suggest that Mahler had made a start on the song that was to be No. 5 in the summer of 1901 but did not resume the composition of it until much later? Or had he sketched it, and these 11 bars were the start of a fair copy left unfinished? There is a mystery here which is still to be solved and the solution of which might easily (and radically) modify or qualify the suggested chronology I outline for the cycle on pp. 34–43. All of which goes to show once again the ambiguities and uncertainties that still surround the chronology of Mahler's music. (The voice and piano MS of the *first* of the *Kindertotenlieder* seems to have vanished. Where is it?)

I have been misled by the English edition (1959) of Alma Mahler's later autobiography. In the German text (*Mein Leben*, Stuttgart, 1960, p. 48) she refers correctly to five songs in all, though disposing the stages of their assembly as 3 + 2, not 2 + 3, as she had in fact written in her earlier book.

p. 97 However, as a comparison of the PS with the EV shows, Mahler arrived at his 'renowned economy and precision' by an *increase* in the resources deployed in the PS:

EV	PS
2 flutes (+ picc. in No. 3)	3 flutes (incl. picc.)
2 oboes	2 oboes (incl. cor anglais)
2 clarinets	2 clarinets
	1 bass clarinet
2 bassoons	2 bassoons
4 horns	4 horns
2 trumpets	2 trumpets
3 trombones (incl. bass tuba)	3 trombones (incl. bass tuba)
Perc.	*Perc.*
Triangle	Triangle
Cymbals	Cymbals

Perc.	Perc.
Bass drum	Glockenspiel
	Bass drum
	Timpani
	Tam-tam
Harp	Harp
Strings	Strings

p. 127   In the MS full score of the five *Wunderhorn* songs that I mention on this page (line 6) as being in the possession of the Gesellschaft der Musikfreunde, Vienna, the title page of the first song reads as follows:

'Der Schildwache Nachtlied'
(aus des 'Knaben Wunderhorn')
Eine Humoreske (Nro. I.)
für eine Singstimme
und Orchester
von
Gustav Mahler

The third song in the MS, 'Trost im Unglück', has a subsidiary title on the first page: 'Wir wissen uns zu trösten'.
All these orchestral songs are written in the same keys as the original voice and piano MSS (see the note in these Addenda for pp. 423–4) and on Hamburg MS paper imprinted Joh. Aug. Böhme (No. 12).
p. 127   I have settled for 'Wer hat dies Liedlein erdacht?' as the title of the fourth *Wunderhorn* song. This is how the title appears on Mahler's voice and piano MS (see p. 423). In the printed U.E. miniature score the title appears as 'Wer hat dies Liedel erdacht?', while Mahler himself performed the song, in Hamburg, in 1893, under the title 'Wer hat dies Liedchen erdacht?'. The title on the MS at least reflects the actual words of the poem itself, i.e. 'Wer hat denn das schön schöne Liedlein erdacht?'.
p. 147   No. 5 in the checklist. A composition sketch for this song is in private ownership. It is undated but written on paper of Hamburg provenance.
p. 155   Perhaps the titles of the songs Mahler was to perform are missing from the concert announcement because he and his singer were late in deciding which songs they would perform (as distinct from how many).
pp. 163–5   Perhaps I should also have mentioned in these brief notes on the symphonic poem that the post-Mahler and Strauss generation too was still enthralled by the possibilities of the form, e.g. Schoenberg's string sextet *Verklärte Nacht* (1899) and *Pelleas und Melisande* (1903), for orchestra.
p. 169   *Der Messias* to which Foerster refers is Klopstock's epic poem (1748–73)— nothing to do with Handel. However, as I point out in Appendix C, it is among Klopstock's *Geistliche Lieder* that his Resurrection hymn will be found.
p. 265   In n. 46, I mean of course the probable first *complete* performance of the *Gesellen* cycle.
p. 266   In the Berlin concert schedule reproduced here the 'Behn' referred to in the title of the upper illustration is, of course, the lawyer Hermann Behn, evidently a generous patron of music, who is mentioned on p. 97 and elsewhere.
p. 291   Note 89: in the last bar of the music example, in the final chord in the bass, for B flat *read* C.
p. 322   Line 21, B major better B major-minor.
p. 354   It is not quite clear to me whether by 'Bach-Konzert' Mahler in his letter is making a general reference to the prominence of Bach in the historical *concert* of 10 November or specifically to the Bach E major violin *concerto*. I have settled for 'concert' but concede that it might well be 'concerto', especially since Mahler's conception of the continuo part in his Bach Suite involves both organ and quasi-harpsichord in the first movement. Did this mean that the concerto would have been similarly accompanied? The mind boggles.
p. 361   Ex. 118: in bar 5, upper part, the first crotchet should be dotted.
p. 403   Line 5 from bottom: Heinrich Effer. I have not been able to clarify this reference. Who was he?

pp. 423–4   The keys in which Mahler wrote these songs in his MSS are as follows:

No. 1:   B flat
No. 2:   A
No. 3:   F
No. 4:   G→E
No. 5:   A
No. 6:   A

Addition to Supplementary Bibliography
p. 435   Fischer, Kurt von: 'Zu GMs Liedern', *Neue
             Zürcher Zeitung*, 5/6 July
             1975, p. 41.
         Murphy, Edward W.: 'Sonata-Rondo Form in
             the Symphonies of GM', Music
             Review, Vol. 36, No. 1, February,
             1975, pp. 54–62.

Index

Compiled by Terence A. Miller
Page numbers in italics indicate literary quotations. Musical examples are in bold type.